Daniel Reveals the Bloodline of the Antichrist

Dr. J. R. Church

All scripture references are from the King James Version unless otherwise stated.

Daniel Reveals the Bloodline of the Antichrist
First Edition, 2010
Copyright © 2010 by Prophecy Publications
Oklahoma City, OK

Printed in the United States of America

Published by:

Prophecy Publications

P. O. Box 7000

Oklahoma City, OK 73153

ISBN 0-941241-22-X

To my children with love and devotion ...

My daughter, Terri Jeanne McInnis
My son, Jerry R. Church, Jr.

Foreword

The book of Daniel offers rare insights into the bloodline of the Antichrist. Written during the Babylonian captivity, Daniel introduces the *"times of the Gentiles"* — and gives the roots of the man who will conclude the era with his diabolical attempt to destroy the Chosen People.

There have been many candidates for the Antichrist down through the ages. Among the most notorious were Antiochus IV Epiphanes, who sacrificed a pig at the Jerusalem Temple in 167 B.C.; Nero, who had the Apostle Paul beheaded in A.D. 66; Titus, who burned Herod's Temple in A.D. 70; Hadrian, who destroyed Jerusalem in A.D. 135; and in more recent years ... Adolf Hitler, who slaughtered a third of the world's Jewish population during World War II.

But all these were mere foreshadows of that future *"man of sin"* ... the *"seed"* of the serpent ... the *"little horn"* of Daniel's visions. Why was Daniel told that the little horn would rise out of the fourth beast (chapter 7), which most consider to be the Roman Empire; then later is told that the little horn will rise out of the goat (chapter 8), symbolic of the Greek Empire? Still later, Gabriel tells Daniel that the *"people of the prince that shall come"* shall destroy the city and the sanctuary (chapter 9), which most scholars agree points to the Roman destruction of Jerusalem. And finally, in chapters 10-12, Daniel is told that the Antichrist will come out of the Seleucid dynasty — again, a Syrian ruler of Greek descent.

Will the Antichrist be from both Greek and Roman descent? How can we reconcile these roots in the bloodline of the Antichrist? This is one of Daniel's most important themes. Therefore, in this commentary, we shall examine all that the prophet has to say about the Antichrist, and compare our findings with New Testament Scriptures in order to build a composite description of this diabolical enemy.

Also included in this book is a chapter on the 243 missing years in the Jewish calendar, giving details about when and why those years were excluded.

Finally, a chart of six thousand years shows where Daniel's Seventy Weeks fit in history. The chart begins with Creation in the autumn of 4004 BC, and contains the Sabbatical Years and Jubilees; seven dispensations; seven church ages; the kings of Judah and Israel; the captivities; and notes on many historical events.

The chart also contains a listing of planetary conjunctions between Jupiter and Saturn, which helps to explain why an ancient legend grew up in Greek Mythology about the war between Saturn (head of the Titans) and Jupiter (head of the Olympians). The Rabbis believed that a triple conjunction between these two planets in the constellation Pisces would herald the coming of the Messiah. In fact, such a conjunction did occur in 7 BC.

This chart will become your most treasured asset in the study of biblical prophecy. It will help you to better understand the book of Daniel and other prophecies, as well as God's overall plan of the ages.

Table of Contents

The Babylonian Captivity

Though the stories of Daniel in the lion's den and the three Hebrew boys in the fiery furnace were widely popular for the better part of two millennia, Daniel's prophecies remained shrouded in mystery. The lock on this treasure trove seems to be located in the last chapter:

"But thou, O Daniel, shut up the words, and seal the book, even to the time of the end: many shall run to and fro, and knowledge shall be increased" (Dan. 12:4).

The symbols and metaphors in Daniel were virtually incomprehensible ... until the Reformation gave rise to a renewed interest in the literal interpretation of Scripture and a renewed understanding of Israel's place in God's plan of the ages. Only in recent times have theologians been challenged to take up the pen and write about Daniel's dreams and visions.

Dr. M. R. DeHaan once wrote: "Of all the beloved characters found in the Scriptures, there is none more interesting, none more appealing, and none more lovable and pure than the man Daniel. Together with Joseph, he stands among the heroes of the

Old Testament as one of whom practically no evil is recorded" (M. R. DeHaan, *Daniel the Prophet*, p. 17). Jesus called Daniel a *"prophet"* (Matt. 24:15), and yet, his book is not included among the *Nevi'im*, "Prophets" of the Jewish Bible — in neither the Major Prophets, nor the Minor Prophets. Instead, Daniel is located in the *Kethubim*, "Writings," along with the Psalms, Proverbs, Job, Song of Solomon, Ruth, Lamentations, Ecclesiastes, Esther, Ezra, Nehemiah and I & II Chronicles.

Perhaps Daniel stands in a league all his own. Though he and Ezekiel were prophets of the exile, Daniel, being of princely descent from the family of King Zedekiah (Flavius Josephus, *Antiquities*, X, X, 1) and the tribe of Judah, was not a member of the exclusive order of the Levites. He was not educated in the school of the prophets, nor did he serve in Solomon's Temple as an ordained priest. The priesthood may have earned Ezekiel the right to be included in the *Nevi'im*, but not Daniel.

However, Daniel seems to stand apart from the other prophets in theme and content. While the others directed scathing messages against the idolatry of the Jewish people, Daniel concentrated on the *"times of the Gentiles,"* the rise of the Antichrist and the coming of the Messiah. Ezekiel wrote that God had included Daniel in a class of such renowned men as Noah and Job:

"The word of the LORD came again to me, saying,
"Son of man, when the land sinneth against me by trespassing grievously, then will I stretch out mine hand upon it, and will break the staff of the bread thereof, and will send famine upon it, and will cut off man and beast from it:
*"Though these three men, Noah, **Daniel**, and Job, were in it, they should deliver but their own souls by their righteousness, saith the Lord GOD"* (Ezk. 14:12-14).

It can be said that few men in history possessed the integrity and courage of Daniel. Perhaps that was the reason God chose to reveal the future to him in ways unlike those of other prophets.

The Times of the Gentiles

The Apostle John referred to Daniel's metaphoric symbols more often than those of any other Old Testament prophet. Daniel became one of John's foundational sources for the book of Revelation. Both Daniel and Revelation, unlike the other prophets, give us a view of the *"times of the Gentiles."* Daniel prophesied in the Babylonian kingdom, while John prophesied in the Roman kingdom — the first and fourth Gentile world empires, as if they were historical bookends for God's plan regarding Jerusalem. Furthermore, John seems to concentrate on explaining Daniel's final seven-year Sabbatical cycle (i.e., the seventieth week). In these two books, Israel's capital city becomes a type of the heavenly city, New Jerusalem. Gentile domination over Jerusalem alludes to the ages-long war in heaven between God and the devil.

The concept, referred to by Jesus as *"the times of the Gentiles"* (Luke 21:24), was introduced in Daniel 2:4, launching a section of six chapters written in Aramaic ("Syriack" — the language of the ancient Syrians) that continues until Daniel 7:28. Half of Daniel's book was written in the language of the Gentiles!

The term, *"times of the Gentiles,"* is not to be confused with the Apostle Paul's use of the term, *"fullness of the Gentiles,"* in Romans 11:25. His *"fullness of the Gentiles"* refers to the age of Gentile Christianity, whereas the *"times of the Gentiles"* refers to profane foreign governments conquering and controlling Jerusalem, and extending from the Babylonian exile to the arrival of the messianic kingdom — the *"stone ... cut out ... without hands"* (Dan. 2:45).

From another perspective, the book of Daniel is divided into two sections: the first six chapters (1-6) deal with current events in Daniel's generation, along with visionary glimpses (into the future) given to a Gentile king; while the final six chapters (7-12) exclusively record Daniel's visions. Those focus on the future rise of world government, along with the background and exploits of the Antichrist.

The Babylonian exile is a major theme in the Old Testament. Out of 39 OT books, twelve of them refer primarily to the years of Judah's defeat, exile and return. They are II Chronicles, II Kings, Ezra, Nehemiah, Esther, Jeremiah, Lamentations, Ezekiel, Daniel, Haggai, Zechariah and Malachi. The OT books of II Chronicles and II Kings record the historical accounts of Judah's defeat and exile, while the others include their return. These books represent a significant portion of the Old Testament Scriptures.

The book of Daniel introduces the *"times of the Gentiles,"* beginning with Nebuchadnezzar conquering Jerusalem and deporting prisoners. Babylon is depicted as the head of gold on the statue in the king's dream. According to the statue, three other kingdoms were to follow — the arms of silver (Medo/Persia); the belly of brass (Greece); the legs of iron (Rome) and the feet and toes of iron and clay (the final world kingdom). These are the empires destined to control Jerusalem during the *"times of the Gentiles."* When the fourth kingdom conquered Jerusalem, it was time for the First Advent of the Messiah. Someday, when ten toes (a united consortium of nations) take over the world, a rock from heaven (the Messiah) will crush the entire proverbial statue and replace it with heaven's kingdom.

The New Testament opens during the fourth kingdom and concludes with the prophecies of Revelation, which expands upon Daniel's prophecies of the ten toes (Dan. 2); his ten-horned beast that rises out of the sea of humanity (Dan. 7); and his most important prophecy — the Tribulation Period, as depicted in the seventieth week (Dan. 9).

Now let us review the historical background:

The First Babylonian Invasion (607-606 B.C.)

"In the third year of the reign of Jehoiakim king of Judah came Nebuchadnezzar king of Babylon unto Jerusalem, and besieged it.

"And the Lord gave Jehoiakim king of Judah into his hand, with part of the vessels of the house of God: which he carried into the land of Shinar to the house of his god; and he brought the vessels into the treasure house of his god" (Dan. 1:1,2).

There were three Babylonian invasions of Judah and Jerusalem. The first invasion secured Judah as a vassal state, thus launching the *"times of the Gentiles."* The dating for these events vary with different historians. Concerning the three sieges of Jerusalem, I have seen the date for the first invasion vary from 607 to 606 B.C.; the date for the second siege from 600 to 597 B.C., and the date for the third siege from 590 to 586 B.C. Though I am skeptical of a few of Bishop Ussher's dating attempts, I agree with most of his findings. In 1658, the year he published *The Annals of the World*, it must have been a monumental task to chronicle every detail with historical accuracy. Under the circumstances, he produced a commendable work. For the sake of continuity, I will use his dating, differing only where I feel the need.

Jehoiakim was the throne name of Eliakim, second son of Josiah, appointed by Pharaoh Necco in the autumn of 610 B.C. His father, Josiah, had been killed in a battle with Necco's forces, in the valley of Megiddo, in the spring of 610 B.C. At first, Pharaoh allowed Jehoahaz to succeed his father, but after three months, the Egyptian king replaced him with his brother, Jehoiakim. Three years later, the king of Egypt had to give up Judah to the Babylonians.

Nebuchadnezzar became viceroy of Babylon in the winter of 607 B.C., and launched a series of invasions against Coelosyria, Phoenicia, Egypt and, eventually, Judah. Daniel reported that Nebuchadnezzar besieged Jerusalem *"in the third year of the reign of Jehoiakim"* (Daniel 1:1). The Babylonian army came against Judah late in the third year of Jehoiakim's reign (autumn 607 B.C.), and succeeded in securing the city of Jerusalem in the ninth month (*Kislev* - December 607 B.C.), which was in the beginning months of Jehoiakim's fourth year. This date was only days away from January 1, 606 B.C. Furthermore, securing Jerusalem and taking the first group of captives may have required several days, if not weeks. Therefore, it is not out of reason to understand why some say that Jerusalem was conquered in 606 B.C.

This was the first of three Babylonian invasions. Daniel was taken in the first deportation (607-606 B.C.), and Ezekiel was enslaved during the second siege (600-599 B.C.). The third siege (590-588 B.C.), led to the burning of Solomon's Temple on the 9th of *Av* (August 27, 588 B.C.).

The Law of the Sabbatical Years

Why did God allow the Babylonian invasion and Judah's subsequent exile? Could not God have protected the tiny nation as He had done in the past? Did He not destroy Egypt with plagues? Did He not destroy the armies of Sennacherib in one night? For the answer, we should consult the Mosaic Law. Almost 900 years before Nebuchadnezzar's invasion, God gave Moses instructions for Israel to keep a series of laws, one of which, was the law of Sabbatical cycles:

"When ye come into the land which I give you, then shall the land keep a sabbath unto the LORD.

"Six years thou shalt sow thy field, and six years thou shalt prune thy vineyard, and gather in the fruit thereof;

"But in the seventh year shall be a sabbath of rest unto the land, a sabbath for the LORD: thou shalt neither sow thy field, nor prune thy vineyard.

"That which groweth of its own accord of thy harvest thou shalt not reap, neither gather the grapes of thy vine undressed: for it is a year of rest unto the land" (Lev. 25:2-5).

To compensate for the land lying fallow during the Sabbatical Year, God promised a bumper crop every sixth year:

"I will command my blessing upon you in the sixth year, and it shall bring forth fruit for three years.
"And ye shall sow the eighth year, and eat yet of old fruit until the ninth year; until her fruits come in ye shall eat of the old store" (Lev. 25:21,22).

However, God threatened to exile the Chosen People and make their land desolate if they failed to observe the sacred Sabbatical cycles:

"But if ye will not hearken unto me, and will not do all these commandments;
"I will make your cities waste, and bring your sanctuaries unto desolation, and I will not smell the savour of your sweet odours.
"And I will bring the land into desolation: and your enemies which dwell therein shall be astonished at it.
"And I will scatter you among the heathen, and will draw out a sword after you: and your land shall be desolate, and your cities waste.
"Then shall the land enjoy her sabbaths, as long as it lieth desolate, and ye be in your enemies' land; even then shall the land rest, and enjoy her sabbaths.
"As long as it lieth desolate it shall rest; because it did not rest in your sabbaths, when ye dwelt upon it" (Lev. 26:14,31-35).

According to Ussher, Joshua led the Israelites across the Jordan River on the tenth day of Nisan (Friday, April 16, 1451 B.C.). On the evening of the 14th (Tuesday, April 20), they celebrated the first Passover in the Promised Land. The manna ceased with the disappearance of Moses. Jewish sources say that the Israelites fought for seven years to secure the land, then took another seven years to divide the land among the various tribes and families. During this time, they ate from the crops that others had left behind. From all accounts, it seems that the people planted their first official crop in the autumn of 1437 B.C. That marked the beginning of the first Sabbatical cycle. They observed their first Sabbatical Year beginning in the autumn of 1431 B.C., and extending through the winter, spring and summer of 1430 B.C. The Israelites observed their first Jubilee in 1388/87 B.C.

Concerning these dates, there is some disagreement among scholars. First of all, as noted above, the *Seder Olam* claims that the first Sabbatical cycle began, not seven years later (as Ussher suggested), but following the fourteenth year after crossing the Jordan River (though they claim that the year was 1258 B.C.). Secondly, the *Seder Olam* charts the years of Jubilee in the fiftieth year (Ussher has them in the forty-ninth). Jewish records report observing the Jubilee in the year following the seventh Sabbatical Year of each cycle. It was considered to be both the fiftieth year and the first year of the next seven-year cycle. Therefore, the first crop should have been planted in 1437 B.C., and the first Sabbatical Year should have been 1431/30 B.C. The first Jubilee should have been observed in 1388/87 B.C., rather than in 1396/95 B.C., as reckoned by Ussher.

In an article entitled *"Chronomessianism"* published in 1976 in the Hebrew Union College annual yearbook, the late Rabbi Ben Zion Wacholder quoted an ancient source, saying that the last Jubilee was recorded during the Bar Kochba revolt in A.D. 132/33, not in A.D. 124/25 as Ussher would have it.

Following the Sabbatical and Jubilee cycles from the days of antiquity to our present generation, 1993/94 was Israel's 490th Sabbatical Year, and 1994/95 should have been Israel's 70th biblical year of Jubilee. I once asked a Rabbi about the observance of Jubilee, to which he replied that Jews do not observe Jubilee since there is no Temple. He asked me to pray that Israel will be allowed to restore Temple worship so that they might once again celebrate the Jubilee.

The Reason for the Babylonian Captivity

Over the course of 826 years, from the planting of their first crop in the autumn of 1437 B.C., to the observance of their 118th Sabbatical year in 612/11 B.C., Israel violated the law of Sabbatical cycles some 70 times — making 70 years of exile necessary. Their seventeenth Jubilee should have been observed in 604/603 B.C., but by this time, God's patience had finally run out. In 607-606 B.C., God allowed the Babylonians to conquer Judah and deport their first group of prisoners, among whom were Daniel and three relatives. The story of the Babylonian invasion is given in the final chapters of both II Kings and II Chronicles. Below is the account in II Chronicles:

"Jehoiakim was twenty and five years old when he began to reign, and he reigned eleven years in Jerusalem: and he did that which was evil in the sight of the LORD his God.

"Against him came up Nebuchadnezzar king of Babylon, and bound him in fetters, to carry him to Babylon.

"Nebuchadnezzar also carried off the vessels of the house of the LORD to Babylon, and put them in his temple at Babylon" (II Chron. 36:5-7).

Nebuchadnezzar had invaded Judah in Jehoiakim's third year (607B.C.), but allowed the Jewish monarch to remain on the throne as a vassal king. However, in his eleventh year (600-599 B.C.), the Babylonian army besieged Jerusalem once again; this time because Jehoiakim had renounced his allegiance to Babylon. The Babylonian army seized and killed Jehoiakim, dragged his body out of the gate of Jerusalem and discarded it without a proper burial. Jeremiah had predicted his death:

"He shall be buried with the burial of an ass, drawn and cast forth beyond the gates of Jerusalem" (Jer. 22:19).

Jehoiakim's eighteen-year-old son, Jehoiachin (also called Jeconiah and Coniah), was installed as a vassal king and ruled for three months and ten days. When Nebuchadnezzar arrived, the naive Jeconiah brought his family out to meet the

Gordon's Calvary: The large cave (left of center) is said to be the remains on an ancient dungeon where Jeremiah was lowered into a miry pit. Today, it is known as Jeremiah's Grotto.

Babylonian king and was promptly taken prisoner. His family was deported and imprisoned in Babylon. Jeremiah recorded God's curse upon Jeconiah's posterity:

"Thus saith the LORD, Write ye this man childless, a man that shall not prosper in his days: for no man of his seed shall prosper, sitting upon the throne of David, and ruling any more in Judah" (Jer. 22:30).

Henceforth, none of Jeconiah's lineage would be qualified to rule upon the throne of David. We should note that Jeconiah is listed in Matthew's genealogy (Matt. 1:11). Therefore, this curse would have affected Jesus had He been the begotten son of Joseph. Because of this ancient curse, we can be assured that Jesus was, indeed, virgin born.

Jeconiah's uncle, the 21-year-old Zedekiah, was given the opportunity to govern Judah, a reign that lasted 11 years. Like others before him, Zedekiah also failed to govern wisely. In fact, he treated Jeremiah terribly. In 590 B.C., he had the prophet imprisoned for a time in a dungeon. In 589 B.C., the princes imprisoned Jeremiah in a miry pit in a prison atop the hill, today called Calvary. In later years, when the hill was cut away, the dungeon was exposed. Today, that shallow cave near the top of skull hill is called Jeremiah's Grotto. It is said to be the remains of the miry pit into which the prophet was lowered and sank in the mud. Ebed-melech, an Ethiopian eunuch in the king's house, took some *"old cast clouts and old rotten rags"* (Jer. 38:11) and pulled Jeremiah out of the dungeon. These failures in leadership brought the Babylonian army to Jerusalem for a third siege in 589 B.C.:

> *"Therefore he brought upon them the king of the Chaldees, who slew their young men with the sword in the house of their sanctuary, and had no compassion upon young man or maiden, old man, or him that stooped for age: he gave them all into his hand.*
>
> *"And all the vessels of the house of God, great and small, and the treasures of the house of the LORD, and the treasures of the king, and of his princes; all these he brought to Babylon.*
>
> *"And they burnt the house of God, and brake down the wall of Jerusalem, and burnt all the palaces thereof with fire, and destroyed all the goodly vessels thereof.*
>
> *"And them that had escaped from the sword carried he away to Babylon; where they were servants to him and his sons until the reign of the kingdom of Persia:*
>
> *"To fulfil the word of the LORD by the mouth of Jeremiah,* **until the land had enjoyed her sabbaths**: *for as long as she lay desolate she kept sabbath, to fulfil threescore and ten years"* (II Chron. 36:17-21).

Nebuchadnezzar's army breached the walls and entered the city on the ninth of Tammuz (July 27) and burned Solomon's Temple on the ninth of Av (August 27, 588 B.C.). Ezekiel received news of its destruction on the fifth day of the tenth month, January 25, 587 B.C. Jeremiah was a noted prophet and scholar on the law of the Sabbatical cycles. He had prophesied:

"And this whole land shall be a desolation, and an astonishment; and these nations shall serve the king of Babylon seventy years.

"And it shall come to pass, when seventy years are accomplished, that I will punish the king of Babylon, and that nation, saith the LORD, for their iniquity, and the land of the Chaldeans, and will make it perpetual desolations" (Jer. 25:11,12).

Four chapters later, Jeremiah repeated his prophecy:

"For thus saith the LORD, That after seventy years be accomplished at Babylon I will visit you, and perform my good word toward you, in causing you to return to this place" (Jer. 29:10).

The seventy-year captivity began in December 607 B.C., and would last until the decree of Cyrus in late 537 B.C., and the return of 42,360 people under the leadership of Zerubbabel in the spring of 536 B.C.

Dating the Babylonian Captivity

"And Daniel continued even unto the first year of king Cyrus" (Dan. 1:21).

Cyrus is the KJV name given to King כורש Koresh, head of the Persian Empire. The English spelling of *"Cyrus"* is simply a preferred pronunciation of the Hebrew text.

One would think that Daniel 1:21 should have referred to the death of the prophet, but that is not the case. Daniel was still alive two years later, as we shall see in chapter 10. The reason Daniel included the statement that he *"continued ... unto the first year of king Cyrus,"* is that the date refers to that all-important prophecy fulfilled by the royal commandment to restore Jerusalem. It seems strange to me that most scholars want to place the date for the beginning of the *"seventy weeks"* (Dan. 9) with Artaxerxes in 445 B.C., instead of with the decree of Cyrus in 537/536 B.C.

If the decree that launched the *"seventy weeks"* is not the one in the first year of Cyrus, then why did Daniel open his first chapter (v. 1) with Nebuchadnezzar besieging Jerusalem in the third year of Jehoiakim, and conclude the chapter (v. 21) in the first year of Cyrus. The answer is obvious. Those are the seventy years of the captivity. The seventy years were up in the first year of Cyrus. His decree was recorded in the first chapter of Ezra:

"Thus saith Cyrus king of Persia, The LORD God of heaven hath given me all the kingdoms of the earth; and he hath charged me to build him an house at Jerusalem, which is in Judah.

"Who is there among you of all his people? his God be with him, and let him go up to Jerusalem, which is in Judah, and build the house of the LORD God of Israel, (he is the God,) which is in Jerusalem.

"And whosoever remaineth in any place where he sojourneth, let the men of his place help him with silver, and with gold, and with goods, and with beasts, beside the freewill offering for the house of God that is in Jerusalem" (Ezra 1:2-4).

Cyrus issued this decree in 537 B.C. It was carried out during the following year — 536 B.C. This was the Cyrus of which Isaiah (712 B.C.) had prophesied:

*"That saith of Cyrus, He is my shepherd, and shall perform all my pleasure: even **saying to Jerusalem, Thou shalt be built; and to the temple, Thy foundation shall be laid**"* (Isa. 44:28).

*"Thus saith the LORD to **his anointed**, to Cyrus, whose right hand I have holden ..."* (Isa. 45:1).

Isaiah wrote that Cyrus would say to Jerusalem, *"Thou shalt be built; and to the temple, Thy foundations shall be laid."* God called him both *"shepherd"* and *"anointed."* Is it not obvious that this is the date God had in mind when Gabriel told Daniel about the *"commandment"* to restore and build Jerusalem?

Why wait another 91 years for the *"commandment?"* The last verse of chapter one tells us that Daniel *"... continued even unto the first year of king Cyrus"* (Dan. 1:21). This was the year of the predicted *"commandment."* It does not mean that Daniel retired or that he died that year. Quite the contrary. It can only refer to the *"commandment"* that Cyrus delivered to Zerubbabel. When we get to chapter 9, we shall review the historical evidence in favor of dating the seventy weeks from the decree of Cyrus.

Captives from the Royal Family

In 713 B.C., King Hezekiah entertained a delegation from Babylon. They had come to congratulate him on his recovery from illness, and bring him a present from Merodach-Baladan, king of Babylon. The naive Hezekiah gave them the royal tour of Jerusalem. Afterward, Isaiah asked Hezekiah if he had shown them the national treasury, to which he replied that he had:

"And Isaiah said unto Hezekiah, Hear the word of the LORD.
"Behold, the days come, that all that is in thine house, and that which thy fathers have laid up in store unto this day, shall be carried into Babylon: nothing shall be left, saith the LORD.
"And of thy sons that shall issue from thee, which thou shalt beget, shall they take away; and they shall be eunuchs in the palace of the king of Babylon" (II Kings 20:16-18).

This same prophecy is recorded in Isaiah 39. Therefore, though we are not told specifically in the Bible, Flavius Josephus reported that Daniel, Hananiah, Mishael, and Azariah were members of the royal family of Zedekiah, thus fulfilling Isaiah's prophecy to King Hezekiah.

During the early years of Babylon's rule over Jerusalem, Nebuchadnezzar allowed Jehoiakim to remain upon the throne of Judea. Upon removing him in 597 B.C., Nebuchadnezzar allowed Jehoiakim's 18-year-old son, Jehoiachin, to rule. After a hundred days, the Babylonian monarch removed Jehoiachin and invested Judea's government into the hands of 21-year-old Zedekiah. It is plain to see that Nebuchadnezzar wanted to groom the youth to serve him. It was far easier to raise a new generation of loyal aids than to try to persuade the adults to assist in the Babylonian government. That also may have been the reasoning behind Nebuchadnezzar's kind treatment of Daniel and his friends:

"And the king spake unto Ashpenaz the master of his eunuchs, that he should bring certain of the children of Israel, and of the king's seed, and of the princes;

"Children in whom was no blemish, but well favoured, and skilful in all wisdom, and cunning in knowledge, and understanding science, and such as had ability in them to stand in the king's palace, and whom they might teach the learning and the tongue of the Chaldeans" (Dan. 1:3,4).

Adolescent Rebellion or Conviction?

Young people have a tendency to test the rules. For example, the eighteen-year-old Jehoiachin had displeased the Babylonian king and the young Zedekiah refused to listen to his godly advisers. During those same years, Daniel and his relatives were also tested. Daniel managed to harness his natural inclination to rebel. He became a man of personal integrity and conviction in ways that pleased his captors:

"And the king appointed them a daily provision of the king's meat, and of the wine which he drank: so nourishing them three years, that at the end thereof they might stand before the king.

"Now among these were of the children of Judah, Daniel, Hananiah, Mishael, and Azariah:

"Unto whom the prince of the eunuchs gave names: for he gave unto Daniel the name of Belteshazzar; and to Hananiah, of Shadrach; and to Mishael, of Meshach; and to Azariah, of Abednego.

"But Daniel purposed in his heart that he would not defile himself with the portion of the king's meat, nor with the wine which he drank: therefore he requested of the prince of the eunuchs that he might not defile himself.

"Now God had brought Daniel into favour and tender love with the prince of the eunuchs.

"And the prince of the eunuchs said unto Daniel, I fear my lord the king, who hath appointed your meat and your drink: for why should he see your faces worse liking than the children which are of your sort? then shall ye make me endanger my head to the king" (Dan. 1:5-10).

Daniel's name meant, "God is my Judge." Upon arriving in Babylon, his name was changed to Belteshazzar, meaning "Baal's protector of, or attendant to, the king." Since Baal was Nebuchadnezzar's god, the Babylonian monarch looked upon

Daniel as "the Babylonian god's attendant to the king." However, we know that Daniel was Jehovah's attendant to the king!

Hananiah's name meant, "Jehovah has been gracious." His name was changed to Shadrach. Mishael's name meant, "who is like God." His name was changed to Meshach. Azariah's name meant, "Jehovah has helped." His name was changed to Abednego. No meanings have been determined for these three Babylonian names.

The Ten-Day Trial

Daniel convinced his guard to allow him and his three relatives to eat a vegetarian diet for ten days — food that would not impair their mental capabilities nor their religious convictions:

"Then said Daniel to Melzar, whom the prince of the eunuchs had set over Daniel, Hananiah, Mishael, and Azariah,

"Prove thy servants, I beseech thee, ten days; and let them give us pulse to eat, and water to drink.

"Then let our countenances be looked upon before thee, and the countenance of the children that eat of the portion of the king's meat: and as thou seest, deal with thy servants.

"So he consented to them in this matter, and proved them ten days.

"And at the end of ten days their countenances appeared fairer and fatter in flesh than all the children which did eat the portion of the king's meat.

"Thus Melzar took away the portion of their meat, and the wine that they should drink; and gave them pulse" (Dan. 1:11-16).

Daniel was not a lifelong vegetarian. We learn from Daniel 10:3 that the aged prophet (about 90 years old) was not opposed to eating meat. He explains his eating habits in the account of a three-week fast: *"I ate no pleasant bread, neither came flesh nor wine in my mouth ... three whole weeks...."* What should be noted in the chapter before us is that the young Daniel purposed in his heart to always eat kosher foods.

Knowledge and Wisdom

It seems that Jewish intellect always rises, like cream, to the top of any society. Not only do Jews have a keen mentality, but education in the Jewish *yeshivah* (school) involves the *"pilpul"* method of reasoning, thus encouraging wisdom along with knowledge. *"Pilpul"* is a method of Talmudic study. The word is derived from the verb "pilpel" (lit. "to spice," "to season," and in a metaphorical sense, "to dispute violently" [Tosef., B. B. vii. 5] or "cleverly" "[Shab. 31a; B. M. 85b]). Since by such disputation the subject is, in a way, spiced and seasoned, the word has come to mean penetrating investigation, disputation, and drawing of conclusions; and is used especially to designate a method of studying the Law (Ab. vi. 5; Baraita; B. B. 145b; Tem. 16a; Ket. 103b; Yer. Ter. iv. 42d).

On the other hand, the Greeks and Romans used deductive reasoning, involving syllogisms (fundamental logic — a major premise with a minor premise, leading to a conclusion). Though knowledge is acquired by instruction, absorbing it requires a keen intellect. Wisdom is the mental ability to apply that knowledge to the problems of life. In the case of Daniel and his three relatives, because of their dedication, God opened their minds in unusual ways:

> *"As for these four children, God gave them knowledge and skill in all learning and wisdom: and Daniel had understanding in all visions and dreams.*
>
> *"Now at the end of the days that the king had said he should bring them in, then the prince of the eunuchs brought them in before Nebuchadnezzar.*
>
> *"And the king communed with them; and among them all was found none like Daniel, Hananiah, Mishael, and Azariah: therefore stood they before the king.*
>
> *"And in all matters of wisdom and understanding, that the king enquired of them, he found them ten times better than all the magicians and astrologers that were in all his realm"* (Dan. 1:17-20).

It seems that their diet had a positive effect on their mental capacities. There were no huge amounts of sugar for these boys! Their balanced vegetable diet was helpful to the brain's ability to function. God had given wisdom to their forefather Solomon … and now to these young men from Zedekiah's royal family.

Wisdom is divinely bestowed. According to Jesus, both knowledge and wisdom are directed by the Holy Spirit. Jesus told His disciples that the Holy Spirit would give them understanding: *"Howbeit when he, the Spirit of truth, is come, he will guide you into all truth"* (John 16:13). Spiritual understanding is also available to us, if we will seek it. It is a wisdom that sees the Bible from an eternal viewpoint, rather than simply looking for practical applications. It is a wisdom that helps us understand God's grand plan — as given through the prophetic implications of biblical passages.

If Daniel was … say about 18 years old … when he was taken to Babylon, then he would have been about 90 when he received his last vision recorded in the book. Daniel's 12 chapters cover a period of 72 years — from 606 to 534 B.C.

It behooves us to aspire to be like Daniel! He refused to be contaminated by the temptations around him. This world needs a group of dedicated Christians who will not compromise in the midst of this off-beat generation. One of the main reasons why Christians have so little influence today is because society can see no difference between the church and the world. Many dress and act just like the ungodly among whom we live. M. R. DeHaan once wrote:

> "Dare to be a Daniel,
> "Dare to stand alone;
> "Dare to have a purpose firm!
> "Dare to make it known!"

The Times of the Gentiles

The story in Daniel's first chapter was only introductory to the more significant theme discussed in chapter two. This chapter offers one of the most important prophecies in the Old Testament. The unusual thing about this story is that God revealed the future, not to a Jewish prophet, but to a Gentile king — Nebuchadnezzar. The Babylonian king had a visionary dream that mapped out *"the times of the Gentiles"* — God's grand plan for Gentile domination over Jerusalem:

"And in the second year of the reign of Nebuchadnezzar Nebuchadnezzar dreamed dreams, wherewith his spirit was troubled, and his sleep brake from him.

"Then the king commanded to call the magicians, and the astrologers, and the sorcerers, and the Chaldeans, for to shew the king his dreams. So they came and stood before the king.

"And the king said unto them, I have dreamed a dream, and my spirit was troubled to know the dream.

*"Then spake the Chaldeans to the king in **Syriack**, O king, live for ever: tell thy servants the dream, and we will shew the interpretation"* (Dan. 2:1-4).

The History of the Aramaic Language

Verse 4 changes the language in the text from Hebrew to Aramaic, the language of the ancient Syrians. Beginning with this verse, the Aramaic continues for six chapters — until the final verse of chapter seven (Dan. 7:28). These prophecies about *"the times of the Gentiles"* are presented in the language of Mesopotamia. Daniel wrote six chapters (half of the book) in Aramaic, an easy second language for Daniel, since it is closely akin to Hebrew. Furthermore, for the first three years of his education in the king's palace, he and his relatives were schooled in *"the tongue of the Chaldeans"* (Dan. 1:4). This gave Daniel a grasp of linguistics, as well.

Aramaic is a Semitic language, very similar to Hebrew. It may have been a post-Babel corruption of ancient Hebrew. The Arameans were an important Semitic people living in the regions of Mesopotamia and Syria in various tribes and settlements. During patriarchal times (Abraham, Isaac and Jacob), Aram lived in the Mesopotamian Valley, while during the monarchy (David and Solomon), his territory seemed to refer more specifically to Damascus and its surrounding area.

Aram was one of five sons of Shem and father of Uz, Hul, Gether and Mash, as given in the table of the nations in Genesis 10:22,23. Abraham descended from Arphaxad, another son of Shem. The name Aram, as a state or region, first appeared in the 23rd-century B.C., cuneiform inscription of the Akkadian King N**aram**-Sin (note the "aram" in Naram-Sin's name). The Bible associates the patriarchs with the **Aram**eans in such cities as Padan-**aram**, and the ancient city of Damascus, then known as **Aram**-Damascus.

By 701 B.C., Aramaic had become the major language of the fertile crescent — the Mesopotamia region from Babylon to Damascus. Though the Aramaic people themselves added little to the political aspects of early civilizations, their language was widely adopted. Aramaic became popular because of its use of an alphabet, in contrast with the cumbersome cuneiform or syllabic system used in the Akkadian language. Aramaic competed with cuneiform until it became the most used language by the middle of the eighth century B.C. The Medo-Persian Empire made it an international diplomatic language popularly used from India to Egypt between the sixth to fourth centuries B.C.

Flavius Josephus offers insight into the relationship between Aramaic and Hebrew. He wrote that Ptolemy had built a great library at Alexandria, Egypt, and had appointed Demetrius as his library-keeper, who was "… endeavoring, if it were possible, to gather together all the books that were in the habitable Earth, and buying whatsoever was anywhere valuable, or agreeable to the king's inclination (who was very earnestly set upon collecting of books), to which inclination of his, Demetrius was zealously subservient" (Josephus, *Antiquities*, XII, II, 1).

Josephus recorded a conversation between Demetrius and King Ptolemy, in which Demetrius said that "… he had been informed that there were many books of laws among the Jews worthy of inquiring after, and worthy of the king's library, but which, being written in characters and in a dialect of their own, will cause no small pains in getting them translated into the Greek tongue: that the character in which they are written seems to be like to that which is the proper character of the Syrians [Aramaic], and that its sound, when pronounced, is like to theirs also; and that this sound appears to be peculiar to themselves."

Many scholars agree that Aramaic heavily influenced Hebrew. The block style of Modern Hebrew came from the Aramaic alphabet during the Babylonian captivity. However, we should note that Aram descended from Shem, who spoke the language of his father, Noah, and those generations who came before him, all the way back to Adam. It is not unreasonable to assume that Hebrew was the original language and that Aramaic was a linguistic corruption after the Tower of Babel.

Dreams and Visions

The book of Daniel is noted for its dreams and visions concerning *"the times of the Gentiles"* and the rise of the Antichrist. There are two dreams by the Babylonian king and four dreams and/or visions by Daniel, himself, offering the single most important set of prophecies in the Old Testament. Only Daniel has been compared to the New Testament book of Revelation. Because of its unusual nature, it is important that we briefly examine the subject of dreams and visions.

During the last century, scientists became interested in dreams when they discovered that during certain times of the sleep cycle, the eyes move rapidly. They dubbed it REM, an acronym for **R**apid **E**ye **M**ovement, and began to study why it occurs. They found that during this period, people are dreaming. If awakened during REM, they remember their dreams, but if allowed to awaken on their own, many forget what they had dreamed.

Eventually, sleep studies discovered four stages of sleep, causing brain waves to vary in each. Brain waves become larger and slower as sleep becomes deeper. After reaching the fourth and deepest level, the pattern reverses and becomes progressively lighter until REM occurs. This cycle takes about 90 minutes. During REM, brain activity begins in the Pons, a structure in the brainstem and neighboring midbrain regions. The Pons sends signals to the Thalamus and to the Cerebral Cortex — the area responsible for thought processes. It also sends a signal to turn off motor neurons in the spinal cord, causing a temporary paralysis that prevents movement.

Most of us experience dreams while sleeping. Those we remember best usually occur early in the morning during the final stage of REM. Most dreams are construed from the previous day's activities or from the occupation of the mind in the last few hours before sleep. Dreams range from pleasant experiences to nightmares. Most terror-ridden dreams occur in the first two hours of sleep, whereas more enjoyable dreams, including inspiration or problem-solving dreams, usually occur during the last hour of a night's sleep.

Nightmares are more common among children between the ages of three to eight years, though adults can also be afflicted as a result of stress, emotional problems, trauma, or illness. Those, whose nightmares seem unrelated to these types of external problems, tend to have a more emotionally sensitive personality. Five to ten percent of the population experience nightmares at least once a month. Combat veterans may be prone to nightmares brought on by the stress of war. Such nightmares tend to occur over and over.

Night Terrors

Nightmares and night terrors arise from different physiological stages of sleep. Nightmares occur after several hours of sleep, whereas night terrors seem to occur within the first hour or two. Night terrors sometime include loud screaming and thrashing, though the person is hard to awaken. Children who have night terrors also have a tendency to sleepwalk. Fortunately, most children outgrow these dreadful dreams by the time they reach their teens.

These nocturnal experiences are a common phenomenon in brain activity. According to The Association for the Study of Dreams, most dreams are forgotten by morning: "There is something about the phenomenon of sleep itself which makes it difficult to remember what has occurred and most dreams are forgotten ..." This may have been the case with King Nebuchadnezzar. Though troubled by his dream, the king could not remember it. On occasion, a person might remember a dream several days later, which means that the memory is not lost, just hard to retrieve. This, too, seems to describe the situation with the Babylonian king.

The Bible records 34 dreams by 24 people, not all of them saints. Twenty-two dreams are recorded in the Old Testament and twelve in the New Testament. There are two *"visions"* in Genesis; but Hebrew terms translated *"vision"* (both singular and plural) are used 32 times in Daniel; and 70 times in the rest of the Bible. The book of Daniel contains a third of all the uses of the Hebrew terms for *"vision"* in Scripture and a fourth of all the uses of the Hebrew terms for *"dream"* in Scripture. Were it not for Genesis, with its introduction of the dream-state, Daniel would have far more than the rest of Scripture.

There are 22 uses of the singular term *"vision"* in the book of Daniel, of which, two are חזו *chezev*; eleven are חזון *chazown*; and nine are מראה *mareh*. In addition, there are ten more uses of the plural term *"visions"* — nine of which are חזו *chezev*, and one is חזון *chazown*. The term *"dream"* (singular) is used 23 times; *"dreamed"* (past tense) twice; and *"dreams"* (plural) four, for a total of 29 times. These plural uses of the dream-state in Daniel are all either חלום *chalowm*, חלם *chalam* or חלם *chelem*.

The first half of the book of Daniel is taken up with the dreams of the Gentile king, while the last half concentrates on the dreams and visions of the Jewish prophet, himself.

The King Could Not Remember His Dream

King Nebuchadnezzar experienced the first dream recorded in the book of Daniel and, as happens so often with dreams, he couldn't remember it the next morning:

"The king answered and said to the Chaldeans, The thing is gone from me: if ye will not make known unto me the dream, with the interpretation thereof, ye shall be cut in pieces, and your houses shall be made a dunghill.

"But if ye shew the dream, and the interpretation thereof, ye shall receive of me gifts and rewards and great honour: therefore shew me the dream, and the interpretation thereof.

"They answered again and said, Let the king tell his servants the dream, and we will shew the interpretation of it.

"The king answered and said, I know of certainty that ye would gain the time, because ye see the thing is gone from me.

"But if ye will not make known unto me the dream, there is but one decree for you: for ye have prepared lying and corrupt words to speak before me, till the time be changed: therefore tell me the dream, and I shall know that ye can shew me the interpretation thereof.

"The Chaldeans answered before the king, and said, There is not a man upon the earth that can shew the king's matter: therefore there is no king, lord, nor ruler, that asked such things at any magician, or astrologer, or Chaldean.

"And it is a rare thing that the king requireth, and there is none other that can shew it before the king, except the gods, whose dwelling is not with flesh" (Dan. 2:5-11).

Calling his staff together, the king asked for an interpretation of the dream. Perhaps he hoped that they could tell him the dream without revealing his own inability to remember it. After all, kings must maintain an air of superiority in the presence of their subjects. History records many instances of kings declaring themselves gods, or the sons of gods.

Most people become irritated when trying to hide something that others are pressing them about. Perhaps, without knowing it, they were irritating the king by asking him to tell them the dream. Try as they might, the Chaldean magicians, astrologers and sorcerers were unable to read the king's mind, or to tell him about his dream.

One of the so-called gifts of court magicians and sorcerers was the perceived ability to read the thoughts of others. The king thought that it should have been a simple thing for them to exhibit their psychic powers and tell him about his dream. However, at last the truth comes out. Those who boast of being psychic, with the ability to read another's thoughts, are usually playing parlor tricks. If any so-called mental telepathy is expressed, it must come through a third party, which could be either from a demonic source (as is the case of court magicians) or an angelic source (as in the case of Daniel). Indeed, such a thing may be possible through a third party, but not directly between the psychic and his subject.

> "For this cause the king was angry and very furious, and commanded to destroy all the wise men of Babylon.
>
> "And the decree went forth that the wise men should be slain; and they sought Daniel and his fellows to be slain.
>
> "Then Daniel answered with counsel and wisdom to Arioch the captain of the king's guard, which was gone forth to slay the wise men of Babylon:
>
> "He answered and said to Arioch the king's captain, Why is the decree so hasty from the king? Then Arioch made the thing known to Daniel.
>
> "Then Daniel went in, and desired of the king that he would give him time, and that he would shew the king the interpretation.
>
> "Then Daniel went to his house, and made the thing known to Hananiah, Mishael, and Azariah, his companions:
>
> "That they would desire mercies of the God of heaven concerning this secret; that Daniel and his fellows should not perish with the rest of the wise men of Babylon" (Dan. 2:12-18).

When faced with the pressure to admit his inability to remember the dream, Nebuchadnezzar flew into a fit of rage and threatened to execute his entire staff of advisers. Evidently, Daniel was not present, but learned about it from Arioch, the captain of the king's guard. Realizing the imminent danger, Daniel requested an audience with the king and asked for a little time that he might consult the God of Israel. Evidently, Daniel had developed an ability to communicate with heaven and interpret dreams, though this is the first time we learn about it. It is possible that Daniel had interpreted a significant number of dreams and visions prior to this account of the king's nightmare, which may have given him a measure of confidence.

Having been given time for consultation about revealing the king's dream, Daniel shared the problem with his three relatives. They prayed for God to grant them mercy and show the dream. That night, God answered their prayer:

"Then was the secret revealed unto Daniel in a night vision. Then Daniel blessed the God of heaven.

"Daniel answered and said, Blessed be the name of God for ever and ever: for wisdom and might are his:

"And he changeth the times and the seasons: he removeth kings, and setteth up kings: he giveth wisdom unto the wise, and knowledge to them that know understanding:

"He revealeth the deep and secret things: he knoweth what is in the darkness, and the light dwelleth with him.

"I thank thee, and praise thee, O thou God of my fathers, who hast given me wisdom and might, and hast made known unto me now what we desired of thee: for thou hast now made known unto us the king's matter" (Dan. 2:19-23).

The fact that Daniel could tap into the source of the king's dream is most interesting. This suggests that the dream did not originate in the king's brain, but was imposed upon him from beyond this world. That is the only way Daniel could have prayed and received the vision into his brain the next night. Furthermore, his divine source also imparted the dream's interpretation — something that was not given to the Gentile king. Daniel didn't have to piece the interpretation together, as some modern psychologists might try to do. In fact, his interpretation was so precise and accurate, some liberal scholars suggest that the book was written in later centuries, after the rise of the Roman Empire.

I can imagine an angel, sitting at something like a heavenly computer terminal connected to Daniel's brain, receiving Daniel's prayer request. Perhaps this angel contacted the angel in charge of monitoring Nebuchadnezzar's brain and downloaded the king's dream into Daniel's brain. It had to be something like that. If Daniel had the ability to tap directly into the king's thoughts, it would have been of little benefit. The king could not remember his own dream. There is no reason to believe that Daniel possessed psychic powers to read men's minds. Jesus demonstrated such abilities, but not Daniel. Technically speaking, it seems reasonable that the transfer was initiated in heaven.

Daniel was quick to give all credit to God, and humble enough not to take any credit for himself:

> *"Daniel answered in the presence of the king, and said, The secret which the king hath demanded cannot the wise men, the astrologers, the magicians, the soothsayers, shew unto the king;*
>
> *"But there is a God in heaven that revealeth secrets, and maketh known to the king Nebuchadnezzar what shall be in the latter days. Thy dream, and the visions of thy head upon thy bed, are these;*
>
> *"As for thee, O king, thy thoughts came into thy mind upon thy bed, what should come to pass hereafter: and he that revealeth secrets maketh known to thee what shall come to pass.*
>
> *"But as for me, this secret is not revealed to me for any wisdom that I have more than any living, but for their sakes that shall make known the interpretation to the king, and that thou mightest know the thoughts of thy heart"* (Dan. 2:27-30).

I am sure the king was astonished to hear Daniel remind him that he had been contemplating such thoughts about the future as he retired that night. The king probably knew that his kingdom would not be able to perpetuate its absolute power over other nations forever, but that someday, Babylon could be replaced by another more powerful conqueror. He probably wondered what nations would succeed Babylon and what fate awaited the human race. Those may have been the thoughts that troubled him as he drifted off to sleep.

He must have been enamored with Daniel's explanation that the secret came, not from himself, but from the great Creator of the universe. What humility! What a sophisticated demeanor this captive from the royal family of Zedekiah was exhibiting! Daniel's manner was both disarming and enchanting. Nebuchadnezzar was thoroughly impressed:

> *"Thou, O king, sawest, and behold a great image. This great*

image, whose brightness was excellent, stood before thee; and the form thereof was terrible.

"This image's head was of fine gold, his breast and his arms of silver, his belly and his thighs of brass,

"His legs of iron, his feet part of iron and part of clay.

"Thou sawest till that a stone was cut out without hands, which smote the image upon his feet that were of iron and clay, and brake them to pieces.

"Then was the iron, the clay, the brass, the silver, and the gold, broken to pieces together, and became like the chaff of the summer threshingfloors; and the wind carried them away, that no place was found for them: and the stone that smote the image became a great mountain, and filled the whole earth.

"This is the dream; and we will tell the interpretation thereof before the king" (Dan. 2:31-36).

Daniel recorded one of the most important prophetic dreams found in Scripture. Nebuchadnezzar had dreamed about the statue of a man, whose head was of gold; with arms and chest of silver; stomach and thighs of brass; legs of iron; and feet mixed with iron and clay. Then he saw something like an asteroid come out of the sky and destroy the image. Upon hearing the dream, the king remembered and was profoundly impressed that Daniel had retrieved his forgotten dream!

These metals were given in a particular order — decreasing in value, but increasing in strength until the statue reached its feet of clay. Gold, the most valuable metal, has a specific gravity of 19.5. Silver, second in value, has a specific gravity of 10.7. Brass, a lesser value, has a specific gravity of 8.0. Iron, the metal with the least value, has a specific gravity of 5.0. Finally, clay, with virtually no value, has a specific gravity of 1.9. Silver is stronger than gold; brass is stronger than silver; and iron is stronger than brass. However, the entire structure has feet of clay, leading to its ultimate weakness and failure. The term "feet of clay" has become a popular cliché for a person's shortcomings.

By now, the astounded king was prepared to accept the

interpretation. Presented in any other way, the king might have simply passed it off as the philosophy of some religious group. But Daniel was telling Nebuchadnezzar about a secret dream that only the king knew. Nebuchadnezzar must have realized that Daniel was privy to his innermost secret thoughts — perhaps not a comfortable feeling for the Babylonian monarch.

Daniel's Interpretation of the Dream

Daniel assured Nebuchadnezzar that he had great respect for the office of the Babylonian king. Also, he said that God had bestowed this great rulership upon him. Cautiously, Daniel told the king that the dream had been divinely given:

"Thou, O king, art a king of kings: for the God of heaven hath given thee a kingdom, power, and strength, and glory.

"And wheresoever the children of men dwell, the beasts of the field and the fowls of the heaven hath he given into thine hand, and hath made thee ruler over them all. Thou art this head of gold" (Dan. 2:37,38).

The Empire of Babylon (627-538 B.C.)

Gentile domination over Jerusalem began with Nebuchadnezzar's Babylon. Why did the dream not begin with the earlier Babylon under Nimrod, or with Egypt and the Pharaohs? Why Nebuchadnezzar's Babylon? Because this prophecy is about God's judgment upon Judea. It has no relationship to the general failures of mankind. This whole emphasis about *"the times of the Gentiles"* has to do only with Israel's violation of the law of the Sabbatical Years (Lev. 25, 26). We shall consider that subject at length when we get to Daniel's ninth chapter.

God began with Babylon because it marked the exile of the Jewish people and the desolation of the Promised Land. However, God promised that this Gentile domination would not be permanent; that Israel would rise again at the appearing of the Messiah. From head to toe, this is the story of foreign domination over Jerusalem. The ten toes make up the kingdom of the Antichrist. His world kingdom will be destroyed by the *"stone"* cut out without hands!

On the other hand, Nebuchadnezzar's famous city, with its hanging gardens and colossal tower certainly offers us a connection with Nimrod's ancient Babylon and MYSTERY BABYLON of the future. We should note that the head virtually controls the rest of the body. A hand or foot cannot see, hear, or provide intelligence, only the head. Therefore, we should be aware that Nimrod established a religious and political culture that formed the concept of centralized government.

Nimrod's Babylon revived an idolatrous pre-flood religion first mentioned in Genesis 6, where certain *"sons of God"* descended to the summit of Mount Hermon and lived for a while among men, taking human wives and producing *"giants."* In addition to the biblical account, several ancient sources mention these *Nephilim*, including Rabbinic literature, the *Zohar*, and the *Book of Enoch*. God incarcerated those fallen angels in *Tartarus*, a subterranean abyss or *"bottomless pit"* (Rev. 9:1,2). Their human offspring were destroyed in the flood. However, Genesis 6:4 indicates that another group of these fallen angels descended after the flood and continued their abominable practices. They also established a form of worship, known as the Canaanite religion of Baal and Ashtaroth. Canaan was one of four sons of Ham, along with Mizraim, Phut and Cush. Nimrod was the son of Cush, and grandson of Ham.

This idoloatrous worship was established by Ham's four sons, and can be seen in the religion of every ancient civilization. Whether it be the Babylonian fertility goddess, Ishtar, or her counterparts, Isis, Artemis, or Diana, the concept is the same. Those religious practices of previous civilizations were passed down to succeeding cultures. Perhaps Nebuchadnezzar's Babylon is represented as the head because its social concepts would remain in virtual control of all civilizations until the whole body is destroyed by the heavenly *"stone."* Also, the head is the obvious place for a babbling mouth! It seems that Babylon just had to be the head!

Nimrod's Babylon was the first city built after the Flood — in defiance of God's command to spread out and populate the Earth. Mankind's first form of idolatry was the "city." This great mystery is advanced in Revelation's MYSTERY BABYLON, the prototype or "mother," so to speak, of all the other cities of the world (with the exception of Jerusalem, God's city). Nimrod (c. 2300 B.C.), grandson of Ham, built the original Babylon and attempted to construct the infamous tower. Therefore, though the golden head of Nebuchadnezzar's kingdom was to be replaced by the arms and chest of silver, Babylon's culture would continue to dominate the world's civilizations.

The Symbolic Leopard

Before leaving our study of *"the belly and thighs of brass,"* let us take this opportunity to consider another metaphoric symbol connected with Nimrod and Mount Hermon — the symbolic "leopard." Solomon once wrote that the three peaks of Mount Hermon were known as *"the mountains of the leopards."* In the Song of Solomon, the king wrote: *"Come with me from Lebanon, my spouse, with me from Lebanon: look from the top of Amana, from the top of Shenir and Hermon, from the **lions' dens**, from **the mountains of the leopards**"* (Song of Solomon 4:8).

Here, Solomon mentioned *"lions' dens"* and *"the mountains of the leopards."* The *"lions' dens"* may be a reference to the prophecy given by Moses, calling Dan a *"lion's whelp"* (Deut. 33:22). Also, it seems that Solomon was aware of the Danite connection to Mount Hermon. When the Danites first arrived in Northern Israel, they conquered the village of *Laish* (meaning "lion") and renamed it "Dan." The book of Judges reports:

*"And they called the name of the city Dan, after the name of Dan their father, who was born unto Israel: howbeit the name of the city was **Laish** at the first"* (Judges 18:29).

Laish appears to be the origin of the terms *"lion's whelp"* (Deut. 33:22) and *"lions' dens"* (Song 4:8). Furthermore, Solomon mentioned Mount Hermon in connection with *"leopards."* It is said that Ham's grandson, Nimrod, wore a leopard skin as a symbol of his kingship.

Evidently, the symbolic leopard had its roots in the earliest stories of human civilization. It is quite possible that leopard skins were worn by the world's first king and queen — Adam and Eve. Though some Christian theologians have suggested that God killed sheep for Adam and Eve's clothing, there is no actual historical evidence. On the other hand, as ancient tribes migrated across the globe, tribal leaders donned leopard skins as symbols of rulership. I once saw a picture of the first king of China wearing a leopard skin. There is a wall painting in the Egyptian tomb of Tutankhamen (King Tut) depicting the successor to his throne wearing a leopard skin. I have also seen portraits of European royals wearing leopard skins. It is apparent that all early civilizations were acquainted with the symbolism of the leopard, thus showing a common ancestry among men.

Furthermore, ancient sources report that Nimrod's leopard skin gave him a political advantage, being accepted as the undisputed ruler of the world. It seems that the political authority, once belonging to Adam, was recognized in Nimrod. According to Alexander Hislop, author of *The Two Babylons*, the name Nimrod means, "the subduer of the leopard." It is said that Nimrod hunted with trained leopards. Accordingly, the ancient Jewish book of *Jasher* also claims that Nimrod wore the royal garments that once belonged to Adam and Eve:

"And Cush the son of Ham, the son of Noah, took a wife in those days in his old age, and she bare a son, and they called his name Nimrod, saying, At that time the sons of men again began to rebel and transgress against God, and the child grew up, and his father loved him exceedingly, for he was the son of his old age.

And the garments of skin, which God made for Adam and his wife, when they went out of the garden, were given to Cush. For after the death of Adam and his wife, the garments were given to Enoch, the son of Jared, and when Enoch was taken up to God, he gave them to Methuselah, his son. And at the death of Methuselah, Noah took them and brought them to the ark, and they were with him until he went out of the ark" (Jasher 7:23-26).

A 13th-century Jewish commentary (*Zohar*) also connected Nimrod's Leopard skins with the coats of skin belonging to Adam and Eve:

"Truly he [Nimrod] was a man of might, because he was clad in the garments of Adam, and was able by means of them to lay snares for mankind and beguile them. Rabbi Eleazar said: 'Nimrod used to entice people into idolatrous worship by means of those garments, which enabled him to conquer the world and proclaim himself its ruler, so that mankind offered him worship. He was called Nimrod for the reason that he rebelled against the most high King above, against the higher angels and against the lower angels.' Rabbi Simeon said: 'Our colleagues are acquainted with a profound mystery concerning these garments.'" (*Zohar*, vol. 1, p. 250). In Daniel 7 and Revelation 13, the Antichrist seems to be connected to the metaphoric leopard.

We cannot say with certainty that Adam and Eve wore leopard skins, but there are a number of sources claiming that Nimrod wore a leopard skin. Among them was Alexander Hislop, in his work, *The Two Babylons*: "This custom of taming the leopard, and pressing it into the service of man in this way, is traced up to the earliest times of primitive antiquity. In the works of Sir William Jones, we find it stated from the Persian legends, that Hoshang (i.e., Nimrod), the father of Tahmurs, who built Babylon, was the 'first who bred dogs and leopards for hunting.' Tahmurs, who built Babylon, could be none other than Nimrod ... this legend only attributes to his father what, as his name imports, he got the fame of doing himself. Now, as the classic god bearing the lion's skin is recognized by that sign as Hercules, the slayer of the Nemean lion, so in like manner, **the god clothed in the leopard's skin would naturally be marked out as Nimrod**, the 'leopard-subduer.' That this leopard skin, as appertaining to the Egyptian god, was no occasional thing, we have clearest evidence. Wilkinson tells us, that on all high occasions when the Egyptian high priest was called to officiate, it was indispensable that he should do so wearing, as his robe of office, the leopard's skin. As it is a universal principle in all idolatries that the high priest wears the insignia of the god he serves, this indicates the importance which the spotted skin must have had attached to it as a symbol of the god himself" (Alexander Hislop, *The Two Babylons*).

Gary Stearman offers an insightful commentary on this story from the book of Jasher, in his article entitled, *"Night of the Leopard"* (*Prophecy in the News*, July 2001). He said, "If this account contains even a grain of historical truth, then many of the old world's happenings are easier to explain. In this case, there was apparently a long-standing reverence for the garments of Adam and Eve. And rightly so, for they had been crafted for the first couple by the Lord, Himself, as seen in Genesis 3:21: *'Unto Adam also and to his wife did the LORD God make coats of skins, and clothed them.'* As the story continues, it becomes filled with political intrigue, trickery and deceit. Apparently, those garments were thought to possess some kind of power that was capable of giving a man strength over his enemies. Their chain of guardianship — through Enoch, Methuselah and Noah — has the ring of truth. That is, assuming the garments were preserved all the way to the Flood, they would have been handed down, exactly as described."

Gary noted that the account in the book of *Jasher* also tells us how the sacred garments found their way into the possession of Nimrod:

"And in their going out, Ham stole those garments from Noah his father, and he took them and hid them from his brothers. And when Ham begat his firstborn Cush, he gave him the garments in secret, and they were with Cush many days. And Cush also concealed them from his sons and brothers, and when Cush had begotten Nimrod, he gave him those garments through his love for him, and Nimrod grew up, and when he was twenty years old he put on those garments. And Nimrod became strong when he put on the garments, and God gave him might and strength, and he was a mighty hunter in the earth, yea, he was a mighty hunter in the field, and he hunted the animals and he built altars, and he offered upon them the animals before the Lord. And Nimrod strengthened himself, and he rose up from amongst his brethren, and he fought the battles of his brethren against all their enemies round about. And the Lord delivered all the enemies of his brethren in his hands, and God prospered him from time to time in his battles, and he reigned upon earth. Therefore, it became current in those days, when a man ushered forth those that he had trained up for battle, he would say to them, like God did to Nimrod, who was a mighty hunter in the earth, and who succeeded in the battles that prevailed against his brethren, that he delivered them from the hands of their enemies, so may God strengthen us and deliver us this day" (*Jasher* 7:27-33).

Gary continued: "Can it be that the skins from which the Lord fashioned garments for Adam and Eve came from the leopard? Hislop writes, '… that on all occasions when the Egyptian high priest was called to officiate, it was indispensable that he should do so wearing, as his robe of office, the leopard's skin. As it is a universal principle in all idolatries that the high priest wears the insignia of the god he serves, this indicates the importance which the spotted skin must have had attached to it as a symbol of the god, himself.' Nimrod had initiated the leopard priesthood. Subsequently, his reputation spread from Babylon, to the priesthoods of Assyria and Egypt. Hislop

The floodgates of
THE BLESSING
of The LORD
are open!

king Up My Faith

AT MY LIFE MAY BE BY GRACE!

The just shall live by faith!
GALATIANS 3:11

Today, I wake up my faith by
declaring—shouting—The WORD
of my Father!

I am healed!
I am prosperous!
I am happy and filled with joy!
My Father loves me as He
does Jesus!

I refuse to remain in any cage of
doubt, fear or unbelief!

I have faith in God—the Most High
God—my Father God!

Kenneth Copeland Ministries
Fort Worth, TX 76192
1-800-600-7395 (U.S. only) or +1-817-852-6000 • kcm.org

79-1427

further comments, 'When we find that Osiris, the grand god of Egypt, under different forms, was thus arrayed in a leopard's skin or spotted dress, and that the leopard-skin dress was so indispensable a part of the sacred robes of this high priest, we may be sure that there was a deep meaning in such a costume. And what could that meaning be, but just to identify Osiris with the Babylonian god, who was celebrated as the 'Leopard-tamer,' and who was worshipped even as he was, as Ninus, the child in his mother's arms.'

"Hislop and others have reflected that the same form of worship came into ancient Greece. Ceres the mother goddess, with Bacchus, the son in her arms, brought the figure of the mother and child cult into Greek culture. The Greek historian Herodotus stated, 'Orpheus [the priesthood] introduced from Egypt the greatest part of the mystical ceremonies, the orgies that celebrate the wandering of Ceres and the whole fable of the shades below. The rites of Osiris and Bacchus are the same; those of Isis and Ceres [Demeter] exactly resemble each other except in name. He noted that in the Greek rite of Bacchus, leopards were used to draw his coach and that Bacchus, himself, was shown clothed in a leopard skin. The priests who performed the rituals were also clothed in leopard skins. It is interesting that the Greek priesthood borrowed another custom from the Assyrians. They used the spotted skins of fawns when leopard skins were unavailable.

"In Babylonian, Assyrian and Greek society, Nimrod, the 'Leopard tamer,' came to be recalled as the subduer of the 'spotted one.' Later he, himself, came to be recognized by that title. Hislop says, 'Thus, then, it became easy to represent Nimrod by the symbol of the spotted fawn, and especially in Greece, and wherever a pronunciation akin to that of Greece prevailed. The name of Nimrod, as known to the Greeks, was Nebrod. The name of the fawn, as the spotted one, in Greece was Nebros; and thus nothing could be more natural than that Nebros, the spotted fawn, should become a synonym for Nebrod, himself. When, therefore, the Bacchus of Greece was symbolized by the Nebros, or spotted fawn, as we shall find he was symbolized, what could be the design but just covertly to identify him with Nimrod?'

"It is interesting that when Daniel prophesied the coming of four great Gentile empires, his vision depicted Greece as a leopard: '*After this I beheld, and lo another, like a **leopard**, which had upon the back of it four wings of a fowl; the beast had also four heads; and dominion was given to it*' (Daniel 7:6).

"The common interpretation of Daniel's passage is that the leopard depicts the military attributes of Alexander the Great, as he conquered the ancient civilized world. More accurately, it places Alexander in the tradition of Nimrod, the hunter/conqueror. The four wings upon the back of the Greek leopard are commonly interpreted as Alexander's four generals. Upon his death, the kingdom was divided among them. Cassander, Lysimachus, Ptolemy and Seleucus tried to maintain Alexander's alliance, but eventually, their power devolved into the hands of Ptolemy in Egypt and Seleucus in Syria.

Gary continued: "As we come to the prophecies that concern the future Antichrist, we see that they evoke references to Nimrod. Among them is a famous biblical statement that is seldom read in full. Usually, it is evoked at a Christmas service, illustrating the prophecy of Christ's birth. Its full meaning is much deeper. Let us look at it again, this time in the context of the resurrection and ascension into heaven, until the time of the end:

'*But thou, Bethlehem Ephratah, though thou be little among the thousands of Judah, yet out of thee shall he come forth unto me that is to be ruler in Israel; whose goings forth have been from of old, from everlasting.*

'*Therefore will he give them up, until the time that she which travaileth hath brought forth: then the remnant of his brethren shall return unto the children of Israel.*

'*And he shall stand and feed in the strength of the LORD, in the majesty of the name of the LORD his God; and they shall abide:*

for now shall he be great unto the ends of the earth.' And this man shall be the peace, when **the Assyrian** *shall come into our land: and when he shall tread in our palaces, then shall we raise against him seven shepherds, and eight principal men.*

'And they shall waste the land of Assyria with the sword, and the land of **Nimrod** *in the entrances thereof: thus shall he deliver us from the Assyrian, when he cometh into our land, and when he treadeth within our borders'* (Micah 5:2-6)."

Here, the Antichrist is associated with Nimrod, the builder of ancient Nineveh, capital of Assyria — the usurper who wore the stolen garments of Adam and Eve.

Gary concluded: "But we know the truth. They are the symbol of global power. As we noted earlier, the final world power also wears the leopard skin: *'And the beast which I saw was like unto a leopard ...'* (Revelation 13:2)."

The Tower of Babel

Upon seeing Nimrod's excursion into idolatry, God confused man's ability to communicate. The babble at Babel led to the dissolution of Nimrod's kingdom. Various clans left for parts unknown. The sons of Japhath moved northward into central Russia. From there, some went westward into Europe, while others moved eastward — across the Bering Strait and populating the Americas. According to the Human Genome Project, the Europeans and America's native Indians emerged from the same ancestry.

Ham's children moved westward into the territory around and to the south of Mount Hermon — into the land that God had promised to Abram. Canaan, Ham's son, called the Holy Land by his own name. Cush, Phut and Mizraim moved on further south, settling in Egypt (Mizraim) and Africa (Cush and Phut). Also, some Hammites migrated southeastward into India, the South Sea Islands and Australia.

Shem's people stayed mostly in the Mesopotamia Valley and the Middle East. Rabbinic literature suggests that Shem, himself, settled in Jerusalem and became known as Melchizedek. It is also said that Isaac, Jacob and Esau received their education in the home of Shem. Meanwhile, back in the fertile region of the Tigris / Euphrates Valley, Sumu-Abum (c. 1894 B.C.), a descendant of Shem, established a Semitic Dynasty and restored the walls of Babylon. The sixth king of this Semitic line, Hammurabi (1792-1750 B.C.), enlarged the city, making it a prosperous capital and trading center. Hammurabi also established a set of ethical laws, notably similar to the ones that ruled society in Egypt and other parts of the world. Some have suggested that the Mosaic Law was inspired by Hammurabi's moral code, but that would discount their Divine origin. It seems feasible that Hammurabi, a descendant of Shem, received his laws from the same source that Moses did — from God! Besides, Moses was not the first person to walk with God, Adam was. Evidently, God had established moral codes for all early civilizations, including that of Hammurabi; but the 613 statutes in the Mosaic Law were designed specifically for Israel.

In the centuries that followed, Babylon was occupied by various Assyrian overlords. Around 870 B.C., the Assyrian, Shalmaneser III, being called upon to settle a dispute, left the city of Babylon under the care of Adad-nirari III. According to the Greek historian Herodotus, Adad-nirari's mother, Samuramat (i.e., Semiramis), embellished the city.

In 734 B.C., certain southern tribes under Ukin-zer of Amukkani seized Babylon. But, a few years later, in 722 B.C., Merodach-baladan liberated Babylon and declared its independence. Claiming that he took "the hand of Bel," Merodach-baladan received the title "king of Babylon" (Isa. 39:1). He is the Babylonian king that sent a delegation with letters and a present to Hezekiah, asking for support to help him withstand the Assyrians. With Elamite support, Merodach-baladan was able to repulse an Assyrian advance and hold the city for a dozen years.

In 710 B.C., Sargon II led a successful Assyrian attack on the south. Rather than resist, the Babylonians welcomed him into their city, where he claimed the title "viceroy of Marduk." Over the next several decades, Babylon became a battleground for Assyrian forces. Esarhaddon (681-669 B.C.) established two kingdoms, putting one son (Shamash-shum-ukin) upon the throne of Babylon and his other son (Ashurbanipal) on the throne of Assyria. In 651 B.C., Ashurbanipal besieged his brother's palace in Babylon for three years until, in despair, Shamash-shum-ukin, burned his palace and perished in the flames.

In 627 B.C., Babylon regained its independence under Nabopolassar, by taking advantage of the internal strife plaguing the Assyrians. Nabopolassar's son, Nebuchadnezzar, enlarged the kingdom, using the city as a home base for his military exploits against Syria, Israel and Egypt.

Nebuchadnezzar brought back the spoils of war, accumulating a great fortune, with which he built many elaborate temples and palaces. No wonder his kingdom was associated with the head of gold. Nebuchadnezzar was a ruthless robber and absolute dictator. His campaigns were designed to grab all the gold, precious metals, jewels and treasures he could get his hands on. As is true with every thief, he had to continually keep looking over his shoulder, so to speak, because he had robbed so many people. Perhaps his mind was troubled because he realized that it might be only a matter of time until some neighboring kingdom would exact their revenge. He was troubled over the thought that Babylon might not last forever.

Today's Babylon is called Iraq. Some years ago, Saddam Hussein announced that he was a descendant of Nebuchad-nezzar and would rebuild ancient Babylon in his honor, the ruins of which are located about 50 miles south of Baghdad. He managed to rebuild the walls and gate, along with several palaces, but the city of Babylon remains today as little more than a museum on the banks of the Euphrates River. Saddam Hussein was convicted of high crimes against the Iraqi people and hanged on December 30, 2006.

Nebuchadnezzar feared that, eventually, some mighty army would overrun his kingdom. That time would come in the winter of 538 B.C., while Belshazzar was hosting a feast. The armies of the Medes and Persians diverted the Euphrates River and entered the city under the cover of darkness through the riverbeds that ran under Babylon's massive walls — the walls that were supposed to protect the city.

The Empire of Medo-Persia (538-331 B.C.)

In giving a prophetic view of the silver kingdom, Daniel was quick to point out that Nebuchadnezzar, himself, would never be defeated. The silver kingdom would come years after his death. Furthermore, Daniel referred to its inferiority:

"And after thee shall arise another kingdom inferior to thee ..." (Dan. 2:39).

It seems appropriate that the combined kingdom of the Medes and Persians should be associated with the two arms of the statue. Before the arrival of the Medes and Persians, the territory east of Babylon was known as an Elamite kingdom. The Elamites used a unique hieroglyphic script that later gave way to the Sumer-Akkadian cuneiform syllabary. The Elamites called their kingdom "Haltamti" (the land of God). According to a list of Sumerian kings, discovered in an archeological dig, Gilgamesh (c. 2600 B.C.) was one of their legendary heroes. While Israel was being ruled by judges, the Elamite kingdom was enjoying its "golden age." Not long after, the Elamites were defeated by Babylonian forces (c. 1100 B.C.).

Eventually, the Elamite kingdom faded away, only to be replaced by a group of Indo-Europeans (Aryans) from the borders of southern Russia. Their territory stretched westward to the land that lay north of the Black Sea. Their origins reached back to the more primitive cultures of the Balkan Peninsula, whose people also migrated southwestward into Greece. Strange as it may seem, the Persians and the Greeks both arose from the same ancestry, with a similar language, culture and set of customs. Two of these Aryan tribes settled within the borders of ancient Elam and became known as the Medes and the Persians.

Because of numerous wars with Assyrian armies, the loosely knit families of the Medes forged a united political regime and began their rise to national statehood. The Persians first appeared in the role of allies against Sennacherib (c. 710 B.C.). Kishpish came to the Persian throne in 675 B.C. By 640 B.C., there were two Persian kings — the two sons of Kishpish. The house of the younger served that of the older until the son and heir of Koresh I married Mandane, the daughter of the Median king. Their firstborn son was Koresh II (*"Cyrus"* - KJV English), one of the most celebrated kings of history, called by Isaiah (44:28; 45:1), *"my Shepherd"* and the LORD's *"anointed."* In 539 B.C., the combined armies of Darius the Mede and Cyrus the Persian overthrew Belshazzar's Babylon. The Medo/Persian Empire lasted for 207 years with thirteen monarchs. Because of their importance to Daniel's prophecies, we shall consider them again at length in Daniel 9-12.

Both the Persians and Greeks stem from the same Indo-European ancestry. Not long after the Persian rise to world prominence, they launched campaigns of aggression against Greece. This led to several wars extending over a period of 150 years, and eventually brought the revenge of Alexander the Great down upon them. Strange as it may seem, the descendants of the Medes and Persians (Aryans from the northern shore of the Black Sea) still live in the territory that once comprised ancient Persia. However, they are no longer called Persians. In 1925, Reza Shah Pahlavi was installed upon the Peacock throne, and Persia adopted the modern name of Iran — a name taken from their tribal origin, the Aryans.

Daniel did not give the names of any of the kingdoms that were destined to follow Babylon. He did not elaborate on the identity of the *"silver"* kingdom, only mentioning that it was *"another kingdom."* He did not tell Nebuchadnezzar that his enemy lay just to the east of Babylon, or that they would invade and conquer Belshazzar in 538 B.C. Daniel quickly moved on to the brass kingdom.

The Empire of Greece (331-168 B.C.)

"... and another third kingdom of brass, which shall bear rule over all the earth" (Dan. 2:39).

The statue's *"belly and thighs of brass"* found their fulfillment in the Greeks. We should note that brass always stands for judgment. Furthermore, the anatomical area known as *"the belly and thighs of brass"* houses the reproductive organ and the ability to produce the *"seed of the serpent."* This offers a strong connection with the tribe of Dan, who left their territory at the foot of Mount Hermon and sailed across the Mediterranean Sea to parts unknown. There is strong evidence that this "lost tribe" sailed to Greece, becoming the Danaans of Homer's *Iliad*, later known as the Spartans. Brass is the symbol of judgment and the name Dan means "judge." Adding these facts to other evidences, we learn from the book of Daniel that the future Antichrist will come from a "Greek/Roman" ancestry — possibly with roots in the *Nephilim* and their consorts from the tribe of Dan.

The Greeks never forgot, nor forgave the Persian attacks on their country. They were convinced that only a strong military could remove the continual threat of another Persian attack. For 150 years, Athenian orators and intellectuals called for an invasion of Persia. Finally, Philip of Macedonia took up the challenge. He planned the venture, but did not live to see it. Upon Philip's death, his son, Alexander, rallied the crusade to bring Persia and the rest of the world under Greek domination.

In 334 B.C., Alexander launched a campaign to conquer

Persia. When he crossed into Asia, he leaped ashore at the site of ancient Troy and danced about in his armor. He offered a sacrifice to the "ghost of Achilles, from whom he was descended on his mother's side, and to other Greek heroes who had died in the war against Troy" (Ussher, *Annals*, p. 215).

Alexander defeated a Persian army at the Granicus River, and soon, all the cities that lay in their path fell to the Greeks. In 333 B.C., Alexander met Darius III at Issus, in one of the decisive battles of world history, and won against incredible odds. Darius lost his wives and treasures to Alexander, but managed to get away. His defeat and death would come two years later, in 331 B.C.

The Macedonian monarch turned south along the Eastern Mediterranean and conquered Damascus, then on to Sidon and Tyre. The siege of Tyre took seven months. Then, Alexander set his sights on Jerusalem! Flavius Josephus gives us the remarkable story. Jerusalem's High Priest, Jaddua, was in agony over the prospects of a Greek invasion and went before the Lord in prayer. God came to him in a dream and told him to "... decorate the city, open the gates, have all the people to dress in white, and that the priesthood should dress appropriately according to their order, without the dread of any ill consequences" (Josephus, *Antiquities*, XI, VIII, 4).

When Jaddua learned that Alexander was near, he led a procession out to meet him. As the Greeks arrived at *Sapha* (Prospect), a hilltop where they could see Jerusalem and the Temple Mount, there stood the people of the city dressed in white robes! The High Priest's robe was purple and scarlet, with the golden mitre, containing the name of Jehovah, on his head. Alexander was delighted at what he saw. He dismounted and walked alone to meet the High Priest, bowed to the ground before him, and extended his hand in friendship. The Jewish people saluted him in unison and the priesthood gathered around him.

Alexander's army was startled at what they saw. Alexander's second in command sent a runner to question how he could adore the Jewish High Priest in this manner, to which Alexander replied: "I did not adore him, but that God who hath honored him with that high-priesthood; for I saw this very person in a dream, in this very habit, when I was at Dios, in Macedonia, who, when I was considering with myself how I might obtain the dominion of Asia, exhorted me to make no delay, but boldly to pass over the sea thither, for that he would conduct my army, and would give me the dominion over the Persians; whence it is, that having seen no other in that habit, and now seeing this person in it, and remembering that vision and the exhortation which I had in my dream, I believe that I bring this army under the divine conduct, and shall therewith conquer Darius, and destroy the power of the Persians, and that all things will succeed according to what is in my own mind" (*Antiquities*, XI, VIII, 5).

Josephus said that Alexander entered the Temple with the High Priest and offered a sacrifice to God. Furthermore, the High Priest brought out the scroll of Daniel and read the prophecy about the Greeks conquering the Persians! For this kind reception, Alexander promised to allow the Jews in Jerusalem and Babylon to worship freely, and that all taxes would be deferred for seven years.

Leaving Jerusalem, Alexander marched to Gaza, then into Egypt, where the Egyptians defected from their Persian rulers and received him gladly. He established the city of Alexandria and moved a colony of Jews there, "whose virtue and good behavior he greatly approved of, deeming them worthy of special trust" (*Annals*, p. 229).

In 331 B.C., Alexander pursued Darius into Babylonia and Persia, and fully conquered those countries. However, Darius managed to escape to Ectbatana, and from there northward toward the Caspian Gates.

In the summer of 330 B.C., Persian soldiers arrested their king and put him in a prison wagon; planning to give him to Alexander. When the Greeks were close, however, the Persian guards drew their bows and shot Darius and the horses. When the abandoned prison wagon was found by Polystratus, a Macedonian, the dying Darius asked that a message be given to Alexander, thanking him for being kind to his mother, wife and children. He begged nothing for himself, but a decent burial. Darius took Polystratus by the hand and asked that he pass on the handshake to Alexander as a pledge of faith, and then, having taken Polystratus' hand, he died.

Alexander's final campaign brought him to Babylon where, it is said, he sat down and wept because he had no more worlds to conquer. He and his men took Persian wives. Alexander's wife, Roxane, produced a son, Alexander IV.

At the age of 33, while planning his next campaign, Alexander became deathly ill. On May 22, 323 B.C., after being sick for only two weeks, he died in Babylon. Some say he died in a drunken stupor; others say he died of a venereal disease. There was speculation that Alexander was poisoned, while others suggest he died of malaria. Some accounts tell of his trying to commit suicide by jumping into the Euphrates River.

One account says that his generals marveled that his body did not decay for several days. In fact, Alexander may not have been dead, but was suffering from an "ascending paralysis" that left him immobile for several days before he died. The generals refused to remove him from his throne, but opened the doors of the palace and allowed his troops to enter and view his body.

In 1658, Bishop James Ussher suggested that Alexander was the victim of typhoid fever. This disease was known for its curious symptom of "ascending paralysis." It is a neurological problem that starts with the feet and moves up the body, paralyzing muscles and slowing down breathing. It can make a person look dead, even if he is not. Alexander may have been in that state for a few days before he died.

Successors to Alexander

Alexander left no instructions about who was to succeed him. However, he gave his royal seal to Perdiccas, who presided over the Council of Generals that met and divided up the kingdom. There were more than four generals who contended for the empire. In fact, there were several men who tried to grab a share of the kingdom. But the term *"horns"* always refers to rulers. Horns cannot simply represent the *"four winds of heaven."* In the end, they speak of four of those generals who succeeded in dividing Alexander's kingdom. Conflicts between Alexander's men led to several wars, but the four generals who ended up with the divided kingdom were Seleucus, Ptolemy, Cassander and Lysimachus. These are the four who are generally attributed to the four horns in Daniel 8:8. However, we shall review several of the contenders, beginning with Antipater, governor of Macedonia.

Antipater

When Alexander left for Asia, he entrusted Antipater (398-319 B.C.), with governing Macedonia and Greece. Antipater often found himself opposed by Alexander's mother, Olympias, who tried to undermine his position, first with Alexander, and later with Perdiccas, to whom Alexander had left his royal seal. After Alexander's death, Antipater led the Macedonian army against a rebellion of Greeks. His stronger forces, defeated the Greeks, and reestablished the Macedonian occupation of Greece.

Antigonus, commander of the Macedonian troops in Asia, served Antipater. He brought back Alexander's Persian wife, Roxane, and their infant son, Alexander IV. Antipater sealed his alliance with Antigonus by allowing the marriage of his daughter, Phila, to Antigonus' son, Demetrius. By then, Antipater was nearing eighty. The period of political stability soon ended with his death in 319 B.C., leaving Polyperchon in charge of the Macedonian army.

King Phillip III Arrhidaeus

Alexander was fond of his half-brother Arrhidaeus (359-317 B.C.). He was an illegitimate son of King Phillip and a dancer. The young man was believed to be mentally retarded and subject to epileptic seizures. To protect his life, Alexander took him along on his trip to conquer the world. After Alexander's death, Arrhidaeus was proclaimed "King Phillip III" on June 10, 323 B.C., by the Macedonian army in Asia. However, he was only a figurehead under the control of Alexander's powerful generals. His reign did not last long. Alexander's mother, Olympias, led an army that defeated and killed him on December 25, 317 B.C.

Polyperchon

Polyperchon (394-303 B.C.) was a Macedonian general who served under King Phillip and his son, Alexander the Great. Having reached Babylon, Alexander sent Polyperchon back to Macedonia to help Antipater defeat a Greek rebellion. When news of Alexander's death arrived, Polyperchon stayed in Macedonia, while Antipater traveled to Asia Minor in an attempt to assert his rulership over the whole Empire.

Upon Antipater's death in 319 B.C., Polyperchon was appointed supreme commander of the entire Empire, but soon fell into conflict with Antipater's son, Cassander. Their civil war quickly spread among all the successors of Alexander, with Polyperchon allying with Eumenes against Cassander, Antigonus and Ptolemy.

Polyperchon was successful in gaining control of the Greek cities, but his victory was short-lived. His fleet was destroyed by the forces of Antigonus in 318 B.C. Cassander took control of Athens the next year and Polyperchon fled to Epirus, where he joined Alexander's mother, Olympias, widow Roxana, and young son, Alexander IV. Olympias led an army into

Macedon and defeated King Philip III Arrhidaeus (Alexander's half-brother). But in 316 B.C., Cassander returned from the Peloponnesus, executed Olympias and captured Roxana and the boy king, both of whom he later killed.

After Olympias was killed, Polyperchon fled to the Peloponnesus, where he still controlled a few areas, and allied himself with Antigonus, who had fallen out with his former allies. Polyperchon soon controlled much of the Peloponnesus, including Corinth and Sicyon. When war again broke out between Antigonus and the others, Antigonus sent Alexander's natural son, Heracles, to Polyperchon as a bargaining chip to use against Cassander. However, Polyperchon decided to break with Antigonus and executed the boy. Polyperchon retained control of the Peloponnesus until his death a few years later, but took no further action against the contenders for the Empire.

Cassander

Cassander (355-297 B.C.), son of Antipater, did not travel with the Macedonian army, but remained in Europe to assist with his father's rule over Macedonia and Greece. However, he was displeased with his father's choice of Polyperchon. In 318 B.C., Cassander persuaded King Philip III to depose Polyperchon. After this, his control over Macedonia remained secure. In 316 B.C., he had Olympias executed for the murders of King Philip III and his brother, Nicanor. He imprisoned her grandson, the young Alexander IV and his mother, Roxane, and some years later had them executed.

Cassander proclaimed himself king of Macedonia and joined the coalition of Ptolemy, Seleucus and Lysimachus against Antigonus. Cassander continued the policy pursued by his father, Antipater, of treating the Greek city-states as subjects rather than allies, in contrast to the policy that Antigonus had followed.

With the death of Antigonus in 301 B.C., Cassander secured

his kingship over Macedonia. He married Thessalonica, the sister of Alexander the Great and, in her honor, founded the city of Thessalonica, which eventually became the greatest Macedonian city.

Perdiccas

Perdiccas (360-321 B.C.) was a member of a princely family of the province of Orestis in upper Macedonia. He served with distinction under Alexander and became his leading general. The dying Alexander entrusted him with his royal seal. However, Perdiccas was unable to keep the empire intact. Alexander's kingdom was divided to the *"four winds of heaven"* (Dan. 8:8).

In 322 B.C., Perdiccas requested the hand of Antipater's daughter, Nicaea. However, before the marriage was arranged, Alexander's mother, Olympias, offered him her daughter (Alexander's sister), Cleopatra. He broke his engagement to Nicaea and married Cleopatra. His rejection of Nicaea caused an irreparable breach with Antipater.

Alexander's royal seal must have given Perdiccas the notion that he could reunite the Empire. In 321 B.C., he marched south into Egypt to attack Ptolemy. However, he failed to defeat Ptolemy's army and lost most of his men in the attempt. Thoroughly discouraged, his troops mutinied and murdered him.

Antigonus I

Antigonus I (382-301 B.C.) was one of the oldest and ablest of Alexander's Macedonian generals. He took part in the early campaigns in Asia and, in 333 B.C., Alexander appointed him governor of Central Phrygia. After Alexander's death, Pamphylia and Lycia were added to his province.

He was unwilling to accept the authority of Perdiccas, to whom Alexander had left his royal seal, so he fled to Macedonia and gained the favor of Antipater. Over the years, he and his son, Demetrius, became the leaders of the Macedonian army and grew very powerful. The prospect that they might try to reunite the Macedonian empire, alarmed Ptolemy, Seleucus, Cassander and Lysimachus.

In 306 B.C., Antigonus became the first Macedonian general to take the royal title, "king of Macedonia." However, at the Battle of Ipsus, in 301 B.C., the combined armies of Ptolemy, Seleucus and Lysimachus defeated Antigonus, while Demetrius was off chasing another army. Without his son to help defend him, Antigonus died in a hail of spears. Soon, Demetrius was also killed. With their deaths, the idea of uniting the Macedonian Empire vanished.

Ptolemy

Ptolemy (360-284 B.C.) was appointed to rule over Egypt. He was the stepson of a Macedonian nobleman, military general and one of the inner circle of Alexander's advisers. Some say he was the illegitimate son of King Philip, making him a half-brother to Alexander.

He fought with distinction in India and wrote a history of Alexander's campaigns. Though the army wanted to bury their monarch in Macedonia, Ptolemy was allowed to take the body to Egypt. It is reported that Alexander's remains were buried at Memphis, and later moved to a grand tomb in Alexandria at the site of the oracle of Amun, Egypt's ram god. However, a few years ago, an empty tomb was discovered at the Siwa Oasis, near the Oracle of Zeus, in the desert of western Egypt, which caused quite a stir. It contained evidence of being a royal tomb — possibly that of Alexander, since no tomb site had ever been confirmed by archeological digs in Memphis or Alexandria.

In 322 B.C., Ptolemy married Eurydice, the daughter of Antipater, whom Alexander had left in charge of Macedonia. In 316 B.C., he joined forces with Antipater's son, Cassander, along with Seleucus and Lysimachus, to resist Antigonus' ambition to reconstitute the Macedonia Empire under his rule. In 306 B.C.,

Ptolemy's fleet was almost wiped out at the battle of Salamis in Cyprus, by Antigonus' son Demetrius, who, by the way, had married Phila, another one of Antipater's daughters.

More successful as a statesman than as a soldier, Ptolemy left behind a kingdom, which was to become the most enduring of the Macedonian monarchies after Alexander the Great. He built the famous Alexandrian lighthouse, considered one of the seven wonders of the ancient world, and a famous library containing literature collected from all over the known world. When the Moslems burned the Alexandrian Library in A.D. 640, there were 700,000 scrolls — among them many original writings that were forever lost. Ptolemy I is the founder of the dynasty that ruled Egypt for three centuries, until the death of the last descendent, Cleopatra, in 30 B.C.

Seleucus

Seleucus (358-281 B.C.), son of Antiochus (one of Philip's generals), fought in the "Companion" cavalry and later became commander of the crack, heavy infantry formation, the Hypaspistae. Antipater appointed him governor of Babylon in 321 B.C. However, in 315 B.C., Antigonus drove him out. He fled to Egypt, where he gained Ptolemy's aid in pursuing his war against Antigonus.

Antigonus eventually grew tired of trying to conquer Babylon and Persia, pulled his troops out and returned to Phrygia. In 312 B.C., Seleucus was able to regain and secure his kingdom. This is the calendar year that the Jews used for centuries to date important events. They called that year "the beginning of the kingdom of the Greeks" (I Maccabees 1:10). In fact, the current Jewish calendar, which purports to date from Creation, uses as its source the *Seder Olam Rabbah*, written about twenty years after the Bar Kokhba rebellion.

The *Seder Olam Rabbah* only began to make inroads into Jewish thinking in the ninth and tenth centuries, but was not widely used until 1517. Previous Jewish dating marked their years from 312 B.C., a system of dating called *Minyan Shtarot* (see pages 240-242).

Seleucus made peace with the Indian ruler, Chandra-gupta, and received a corps of elephants, which played a large part in his victory over Antigonus at Ipsus (301 B.C.). At the partition of Antigonus' domains, Seleucus added Syria to his territories and founded his western capital at Antioch. In 285 B.C., his most threatening rival, Antigonus' son, Demetrius, surrendered.

In 281 B.C., Seleucus turned on his former ally, Lysimachus. He invaded Lysimachus' territories in Western Asia Minor and, at the battle of Corupedium, defeated and killed him. But when he crossed to Europe to claim Lysimachus' Thracian kingdom, he was assassinated by Ptolemy Ceraunus, the son of Ptolemy I.

His heirs continued to rule a Syrian Empire from Damascus, and eventually produced Antiochus IV Epiphanes who, in 168 B.C., erected a statue of Zeus and sacrificed a sow on the site of the great altar in the courtyard of the Jerusalem Temple.

Rabbinical writings say that Antiochus IV fulfilled Daniel's prophecy about the abomination of desolation. However, Jesus taught that the prophecy would be ultimately fulfilled by a future Antichrist. We shall have more to say about Antiochus IV Epiphanes when we study Daniel 9-12.

Lysimachus

Lysimachus (361-281 B.C.) was also a member of Alexander's "Companion" cavalry, and distinguished himself in campaigns in India. Following Alexander's death, he became governor of Thrace. After Perdiccas had rejected the hand of Antipater's daughter, Nicaea, Lysimachus married her. In 315 B.C., he joined the coalition of Ptolemy, Seleucus and Cassander, against their mutual enemy, Antigonus. For many years, he was preoccupied with trying to hold on to his territory in Thrace against rebellious Thracian tribes and coastal Greek cities.

In 301 B.C., he launched a perfectly-timed surprise invasion of Asia Minor and in the following year, helped to defeat and kill Antigonus. Following the battle, Lysimachus became the principal beneficiary of Antigonus' territories. His newly acquired dominions stretched from north to south across Asia Minor, shut out Seleucus from the western seaboard and thus, sowed the seeds of future conflict. In the last years of his reign, Lysimachus' autocratic methods of government became increasingly unpopular. When Seleucus invaded his territory in 282 B.C., he met little resistance. Lysimachus made a stand at Corupedium near Magnesia in Asia Minor, but was killed in the battle.

The Roman Empire (168 B.C. - Mid 4th Century)

Using Nebuchadnezzar's dream statue as an outline of world kingdoms, Daniel described the fourth kingdom as being more brutal than the others — as strong as iron:

"And the fourth kingdom shall be strong as iron: forasmuch as iron breaketh in pieces and subdueth all things: and as iron that breaketh all these, shall it break in pieces and bruise" (Dan. 2:40).

The legs are the longest part of the body, representing the concept that the fourth kingdom would dominate Jerusalem for many centuries. Also, the two legs allude to the idea that the iron kingdom would be divided into two formidable forces. During the reign of Constantine in the fourth century A.D., the Roman kingdom split into two factions, the Byzantine Empire in the East and the weakened Roman government in the West.

Rome's Historical Background

The origin of Rome is shrouded in legend. Without being too detailed with its long history, suffice it to say that Roman history claims its origin in the eighth century B.C., with the births of Romulus and Remus — twin brothers who founded the ancient capital. They were said to be the "virgin-born" sons of Rhea Silvia, whose father was Mars, the Roman god of war.

Romulus marked the city's boundaries with a plough drawn by a white bull and a white cow. Today, the symbol of the new United Europe shows Europa, the mother of European royalty, riding a white bull, symbol of the Greek god, "Zeus" (the Roman "Jupiter"). According to the legend, Remus leaped over the furrow, probably in jest, but Romulus lost his temper and killed his twin brother (suspiciously similar to the story of Cain and Abel).

According to historical sources, Rome was founded on April 21, 753 B.C. The city atop Palatine Hill was little more than a small settlement and had almost no women. To solve this problem, Romulus invited the neighboring tribe of "Sabines" to a harvest festival. Once their guests arrived, the Romans abducted 600 Sabine daughters. These legends seem to be corrupted stories that came right out of Israel's ancient sacred scrolls! Where else could they have come from? Israel's messiah was predicted to be virgin born (Isaiah 7:14); and in Judges 21:12, the Israelites abducted 400 virgins from a neighboring tribe to supply wives for the tribe of Benjamin. It seems that someone, familiar with Israel's history, corrupted those stories while telling them around the campfires of ancient Rome.

Who could have twisted Jewish facts to launch the Roman legends? Could it have been the Trojan prince, Aeneas, who was credited with being the progenitor of Romulus and Remus? According to legend, Aeneas escaped the destruction of Troy around 1187 B.C. and fled to central Italy, where his descendants produced Romulus and Remus. His story is recorded in Virgil's *Aeneid*, a famous poem about the Roman era. Aeneas had his family roots in the Spartans, who, at first, had called themselves Danaans (*The Iliad and Odyssey*, by Homer). If he was a descendant of the lost tribe of Dan, then it is quite feasible that such legends could have been concocted from stories out of the Bible. You can read more about the Danaans in our study of Daniel, chapter 11.

How could such primitive beginnings produce the glory of Rome — a city and empire with the military might to rule the world? First of all, Rome lies inland from the Mediterranean, offering a measure of protection from aggressors traveling by sea. In fact, the Italian peninsula is protected by water on three sides, and by the mountainous Alps on the north. Furthermore, Italy lies in the center of the Mediterranean world. These conditions were in Rome's favor. Their great culture came from the Greeks, who taught them how to read and write — and provided them with a pantheon of gods. The Greek Zeus became Jupiter, Ares became Mars, Aphrodite became Venus, etc.

Over the centuries, Rome fought one war after another. Either they were being invaded, or they were invading someone else. They fought against Carthage on the northern shore of Africa, Spain in the west, and Greece in the east. They launched campaigns against Asia Minor and Syria. It seemed that their wars would never end. Eventually, the landowners in Italy had few workers to help them plant, or customers to buy their crops. Since Rome's army was recruited from among its landowners, many farmers left their farmlands and moved to urban centers in order to avoid the draft. It is hard to imagine how they managed to become such a formidable world kingdom, but the Romans lived and breathed … ate and slept "war."

In 168 B.C., the Roman army won a decisive battle against the Greeks. The Macedonian king, Perseus, was banished to a small town where he spent the rest of his life. The Greek peninsula was divided into four "republics," each forbidden to have any political or commercial relations with the other. Some regard this date as the end of the Greek Empire and the beginning of the Imperial Roman Empire.

Roman wars continued throughout the next century. In 84 B.C., the Roman general, Sulla, decided that he would return to Rome and become its dictator. In August 82 B.C., Sulla fought the "Battle of the Colline Gate," where he slaughtered 50,000 men and became the undisputed master of the Roman Empire. Three days after the battle, he ordered all 8,000 prisoners taken onto the battlefield and massacred. Over the following months, he gave his army a list of people he wanted eliminated. They included supporters of his enemies and others he simply didn't like. He became Rome's absolute dictator, having people killed on a whim. But one person he chose to spare was a young patrician — Gaius Julius Caesar, who eventually became the most famous Roman emperor in history.

Within a few short years, the Romans would become the ruthless rulers of the known world. In 67 B.C., the Roman general, Pompey, was given supreme power to conquer all lands to the East. He annexed Syria in 65 B.C., and Jerusalem in 63 B.C., leaving Hyrcanus to govern Judea. The Jewish state had long been an ally to Rome, but Pompey made it a "protectorate" — a fancy name for a slave state.

Rome ruled Jerusalem with an iron hand, crucifying Jesus around A.D. 30; burning Herod's Temple in A.D. 70; and putting down the Bar Kochba revolt in A.D. 135. They emptied the Holy Land of its inhabitants and sold them on the slave markets of the world. However, in A.D. 313, Constantine halted the persecution of Christians and Jews. In A.D. 325, he organized the Council of Nicaea and led the Empire toward a decidedly Christianized Roman System. He built a new city on the northern shore at the eastern end of the Dardanelles waterway and called it Constantinople (today's Istanbul). The Roman Empire was effectively split between the East and the West, as seen in the two legs of iron in the statue of Nebuchadnezzar's dream.

The Feet and Toes of Iron and Clay

Looking into the far future, Daniel disclosed the meaning of the ten toes as a final world kingdom. Ten short toes represent a world kingdom of relatively short duration:

"And whereas thou sawest the feet and toes, part of potters' clay,

*and part of iron, the kingdom shall be divided; but there shall be
in it of the strength of the iron, forasmuch as thou sawest the iron
mixed with miry clay.*

*"And as the toes of the feet were part of iron, and part of clay, so the
kingdom shall be partly strong, and partly broken"* (Dan. 2:41,42).

Daniel explained that the weakness of the future world
kingdom lay in its mixture of iron and clay, noting that the
iron represented a strong government and the clay, a weak
and fragmented system. Daniel called it *"partly strong, and
partly broken."* Most eschatologists agree that the iron speaks
of totalitarian dictatorships, while the clay denotes inherit
weaknesses evident in the political structures of democracies.
In fact, Hippolytus introduced this concept: "As these things,
then, are destined to come to pass, and as the toes of the image
turn out to be democracies, and the ten horns of the beast are
distributed among ten kings" (Hippolytus, *On Daniel*, ch. 2,
para. 2). However, the true meaning of the iron and clay may
be far more sinister than simply a mixture of democracies with
totalitarian regimes.

The Seed of the Serpent

Daniel offered a very strange statement concerning the iron
and clay:

*"And whereas thou sawest iron mixed with miry clay, **they shall
mingle themselves with the seed of men**: but they shall not cleave
one to another, even as iron is not mixed with clay"* (Dan. 2:43).

He said that *"they"* would mingle with *"the seed of men."* It
is possible that he was referring to a situation similar to the one
that occurred in the days before the Flood, when the *"sons of God"*
(i.e., fallen angels) took human wives. Ancient sources tell us that
fallen angels descended to the summit of Mount Hermon and
lived in the area that eventually became the territory of Dan.

According to the Encyclopedia Britannica, Hermon means
"forbidden place." Jerome (4th-century translator of the Latin

Vulgate Bible) interpreted Hermon as "anathema." Evidently, Mount Hermon was the port of entry for a group of wicked angels, who corrupted the human race in the days of Noah. Moses wrote:

"That the sons of God saw the daughters of men that they were fair; and they took them wives of all which they chose ....

"There were giants in the earth in those days, and also after that, when the sons of God came in unto the daughters of men, and they bare children to them, the same became mighty men which were of old, men of renown" (Gen. 6:2,4).

The fallen angels bore children called *"Nephilim."* Their giant grandchildren were the *"Anakim"* and *"Raphaim."* There is a rabbinical remark about this story in an ancient Jewish commentary (*Zohar*), in which two rabbis added the following insight:

"Rabbi Jose says, following a tradition, that these were *Uzza* and *Azazel*, whom, God deprived of their supernal sanctity. How, it may be asked, can they exist in this world? Rabbi Hiya answers, that they were of a class of spirits referred to in the words, *'and birds which fly on the earth'* (Gen. 1:20), and these, as we have said, appear to men in the form of human beings. If it is asked, how can they transform themselves? The answer is, that they do, in fact, transform themselves into all kinds of shapes, because when they come down from heaven they become as concrete as air and take human shape. These are *Uzza* and *Azazel*, who rebelled in heaven, and were cast down by God, and became corporeal on the earth and remained on it, not being able to divest themselves of their earthly form. Subsequently, they went astray after women, and up to this day they exist and teach men the arts of magic. They begat children whom they called *Anakim* (giants), while the *Nephilim* themselves were called *'sons of God'"* (*Zohar*, vol. 1, p. 186).

Note that one rabbi alluded to a class of spirits described as *"birds"* in Genesis 1:20. Perhaps this was the origin of the story that angels had bird-like wings. To this day, white doves are symbolic of good, while black crows are typical of evil. It should also be noted that birds seem to have a reptilian connection. The Phoenix was depicted as an eagle in the West, but in the East, it was a winged dragon. From ancient lore, Satan was thought to be a gargoyle with bat-like wings.

The Book of Enoch

The apocryphal Book of Enoch enlarges upon the story of the *Nephilim*. First, allow me give you a little background on this mysterious book. Scholars have traced its origin back past the first century:

> "In the early literature of the church there is a whole chain of evidences to this effect. Nearly all of the church [leaders] knew of an apocryphal Book of Enoch. Among the Apostolic [leaders], the Epistle of Barnabas refers to such a work. From that time on to about the seventh-century, Christian literature produces ample proof of the constant use and high standing of this book. The early theologians Justin Martyr, Clement of Alexandria, Origen, Irenaeus, Tertullian, Eusebius, Jerome, Hilary, Epiphanius, Augustine, and others refer to and use it ... following the example of Jude, whose citation is taken from Enoch 1:9. (George H. Schodde, Nov. 21, 1881, General Introduction to the Book of Enoch).

The following is quoted from the Book of Enoch:

> "And it came to pass, after the children of men had increased in those days, beautiful and comely daughters were born to them.
> "And the angels, the sons of the heavens, saw and lusted after them, and said one to another: 'Behold, we will choose for ourselves wives from among the children of men, and will beget for ourselves children.'
> "And they descended on Ardîs, which is the summit of Mount Hermon; and they called it Mount Hermon, because they had sworn on it and bound themselves mutually by a curse" (Enoch 6:1-6).

Of all places on this planet where angels could have descended, it was on the northern border of the Promised Land.

Perhaps knowing something about God's future plans to give territory to Abraham's descendants, these angels plotted their strategy to introduce *"the seed of the serpent"* into the human race. Also, Mount Hermon lay in the territory where Ham and his family migrated after God's judgment at the Tower of Babel. According to Genesis 10:6, Ham had four sons: *"And the sons of Ham; Cush, and Mizraim, and Phut, and Canaan."*

Canaan settled in the area of Mount Hermon and southward into the territory that was to become Abraham's Promised Land. This is why the Promised Land was called "Canaan" in the days of Moses and Joshua. Mizraim continued to move southward into Egypt. Coincidentally, Mount Hermon has three peaks, and Ham's family encountered another set of "three peaks" that had been built before the Flood (those being three great pyramids). Evidently, Mizraim was fascinated by the pyramids and developed a system of worship based on those ancient structures. Cush and Phut continued the family migration southward and settled in Ethiopia and throughout the continent of Africa.

To this day, Mount Hermon is still the place where evil continually rains down upon Israel. It is the area of the Syrians, and Hezbollah. The Book of Enoch continues:

"And they took unto themselves wives, and each chose for himself one, and they began to go in to them, and mixed with them, and taught them charms and conjurations, and made them acquainted with the cutting of roots and of woods. And they became pregnant and brought forth great giants whose stature was three thousand ells. These devoured all the acquisitions of mankind till men were unable to sustain themselves. And the giants turned themselves against mankind in order to devour them" (Enoch 7:1-4).

It seems that these fallen angels contaminated both men and animals with genetic manipulation. Perhaps the fossil evidence of giant animals points to the work of the fallen angels. We do not know how many people were contaminated, but we are told that at least Noah's family remained genetically pure. For that reason, God destroyed the world with the Flood. Had it not been for Noah and his three sons, those fallen angels might have brought an end to all life on the planet. Noah, Shem, Ham and Japheth helped save the animals and repopulate the Earth.

God Judged the Angels

Both Peter and Jude added further insight about these fallen angels. Peter said:

"God spared not the angels that sinned, but cast them down to hell [Tartarus], and delivered them into chains of darkness, to be reserved unto judgment; and spared not the old world, but saved Noah the eighth person, a preacher of righteousness, bringing in the flood upon the world of the ungodly" (II Peter 2:4,5).

Jude put it this way:

"And the angels which kept not their first estate, but left their own habitation, he hath reserved in everlasting chains under darkness unto the judgment of the great day" (Jude 6).

Both passages tell of severe punishment upon the Nephilim. Yet, Moses said that *"sons of God"* reappeared after the Flood (Gen. 6:4). How can this be? The *Book of Enoch* only mentioned 200 angels, and Satan was not among them. Bear in mind, Satan's forces were much larger then a mere 200. Perhaps the original group of *Nephilim* were scouts for a much larger force of demonic angels who, under the leadership of Satan, returned to Earth after the Flood. It seems to me that the Tower of Babel (meaning "Gate to God") may have been built in an effort to contact these dark forces and forge a defense against the threat of another judgment. As noted in the *Zohar* (above) Rabbi Hiya said, "... to this day they exist and teach men the arts of magic."

Genesis 6:4 adds, "... *and also after that*" — meaning that more fallen angels returned to this area after the Flood and established what Joshua called the *"land of giants."* Moses and Joshua conquered those giants, of whom, Og was king. Moses

wrote that Og's bed was almost 15 feet long! (Deut. 3:11). Og
reigned in Mount Hermon. Joshua wrote:

> *"And the coast of Og king of Bashan, which was of the remnant
> of the giants, that dwelt at Ashtaroth and at Edrei,*
>
> *"And **reigned in mount Hermon**, and in Salcah, and in all
> Bashan, unto the border of the Geshurites and the Maachathites,
> and half Gilead, the border of Sihon king of Heshbon.*
>
> *"Them did Moses the servant of the LORD and the children of
> Israel smite ..."* (Joshua 12:4-6).

The tribe of Dan moved to this area during the days of the
Judges, and adopted the Canaanite worship of these angels. It
was an ancient idolatry that opposed the worship of Jehovah. In
fact, Baal and Ashtaroth were Canaanite deities, whose origin
was in the vacinity of Mount Hermon! The book of Judges even
calls Mount Hermon *"Baalhermon,"* saying:

> *"Namely, five lords of the Philistines, and all the Canaanites,
> and the Sidonians, and the Hivites that dwelt in mount Lebanon,
> from **mount Baalhermon** unto the entering in of Hamath"*
> (Judges 3:3).

Furthermore, the fallen angels living on and around Mount
Hermon adopted a biblical name for the mountain. They had
the audacity to plagiarize a name that God had given to Mount
Moriah — Mount Sion! Moses wrote:

> *"And they possessed his [Sihon's] land, and the land of Og
> king of Bashan, two kings of the Amorites, which were on this side
> Jordan toward the sun rising;*
>
> *From Aroer, which is by the bank of the river Arnon, even unto
> **Mount Sion, which is Hermon**"* (Deut. 4:47,48).

Sion means "lofty," whereas, Zion means "stronghold." It is
evident that Satan was pushing for a counterfeit of God's plan
for man's redemption. The devil was determined to replace the
"seed" of the woman with the *"seed"* of the serpent.

In a book entitled, *The Gods of the Lodge*, author Reginald C.

Haupt, Jr., described what he found during his trip to Mount Hermon:

"In the excavations of Baalbek, renamed Heliopolis by the Greeks, temples were uncovered honoring Baal and Bachus. The same is true of the site at Sidon. The Temple there is named the Temple of Baal of Sidon. But by far, of greater importance was the temple of Baal found on Mt. Hermon. Perhaps it would be more meaningful to you if I [Reginald Haupt] quote direct from my source. In the 1982 edition of the *Thompson Chain Reference Bible* (Fourth Improved Edition), the archaeological supplement was provided by G. Fredrick Owen, D.D., Ed.D. Dr. Owen wrote on page 376 of his supplement the following:

"Mount Hermon, the 'chief' of the mountains of Palestine is five miles wide and twenty miles long. It has three peaks, the tallest of which is 9,166 feet above the Mediterranean Sea. For centuries before Abraham's time, the mountain had been venerated in connection with Baal.

"Baal worship was the leading religion of Canaan. On most of the high peaks of the country were shrines known as 'high places,' the higher the holier. Here, groves were planted and shrines erected for worship. Since Mount Hermon towered above all the other mountains in the region, it was the chief high place, the shrine of shrines. Canaanites looked to Mount Hermon much as the Moslems face Mecca when they pray.

"During the summer of 1934, Dr. Stewart Crawford and this writer [Reginald Haupt] led a small expedition, in which we studied the ancient Baal shrines surrounding Mount Hermon. We located many ruins and in each case the shrine was so oriented that when the priests and the devotees were at the altar, they faced the chief Baal sanctuary, or Quibla, located on the highest of the three peaks of Hermon.

"We then ascended the mountain and found the ruined temple of Baal, constructed of Herodian masonry, which dated it to just previous to and during the early Christian era. In a low place near the northwest corner of the temple, we excavated and found loads of ash and burnt bone, which had been dumped there as a refuse from sacrifices" (Reginald C. Haupt, Jr., *The Gods of the Lodge*, p. 126).

During the ministry of Jesus, He and His disciples visited Caesarea Philippi where the Jordan River springs forth from the slopes of Mount Hermon. While observing these shrines; and knowing that He was standing in the territory of His great enemy, Satan, and his idolatrous *Nephilim*; and knowing that they provided the *"seed of the serpent,"* out of which the Antichrist would arise. Jesus rightly posed the question: *"Whom do men say that I the Son of man am?"* (Matt. 16:13)

The French Connection

In 1666, Louis XIV of France, authorized the building of an observatory in Paris to measure longitude. This was the beginning of the "Paris Zero Meridian." Believe it or not, according to the Paris Zero Meridian, Mount Hermon (and the ancient territory of Dan) is located 33 degrees east of the Paris Zero Meridian (longitude), and 33 degrees latitude north of the Equator! The 33rd degree became an important part of Freemasonry, probably due to a history that dates back to the Knights Templar, the French Merovingian Dynasty and their family ties to the Danites.

However, the British would not be outdone. In 1675, England's first Astronomer Royal, Sir Flamsteed, established a Prime Meridian in London to rival the one in Paris. In 1725, Edmund Halley, the second Astronomer Royal established a second Meridian. In the mid-18th century, another Astronomer Royal, James Bradley, established a third. And, in 1851, another Astronomer Royal, Sir George Airy, set up new measuring equipment in a room alongside Bradley's original equipment (just 19 feet away), which eventually became the basis for international time zones.

It soon became clear that the world needed to adopt a worldwide standard for the Zero Meridian, so in 1884, 25 countries met in Washington, DC, and voted to accept Airy's meridian at London's Greenwich Observatory as the Prime Meridian. France abstained from the vote. The French held to the Paris Zero Meridian as a rival to Greenwich until 1911 for timekeeping purposes and 1914 for navigation. To this day, French cartographers continue to indicate the Paris Meridian on some maps.

In the opening years of the twentieth century, a booklet appeared in Russia by the title, *"The Protocols of the Learned Elders of Sion."* It was touted as the exposure of a Jewish plot to rule the world. However, its Masonic connection is obvious. The booklet ends with the statement: "Signed by the representatives of Sion of the 33rd Degree" (Michael Baigent, *Holy Blood Holy Grail*, p. 193).

Note that the name "Sion" is spelled with an "S" (a reference to Hermon) rather than "Zion" with a "Z" (a reference to Jerusalem and the Temple Mount). Also, the "33rd Degree" connection with Mount Hermon is obvious. The booklet was published for the purpose of accusing the Jews of plotting to rule the world when, in fact, it appears to be a series of Masonic protocols.

The Tribe of Dan

Jacob prophesied that Dan would be *"a serpent by the way, an adder in the path"* (Gen. 49:17), and Moses prophesied, *"Dan is a lion's whelp: he shall leap from Bashan"* (Deut. 33:22). These two prophecies are remarkable, in that they connect Dan with the *"seed of the serpent,"* from which the Antichrist will emerge to claim the title "lion of Judah." We should note that the dying Jacob referred to Judah as a *"lion's whelp"* (Gen. 49:9), while Moses referred to Dan as a *"lion's whelp"* (Deut. 33:22). It appears that Judah will own the royal title for their Messiah, while Dan will merely claim the royal title for one of their own, namely, the Antichrist.

In the book of Judges we are told that the Danites relocated to the northern reaches of the Promised Land. They settled at the foot of Mount Hermon in the territory of Bashan, and adopted the idolatrous Canaanite religion of Baal and Ashtaroth. Eventually, they left for parts unknown and became the proverbial "Lost Tribe."

However, the Danaans (i.e., Spartans) of Greece, established the same religious practices that the Danites had followed at Mount Hermon. Greek Mythology appears to be an elaborate reinvention of the Danite religion. The Spartans created the myth of a "messenger of the gods" and called him Hermes (a possible variation of Hermon), whom the Romans called Mercury. Supposedly, Hermes had a son named Pan. The name "Pan" could be a corruption of the name "Dan." Today, the Arabs call Caesarea Philippi, "Banias," but that is because there is no "P" sound in Arabic. The older form was "Paneas" (meaning "city of Pan") from "Paneion." The name comes from Pan, the pagan god who was worshiped at Mount Hermon.

In 4 B.C., this area became the tetrarchy of Herod's son Philippus, who renamed Paneas, "Caesarea Philippi." This name continued until the reign of Nero, when it was changed to "Neronias," (meaning "city of Nero") (*Encyclopedia Judaica*, "Banias," p. 162). Could Nero have believed that his family roots went back to that mountain? Was Nero a descendant of the *"seed of the serpent?"* According to the writings of Augustine (c. fifth century) it was a common belief that Nero would return someday as the Antichrist: "Some think that the Apostle Paul referred to the Roman Empire, and that he was unwilling to use language more explicit, lest he should incur the calumnious charge of wishing ill to the Empire, which it was hoped would be eternal; so that in saying, 'For the mystery of iniquity doth already work,' he alluded to Nero, whose deeds already seemed to be as the deeds of Antichrist. And hence some suppose that he shall rise again and be Antichrist. Others, again, suppose that he is not even dead, but that he was concealed that he might be supposed to have been killed, and that he now lives in concealment in the vigor of that same age which he had reached when he was believed to have perished, and will live until he is revealed in his own time and restored to his kingdom" (Augustine, *The City of God*, bk. 20, ch. 19).

The name Pan means, "all things, all gods, or all life." Therefore, when the Romans built a domed temple to commemorate all their gods, they named it the "Pantheon." It is a combination of two root words, "Pan," standing for the son of Hermes (Mercury) and "theo" meaning "gods." It is clear that Mount Hermon, with its infamous fallen angels and their offspring, the *Nephilim*, found its way into the mythologies of many ancient cultures.

The Danite Antichrist

The early church theologians, Irenaeus and Hippolytus, agreed that the Antichrist would come from these *Nephilim* and their connection with the tribe of Dan, based upon Jeremiah 8:16: *"The snorting of his horses was heard from Dan: the whole land trembled at the sound of the neighing of his strong ones."* Irenaeus quoted this verse from Jeremiah and applied it to the man on the white horse, who rides forth with the other horsemen of the Apocalypse: "And Jeremiah does not merely point out his sudden coming, but he even indicates the tribe from which he shall come, where he says, 'We shall hear the voice of his swift horses from Dan; the whole earth shall be moved by the voice of the neighing of his galloping horses: he shall also come and devour the earth, and the fullness thereof, the city [Jerusalem] also, and they that dwell therein.' This, too, is the reason that this tribe is not reckoned in the Apocalypse along with those which are saved" (Irenaeus, *Against Heresies*, bk.5, ch.30).

Irenaeus continued: "But when this Antichrist shall have devastated all things in this world, he will reign for three years and six months, and sit in the temple at Jerusalem; and then the Lord will come from heaven in the clouds, in the glory of the Father, sending this man and those who follow him into the lake of fire; but bringing in for the righteous the times of the kingdom, that is, the Rest, the hallowed Seventh Day; and restoring to Abraham the promised inheritance, in which kingdom the Lord declared, that 'many coming from the east and from the west should sit down with Abraham, Isaac, and Jacob'" (*Against Heresies*, bk.5, ch.30).

Irenaeus concludes by telling us that the kingdom will last for a thousand years, and that it will come to pass during the seventh millennium of human history, corresponding to the seventh day, in which God rested. This will be the ultimate fulfillment of the Abrahamic covenant. Hippolytus, a student and disciple of Irenaeus, also taught this. In the following passage, his words bring together a number of ideas in support of the Danite lineage of the Antichrist:

"Thus did the Scriptures preach before-time of this lion and lion's whelp. And in like manner also we find it written regarding Antichrist. For Moses speaks thus: *'Dan is a lion's whelp, and he shall leap from Bashan.'* But that no one may err by supposing that this is said of the Savior, let him attend carefully to the matter. *'Dan,'* he says, *'is a lion's whelp'*; and in naming the tribe of Dan, he declared clearly the tribe from which Antichrist is destined to spring. For as Christ springs from the tribe of Judah, so Antichrist is to spring from the tribe of Dan. And that the case stands thus, we see also from the words of Jacob: *'Let Dan be 'a serpent, lying upon the ground, biting the horse's heel.'* What, then, is meant by the serpent but Antichrist, that deceiver who is mentioned in Genesis, who deceived Eve and supplanted Adam? But since it is necessary to prove this assertion by sufficient testimony, we shall not shrink from the task. That it is in reality out of the tribe of Dan, then, that the tyrant and king, that dread judge, that son of the devil, is destined to spring and arise, the prophet testifies when he says, *'Dan shall judge his people, as (he is) also one tribe in Israel.'* But some one may say that this refers to Samson, who sprang from the tribe of Dan, and judged the people twenty years. Well, the prophecy had its partial fulfillment in Samson, but its complete fulfillment is reserved for Antichrist. For Jeremiah also speaks to this effect: *'From Dan we are to hear the sound of the swiftness of his horses: the whole land trembled at the sound of the neighing, of the driving of his horses'"* (Hippolytus, *The Extant Works and Fragments*, Part 2, Paragraph 14).

Note that Hippolytus links the serpent in Jacob's prophecy (Gen. 49:17) with the serpent in the Garden of Eden, and thereby connects the Antichrist with Satan. Dan will fulfill the prophecy concerning the *"seed"* of the serpent (Gen. 3:15).

The following comments are also taken from the writings of Hippolytus concerning the prophecies of Daniel: "In speaking of a *'lioness from the sea,'* he meant the rising of the kingdom of Babylon, and that this was the *'golden head of the image.'* And in speaking of its *'eagle wings,'* he meant that king Nebuchadnezzar was exalted and that his glory was lifted up against God. Then he says *'its wings were plucked off,'* i.e., that his glory was destroyed; for he was driven out of his kingdom. And the words, *'A man's heart was given it, and it was made to stand upon the feet of a man,'* mean that he came to himself again, and recognized that he was but a man, and gave the glory to God.

"Then after the lioness he sees a second beast, *'like a bear'* which signified the Persians. For after the Babylonians the Persians obtained the power. And in saying that *'it had three ribs in its mouth,'* he pointed to the three nations, Persians, Medes, and Babylonians, which were expressed in the image by the silver after the gold. Then comes the third beast, *'a leopard,'* which means the Greeks; for after the Persians, Alexander of Macedon had the power, when Darius was overthrown, which was also indicated by the brass in the image. And in saying that the beast *'had four wings of a fowl, and four heads,'* he showed most clearly how the kingdom of Alexander was parted into four divisions. For in speaking of four heads, he meant the four kings that arose out of it. For Alexander, when dying, divided his kingdom into four parts. Then he says, *'The fourth beast (was) dreadful and terrible: it had iron teeth, and claws of brass.'* Who, then, are meant by this but the Romans, whose kingdom, the kingdom that still stands, is expressed by the iron? *'for,'* says he, *'its legs are of iron.'*

"After this, then, what remains, beloved, but the toes of the feet of the image, in which *'part shall be of iron and part of clay mixed together?'* By the toes of the feet he meant, mystically, the ten kings that rise out of that kingdom. As Daniel says, *'I considered the beast; and, lo, (there were) ten horns behind, among which shall come up another little horn springing from them;'* by which none other is meant than the Antichrist that is to rise; and he shall set up the kingdom of Judah. And in saying that *'three horns'* were *'plucked up by the roots'* by this one, he indicates the three kings of Egypt, Libya, and Ethiopia, whom this one will slay in the array of war. And when he has conquered all, he will prove himself a terrible and savage tyrant, and will cause tribulation and persecution to the saints, exalting himself against them. And after him, it remains that *'the stone'* shall come from heaven, which *'smote the image'* and shivered it, and subverted all the kingdoms, and gave the kingdom to the saints of the Most High. This *'became a great mountain, and filled the whole earth.'*

"As these things, then, are destined to come to pass, and as the toes of the image turn out to be democracies, and the ten horns of the beast are distributed among ten kings, let us look at what is before us more carefully, and scan it, as it were, with an open eye. The *'golden head of the image'* is identical with the *'lioness,'* by which the Babylonians were represented. *'The golden shoulders and the arms of silver'* are the same with the *'bear,'* by which the Persians and Medes are meant. *'The belly and thighs of brass'* are the *'leopard,'* by which the Greeks who ruled from Alexander onward are intended. The *'legs of iron'* are the *'dreadful and terrible beast,'* by which the Romans who hold the empire now are meant. The *'toes of clay and iron'* are the *'ten horns,'* which are to be. The *'one other little horn springing up in their midst'* is the *'Antichrist.'* The stone that *'smites the image and breaks it in pieces,'* and that filled the whole earth, is Christ, who comes from heaven and brings judgment on the world" (Hippolytus, *On Daniel*, ch. 2, para. 2).

Furthermore, the Greek monarch, Alexander the Great, claimed to be born of the *"seed"* of the serpent. Greek history records a story that Philip of Macedon, father of Alexander the Great, doubted that Alexander was his son. So he spied on his wife, Olympias. One morning, he found a snake in her bed and consulted the oracle at Delphi about what this meant. He was told that the snake was the god Zeus/Amun, and that Alexander was the son of this serpent/god. Before Alexander set off on his quest to destroy the Persian Empire, Olympias told her son that he was the son of Amun, not Philip. When Alexander arrived in Egypt, he visited the Oracle of Amun in Siwa, near the western border of Egypt, and declared that he was the son of that god.

Finally, an ancient Jewish Midrash likens Samson to their expected messiah, claiming that Samson's father was a Danite, but that his mother was from the tribe of Judah. Furthermore, they say, "Samson in some respects was considered a forerunner of the Messiah who will come from Judah, but his mother, according to the Midrash, will be of the tribe of Dan" (Yair Davidy, *"Dan"*). Amazing! The Jews are looking for a messiah whose father is from the royal family of Judah, but whose mother is from the tribe of Dan!

Those fallen angels who descended to Mount Hermon introduced the *"seed"* of the serpent into the human race. Evidently, after the Flood, the *Nephilim* consorted with members of the tribe of Dan, mixing the *"seed"* of the serpent into the human genome once again. The first time it happened, God judged the world with water. When the Antichrist arrives, God will judge the world by fire.

The European Parliament, Strasbourg, France, and Europa (inset).

Mystery Babylon

Today, Europe is attempting to revive the glory of the Roman Empire while, at the same time, giving the appearance of being MYSTERY BABYLON. The European Parliament building in Strassbourg, France, is designed to look like an unfinished tower — shades of Babel. They brag that the diversity of languages across Europe will be solved through political and cultural unity. In other words, they are trying to reverse the Babel effect. The new European logo depicts a woman riding a beast. Her name is Europa. She is depicted as riding upon the back of Zeus, who changed himself into a white bull.

At the same time, they are sponsors of the United Nations, a beastly entity with a proposed world government on its agenda. Could Europe be that mystery woman? Just inside the entrance to the UN stands a large statue of Zeus. Could the UN be that beast upon which she rides? If so, then their proposed "New World Order" should not last very long. The ten toes are quite small, depicting a kingdom of short duration. The current plan for world government involves dividing the world into ten political-economic regions. Daniel's prophecy could come to pass in our generation.

The Stone Cut Out Without Hands

Daniel told King Nebuchadnezzar that, in the end, God would judge the nations and establish a worldwide messianic kingdom:

"And in the days of these kings shall the God of heaven set up a kingdom, which shall never be destroyed: and the kingdom shall not be left to other people, but it shall break in pieces and consume all these kingdoms, and it shall stand for ever.

"Forasmuch as thou sawest that the stone was cut out of the mountain without hands, and that it brake in pieces the iron, the brass, the clay, the silver, and the gold; the great God hath made known to the king what shall come to pass hereafter: and the dream is certain, and the interpretation thereof sure" (Dan. 2:44,45).

Without a doubt, Jesus is the fulfillment of that *"stone."* Isaiah wrote:

*"Therefore thus saith the LORD God, Behold I lay in Zion for a foundation a **stone**, a tried **stone**, a precious corner **stone**, a sure foundation: he that believeth shall not make haste"* (Isa. 28:16).

And the Apostle Paul wrote:

*"And did all drink the same spiritual drink: for they drank of that spiritual Rock that followed them: and that **Rock** was Christ"* (I Cor. 10:4).

Jesus used the metaphor of the stone:

*"Jesus saith unto them, Did ye never read in the scriptures, The **stone** which the builders rejected, the same is become the head of the corner: this is the Lord's doing, and it is marvelous in our eyes?*

And whosoever shall fall on this stone shall be broken: but on whomsoever it shall fall, it will grind him to powder" (Matt. 21:42,44).

Zechariah used the stone as a metaphor:

*"And in that day will I make Jerusalem a burdensome **stone** for all people: all that burden themselves with it shall be cut in pieces, though all the people of the earth be gathered together against it"* (Zech. 12:3).

When Jesus returns as King of kings and Lord of lords, He will judge the nations and establish heaven's kingdom. Without a doubt, Jesus is the stone!

The King Honored Daniel

It was customary in the early days of civilization to honor a person by bowing down to them. Through this act of worship, Nebuchadnezzar was recognizing Daniel's God:

"Then the king Nebuchadnezzar fell upon his face, and worshipped Daniel, and commanded that they should offer an oblation and sweet odors unto him.

"The king answered unto Daniel, and said, Of a truth it is, that your God is a God of gods, and a Lord of kings, and a revealer of secrets, seeing thou couldest reveal this secret.

"Then the king made Daniel a great man, and gave him many great gifts, and made him ruler over the whole province of Babylon, and chief of the governors over all the wise men of Babylon.

"Then Daniel requested of the king, and he set Shadrach, Meshach, and Abednego, over the affairs of the province of Babylon: but Daniel sat in the gate of the king" (Dan. 2:46-49).

An offering was made in honor of Daniel's God. Daniel was elevated to a position of prominence in the province of Babylon. Upon Daniel's request, his three relatives were also given promotions to important positions in the government. Nebuchadnezzar was thoroughly impressed! One would think that Nebuchadnezzar would become a believer and serve God for the rest of his life. But, the king was not yet predisposed to do that. In fact, the Babylonian king was mentally unstable. Over the next several years, Nebuchadnezzar decided that God was not going to give his "golden" kingdom to a "silver" aggressor. In the next chapter, Nebuchadnezzar builds a statue like the one in his dream, only it will be all of gold, to the exclusion of silver, brass, iron, or clay. The Babylonian monarch thought he could live forever and no one ... not God ... or anybody else, would take his kingdom from him!

Nebuchadnezzar's Golden Image

King Nebuchadnezzar had a flair for the auspicious and grand. Not unlike many monarchs, he set out to beautify Babylon and make it a showcase for the world. He built the famous hanging gardens and a 350-foot colossal pyramid to his patron god, Marduk. In this chapter we find him building a statue 60 cubits high and 6 cubits wide (approximately 102.5 feet high and 10.25 feet wide, using the Babylonian cubit, which was 15/16" less than the Egyptian Royal Cubit of 20.64").

It is entirely possible that this statue was fashioned after the one in his dream. It seems to me that he wanted to show Daniel's God how angry he was over the prophecy that Babylon would not last forever. It had been several years since his dream of the statue with a head of gold and feet of clay, but it must have haunted him night and day.

In 588 B.C., he sent the Babylonian army to decimate Jerusalem, destroy Solomon's Temple and confiscate its gold. In about 580 B.C., in defiance of God, he built his dream statue all of gold, determined that no silver kingdom would replace Babylon — no brass, no iron, and no clay! I suspect that much of that gold came from the ruins of Solomon's Temple. Daniel wrote:

"Nebuchadnezzar the king made an image of gold, whose height was threescore cubits, and the breadth thereof six cubits: he set it up in the plain of Dura, in the province of Babylon.

"Then Nebuchadnezzar the king sent to gather together the princes, the governors, and the captains, the judges, the treasurers, the counsellors, the sheriffs, and all the rulers of the provinces, to come to the dedication of the image which Nebuchadnezzar the king had set up.

"Then the princes, the governors, and captains, the judges, the treasurers, the counsellors, the sheriffs, and all the rulers of the provinces, were gathered together unto the dedication of the image that Nebuchadnezzar the king had set up; and they stood before the image that Nebuchadnezzar had set up.

"Then an herald cried aloud, To you it is commanded, O people, nations, and languages,

"That at what time ye hear the sound of the cornet, flute, harp, sackbut, psaltery, dulcimer, and all kinds of musick, ye fall down and worship the golden image that Nebuchadnezzar the king hath set up:

"And whoso falleth not down and worshippeth shall the same hour be cast into the midst of a burning fiery furnace.

"Therefore at that time, when all the people heard the sound of the cornet, flute, harp, sackbut, psaltery, and all kinds of musick, all the people, the nations, and the languages, fell down and worshipped the golden image that Nebuchadnezzar the king had set up" (Dan. 3:1-7).

He built a large furnace nearby, probably for the purpose of casting the golden statue. Maybe it looked like a huge barbecue pit designed to cook a feast for the party. He brought in an orchestra to provide music for the entertainment of his guests. He invited the leaders of all nations under his control to attend the celebration — all but Daniel. The king probably sent Daniel off to some remote part of the kingdom on some pretended diplomatic mission to keep him from being on hand to haunt the king's conscience. But all others must attend!

Nebuchadnezzar's invitation may have included a subtle reminder that what happened to Jerusalem might happen to their countries if they did not attend. Note that all leaders of all nations had to come, from the most important rulers and princes, to all military leaders, to all domestic keepers of the peace, to all bureaucrats, to all counselors — all politicians had to be there.

Once the celebration commenced, he sprang the surprise. He informed his guests that they must bow before Babylon and pledge allegiance, or burn! Alas, that barbecue pit was built with an alternate purpose! That must have put a slight crimp in their festivities! I am sure the kings of the Medes and Persians must have been there that day. I can imagine that one probably said to the other, "Wow! Look at all that gold! Fifty-two years later, in 538 B.C., the Medes and Persians would come to confiscate all that gold for themselves.

After all this time, Nebuchadnezzar was still obsessed with the fear that Babylon should be replaced by another kingdom. For 23 years, Nebuchadnezzar had worked on his plan to prevent the inevitable. He may have set up a vast spy network in all surrounding nations in order to gather intelligence and insure that his position would not be challenged. He might have thought that he was immortal — that he would live forever. In those days, politicians were instructed to say, *"Oh king, live forever!"* But today, they only say, "Long live the king!" The history of mankind's inevitable fate had not yet convinced the king that no one lives forever — not Adam, not Nimrod, and not him.

To build a statue cast in gold required a vast amount of the rare yellow metal. In fact, some have suggested that there was not enough gold in the world at that time to build such a statue. However, we should remember that Nebuchadnezzar had plundered most of the other nations in the known world. Solomon's Temple was quite a golden edifice itself. The roof of the Jewish Temple was ornamented with it. The walls inside were covered with it. So, it seems that Nebuchadnezzar had two motives for burning the Jerusalem Temple. He was determined to get rid of Daniel's God, and then bring back enough gold to build his statue. There was no silver, brass or iron in this statue.

King Solomon did not have to plunder other nations in order to accumulate the gold that adorned the Jerusalem Temple. He had gold mines in a mysterious country called Ophir that supplied him with all the gold he needed. Both King Hiram of Tyre and Solomon had access to these mines. Their ships would set sail for parts unknown. Months later, they would return with large quantities of gold. It is possible that they headed westward across the Atlantic and up the Amazon River to the gold mines high in the Andes Mountains of Peru. The Chronicles of the Jewish kings reported: *"And the king made silver and gold at Jerusalem as plenteous as stones"* (II Chron. 1:15).

Nebuchadnezzar managed to get enough gold to build his statue. In fact, he could have exclusively used Jewish gold to build the whole thing! After all, this obsession of his may have become a contest between him and Daniel's God.

The statue could not have been made with thin sheets of gold without collapsing. Gold is too heavy and not that strong a metal. It had to be extra thick to support the weight of the statue! It is possible that the pedestal that bore the statue could have been included in the 60 cubits high array. If so, then the statue didn't have to be ten stories high. It could have been a smaller statue standing atop a tall pedestal. The prudent thing to do might be to make the statue out of brass, iron, or baked clay, then overlay it with a thin layer of gold. But that would have defeated the king's purpose. He could have none of those other elements in the statue.

Fausett's Bible Dictionary and Encyclopedia states that an archeologist by the name of Oppert found a large pedestal on the plains of Dura, south of Babylon, now called Duair, on which a colossal statue could have been supported. The pedestal may still be there, but no statue, no gold and no Nebuchadnezzar! It's all gone. So, who won this little skirmish — God or the Babylonian monarch? Obviously, God won. Only the pedestal still stands!

It seems to me that Nebuchadnezzar had harbored bitterness against God since the dream. He may have been determined that Babylon should stand forever. Furthermore, from the context of this chapter, along with the king's outburst in the previous chapter, it seems that Nebuchadnezzar was more than merely impatient or hotheaded. He was prone to fits of uncontrollable rage. Perhaps, he suffered from a mental problem — one that eventually caused his seven-year insanity. The old adage, "power corrupts and absolute power corrupts absolutely," can be said of Nebuchadnezzar.

The Defiant Hebrews

When the band played, everyone hit the sand — all but three Jews — Daniel's relatives. They stood as a testimony that the dream was real and that the interpretation was accurate. This was no mere demonstration of loyalty. This was Nebuchadnezzar's outrage against all that Daniel and his relatives had stood for. They really had no choice in the matter. They had to come down on the side of the great Creator God, who gave the king the dream of his statue in the first place. Notice that these Jews were betrayed by Chaldeans — their own associates within the Babylonian government:

"Wherefore at that time certain Chaldeans came near, and accused the Jews.

"They spake and said to the king Nebuchadnezzar, O king, live for ever.

"Thou, O king, hast made a decree, that every man that shall hear the sound of the cornet, flute, harp, sackbut, psaltery, and dulcimer, and all kinds of musick, shall fall down and worship the golden image:

"And whoso falleth not down and worshippeth, that he should be cast into the midst of a burning fiery furnace.

"There are certain Jews whom thou hast set over the affairs of the province of Babylon, Shadrach, Meshach, and Abednego; these men, O king, have not regarded thee: they serve not thy gods, nor worship the golden image which thou hast set up.

"Then Nebuchadnezzar in his rage and fury commanded to bring Shadrach, Meshach, and Abednego. Then they brought these men before the king.

"Nebuchadnezzar spake and said unto them, Is it true, O Shadrach, Meshach, and Abednego, do not ye serve my gods, nor worship the golden image which I have set up?

"Now if ye be ready that at what time ye hear the sound of the cornet, flute, harp, sackbut, psaltery, and dulcimer, and all kinds of musick, ye fall down and worship the image which I have made; well: but if ye worship not, ye shall be cast the same hour into the midst of a burning fiery furnace; and who is that God that shall deliver you out of my hands?

"Shadrach, Meshach, and Abednego, answered and said to the king, O Nebuchadnezzar, we are not careful to answer thee in this matter.

"If it be so, our God whom we serve is able to deliver us from the burning fiery furnace, and he will deliver us out of thine hand, O king.

"But if not, be it known unto thee, O king, that we will not serve thy gods, nor worship the golden image which thou hast set up" (Dan. 3:8-18).

Nebuchadnezzar did not plan on having any opposition from his own appointees. Regardless of how much he may have personally admired Shadrach, Meshach and Abednego (and Daniel) for their exemplary service in His kingdom, he could not ignore his own decree to exterminate anyone who refused to bow before the statue.

To these Jewish men, it was a matter of keeping the Ten Commandments. They could not conscientiously violate the Second Commandment about bowing down to graven images (Exodus 20:5). If there had been any other way to pledge their allegiance to Babylon, they probably would have been free to do so. Going the extra mile, so to speak, Nebuchadnezzar gives them a second chance. But, to his dismay, they refused the offer.

They would obey God, no matter what the cost in human terms. That is genuine integrity!

We must remember that Daniel was written as a prophecy. Therefore, this whole chapter sets forth a prophetic message. There is more here than just primary interpretation and practical application. There is a prophetic implication to be discovered in the kingdom, the nations, the willful king, the image, the Chosen People, the furnace and the *"Son of God."*

Babylon and the Nations

The king was determined that Babylon should always rule over the nations. He wanted to eliminate the silver, brass, iron and clay lest they rise up someday and replace the glory of Babylon. Today, after 2,500 years, the concept of Babylon's fabled tower still holds an important place in the affairs of nations. Not only are political concepts still evident, but European politicians are openly voicing their allegiance for the unity once promoted in Babylon. They built their new European Parliament building in the design of an unfinished tower. Former president Bill Clinton built his presidential library in the form of an unfinished bridge. The great seal of the United States contains the relief of an unfinished Pyramid with the capstone floating above it. The idea is that the work of producing utopia is not yet complete. What started at the tower of Babel was only a beginning. The world is striving for one language, one economy, one government and one god … to the exclusion of the Jew.

The Antichrist

The world is looking for a leader to complete the quest for the glory of Babylon. Nebuchadnezzar was a prototype of that future world leader whom the Bible calls, "Antichrist." When he arrives on the world scene, he will consolidate the governments in such a way that to oppose him will mean certain death. He will allow no dissent. However, as always, one group will stand out in opposition to his plan. In order to subvert their prophets and undermine God's ancient promise of His coming Messiah to judge the nations and establish a messianic kingdom, he will take over Jerusalem and desecrate the future Jewish Temple, just as Nebuchadnezzar had done.

The Image of the Beast

In the midst of the Tribulation Period, the Antichrist will set up an *"image to the beast"* (Rev. 13:14) and demand allegiance from all nations. Nebuchadnezzar's image was a prophetic type of that future image. What the Antichrist's image will look like is not given, but it will be a clear violation of the Second Commandment. When the future image is set up on the Temple Mount, Israel's enemies will know that the Jews cannot comply. They will be delighted that the image will at last create an impasse for Israel, thinking that it will lead to their final and utter destruction.

"Nebuchadnezzar's statue was six cubits wide and sixty cubits high. According to the second-century theologian, Irenaeus (A.D. 120-202), student of Polycarp, these numbers allude to 666 — the mark of the beast and the number of his name. Irenaeus wrote:

"In the previous books I have set forth the causes for which God permitted these things to be made, and have pointed out that all such have been created for the benefit of that human nature which is saved, ripening for immortality that which is [possessed] of its own free will and its own power, and preparing and rendering it more adapted for eternal subjection to God. And therefore the creation is suited to [the wants of] man; for man was not made for its sake, but creation for the sake of man. Those nations however, who did not of themselves raise up their eyes unto heaven, nor returned thanks to their Maker, nor wished to behold the light of truth, but who were like blind mice concealed in the depths of ignorance, the word justly reckons 'as waste water from a sink, and as the turning-weight of a balance — in fact, as nothing;' so far useful and serviceable to the just, as stubble conduces towards the growth of the wheat, and its straw, by means of combustion, serves for working gold. And therefore, when in the end the Church shall be suddenly caught up from this, it is said, 'There shall be tribulation such as has not been since the beginning, neither shall be.' For this is the last contest of the righteous, in which, when they overcome they are crowned with incorruption.

"And there is, therefore, in this beast, when he comes, a recapitulation made of all sorts of iniquity and of every deceit, in order that all apostate power, flowing into and being shut up in him, may be sent into the furnace of fire. Fittingly, therefore, shall his name possess the number six hundred and sixty-six, since he sums up in his own person all the commixture of wickedness, which took place previous to the deluge, due to the apostasy of the angels. For Noah was six hundred years old when the deluge came upon the earth, sweeping away the rebellious world, for the sake of that most infamous generation which lived in the times of Noah. And [Antichrist] also sums up every error of devised idols since the flood, together with the slaying of the prophets and the cutting off of the just.

"For that image which was set up by Nebuchadnezzar had indeed a height of sixty cubits, while the breadth was six cubits; on account of which Ananias, Azarias, and Misael, when they did not worship it, were cast into a furnace of fire, pointing out prophetically, by what happened to them, the wrath against the righteous which shall arise towards the [time of the] end. For that image, taken as a whole, was a prefiguring of this man's coming, decreeing that he should undoubtedly himself alone be worshipped by all men. Thus, then, the six hundred years of Noah, in whose time the deluge occurred because of the apostasy, and the number of the cubits of the image for which these just men were sent into the fiery furnace, do indicate the number of the name of that man in whom is concentrated the whole apostasy of six thousand years, and unrighteousness, and wickedness, and false prophecy, and deception; for which things' sake a cataclysm of fire shall also come [upon the earth]" (Irenaeus, *Against Heresies*, bk 5, ch.29).

Among his comments, we should note that Irenaeus points out the roots of the Antichrist as having originated during the "apostasy of the angels," who first appeared in the "times of Noah" and returned to establish themselves as "idols since the flood." He links the 600 years of Noah to the 66 cubits in Nebuchadnezzar's golden statue, to form the infamous number 666. He also notes that the Antichrist will contain "the whole apostasy of 6,000 years." By this, Irenaeus tells us when he expected the prophecy to be fulfilled. Since 6,000 years have transpired from Adam until now, the Antichrist should soon appear. Note also, that Irenaeus said that Christians would be caught up — "when in the end the Church shall be suddenly caught up from this." He said that this would happen before the Tribulation Period sets in. That is a second-century theologian's view of the pre-tribulation rapture. Remember, Irenaeus was a student of Polycarp, who was a student of the Apostle John. This provides no room for error to creep into New Testament Christianity — not this early. This is the strongest evidence that John taught a pre-tribulation rapture.

The Chosen People

Throughout history, the Jews have stood in the way of Satan's plan for this world. The only way for the devil to win his war against God is to eliminate the Jews. If he can get rid of the Jews, everyone else will fall down and worship him. Nebuchadnezzar may have sent Daniel off to some unknown part of the kingdom on some trumped up mission to get him out of the way, but he forgot that Shadrach, Meshach and Abednego would be there to give him a hard time.

Why three? Perhaps, those three men represent the historic Jewish exile — being scattered throughout the nations — the nations that are made up of Noah's three sons, Shem, Ham and Japheth. God promised that in the last days He would bring the Jews back from among the nations where they were scattered. They would return to their ancient homeland where the prophetic furnace of affliction would be ignited during the Tribulation Period. However, God will protect them and send the Messiah, the Son of God to deliver them.

The Furnace of Affliction

Nebuchadnezzar flew into a rage again. I am confident that this was not just the second time in 23 years. I suspect it happened often. That was one way the king had of instilling fear in those around him. We are told that *"the form of his visage was changed"* (v. 19), indicating a volatile mental imbalance. Without any further chance for appeal, he had them thrown into the furnace:

"Then was Nebuchadnezzar full of fury, and the form of his visage was changed against Shadrach, Meshach, and Abednego: therefore he spake, and commanded that they should heat the furnace one seven times more than it was wont to be heated.

"And he commanded the most mighty men that were in his army to bind Shadrach, Meshach, and Abednego, and to cast them into the burning fiery furnace.

"Then these men were bound in their coats, their hosen, and their hats, and their other garments, and were cast into the midst of the burning fiery furnace.

"Therefore because the king's commandment was urgent, and the furnace exceeding hot, the flame of the fire slew those men that took up Shadrach, Meshach, and Abednego.

"And these three men, Shadrach, Meshach, and Abednego, fell down bound into the midst of the burning fiery furnace" (Dan. 3:19-23).

The furnace is typical of all the persecutions suffered by the Chosen People since the call of Abraham. In fact, the first furnace was built by Nimrod, and Abraham was its first victim. This story is told in the book of *Jasher.* Whether or not it actually happened, we don't know; but the book of *Jasher* is referenced in Joshua 10:13 and II Samuel 1:18. As the story goes, Abram chopped up his father's idols and King Nimrod had Abram and his brother Haran thrown into a furnace:

"And they bound their hands and feet with linen cords, and the servants of the king lifted them up and cast them both into the furnace.

"And the Lord loved Abram and he had compassion over him, and the Lord came down and delivered Abram from the fire and he was not burned.

"But all the cords with which they bound him were burned, while Abram remained and walked about in the fire.

"And Haran died when they had cast him into the fire, and he was burned to ashes, for his heart was not perfect with the Lord; and those men who cast him into the fire, the flame of the fire spread over them, and they were burned, and twelve men of them died.

"And Abram walked in the midst of the fire three days and three nights, and all the servants of the king saw him walking in the fire, and they came and told the king, saying, Behold we have seen Abram walking about in the midst of the fire, and even the lower garments which are upon him are not burned, but the cord with which he was bound is burned" (*Jasher* 12:23-25).

This story may be a corrupted version of Nebuchadnezzar's furnace — or it may have happened. It would not be out of character for Abram, the progenitor of the Jewish people, to endure the fiery furnace as a prophecy of the persecutions that would befall his progeny down through history.

No other nation or ethnic group has suffered as the Jews have suffered. Aside from the stories in the Bible, profane history attests to the fact that the Jews have suffered terribly in every generation. In spite of Pharaoh's drowning of Jewish boys, Haman's gallows, Rome's deportations, the Pope's inquisitions, Russia's pograms and Hitler's furnaces, the Jews have survived. Babylon's furnace is a symbolic prophecy that in their worst persecutions (yet to come), the Son of God will deliver them — just as he delivered Shadrach, Meshach and Abednego.

The Son of God

The king was astonished to see, not three people in the furnace, but four!

"Then Nebuchadnezzar the king was astonied, and rose up in haste, and spake, and said unto his counsellors, Did not we cast three men bound into the midst of the fire? They answered and said unto the king, True, O king.

"He answered and said, Lo, I see four men loose, walking in the midst of the fire, and they have no hurt; and the form of the fourth is like the Son of God.

"Then Nebuchadnezzar came near to the mouth of the burning fiery furnace, and spake, and said, Shadrach, Meshach, and Abednego, ye servants of the most high God, come forth, and come hither. Then Shadrach, Meshach, and Abednego, came forth of the midst of the fire.

"And the princes, governors, and captains, and the king's counsellors, being gathered together, saw these men, upon whose bodies the fire had no power, nor was an hair of their head singed, neither were their coats changed, nor the smell of fire had passed on them" (Dan. 3:24-27).

Evidently, only three men emerged from the flames. The fourth man was either an angelic type of the Son of God or the Son, Himself. Once he had delivered these three Hebrew men, he simply disappeared — slipping back into heaven's realm. This is a prophecy of the Second Coming of Christ. Our Lord will come as the keeper of Israel in the midst of the fires of history.

Whether or not the Jewish people realize it, Jesus has always been there for them. After all, He is the Holy One of Israel. He is the King of glory. Someday, in the midst of Israel's worst fears — the proposed genocide of Armageddon — Christ will rescue them and establish heaven's kingdom.

The Decree for Religious Freedom

The king had no choice but to admit in his heart that God had won his little 23-year-long battle. From that day forward, Nebuchadnezzar must have wondered when God was going to kill him for burning His Temple and stealing His gold. To make amends, the king promoted these Jewish men and declared religious freedom for all Jews throughout the kingdom:

"Then Nebuchadnezzar spake, and said, Blessed be the God of Shadrach, Meshach, and Abednego, who hath sent his angel, and delivered his servants that trusted in him, and have changed the king's word, and yielded their bodies, that they might not serve nor worship any god, except their own God.

"Therefore I make a decree, That every people, nation, and language, which speak any thing amiss against the God of Shadrach, Meshach, and Abednego, shall be cut in pieces, and their houses shall be made a dunghill: because there is no other God that can deliver after this sort.

"Then the king promoted Shadrach, Meshach, and Abednego, in the province of Babylon" (Dan. 3:28-30).

Shadrach, Meshach, and Abednego must have had a lot to tell Daniel upon his return!

The Testimony of a Gentile Believer

It is not normal for an entire chapter in the Bible to be about a Gentile, much less by the very man who burned Solomon's Temple to the ground, but here it is. Daniel reserved this fourth chapter for a testimony, either dictated or written, by King Nebuchadnezzar, giving details about another dream — this one about his mental breakdown and subsequent conversion! This king became a believer! Ten years have passed since the incident of the fiery furnace, as this story gets underway (570 B.C.).

For the Jews, this testimony from a Gentile convert must be disturbing. How could they ever accept the man who destroyed their Temple, slaughtered their families, enslaved their children, and plundered their nation's wealth? How could they ever accept him as a brother beloved? Another question: How could God ever forgive such a man as King Nebuchadnezzar? Such a thing for someone, like God, to forgive a wicked man of his caliber — why, that would take — pure grace! And yet, Daniel lets the Babylonian monarch tell his story! The book of Daniel only has twelve chapters. Why give one of them to him? Why give

Nebuchadnezzar such a worldwide, centuries-long, expanded opportunity to address the human race for generations to come? Here's why. Daniel is a prophet. This chapter alludes to a political insanity that will run rampant during the Tribulation Period — a seven-year-long period of mental and emotional confusion, in which all Gentile nations will take leave of their senses. At the end of the Tribulation Period, the nations will be converted. At last, they will acknowledge the Deity of Christ. This is the story of mankind's opportunity to admire the truth and power of Almighty God. Nebuchadnezzar wrote:

"NEBUCHADNEZZAR the king, unto all people, nations, and languages, that dwell in all the earth; Peace be multiplied unto you.

"I thought it good to shew the signs and wonders that the high God hath wrought toward me.

"How great are his signs! And how mighty are his wonders! His kingdom is an everlasting kingdom, and his dominion is from generation to generation" (Dan. 4:1-3).

This message is addressed to everyone who has ever lived from the Babylonian kingdom forward — to this very day. It was written after Nebuchadnezzar was restored and converted — the story of a new man — one who finally appreciated God's love and grace. This also represents the final story in the life of Nebuchadnezzar. In Daniel's next chapter, a new king will come to power — Belshazzar. So, for now, this is how Nebuchadnezzar ends the saga of a Babylonian monarch — praising God.

"I Nebuchadnezzar was at rest in mine house, and flourishing in my palace:

"I saw a dream which made me afraid, and the thoughts upon my bed and the visions of my head troubled me.

"Therefore made I a decree to bring in all the wise men of Babylon before me, that they might make known unto me the interpretation of the dream.

"Then came in the magicians, the astrologers, the Chaldeans, and the soothsayers: and I told the dream before them; but they did not make known unto me the interpretation thereof" (Dan. 4:4-7).

Though this was written after the king's conversion, he is telling what happened before he got his theology straightened out. So, naturally, he would be consulting magicians, astro-logers and soothsayers. Furthermore, he will tell us in the following verses that Daniel's Babylonian name, Belteshazzar, came from the name of his former pagan god, and that he once thought of Daniel as having the spirit of the "holy gods." This would be the terminology of an idolater — before conversion, when he did not know how to express himself in theological terms:

> "But at the last Daniel came in before me, whose name was Belteshazzar, according to the name of my god, and in whom is the spirit of the holy gods: and before him I told the dream, saying,
>
> "O Belteshazzar, master of the magicians, because I know that the spirit of the holy gods is in thee, and no secret troubleth thee, tell me the visions of my dream that I have seen, and the interpretation thereof.
>
> "Thus were the visions of mine head in my bed; I saw, and behold a tree in the midst of the earth, and the height thereof was great.
>
> "The tree grew, and was strong, and the height thereof reached unto heaven, and the sight thereof to the end of all the earth:
>
> "The leaves thereof were fair, and the fruit thereof much, and in it was meat for all: the beasts of the field had shadow under it, and the fowls of the heaven dwelt in the boughs thereof, and all flesh was fed of it" (Dan 4:8-12).

There are two scenarios at work here. The first concerns Nebuchadnezzar, himself. His life was like a tree growing in a pleasant land. All was going well, until …

On the other hand, Nebuchadnezzar represented the worldwide Middle Eastern kingdom of Babylon. Therefore, the tree also represents the head of all Gentile world powers throughout the ages, until that day when mankind will be cast into the political insanity of the Tribulation Period.

The Tree Alludes to an End-Time Prophecy

The leaves of this tree were fair; the fruit plentiful; and the population, represented by animals and birds, enjoyed its bounty. One would think that all was well with the world. But trouble seethes just below the surface. In the twentieth century, industrialized nations grew wealthy. Manufacturing offered more jobs than ever before. People were able to buy homes, automobiles, electronics, nice clothes, etc. Well-meaning world leaders joined a sophisticated organization that promised peace and equity. They even called it by a name that stood for brotherhood — the "United Nations." On the surface, it seems that the world is moving toward that grand utopia that has eluded humanity for millennia.

However, just below the facade of tranquility, warlords were plotting to take peace from the Earth. In 1914, Germany struck out against several nations and plunged Europe into the quagmire of World War I. The vast land of Russia was conquered by an ideology that ruined a generation and frightened Western nations. Some twenty years later, Germany, in the West (1939), and Japan, in the East (1941), managed to drag mankind through another horrendous worldwide bloodbath. After that, communist puppets wracked their societies and brought murder and mayhem to China, Korea and Vietnam. Just when the world thought it would have peace at last, some insanity-driven Middle Eastern oil-rich nations funded Islamic terrorists to step up their campaign for world domination. Today, crime is rampant. Marriages are falling apart. Young people are bent on wayward living. Abortion is killing off the next generation. It's a crazy world! The prophecy is all too accurate:

"I saw in the visions of my head upon my bed, and, behold, a watcher and an holy one came down from heaven;

"He cried aloud, and said thus, Hew down the tree, and cut off his branches, shake off his leaves, and scatter his fruit: let the beasts get away from under it, and the fowls from his branches:

"Nevertheless leave the stump of his roots in the earth, even with a band of iron and brass, in the tender grass of the field; and let it be wet with the dew of heaven, and let his portion be with the beasts in the grass of the earth:

"Let his heart be changed from man's, and let a beast's heart be given unto him; and let seven times pass over him.

"This matter is by the decree of the watchers, and the demand by the word of the holy ones: to the intent that the living may know that the most High ruleth in the kingdom of men, and giveth it to whomsoever he will, and setteth up over it the basest of men.

"This dream I king Nebuchadnezzar have seen. Now thou, O Belteshazzar, declare the interpretation thereof, forasmuch as all the wise men of my kingdom are not able to make known unto me the interpretation: but thou art able; for the spirit of the holy gods is in thee" (Dan. 4:13-18).

Nebuchadnezzar told his dream to Daniel, hoping to find an answer. One thing he knew for sure. The angel told him that God wanted men to know that the great Creator is in control of kingdoms and makes kings out of the "basest" — the most wicked — the most arrogant of men! From a human standpoint kings do not rise to power because of how many friends they have, but how straight they can shoot. The "dog-eat-dog" mentality is so true of politicians. Furthermore, Nebuchadnezzar was troubled that an angel would descend from heaven with instructions to cut it down. He was puzzled by the band of iron and brass that preserved its base and roots. And he was curious about the *"seven times"* (seven years) that would pass over it.

The Band of Iron and Brass

It is possible that the band of iron and brass was a reference to Greece (brass) and Rome (iron). The story seems to say that an infamous end-time world ruler would have family roots in Greek and Roman royalty, just as the band was seen to lay around the roots of the severed tree. Its message seems to be that a Greco/Roman Antichrist would be in charge during this time of the world's political insanity — the seven-year Tribulation Period.

Daniel was stunned by what he heard. He knew that the king was mentally unstable, as evidenced by Nebuchadnezzar's 23-year-long obsession with building a golden statue. Daniel had never seen anyone so foolish as to challenge God. Daniel also knew that the king was prone to fits of unbridled rage. How was he going to tell the interpretation to the king?

"Then Daniel, whose name was Belteshazzar, was astonied for one hour, and his thoughts troubled him. The king spake, and said, Belteshazzar, let not the dream, or the interpretation thereof, trouble thee. Belteshazzar answered and said, My lord, the dream be to them that hate thee, and the interpretation thereof to thine enemies.

"The tree that thou sawest, which grew, and was strong, whose height reached unto the heaven, and the sight thereof to all the earth;

"Whose leaves were fair, and the fruit thereof much, and in it was meat for all; under which the beasts of the field dwelt, and upon whose branches the fowls of the heaven had their habitation:

"It is thou, O king, that art grown and become strong: for thy greatness is grown, and reacheth unto heaven, and thy dominion to the end of the earth.

"And whereas the king saw a watcher and an holy one coming down from heaven, and saying, Hew the tree down, and destroy it; yet leave the stump of the roots thereof in the earth, even with a band of iron and brass, in the tender grass of the field; and let it be wet with the dew of heaven, and let his portion be with the beasts of the field, till seven times pass over him;

"This is the interpretation, O king, and this is the decree of the most High, which is come upon my lord the king:

"That they shall drive thee from men, and thy dwelling shall be with the beasts of the field, and they shall make thee to eat grass as oxen, and they shall wet thee with the dew of heaven, and seven times shall pass over thee, till thou know that the most High ruleth in the kingdom of men, and giveth it to whomsoever he will.

"And whereas they commanded to leave the stump of the tree roots; thy kingdom shall be sure unto thee, after that thou shalt have known that the heavens do rule.

"Wherefore, O king, let my counsel be acceptable unto thee, and break off thy sins by righteousness, and thine iniquities by shewing mercy to the poor; if it may be a lengthening of thy tranquility" (Dan. 4:19-27).

This dream occurred in the Sabbatical Year of 570/569 B.C. The king's insanity began one year later — the first year of a seven-year *shavuah*, and was concluded in the Sabbatical Year of 563/562 B.C. The near fulfillment of this dream fits within the framework of a Sabbatical cycle, alluding to the possibility that the far fulfillment — the Tribulation Period — will also occur within the framework of a Sabbatical cycle.

Daniel's Dilemma

Daniel contemplated for an hour, not on the interpretation, but on how to tell this mentally unstable king. Finally, Daniel began by telling the king that such a thing should happen to his enemies! Daniel gently related the decree. Because of Nebuchadnezzar's arrogance, God had decided that he should be plagued with insanity for seven years. This was to be no simple bout with depression, but a full-blown mental breakdown. The king would act like an animal, with no recognition of those around him. Fortunately, he would be healed after seven years. Daniel assured him that his kingdom would remain intact and that, if he would straighten up, stop his wickedness, and show righteousness and mercy to the poor, perhaps God would postpone the sentence for a while.

The Story Continues

This part refers to the king in a detached "third person" view of telling of the story. Either the king sees his former self as if he were a different person, or Daniel, acting as editor, did the writing:

"All this came upon the king Nebuchadnezzar.

"At the end of twelve months he walked in the palace of the kingdom of Babylon.

"The king spake, and said, Is not this great Babylon, that I have built for the house of the kingdom by the might of my power, and for the honour of my majesty?

"While the word was in the king's mouth, there fell a voice from

heaven, saying, O king Nebuchadnezzar, to thee it is spoken; The
kingdom is departed from thee.

"And they shall drive thee from men, and thy dwelling shall be with
the beasts of the field: they shall make thee to eat grass as oxen, and
seven times shall pass over thee, until thou know that the most High
ruleth in the kingdom of men, and giveth it to whomsoever he will.

"The same hour was the thing fulfilled upon Nebuchadnezzar:
and he was driven from men, and did eat grass as oxen, and his body
was wet with the dew of heaven, till his hairs were grown like eagles'
feathers, and his nails like birds' claws" (Dan. 4:28-33).

Giving God no glory, Nebuchadnezzar gloated over what he
had built. He had forgotten that God raises up kings — that God
is in complete control over the affairs of kingdoms. Suddenly,
he heard a voice! But this was no paranoid delusion. This was
God speaking! For the next seven years, Nebuchadnezzar was
a basket case. He didn't know his own name, or that he was
the king over a vast empire. No wonder Nebuchadnezzar had
these verses written in the third person. He didn't want us to
think that he was still the same man. If ever there was a man
who deserved to suffer eternal torment in the fires of hell, the
old Nebuchadnezzar was that man. Few people in this world
have ever been as wicked as he was.

The Dispensation of Grace Foretold

This chapter gives us one of the most profound examples of
grace in the Bible. If God can save a man like him, then there is
hope for us all. The conversion of this Gentile king alludes to a
prophecy of God's incredible grace made available during this
dispensation. Nebuchadnezzar continues:

"And at the end of the days I Nebuchadnezzar lifted up mine
eyes unto heaven, and mine understanding returned unto me,
and I blessed the most High, and I praised and honoured him that
liveth for ever, whose dominion is an everlasting dominion, and his
kingdom is from generation to generation:

"And all the inhabitants of the earth are reputed as nothing: and
he doeth according to his will in the army of heaven, and among the

inhabitants of the earth: and none can stay his hand, or say unto him, What doest thou?

"At the same time my reason returned unto me; and for the glory of my kingdom, mine honour and brightness returned unto me; and my counsellors and my lords sought unto me; and I was established in my kingdom, and excellent majesty was added unto me.

"Now I Nebuchadnezzar praise and extol and honour the King of heaven, all whose works are truth, and his ways judgment: and those that walk in pride he is able to abase" (Dan. 4:34-37).

Before we condemn Nebuchadnezzar for his crimes against humanity, we should examine ourselves. Are not all men a bit like him — or would be, if we could get away with it? If given similar circumstances, would we do the kinds of things he did? We would not like to think so, but throughout life we are continually tested. We are given opportunities to exhibit integrity and honesty, or greed and avarice. And, in our hearts, we know just how well (or poorly) we fare. Know this — eventually, we will all stand before our Creator and be judged for our conduct. Just be glad our Savior offers grace!

At the close of the Tribulation Period, Christ will return to restore political and moral sanity. He will arrive in the midst of the world's most dreadful genocidal war. Any further delay would spell the end to all life on this planet. It will be just that bad. Jesus said, *"Except those day should be shortened, there should no flesh be saved"* (Matt. 24:22). Adam's poor decision to rebel against God will have been played out to its fullest extent. His progeny will fail so badly — so utterly — that only Jesus will be able to save the day. At that time, Christ will judge the nations for the way they treated His people. When all is said and done, men will know that only grace has saved the human race. Those who are spared from extinction will gladly crown Him King of kings. The proverbial family tree will grow again.

The Rise of the Silver Kingdom

In writing these twelve chapters, Daniel was mindful that he did not have the time or space to simply deal with historical events. If these chapters were not prophecies about the *"times of the Gentiles,"* the Lord would not have wasted Daniel's time, or ours. Therefore, this chapter offers more than merely an historical account of Belshazzar's feast and the overthrow of his kingdom. This is the fulfillment of the prophecy set forth in the dream of Nebuchadnezzar's head of gold and arms of silver. Daniel's chapter five is about the rise of the silver kingdom.

The fall of Belshazzar's Babylon to the Medes and Persians fulfilled the second part of the prophecy concerning the *"times of the Gentiles."* Babylon's greatness began to emerge among its neighboring kingdoms under the rule of Nabopolassar. Upon his death (605 B.C.), his son Nebuchadnezzar brought greatness to the kingdom by conquering many nations and using the booty to beautify his capital city.

Nebuchadnezzar had reigned for twenty months as viceroy in the kingdom with his father and another 43 years by himself, dying in 562 B.C. As we observed in the previous chapter, toward the end of his reign, he was driven insane. For seven years (570-563 B.C.), his son, Evilmerodach watched over the kingdom. Then, upon Nebuchadnezzar's death in 562 B.C., Evilmerodach ruled for two years and was murdered by Neriglissar, the husband of Evilmerodach's sister.

Neriglissar ruled for four years (560-556 B.C.), but died in a battle with the Medo/Persian army, leaving his throne to his son, Laborosoarchodus, Nebuchadnezzar's grandson by his daughter. After ruling for only nine months, he was deposed for acts of villany. Nebuchadnezzar's grandson by Evilmerodach succeeded him. The Chaldean historian Berosus called the son of Evilmerodach, Nabonidus. But the Greek historian Herodotus called him Labynetus. According to Bishop Ussher, Nabonidus was thought to be the Belshazzar of this chapter.

Nabonidus (Belshazzar), ascended the throne in 556 B.C. He was overthrown by the Medes and Persians on October 13, 539 B.C. According to *The Jewish Timeline Encyclopedia*, Belshazzar had recently repelled the initial Medo-Persian invasion of Babylon. On this night, Belshazzar was celebrating his victory. Daniel wrote: *"Belshazzar the king made a great feast to a thousand of his lords, and drank wine before the thousand.*

"Belshazzar, whiles he tasted the wine, commanded to bring the golden and silver vessels which his father Nebuchadnezzar had taken out of the temple which was in Jerusalem; that the king, and his princes, his wives, and his concubines, might drink therein.

"Then they brought the golden vessels that were taken out of the temple of the house of God which was at Jerusalem; and the king, and his princes, his wives, and his concubines, drank in them.

"They drank wine, and praised the gods of gold, and of silver, of brass, of iron, of wood, and of stone" (Dan. 5:1-4).

At sunset, all seemed well. However, as soon as darkness fell, the Medo-Persian plan swung into action. Those inside the great city were unaware of the approaching danger. Under the cover of darkness, the armies of the Medes and Persians, led by

Cyrus, nephew and son-in-law of Darius (also called Cyaxares), diverted the flow of the Euphrates River. It seems that no one noticed that the level of the river was going down. Where were the guards at the entrance and exit of the canal that ran under the massive walls? If there were guards upon those walls, they certainly weren't paying attention. Following sunset, there was total darkness for a few hours, until the 18 day-old moon rose just after 11 P.M. Perhaps the noise of celebration and revelry was so loud no one could hear the Medes and Persians approaching.

The defeat of the city was probably due more to the complacency of the Babylonians than it was to the military strategy of the Persians. It had been 42 years since the Medes and Persians were forced to bow before Nebuchadnezzar's golden statue. At that time, the king of the Medes probably said to the king of the Persians, "Wow! Look at all that gold!" Forty-two years later, they came and got it!

Belshazzar Touched Holy Vessels

God allowed Nebuchadnezzar to conquer the known world, destroy Jerusalem and enslave the Chosen People. However, the day of reckoning finally came. When Belshazzar brought out the Temple vessels and began to drink wine from them, God brought down the curtain on Babylon.

This warrants a brief review of the statue in Nebuchadnezzar's dream. God had planned to bring down the *"times of the Gentiles"* during the days of the feet and toes of iron and clay, but Nebuchadnezzar built a statue with the feet and toes made all of gold. Therefore, it seems that God combined the concepts set forth in the two statues, and allowed "golden" Babylon to continue in a "mystery" form until the future destruction of the toes. In other words, God made the destruction of Belshazzar's Babylon to become a foreshadow of the final destruction of MYSTERY BABYLON that will occur at the time of the conclusion of the *"times of the Gentiles."*

Belshazzar appears to be a type of the Antichrist who will bring on the final judgment when he touches the sacred things that belong to God. In this story, God did not let Belshazzar go unpunished. Judgment fell swift and sure. In the ultimate fulfillment of this prophetic scenario, the Antichrist will incur Divine retribution when he tries to divide Jerusalem and the Holy Land. The world will learn that men cannot touch that which belongs to God without invoking His wrath. I do not wish to appear unkind about current plans for peace in the Middle East, but we must understand that the Holy Land belongs to God and should not be divided between the Jews and Palestinians.

According to Daniel, God will judge those who divide the land. In Daniel 11, the prophet gives us a view of the Antichrist and his efforts in dividing the Holy Land. Verses 37 and 38 tell about the Antichrist having little regard for the *"God of his fathers, nor the desire of women,"* and in the following verse, Daniel said that he will *"divide"* the land:

> *"Thus shall he do in the most strongholds with a strange god, whom he shall acknowledge and increase with glory: and he shall cause them to rule over many, and shall **divide** the land for gain."* (Dan. 11:39).

Dividing the Holy Land has always been dangerous, but this prophecy concerns a special time in history — when the Antichrist will divide the land.

Joel also alludes to this time as the period in which *"the sun shall be turned into darkness, and the moon into blood ..."* (Joel 2:31), noting, only three verses later, that when this astronomical display of God's judgment occurs, men will have *"parted"* the land. Joel wrote:

> *"I will also gather all nations, and will bring them down into the valley of Jehoshaphat and will plead with them there for my people and for my heritage Israel, whom they have scattered among the nations, and **parted** my land"* (Joel 3:2).

Jerusalem is the apple of God's eye. Furthermore, the land was given to the progeny of Abraham, Isaac and Jacob. Not only that, David bought the Temple site with hard cash. The transaction is recorded in II Sam. 24:24. It is one of many such land abstracts recorded in the Bible to prove Jewish ownership. Anyone who tries to divide the land will be inviting God's swift and certain judgment. Zechariah wrote:

*"For thus saith the LORD of hosts; After the glory hath he sent me unto the nations which spoiled you: for he that toucheth you toucheth the **apple** of his eye"* (Zech. 2:8).

When something touches the surface of the eye, a reaction is automatic and immediate. The eyelid flinches and the whole body comes to the rescue. That is exactly how God will react over efforts to divide the Holy Land.

During August 2001, only a few weeks before the terrorist attack on September 11, our political leaders met with representatives from Saudi Arabia in extended sessions to lay out plans for the infamous "Roadmap," in which Jews would be dispossessed of their covenant heartland in favor of a Palestinian state. That is when our troubles began. On the very next day after the decision was made, terrorists from Saudi Arabia captured four airliners, flew two of them into New York's World Trade Center and one into the Pentagon, killing some 3,000 innocent people. Since that day, America experienced a Stock Market crash that wiped out billions of dollars in private savings; four hurricanes slammed into America within a single month destroying the homes that people had worked so hard to acquire; and two of the largest F5 category tornadoes introduced a phenomenon that witnessed as many as 85 tornadoes in a single night.

Within a week after Israel began dismantling Gush Katif and pulling their people out of some 21 Jewish communities in the so-called occupied territories, the United States was hit with two huge hurricanes — Katrina and Rita. New Orleans was heavily damaged and recovery will take years. Our State Department had demanded that Israel remove 10,000 people from their homes along the Mediterranean coast, and it seems that God retaliated by dispossessing our people from their homes along the Gulf coast. Our politicians may not be hurting over their decision to establish a Palestinian state, but our citizens certainly are.

The Handwriting on the Wall

As Belshazzar drank from God's holy vessels during this festival, an unseen guest made His appearance:

"In the same hour came forth fingers of a man's hand, and wrote over against the candlestick upon the plaister of the wall of the king's palace: and the king saw the part of the hand that wrote.

"Then the king's countenance was changed, and his thoughts troubled him, so that the joints of his loins were loosed, and his knees smote one against another.

"The king cried aloud to bring in the astrologers, the Chaldeans, and the soothsayers. And the king spake, and said to the wise men of Babylon, Whosoever shall read this writing, and shew me the interpretation thereof, shall be clothed with scarlet, and have a chain of gold about his neck, and shall be the third ruler in the kingdom.

"Then came in all the king's wise men: but they could not read the writing, nor make known to the king the interpretation thereof.

"Then was king Belshazzar greatly troubled, and his countenance was changed in him, and his lords were astonied" (Dan. 5:5-9).

Belshazzar cared little for righteous living. He was more interested in devilish pleasures. Though he had not realized it, God was there that night. The king was soon to learn that God knew everything that was going on. Belshazzar might have tried to hide his debauchery, but God recorded it. That is a good lesson for us to remember. No one can get away with wickedness. A record is being kept. Someone is watching from just beyond the veil. God knows about everything.

When Belshazzar saw the appearance of a hand without a

body attached to it, writing upon the wall of the banquet hall, he became deathly afraid. Think of it! This was probably the same hand that wrote the Ten Commandments on tablets of stone! Daniel does not tell us how big the hand was, but I suspect God could have made it any size He wanted. It was certainly large enough to capture Belshazzar's attention. He had never been so frightened in his life! He had to be standing, because his knees knocked together! This brought him down in a collapse that startled his guests.

Immediately, he called for his advisers and asked for an interpretation. They came, but could not read the language. In the city noted for its history, when all men spoke one language, the king and his greatest intellectuals could not read the message. The God who wrote this message is the same God that confounded the language in this city almost two thousand years before!

Suddenly, this wealthy potentate — this self-expressed party animal — was scared out of his wits! His guests were also astonished. The queen heard about the strange writing and came to see it. She was not there when it happened. She probably did not want to be there to see Belshazzar's disgraceful behavior. Nor was Daniel there, though he had been a high-level official in Nebuchadnezzar's administration. He, too, probably stayed away because he knew about Belshazzar's notorious lifestyle.

The Call for Daniel

"Now the queen, by reason of the words of the king and his lords, came into the banquet house: and the queen spake and said, O king, live for ever: let not thy thoughts trouble thee, nor let thy countenance be changed:

"There is a man in thy kingdom, in whom is the spirit of the holy gods; and in the days of thy father light and understanding and wisdom, like the wisdom of the gods, was found in him; whom the king Nebuchadnezzar thy father, the king, I say, thy father, made master of the magicians, astrologers, Chaldeans, and soothsayers;

"Forasmuch as an excellent spirit, and knowledge, and understanding, interpreting of dreams, and shewing of hard sentences, and dissolving of doubts, were found in the same Daniel, whom the king named Belteshazzar: now let Daniel be called, and he will shew the interpretation" (Dan. 5:10-12).

Though he was living in the midst of a metropolitan city bent on ungodly conduct, Daniel's righteous demeanor was well known. Holiness is a quality of character that will rise, as cream rises, to the top of society every time. Daniel was such a man. Belshazzar may not have wanted him there to see his drunken revelry, but when things got serious, Daniel became the man of the hour. Agreeing with her advice, and not knowing what else to do, Belshazzar called for Daniel to come and help him understand the mysterious message.

"Then was Daniel brought in before the king. And the king spake and said unto Daniel, Art thou that Daniel, which art of the children of the captivity of Judah, whom the king my father brought out of Jewry?

"I have even heard of thee, that the spirit of the gods is in thee, and that light and understanding and excellent wisdom is found in thee.

"And now the wise men, the astrologers, have been brought in before me, that they should read this writing, and make known unto me the interpretation thereof: but they could not shew the interpretation of the thing:

"And I have heard of thee, that thou canst make interpretations, and dissolve doubts: now if thou canst read the writing, and make known to me the interpretation thereof, thou shalt be clothed with scarlet, and have a chain of gold about thy neck, and shalt be the third ruler in the kingdom" (Dan. 5:13-16).

Belshazzar had heard about Daniel, yet had never met him. Nor did he ever really want to meet him. Like many people, Belshazzar probably had an innate dislike for men of God. The king called for all of the other advisers first, hoping not to have to ask advice from God's prophet. Once the preacher arrived, this wicked man, who had just sipped wine out of God's holy vessels, had the audacity to offer Daniel a golden chain and the office that went with it.

Being a man of integrity, Daniel declined the offer from one who had violated Temple vessels. Nevertheless, he agreed to interpret the message. Perhaps the prophet recognized the language as ancient Hebrew, a language the Babylonians could not comprehend. Jewish sages suggest that it was written in an ancient calligraphic style (*Ashurit*) used only for very holy writings:

"Then Daniel answered and said before the king, Let thy gifts be to thyself, and give thy rewards to another; yet I will read the writing unto the king, and make known to him the interpretation.

"O thou king, the most high God gave Nebuchadnezzar thy father a kingdom, and majesty, and glory, and honour:

"And for the majesty that he gave him, all people, nations, and languages, trembled and feared before him: whom he would he slew; and whom he would he kept alive; and whom he would he set up; and whom he would he put down.

"But when his heart was lifted up, and his mind hardened in pride, he was deposed from his kingly throne, and they took his glory from him:

"And he was driven from the sons of men; and his heart was made like the beasts, and his dwelling was with the wild asses: they fed him with grass like oxen, and his body was wet with the dew of heaven; till he knew that the most high God ruled in the kingdom of men, and that he appointeth over it whomsoever he will" (Dan. 5:17-21).

The Interpretation

By now, I suppose Daniel was old enough and wise enough to know that he did not need to mince words with this king, as he had done with Nebuchadnezzar. We recall how Daniel, in the previous chapter, was silent for about an hour while trying to figure out how he might keep from hurting Nebuchadezzar's feelings and maybe losing his own head. But, this time, he did not fear hurting the king's feelings. Therefore, he told the king just how wicked he had been, He probably said these things in the presence of all the people in the banquet hall. He related how

Nebuchadnezzar had been driven insane by his own arrogance, and told him that God was sovereign, bringing judgment upon those who would dare to touch His sacred vessels:

"And thou his son, O Belshazzar, hast not humbled thine heart, though thou knewest all this;

"But hast lifted up thyself against the Lord of heaven; and they have brought the vessels of his house before thee, and thou, and thy lords, thy wives, and thy concubines, have drunk wine in them; and thou hast praised the gods of silver, and gold, of brass, iron, wood, and stone, which see not, nor hear, nor know: and the God in whose hand thy breath is, and whose are all thy ways, hast thou not glorified:

"Then was the part of the hand sent from him; and this writing was written.

"And this is the writing that was written, MENE, MENE, TEKEL, UPHARSIN.

"This is the interpretation of the thing: MENE; God hath numbered thy kingdom, and finished it.

"TEKEL; Thou art weighed in the balances, and art found wanting.

"PERES; Thy kingdom is divided, and given to the Medes and Persians" (Dan. 5:22-28).

Daniel gave the interpretation of the handwriting on the wall. Even as he spoke, the Medo-Persian army was entering the city and taking out soldiers on the fortress walls. Daniel may have told Belshazzar that the time of the seventy-year Jewish captivity was almost up; that Babylon must now pay the price for desecrating God's land and persecuting God's people; and that the land of Babylon would now be conquered by the Medes and Persians.

Being numerical terms, some have suggested that perhaps the etchings on the wall offers a clue as to just how long the *"times of the Gentiles"* might extend across the centuries until the revival of MYSTERY BABYLON. In Babylon, the basic unit of measurement was a gold "shekel" or *"tekel."* The *"mene"* represented 50 shekels; and the *"upharsin"* stood for 25 shekels. Added together, they totaled 126 shekels. According to Ezekiel 45:12, a shekel consisted of 20 gerahs, making a sum total of 2,520 gerahs in 126 shekels. Could this be a prophecy that Babylon would be revived in 2,520 years?

We cannot be dogmatic about such a hidden meaning, but neither should we dismiss the possibility out of hand. Adding 2,520 years to 538 B.C., adds up to around 1982. Generally speaking, the date falls within the generation that is currently witnessing the rise of the European Union. In January 1981, Greece became the 10th member nation to join the Union. The adopted logo for the new Europe shows a woman (Europa) riding a beast (Zeus). The new parliament building in Strasbourg, France, is designed to look like an unfinished tower — as in the unfinished tower of Babel (see photo page 84). Those are fairly significant developments toward an end-time MYSTERY BABYLON.

After hearing this ominous news, Belshazzar may have been too intoxicated to grasp the fact that his kingdom was about to fall. He proceeded to call for a robe and gold chain for Daniel:

"Then commanded Belshazzar, and they clothed Daniel with scarlet, and put a chain of gold about his neck, and made a proclamation concerning him, that he should be the third ruler in the kingdom.

"In that night was Belshazzar the king of the Chaldeans slain.

"And Darius the Median took the kingdom, being about threescore and two years old" (Dan. 5:29-31).

We should note that Daniel's prophecies were well received by Nebuchadnezzar, Belshazzar, Darius, Cyrus and Alexander the Great. None of these monarchs were angry or displeased with Daniel's predictions. In fact, they were favorably impressed. This was not the case with other prophets. Moses was not well received by Pharaoh. Isaiah was executed by being cut in half with a saw. Jeremiah was thrown into prison and King Zedekiah burned his sacred scrolls. Example after example could be given to show how the prophets were ill treated. Therefore, it is remarkable that Daniel could express the mind of God and still be received with favor by the leaders of the gold, silver and brass kingdoms.

Furthermore, Flavius Josephus, who was a beloved servant to the Roman general and future Caesar, Titus, son of Caesar Vespasian, wrote that in his day (c. A.D. 80) Daniel was still "admirable to hear." It is possible that the ruler of the iron kingdom was also interested in Daniel's prophecies—especially that part about the destruction of Jerusalem by *"the people of the prince that shall come"* (Dan.9:26).

This should encourage us to study the book and use it to tell others about the coming judgments upon our world and the return of Christ. If taught properly, Daniel should still be "admirable to hear."

It is said that Belshazzar was accidentally killed by his own soldiers amidst the confusion that broke out that night. Thus ended the reign of the head of gold. Darius and Cyrus established the enlarged Medo-Persian kingdom, fulfilling the prophecy set forth in the chest and arms of silver. The prophecy happened just as God said it would.

The remaining prophetic scenario regarding the Antichrist touching God's land, is yet to come to pass. However, in light of today's so-called "Roadmap" to peace in the Middle East, with its proposal for a Palestinian state — perhaps, the prophetic implications set forth in this chapter could occur in the near future!

Daniel and The Lion's Den

There are several aspects to this story, which should be considered — Daniel's excellent character; his prayer life; his elevation to high authority in the kingdom; the plot on his life; God's faithfulness; Daniel's deliverance; etc. But, even more importantly than the primary interpretation and practical application, is its prophetic implication. Darius becomes a type of the Antichrist; the decree foreshadows the mark of the beast; and Daniel becomes a type of the faithful remnant — similar to Revelation's 144,000 righteous Jews. The plot begins with:

"Honor the King" Month

"It pleased Darius to set over the kingdom an hundred and twenty princes, which should be over the whole kingdom;

"And over these three presidents; of whom Daniel was first: that the princes might give accounts unto them, and the king should have no damage.

"Then this Daniel was preferred above the presidents and princes, because an excellent spirit was in him; and the king thought to set him over the whole realm.

*"Then the presidents and princes sought to find occasion against
Daniel concerning the kingdom; but they could find none occasion
nor fault; forasmuch as he was faithful, neither was there any error
or fault found in him.*

*"Then said these men, We shall not find any occasion against
this Daniel, except we find it against him concerning the law of his
God"* (Dan. 6:1-5).

The newly expanded kingdom of Darius the Mede and
his son-in-law, Cyrus the Persian, was divided into provinces
with governors, over which Daniel and two others were put in
charge. Perhaps one president was a Mede, the other a Persian,
but Daniel, a Jew, was over them all.

The Bible speaks of 120 princes. However, Josephus took
this to mean 120 princes under each of three presidents, for
a total of 360 princes — each over their respective provinces.
The government was established as a republican form of
administration, thus lifting the burden of maintaining the
empire from the shoulders of a single man.

According to the historian, Xenophon, Darius had no male
heirs. He looked to his son-in-law, Cyrus, as the heir to his throne.
Some say that the term "Darius" was a title for "king" rather
than the name of the man. The agreement between Darius, now
62 years old, was for the Mede to rule for one year, then turn the
throne over to his Persian son-in-law as a wedding present.

Daniel was elevated to the highest position in the kingdom
for several possible reasons. Darius and Cyrus certainly didn't
want a Babylonian in their administration, but Daniel, though
a Jew, knew every facet of the Babylonian government, having
served its kings and having been elevated to Babylon's second
highest political position by Belshazzar. Daniel, being almost
90 years old, had served with distinction. I am sure that the
two monarchs had been familiar with Daniel's fame for several
years. Their spies had gathered intelligence on those that could
be trusted; and Daniel was clearly the frontrunner.

The Plot Against Daniel

As always, there were bureaucrats, who, instead of being diligent about their loyalty to the king, bullied their way to the top by stepping on people. The other two presidents hated the idea that Daniel was their superior. Had they managed to remove Daniel, they would have fought each other for the top position. What they did not consider was that Daniel had three times the workload. They plotted against the one person they should have admired. Such is the case with small-minded people.

"Then these presidents and princes assembled together to the king, and said thus unto him, King Darius, live for ever.

"All the presidents of the kingdom, the governors, and the princes, the counsellors, and the captains, have consulted together to establish a royal statute, and to make a firm decree, that whosoever shall ask a petition of any God or man for thirty days, save of thee, O king, he shall be cast into the den of lions.

"Now, O king, establish the decree, and sign the writing, that it be not changed, according to the law of the Medes and Persians, which altereth not.

"Wherefore king Darius signed the writing and the decree.

"Now when Daniel knew that the writing was signed, he went into his house; and his windows being open in his chamber toward Jerusalem, he kneeled upon his knees three times a day, and prayed, and gave thanks before his God, as he did aforetime" (Dan. 6:6-10).

It did not take them long to hatch a plan. Knowing about Daniel's prayer life, they went to the king and lied, saying that *"all"* the presidents had consulted on this proposal. That was not true. There were only three of them, two of whom were standing before the king! Daniel had not agreed to this. In fact, he was not aware of the proposal!

I suspect that Daniel was not without his own intelligence network. Unfortunately, his people were probably surprised by the decree. No governors, princes, counselors, or captains had been consulted. These two conniving politicians had secretly conspired to lie to the king. As soon as the meeting was over, someone went to tell Daniel. Being a man of personal integrity, he determined to continue his prayers in spite of the decree. Daniel violated a law, but it was a bad law.

Their scheme to honor the king was nothing less than a plot to get rid of Daniel. Darius should have known that a decree threatening to cast people into the lion's den offered too harsh a punishment. Their flattery clouded the king's reasoning. He did not consider the consequences involved in such a celebration. Pushing the written decree in front of the king and urging him to sign it, was something these mid-level bureaucrats were good at, having done this many times before. To the king, this was just another decree. But it carried the weight of the *"law of the Medes and the Persians."* Once signed, it could not be changed.

Daniel's Prayer Life

Daniel had established a regimen for prayer. He prayed three times a day, opening his westward window and kneeling toward Jerusalem. In II Chronicles 6:26, at the dedication of the new Temple, King Solomon asked the Lord to hear the people when they prayed facing Jerusalem. That is what Daniel was doing three times a day. Just a side note: when Cyrus came to the throne the next year, he allowed Zerubbabel to lead a group of over 40,000 Jews back to Jerusalem to rebuild the Temple. Daniel's loyal service may have had a positive influence on the king's decision.

As a man of prayer, Daniel is an excellent example for us all. It seems that the average Christian neglects the importance of prayer and Bible study. Prayer offers the opportunity for us to talk to God, while Bible study provides a method for God to communicate with us. This arrangement gives the Christian a sense of personal relationship with Christ. Furthermore, to have a prayer answered is one of the most rewarding moments in a person's life. How would you like to have the spiritual power of a Daniel? You can! Begin today to develop the prayer life of a Daniel, and you will find that there really is someone listening on the other end of that spiritual exercise we call prayer!

The Arrest

"Then these men assembled, and found Daniel praying and making supplication before his God.

"Then they came near, and spake before the king concerning the king's decree; Hast thou not signed a decree, that every man that shall ask a petition of any God or man within thirty days, save of thee, O king, shall be cast into the den of lions? The king answered and said, The thing is true, according to the law of the Medes and Persians, which altereth not.

"Then answered they and said before the king, That Daniel, which is of the children of the captivity of Judah, regardeth not thee, O king, nor the decree that thou hast signed, but maketh his petition three times a day.

"Then the king, when he heard these words, was sore displeased with himself, and set his heart on Daniel to deliver him: and he laboured till the going down of the sun to deliver him.

"Then these men assembled unto the king, and said unto the king, Know, O king, that the law of the Medes and Persians is, That no decree nor statute which the king establisheth may be changed.

"Then the king commanded, and they brought Daniel, and cast him into the den of lions. Now the king spake and said unto Daniel, Thy God whom thou servest continually, he will deliver thee.

"And a stone was brought, and laid upon the mouth of the den; and the king sealed it with his own signet, and with the signet of his lords; that the purpose might not be changed concerning Daniel" (Dan. 6:11-17).

The two presidents assembled a group and, as they expected, caught Daniel praying. Then they pressed the matter with the king, probably waving the decree as they told their sordid story about finding the most trusted president in the kingdom in communication with an alien potentate — the God of the Jews. They made it sound like treason.

Darius knew about Daniel's prayers and was in full agreement with his devotion to the one source that could reveal great wisdom. This gave Daniel a wealth of knowledge that no one else could offer. Yet, he had to admit that Daniel had broken the law. Realizing that he had been tricked, the king tried every avenue of reasoning in an effort to undo the situation. But these men were adamant that Daniel should pay the price stipulated in the law. After all, it was the law of the Medes and Persians! It could not be changed!

The Miracle in the Lion's Den

Finally, Darius offered his apology to Daniel and told him that he was confident that God could deliver him. They may have sounded like encouraging words, but the king was very worried. Daniel entered the den of lions; a stone was rolled over the entrance and sealed with two seals — the king's and the seal of the accusers.

"Then the king went to his palace, and passed the night fasting: neither were instruments of music brought before him: and his sleep went from him.

"Then the king arose very early in the morning, and went in haste unto the den of lions.

"And when he came to the den, he cried with a lamentable voice unto Daniel: and the king spake and said to Daniel, O Daniel, servant of the living God, is thy God, whom thou servest continually, able to deliver thee from the lions?" (Dan. 6:18-20).

Darius was so worried about Daniel, he could not sleep. Nor did he want to listen to any chamber music. The long hours dragged on until morning light was approaching. Hoping for the best, but fearing the worst, the king hurried to the lion's den to see if Daniel had survived.

Almost in tears, he called to Daniel. One can imagine how relieved he must have been to hear the prophet's cheerful voice. God had sent an angel to calm the lions. Daniel told the king that God had found him to be innocent! After all, God presided over the Supreme Court!

"Then said Daniel unto the king, O king, live for ever.

"My God hath sent his angel, and hath shut the lions' mouths, that they have not hurt me: forasmuch as before him innocency was found in me; and also before thee, O king, have I done no hurt.

"Then was the king exceeding glad for him, and commanded that they should take Daniel up out of the den. So Daniel was taken up out of the den, and no manner of hurt was found upon him, because he believed in his God.

"And the king commanded, and they brought those men which had accused Daniel, and they cast them into the den of lions, them, their children, and their wives; and the lions had the mastery of them, and brake all their bones in pieces or ever they came at the bottom of the den" (Dan. 6:21-24).

Darius was delighted that Daniel was alive and ordered his immediate release. By this time, the accusers had arrived. Though this passage does not give the details of what happened next, Flavius Josephus adds that the accusers "... would not own that he was preserved by God, and by his providence; but they said, that the lions had been filled full with food, and on that account it was ... that the lions would not touch Daniel, nor come to him; and this they alleged to the king; but the king out of an abhorrence of their wickedness, gave order that they should throw in a great deal of flesh to the lions; and when they had filled themselves, he gave further order that Daniel's enemies should be cast into the den that he might learn whether the lions, now that they were full, would touch them or not' (Josephus, *Antiquities*, X, XI, 6). The lions attacked Daniel's accusers immediately and devoured them.

The King's Decree

"Then king Darius wrote unto all people, nations, and languages, that dwell in all the earth; Peace be multiplied unto you.

"I make a decree, That in every dominion of my kingdom men tremble and fear before the God of Daniel: for he is the living God, and stedfast for ever, and his kingdom that which shall not be

destroyed, and his dominion shall be even unto the end.

"He delivereth and rescueth, and he worketh signs and wonders in heaven and in earth, who hath delivered Daniel from the power of the lions.

"So this Daniel prospered in the reign of Darius, and in the reign of Cyrus the Persian" (Dan. 6:25-28).

Earlier in Daniel's book, Nebuchadnezzar had made a *"decree"* that all should fear the God who delivers His Chosen People from the fires of persecution, on pain of falling under severe judgment (Dan. 3:29). Now, for the second time in this prophetic book, Darius the Mede makes a similar decree — that all men should respect the God of Daniel as *"the living God"* who *"delivered Daniel from the power of the lions."* This being a book of prophecy about the *"times of the Gentiles,"* it seems that God was warning all nations about anti-Semitism. It is a double warning for all of the generations involved during this extended period of time. Today, the decrees carry as much weight as they did back then. Woe to the nation who curses the Jews!

Four Beasts From the Sea

The book of Daniel is divided into two parts. In the first six chapters, Daniel records the dreams and visions of others, while reserving the second half of the book for his own visions about the end of days. The first six chapters discuss the kings that foreshadow the Antichrist, while the last six chapters reveal his diabolical bloodline.

In this chapter, Daniel describes the first of his personal visionary dreams — although it occurred before the events of chapter 5. Chapter 7 dates to the first year of Belshazzar (555 B.C.); chapter 8 in the third year of Belshazzar (553 B.C.); chapter 9 in the first year of Darius (538 B.C.); and chapters 10-12 in the third year of Cyrus (534 B.C.).

As we shall see in Daniel 7, when Belshazzar first ascended the Babylonian throne, the prophet dreamed about four beasts rising out of a stormy sea. He described ten horns, a little horn, the Ancient of Days and the Son of man coming in the clouds of heaven to establish the messianic kingdom. Yet, he told no one — he kept the details to himself. For several years prior to the handwriting on the wall, Daniel was aware that the Medes and Persians would conquer Babylon and that the Greeks would conquer the Persians. Daniel knew all of this before Belshazzar saw the handwriting on the wall. Now, let us review what Daniel saw:

"In the first year of Belshazzar king of Babylon Daniel had a dream and visions of his head upon his bed: then he wrote the dream, and told the sum of the matters.

"Daniel spake and said, I saw in my vision by night, and, behold, the four winds of the heaven strove upon the great sea.

"And four great beasts came up from the sea, diverse one from another.

"The first was like a lion, and had eagle's wings: I beheld till the wings thereof were plucked, and it was lifted up from the earth, and made stand upon the feet as a man, and a man's heart was given to it.

"And behold another beast, a second, like to a bear, and it raised up itself on one side, and it had three ribs in the mouth of it between the teeth of it: and they said thus unto it, Arise, devour much flesh.

"After this I beheld, and lo another, like a leopard, which had upon the back of it four wings of a fowl; the beast had also four heads; and dominion was given to it.

"After this I saw in the night visions, and behold a fourth beast, dreadful and terrible, and strong exceedingly; and it had great iron teeth: it devoured and brake in pieces, and stamped the residue with the feet of it: and it was diverse from all the beasts that were before it; and it had ten horns.

"I considered the horns, and, behold, there came up among them another little horn, before whom there were three of the first horns plucked up by the roots: and, behold, in this horn were eyes like the eyes of man, and a mouth speaking great things" (Dan. 7:1-8).

Daniel's seventh chapter contains one of the most famous prophecies in the Bible. Some 651 years later, the Apostle John alluded to this chapter in his vision of a beastly world government rising out of the sea (Rev. 13). However, though Daniel described four beasts rising out the sea in succession, John saw them as one composite creature. Daniel listed them as a lion, bear and leopard; but John referred to them in reverse order — a beast like a leopard, with the feet of a bear, and the mouth of a lion. In each case, the sea, out of which the beasts emerged, is depicted as representing humanity's massive population. Some have suggested that Daniel was looking into the future, seeing four kingdoms that would span the *"times of the Gentiles"* in chronological order; whereas, John was looking back upon each historical appearance, which accounted for his naming them in reverse order. On the other hand, could John have been focusing only upon Daniel's fourth beast, describing it as a composite of the other three?

Daniel does not assign an animal motif to his fourth beast, thus leaving the possibility that it could be a composite of the previous lion, bear and leopard. Daniel described it as having *"teeth of iron"* (Dan. 7:19), which is indicative of Rome, thus corresponding to the legs of iron in Nebuchadnezzar's statue. He also described it as having *"nails of brass"* (Dan. 7:19), which is indicative of Greece, also corresponding to the belly of brass in Nebuchadnezzar's statue. We are told that Daniel's beast will *"speak great words against the most High"* (Dan. 7:25). In like manner, John's beast is given the *"mouth of a lion"* (Rev. 13:2) *"... speaking great things and blasphemies"* (Rev. 13:5), that *"... he opened his mouth in blasphemy against God, to blaspheme his name"* (Rev. 13:6). We should also note that Babylon was represented by the head of the statue in Nebuchadnezzar's dream; and that the head is the location of the mouth. Therefore, it seems that Daniel's fourth beast may be a composite of the other three. Could this be the reason why John sees them as parts of a single beast, whose power will extend over all nations for three and a half years?

Most present-day theologians agree that Daniel's vision of the lion, bear, leopard and dreadful beast corresponds closely to Nebuchadnezzar's statue, whose head was of gold, with arms of silver, a belly of brass, legs of iron and feet of iron and clay. Bishop James Ussher, author of *The Annals of the World* (published in 1658) wrote: "In the first year of his [Belshazzar's] reign, Daniel had a vision of four beasts, which signified the four empires of the world." This view is also consistent with an early third-century writing by Hippolytus, one of Christianity's highly acclaimed theologians.

Hippolytus on Daniel's Vision

Outside of John's Apocalypse, one of the earliest extra-biblical views of Daniel's vision came from Hippolytus (A.D. 170-236), bishop of Rome. It is recorded that he was of Greek descent and a disciple of Irenaeus, bishop of Lyons; who, in turn, was a disciple of Polycarp, bishop of Smyrna; who, in turn, was a disciple of the Apostle John. In the introduction to the study of Hippolytus, we are told that the "spirit of his life's work reflects that of [Irenaeus] his master." Therefore, his commentary on Daniel's vision appears to be the product of his predecessors. Note that John, author of the Apocalypse, taught Polycarp, who passed along his work to Irenaeus, who, in turn, taught Hippolytus. That does not mean that everything you read in the following commentary came from John. But it does mean that the same general study of eschatology was prominently held by these men.

As we review the commentary by Hippolytus, we will find ourselves agreeing with some points of interest and disagreeing with other points. Above all, we will understand why modern scholars are reluctant to hold any opposing views. Hippolytus wrote:

"In speaking of a *'lioness from the sea,'* he meant the rising of the kingdom of Babylon, and that this was the *'golden head of the image.'* And in speaking of its *'eagle wings,'* he meant that king Nebuchadnezzar was exalted and that his glory was lifted up against God. Then he says, *'the wings thereof were plucked,'* i.e., that his glory was destroyed, for he was driven out of his kingdom. And the words, *'and made to stand upon the feet as a man, and a man's heart was given to it,'* mean that he came to himself again, and recognized that he was but a man, and gave the glory to God. Then after the lioness he sees a second beast, *'like a bear,'* which signified the Persians. For after the Babylonians the Persians obtained the power. And in saying that *'it had three ribs in its mouth,'* he pointed to the three nations, Persians, Medes, and Babylonians, which were expressed in the image by the silver after the gold. Then comes the third beast, *'a leopard,'* which means the Greeks; for after the Persians, Alexander of Macedon had the power, when Darius was overthrown, which was also indicated by the brass in the image. And in saying that the beast *'had four wings of a fowl, and four heads,'* he showed most clearly how the kingdom of Alexander was parted into four divisions. For in speaking of four heads, he meant the four kings that arose out of it. For Alexander, when dying, divided his kingdom into four parts. Then he says, *'The fourth beast (was) dreadful and terrible: it had iron teeth, and claws of brass.'* Who, then, are meant by this but the Romans, whose kingdom, the kingdom that still stands, is expressed by the iron? *'For,'* says he, *'its legs are of iron'"* (Hippolytus on Daniel, *The Ante-Nicene Fathers*, Vol. 5, pp. 364-367).

Before continuing, we should note that Hippolytus referred to the *"lion"* as a lioness. The Hebrew term — *Ariyah* [אריה] for *"lion"* — ends with ה *hay*, a letter that Hippolytus viewed as feminine. However, though it is agreed that the ה *hay* is feminine, all lexicon references to the Hebrew *Ariyah* [אריה] are decidedly masculine. The Hebrew language has a different word — *Lavia* [לביא] for "lioness." Secondly, he made the three ribs in the mouth of the bear to represent three ancient groups — Persians, Medes and Babylonians. The Babylonians we can understand, but why should the bear be eating two of its own ribs? I am not sure that Hippolytus is correct in this case. The Persian Empire also included the population centers of Asia Minor and Egypt. They could have been included among those three ribs.

Aside from these two problem areas, Hippolytus seems to be on to something here. To his credit, he noted that the dreadful beast had *"nails of brass,"* as well as *"teeth ... of iron"* (Dan. 7:19). This seems to tell us that the dreadful beast is formed from a composite of Greece and Rome and corresponds with the band of iron and brass wrapped around the trunk of the tree in Daniel

4:15. Again, it seems to me that this is a clue to the lineage of the Antichrist. I think he will emerge out of the royal houses of Greece and Rome. Also, he may not be entirely human. His ancestry remains shrouded in mystery — perhaps in the mystery of those ancient fallen angels of Genesis 6. Hippolytus continues:

"After this, then, what remains, beloved, but the toes of the feet of the image, in which *'part shall be of iron and part of clay mixed together?'* By the toes of the feet he meant, mystically, the ten kings that rise out of that kingdom. As Daniel says, *'I considered the beast; and, lo, (there were) ten horns and behold there came up among them another little horn;'* by which none other is meant than the Antichrist that is to rise; and he shall set up the kingdom of Judah. And in saying that *'three horns'* were *'plucked up by the roots'* by this one, he indicates the three kings of Egypt, Libya, and Ethiopia, whom this one will slay in the array of war. And when he has conquered all, he will prove himself a terrible and savage tyrant, and will cause tribulation and persecution to the saints, exalting himself against them. And after him, it remains that *'the stone'* shall come from heaven, which *'smote the image'* and shivered it, and subverted all the kingdoms, and gave the kingdom to the saints of the Most High. This *'became a great mountain and filled the whole earth'*" (Ibid.).

Let us pause here to note that Hippolytus suggested that the three kings, depicted by three horns, are to be the kings of Egypt, Libya and Ethiopia. These were probably good guesses in his day, but I am not sure that we should be held to that interpretation today. Hippolytus does not tell us why he chose these countries, nor does he identify the countries of the other seven kings. It is also noted that he is not clear on the national origin of the Antichrist. Should we assume, since he "set up the kingdom of Judah," that he is Jewish? It would have been helpful had he explained his thoughts in this regard. Hippolytus continues:

"As these things, then, are destined to come to pass, and

as the toes of the image turn out to be democracies, and the ten horns of the beast are distributed among ten kings, let us look at what is before us more carefully, and scan it, as it were, with open eye. The *'golden head of the image'* is identical with the *'lioness,'* by which the Babylonians were represented. *'The golden shoulders and the arms of silver'* are the same with the *'bear,'* by which the Persians and Medes are meant. *'The belly and thighs of brass'* are the *'leopard,'* by which the Greeks who ruled from Alexander onwards are intended. The *'legs of iron'* are the *'dreadful and terrible beast,'* by which the Romans who hold the empire now are meant. The *'toes of clay and iron'* are the *'ten horns,'* which are to be. The *'one other little horn springing up in their midst'* is the *'Antichrist.'* The stone that *'smites the image and breaks it in pieces,'* and that filled the whole earth, is Christ, who comes from heaven and brings judgment on the world" (Ibid.).

Hippolytus refers to the clay as representing "democracies," an interpretation widely held to this day. He seems to suggest that the clay represents an inherent political weakness in democratic forms of government and that the iron represents the strength of totalitarian regimes. It is obvious that a heavy metalic statue could not be sustained by feet of clay, thus giving rise to thoughts of its inherent structural weakness. However, Hippolytus does not address the meaning of the accompanying passage that says, *"they shall mingle themselves with the seed of men, but they shall not cleave one to another"* (Dan. 2:43). If the *"seed of men"* is depicted by the iron, then does the clay represent something other than the *"seed of men"*? Could this be a reference to the prophetic *"seed of the serpent"* — those fallen angels of Genesis 6, who consorted with human women? His mentor, Irenaeus, said that the Antichrist would come from the tribe of Dan, then discusses the Greek Titans, saying that the Antichrist might be known by the name "Titan," since the term has a numerical value of 666 in the Greek alphabet (Irenaeus, *Against Heresies*, Book 5, paragraphs 2 and 3). The Titans were the fallen angels who descended to Mount Hermon, took human wives, and produced giants, both in the days before the flood, and also after that. Hippolytus continues:

"But that we may not leave our subject at this point undemonstrated, we are obliged to discuss the matter of the times, of which a man should not speak hastily, because they are a light to him. For as the times are noted from the foundation of the world, and reckoned from Adam, they set clearly before us the matter with which our inquiry deals. For the first appearance of our Lord in the flesh took place in Bethlehem, under Augustus, in the year 5,500; and He suffered in the thirty-third year. And 6,000 years must needs be accomplished, in order that the Sabbath may come, the rest, the holy day *'on which God rested from all His works.'* For the Sabbath is the type and emblem of the future kingdom of the saints, when they *'shall reign with Christ,'* when He comes from heaven, as John says in his Apocalypse: for *'a day with the Lord is as a thousand years.'* Since, then, in six days God made all things, it follows that 6,000 years must be fulfilled. And they are not yet fulfilled, as John says: *'five are fallen; one is,'* that is, the sixth; *'the other is not yet come.'*

"In mentioning the *'other,'* moreover, he specifies the seventh, in which there is rest. But some one may be ready to say, 'How will you prove to me that the Savior was born in the year 5,500?' Learn that easily, O man; for the things that took place of old in the wilderness, under Moses, in the case of the tabernacle, were constituted types and emblems of spiritual mysteries, in order that, when the truth came in Christ in these last days, you might be able to perceive that these things were fulfilled. For He says to him, *'And thou shalt make the ark of imperishable wood, and shalt overlay it with pure gold within and without; and thou shalt make the length of it two cubits and a half, and the breadth thereof one cubit and a half, and a cubit and a half the height;'* which measures, when summed up together, make five cubits and a half, so that the 5,500 years might be signified thereby.

"At that time, then, the Savior appeared and showed His

own body to the world, (born) of the Virgin, who was the *'ark overlaid with pure gold,'* with the Word within and the Holy Spirit without; so that the truth is demonstrated, and the *'ark'* made manifest. From the birth of Christ, then, we must reckon the 500 years that remain to make up the 6,000, and thus the end shall be. And that the Savior appeared in the world, bearing the imperishable ark, His own body, at a time which was the fifth and half, John declares: *'Now it was the sixth hour,'* he says, intimating by that, one-half of the day. But a day with the Lord is 1,000 years; and the half of that, therefore, is 500 years. For it was not meet that He should appear earlier, for the burden of the law still endured, nor yet when the sixth day was fulfilled (for the baptism is changed), but on the fifth and half, in order that in the remaining half time the gospel might be preached to the whole world, and that when the sixth day was completed He might end the present life" ("Hippolytus on Daniel", *The Ante-Nicene Fathers*, Vol. 5, pp. 364-367).

Hippolytus was right on one thing — he should not have spoken hastily on this subject. He was quite elaborate on his use of typology — especially on the dimensions of the Ark of the Covenant (five and a half cubits) representing 5,500 years. He also interpreted John's use of the *"sixth hour"* from John 19:14 as representing the sixth millennium. Furthermore, he referred to Revelation 17:10, in which John wrote, *"... there are seven kings: five are fallen, and one is ..."* and makes them out to be thousand-year time periods. Hippolytus thought that Christ would return in A.D. 500, which didn't happen. Finally, he attributed the passage, *"a day with the Lord is as a thousand years,"* to John, rather than Peter. Oh well, I think he was right about the return of Christ being at the end of six thousand years, but he and his contemporaries had no historical sources upon which they could rely when it came to counting the years. Their sources had stretched human history beyond reasonable limits. The writings of Hippolytus serve to remind us that we are all groping in the darkness, looking for the light switch!

The Legacy of Hippolytus

Many scholars agree with Hippolytus and compare Daniel's four beasts with the metals in Nebuchadnezzar's statue. Under this method of interpretation, the lion with eagle's wings represents Babylon; the bear corresponds to Medo-Persia; the leopard stands for Greece; and the fourth beast points to Rome.

I also hold this position. However, I suppose there will always be some nagging, yet unanswered questions. For example, why would Daniel repeat the whole scenario about the *"times of the Gentiles,"* after already doing so in chapter 2? Why would his dream experience a change in metaphoric symbols — from the figure of a man to those of animals? Why would Daniel dream of a Medo-Persian *"bear"* in chapter 7 and a Medo-Persian *"ram"* in chapter 8? Why would he dream about a Grecian *"leopard"* in chapter 7 and a Grecian *"goat"* in chapter 8? I suppose there are no good answers to these questions. We have no alternative references throughout history.

We should note that John's *"beast"* (Rev. 13) may not describe the whole history of the *"times of the Gentiles,"* but rather a worldwide bureaucracy under the authority of the Antichrist. Therefore, John's beast seems to conform only to Daniel's fourth beast — the final Gentile world power that will drag all nations down to Armageddon. It seems to me that John's beast is a latter-day composite of all four Gentile world powers, leading to my conclusion that it could also represent a prophetic view of today's United Nations — a world body made up of all of those nations who languished under the rules of Babylon, Medo-Persia, Greece and Rome.

The Man Nearby

In his dream, Daniel saw a man standing nearby and asked him about these beasts; to which he replied, *"These great beasts, which are four, are four kings, which **shall arise** out of the earth"* (v.17). If these beasts represent future kings that *"shall arise,"* could the *"lion"* still represent the king of Babylon? After all, Daniel had this dream several years after Nebuchadnezzar's death and just a few years before the end of the Babylonian kingdom. Since this vision was given in the first year of King Belshazzar, it seems that Babylon could not have a king that *"shall arise."* The visitor in Daniel's dream told him that the fourth beast represented, not only a fourth king, but also a fourth kingdom: *"The fourth beast shall be the fourth kingdom upon earth, which shall be diverse from all kingdoms ..."* (v.23).

The heavenly visitor told Daniel that the fourth kingdom would be different from *"all kingdoms,"* which, though not specifically explained, could imply that the phrase *"all kingdoms"* corresponded to those previous beasts in Daniel's dream. If the fourth beast (the Roman Empire and its future revival) is different from the other three, how, then, could they represent those same kingdoms? Could they also represent modern contemporary kingdoms?

To suggest that Daniel has seen something other than the ancient empires of Babylon, Medo-Persia and Greece in these first three beasts, goes against the consensus of the great theological minds of the nineteenth and twentieth centuries. Therefore, the comfortable position is to assume that Daniel has simply dreamed about the *"times of the Gentiles."* Aside from the general view, however, could the beasts have more than one interpretation? Could they represent both — a view of those ancient kingdoms and a futurist view of great nations that will exist in the days of the fourth kingdom? Before looking at each beast, we should consider the *"four winds"* and the *"great sea."*

The Four Winds and the Great Sea

Though the images of the wind and sea are not explained in this chapter; it is generally believed that the four winds represent turmoil — *"winds"* of war, so to speak; and that the *"great sea"* depicts the ever-increasing population of a warring humanity.

The late Dr. M. R. DeHaan once suggested that the *"sea"* represents the Mediterranean and that the *"land"* refers to Israel. He was a great theologian and, as a young minister, I loved to listen to his radio broadcasts regularly. He had so many terrific insights on eschatology. However, in this particular case, if we confine the dream to the Mediterranean world, then it seems to me that the interpretation would also need to be confined. Personally, after many years of study, I think the vision involves the entire planet.

We learn that the four winds *"strove"* upon the great sea, thus implying great distress. Jesus used such a metaphor in His Olivet Discourse. He taught that, in the last days, there would be: *"… upon the earth distress of nations, with perplexity; the sea and the waves roaring"* (Luke 21:25).

Throughout the twentieth century, and until this very day, evil men have inflicted the human race with two world wars and continual bloodletting with no reprieve in sight. Rogue nations are currently building weapons of mass destruction. Therefore, we may want to look at the twentieth and twenty-first centuries for the answers to Daniel's dream.

The Lion with Eagle's Wings

"The first was like a lion, and had eagle's wings: I beheld till the wings thereof were plucked, and it was lifted up from the earth, and made stand upon the feet as a man, and a man's heart was given to it" (Dan. 7:4).

Though Daniel asked the visitor in his dream for an explanation of the beasts, he was told only that they represented four kingdoms. There were no specifics, thus leaving us with few answers. Therefore, we can only speculate on possibilities. Is it possible to link these beasts to John's vision and bring them all into the last generation — the end-time?

If this view is feasible, then we should consider the nations whose symbols correspond to these creatures. For example, the symbol of a lion is indicative of Great Britain, a major player in the return of the Jews to their ancient homeland. In 1917, the British army liberated Jerusalem under the Balfour Declaration, promising to establish a homeland for the Jews.

Note that Daniel saw eagle's wings torn away from the lion. Could this refer to the fact that Great Britain lost its many colonies around the world during the twentieth century? It was once said that "the sun never sets on the British Empire," but no longer. Or, could the eagle's wings be a symbol of the United States — a major colony torn away from Great Britain in the years following 1776? Perhaps.

On the other hand, the symbol of a lion was long ago attributed to the tribe of Judah, and still represents the motif for modern Israel. Could this vision speak of the return of the Jews on the *"wings"* of eagles (Deut. 32:11)? Could the shore upon which it emerges from the sea represent their ancient Promised Land? Could the *"man's heart"* represent the revival of the nation in 1948? Maybe.

The Bear with Three Ribs

"And behold another beast, a second, like to a bear, and it raised up itself on one side, and it had three ribs in the mouth of it between the teeth of it: and they said thus unto it, Arise, devour much flesh" (Dan. 7:5).

The bear was a major player in the twentieth century as a symbol of Soviet Communism. History attests to the fact that the communist menace terrorized many nations and *"devour*[ed] *much flesh."* Raising itself up on one side could refer to Russia's ability to keep the world frightened as to its intentions. The three ribs in its mouth could refer to its conquests. Russian aggression turned westward and incorporated the Slavic countries of Eastern Europe; occupied the Islamic countries across its southern borders; and then absorbed Siberia on its east. The threat of nuclear war hung over the West for most of the last half of the twentieth century.

We should note that Jews in Russia suffered severe persecution as the twentieth century commenced. Furthermore, Russian Jews supplied the first immigrants to the Holy Land. They started the first kibbutz. Over the course of the century, Russian Jews supplied much of Israel's population.

Jeremiah prophesied that Jews would return from there in the last days. He called it, *"the north country"*:

"But, The LORD liveth, which brought up and which led the seed of the house of Israel out of the north country, and from all countries whither I had driven them; and they shall dwell in their own land" (Jer. 23:8).

We are not trying to stretch these symbols into something that is not readily apparent throughout the twentieth century. The Russian bear was a powerful metaphor. As a key player in the twentieth century, it should be considered. With all of the other pieces of the prophetic puzzle coming together, the bear fits Russia with uncanny accuracy.

The Leopard with Four Wings

"After this I beheld, and lo another, like a leopard, which had upon the back of it four wings of a fowl; the beast had also four heads; and dominion was given to it" (Dan. 7:6).

The third metaphor appearing in Daniel's dream was a leopard with four wings and four heads. Some have suggested that it might be a prophetic view of militant Islam. The leopard is a symbol of conquest that goes all the way back to Nimrod's ancient Babylon. The name Nimrod means, *"rebellious leopard."* It was said that Nimrod hunted with leopards in the same manner as today's sportsmen use hunting dogs. Also, Nimrod wore a leopard skin as a symbol of his royal apparel, in the same manner that European royalty would wear purple robes. If the leopard symbolizes militant Islam, then to what do we ascribe the four wings and four heads? I haven't a clue, but cannot dismiss the possibility that Islam may have four heads.

However, there is an alternate view. There is a nation that used the symbol of a leopard during the twentieth century. It was also the nation that slaughtered a third of the world's Jewish population — Germany. During World Wars I and II, German tanks were called "panthers." Today, the German tank is known as the "leopard."

Each member of Adolf Hitler's SS troops wore a dress-sword with the relief of a leopard's head on the handle. Furthermore, Hitler established the short-lived "Third Reich." The term "Reich" refers to an "empire." The German emperor Charlemagne established the "First Reich" in A.D. 800, and called it the "Holy Roman Empire." The "Second Reich" unified Germany in 1871, and fell with the abdication of Wilhelm II following his defeat in World War I. Adolf Hitler established the "Third Reich" and launched a reign of terror throughout Europe.

If the leopard represents Germany, then we should take note that, to date, there have been three heads (i.e., Reichs) on this beast. If the prophecy refers to Germany's role in a united Europe, then a "Fourth Reich" is destined to emerge. Just as the "First Reich" was known as the "Holy Roman Empire," it stands to reason that a "Fourth Reich" should also attempt to unite Europe. Perhaps the new United Europe, of which Germany is a member, will be the final fulfillment of the prophecy.

The new Europe is a leading sponsor of the upcoming New World Order. Perhaps Europe with its Parliament building designed to look like an unfinished tower and sporting the logo of a woman (Europa) on the back of a white bull (Zeus) will fulfill the prophecy of MYSTERY BABYLON, the proverbial woman who rides and guides the beastly world empire. Germany could still play a significant role in the upcoming New World Order — the published goal of the United Nations. We should not forget that John's prophetic beastly world empire looks like a leopard! Oh, it has the feet of a bear (i.e., Russia) and the mouth of a lion (i.e., Great Britain), but its primary features are that of a leopard.

Now, we cannot say with certainty that these beasts represent those three twentieth-century nations. Only time will tell. However, the fourth beast definitely represents the world government of the Antichrist.

The Dreadful Beast with Ten Horns

"After this I saw in the night visions, and behold a fourth beast, dreadful and terrible, and strong exceedingly; and it had great iron teeth: it devoured and brake in pieces, and stamped the residue with the feet of it: and it was diverse from all the beasts that were before it; and it had ten horns.

"I considered the horns, and, behold, there came up among them another little horn, before whom there were three of the first horns plucked up by the roots: and, behold, in this horn were eyes like the eyes of man, and a mouth speaking great things" (Dan. 7:7,8).

It seems that John saw this beast as a composite of the other three — organized as a multifaceted bureaucracy. John's corresponding beast had seven heads, as well as ten horns. Today, there are seven major nations, whose representatives meet yearly to plan for world government. They have been dubbed the G-7. Could the G-7 fulfill the prophecy of the seven heads, since they are the sponsors of the New World Order?

In 1974, a group of industrialists met in Rome to formulate a new world economic system. Dubbed the "Club of Rome," they published their recommendation that the United Nations divide the world into ten zones — ten political/economic regions, which, at first, they called "kingdoms," until they thought better of it. The uniting of Europe was the first move in that direction. They represent the first region. The recent move by the U. S., Canada and Mexico to establish the "North American Community" could be a move to establish the second political/economic region. These attempts to merge world economies generally follow a 1974 map of the world, designed and published by the Club of Rome.

Could Daniel's vision of ten horns represent a worldwide

division of all nations into ten political/economic regions?
Daniel was told that the ten horns represented ten kings. In
his dream, Daniel met a visitor who explained the fourth beast
with its ten horns:

*"Thus he said, the fourth beast shall be the fourth kingdom upon
earth, which shall be diverse from all kingdoms, and shall devour
the whole earth, and shall tread it down, and break it in pieces.*

*"And the ten horns out of this kingdom are ten kings that shall
arise: and another shall rise after them; and he shall be diverse from
the first, and he shall subdue three kings.*

*"And he shall speak great words against the most High, and
shall wear out the saints of the most High, and think to change
times and laws: and they shall be given into his hand until a time
and times and the dividing of time"* (Dan. 7:23-25).

Since Daniel's vision of the fourth beast was not associated
with any particular animal, we may assume that it represents a
consortium of nations. One prime suspect is the United Nations.
The continuing goal of the UN is to produce a New World Order,
or global government. Since 1974, its agenda has included a plan
to divide the world into these ten political/economic regions
with a ruler over each — all under the auspices of the United
Nations. Out of this global alliance, a world leader could emerge.
Daniel saw him as *"a little horn"* — a ruler who becomes the
predicted world dictator, positioned in the head of this beast. He
will consolidate his reign by destroying three opponents.

This beast will *"devour the whole earth"* — not just Europe or
the Middle East. It will *"tread it down and break it in pieces,"* thus
indicating the possibility of fomenting a third world war. This
could lead to the establishment of a global government based at
the United Nations. After the war, these ten political/economic
regions (the ten horns) could be organized. In the middle of
the Tribulation Period, the Antichrist (the little horn) will take
over control of the world government. He will bring it to life, so
to speak. The leaders of three of these ten regions will oppose
him, but without success. This scenario could be fulfilled by

the appointment of a rogue Secretary-General of the United Nations, after the ten regions are established.

At the top of his game, the Antichrist will set his sights on Jerusalem. He will divide the Holy Land and persecute the Jews. He will think that his new kingdom will last forever. He might even change the calendar to commemorate it. What he does not know, is that his diabolical kingdom will only last three years and six months. Again, we cannot be dogmatic about this scenario, but something like this will occur. Daniel's prophecy is accurate.

The Ancient of Days

"I beheld till the thrones were cast down, and the Ancient of days did sit, whose garment was white as snow, and the hair of his head like the pure wool: his throne was like the fiery flame, and his wheels as burning fire.

"A fiery stream issued and came forth from before him: thousand thousands ministered unto him, and ten thousand times ten thousand stood before him: the judgment was set, and the books were opened" (Dan. 7:9,10).

Daniel's description of God's throne is remarkably like the one in John's Revelation. God is referred to as *"the Ancient of days,"* recognizing that the One upon the throne is the eternal Creator-God who existed from eternity past and will continue forever. Daniel writes that the judgment of this world will be set and the books (scrolls) opened. John describes the book as being sealed with seven seals and opened by the Lamb, thus allowing the four horsemen of the apocalypse to ride forth. The wording may be slightly different, but the scene is the same.

According to rabbinical commentaries, God will someday sit down upon His judgment throne and take three books — the book of life, in which the saints are written; the book of death, in which the wicked are written; and a third book, in which those who are neither totally righteous, nor completely wicked are written. These people will be given a short period of time to repent before their fate is sealed. Of course, the rabbis say that the people in that book are all Jews. They are the ones who need redemption and, therefore, are not yet included in the books of life or death.

Thy Kingdom Come!

Daniel writes that heaven's army, headed up by the *"Son of man"* will destroy this fourth beast:

"I beheld then because of the voice of the great words which the horn spake: I beheld even till the beast was slain, and his body destroyed, and given to the burning flame.

"As concerning the rest of the beasts, they had their dominion taken away: yet their lives were prolonged for a season and time."

"I saw in the night visions, and, behold, one like the Son of man came with the clouds of heaven, and came to the Ancient of days, and they brought him near before him.

"And there was given him dominion, and glory, and a kingdom, that all people, nations, and languages, should serve him: his dominion is an everlasting dominion, which shall not pass away, and his kingdom that which shall not be destroyed" (Dan. 7:11-14).

This is Daniel's view of the glorious appearing of Jesus Christ. He will come with the clouds of heaven, just as the two witnesses told the disciples in the first chapter of the book of Acts. He will appear before the Father's throne to receive his title: King of kings and Lord of lords. He will establish the kingdom of heaven in power and great glory and reign for a thousand years. This will be the fulfillment of Nebuchadnezzar's prophetic *"stone cut out without hands."*

The man in Daniel's dream explained that the kingdom of heaven will put an end to six thousand years of chaos and ruin for the human race. The *"Son of man"* will judge the Antichrist and take away his dominion. The new millennial kingdom will be given to the saints. All nations will serve the Savior in peace and prosperity for a thousand years — here called *"an everlasting kingdom"* (Dan 7:27). After a thousand years of reigning on this planet, a new heaven and new earth will emerge, with a heavenly Jerusalem coming down from above. This everlasting kingdom, established out of the millennial reign, will continue forever.

> *"But the judgment shall sit, and they shall take away his dominion, to consume and to destroy it unto the end.*
>
> *"And the kingdom and dominion, and the greatness of the kingdom under the whole heaven, shall be given to the people of the saints of the most High, whose kingdom is an everlasting kingdom, and all dominions shall serve and obey him.*
>
> *"Hitherto is the end of the matter. As for me Daniel, my cogitations much troubled me, and my countenance changed in me: but I kept the matter in my heart"* (Dan. 7:26-28).

With the concluding verse of this chapter, Daniel ends the portion that was written in Aramaic, the language of the Mesopotamia region. This change from Hebrew began in Daniel 2:4, with the introduction of the *"times of the Gentiles."* It is obvious that Gentile domination over Jerusalem is finished with this chapter. The *"Son of man"* will establish heaven's everlasting kingdom. Six chapters are written in Aramaic. It seems as if we are being told that after six thousand years, the great Sabbath rest will be established for a beleaguered humanity.

Daniel was amazed at this new information. His prayer life had paid off. His mind was opened to see the events of the future and God was in complete control! The chapter ends with Daniel telling us that he *"kept the matter"* in his heart. He did not tell Belshazzar what the future held for him and Babylon.

The Vision of the Ram and Goat

Daniel dated this vision in the third year of Belshazzar's reign (553 B.C.) and explained that it had a relationship to his previous visionary dream about the rise of the *"little horn"* in chapter 7. Throughout these last six chapters (7-12), Daniel revealed the roots and exploits of the Antichrist. We will read about things in these chapters that no other prophet saw or recorded.

It should be noted that Daniel did not present a detailed account of world history from Babylon to the Antichrist. He skipped over the dispensation of grace and focused only upon the events that would affect Jerusalem and the Jewish people leading up to the coming of Israel's promised Messiah.

In this chapter, Daniel recorded the names of Persia and Greece, two kingdoms that would follow Babylon. According to Bishop James Ussher (died 1656), Daniel's vision took place in the city of Susa (KJV Shushan), then a Babylonian city in the province of Elam, which was built on a high plateau along the banks of the Ulai River. According to Bishop James Ussher, Daniel was living in a palace that was probably built by Elamite royalty before Babylon annexed it into their empire. Susa would later become the capital of Persia. The palace where Daniel resided was probably the same palace where Esther would someday live and at whose gates Mordecai would minister (c. 521 B.C.). It was also the palace where Nehemiah would be given permission to return to Jerusalem in 445 B.C. Also, it was the palace where Alexander and 80 of his officers married Persian royal women in a mass ceremony in 331 B.C.

The Persian Ram

"In the third year of the reign of king Belshazzar a vision appeared unto me, even unto me Daniel, after that which appeared unto me at the first.

"And I saw in a vision; and it came to pass, when I saw, that I was at Shushan in the palace, which is in the province of Elam; and I saw in a vision, and I was by the river of Ulai" (Dan. 8:1,2).

Daniel compared this vision to the vision he had *"at the first,"* in which four beasts rose out of the sea and the little horn appeared. In this second vision, Daniel was taken in the spirit to the Ulai River below the city and …

"Then I lifted up mine eyes, and saw, and, behold, there stood before the river a ram which had two horns: and the two horns were high; but one was higher than the other, and the higher came up last.

"I saw the ram pushing westward, and northward, and southward; so that no beasts might stand before him, neither was there any that could deliver out of his hand; but he did according to his will, and became great" (Dan. 8:3,4).

As Daniel considered the vision, he saw Gabriel standing on the shore nearby and heard the voice of the Lord speaking from the river:

"And it came to pass, when I, even I Daniel, had seen the vision, and sought for the meaning, then, behold, there stood before me as the appearance of a man.

"And I heard a man's voice between the banks of Ulai, which called, and said, Gabriel, make this man to understand the vision.

"So he came near where I stood: and when he came, I was afraid, and fell upon my face: but he said unto me, Understand, O son of man: for at the time of the end shall be the vision.

"Now as he was speaking with me, I was in a deep sleep on my face toward the ground: but he touched me, and set me upright.

"And he said, Behold, I will make thee know what shall be in the last end of the indignation: for at the time appointed the end shall be" (Dan. 8:15-19).

The Lord instructed Gabriel to explain the vision. We are not left to mere conjecture. Gabriel explained the meaning of the ram: *"The ram which thou sawest having two horns are the kings of Media and Persia"* (v. 20). On this particular ram, one horn was larger than the other. The smaller horn stood for Darius the Mede, while the larger horn represented Cyrus the Persian and all the Persian kings who would follow him. The ram in this vision was, in fact, the historic symbol of the ancient Persian Empire. Persia had adopted the sign of Aries the Ram as its national symbol. Persian kings would wear a ram's head headdress, complete with horns, instead of a crown, when leading their troops into battle.

The Grecian Goat

"And as I was considering, behold, an he goat came from the west on the face of the whole earth, and touched not the ground: and the goat had a notable horn between his eyes.

"And he came to the ram that had two horns, which I had seen standing before the river, and ran unto him in the fury of his power.

"And I saw him come close unto the ram, and he was moved with choler against him, and smote the ram, and brake his two horns: and there was no power in the ram to stand before him, but he cast him down to the ground, and stamped upon him: and there was none that could deliver the ram out of his hand.

"Therefore the he goat waxed very great: and when he was strong, the great horn was broken; and for it came up four notable ones toward the four winds of heaven" (Dan. 8:5-8).

Gabriel explained the meaning of the goat:

"And the rough goat is the king of Grecia: and the great horn that is between his eyes is the first king.
"Now that being broken, whereas four stood up for it, four kingdoms shall stand up out of the nation, but not in his power" (Dan. 8:21,22).

The male goat from the west represented Alexander the Great, who had nicknamed himself "the goat," after the capital of ancient Greece, Aegae, which means, "the goat city." Also, Alexander had a son by his Persian wife, Roxana, who named the child, Alexander Aegus, "the son of the goat." I am sure that Alexander recognized the goat in the passage from Daniel on the day Jaddua, the high priest in Jerusalem, read it to him. However, I doubt that Jaddua explained the four horns that grew up in its place!

According to Gabriel, the single horn on the goat's head would be broken in the height of its power, giving way to four horns. History attests to the fact that Alexander died in Babylon and the kingdom was divided. Four kingdoms arose out of the Greek Empire. In a previous article, we reviewed the history of the infighting between Alexander's generals; but, it is generally agreed that Cassander conquered Macedonia and Greece; Lysimachus laid claim to Asia Minor; Seleucus kept Syria, Babylon, Persia and the kingdoms to the east; and Ptolemy reigned over Egypt. After years of waging numerous wars, the Roman army eventually absorbed Greece and Asia Minor, leaving only the Seleucid dynasty in Syria and the Ptolemy dynasty in Egypt for awhile until they too, were absorbed into the Roman Empire. As we shall see in Daniel 11, Egypt and Syria continued fighting each other — pity the poor country that lay between them, namely Israel.

Roots of the Antichrist

As we shall see, the ram and goat were only significant as background material for the most important part of this vision

— the rise of the Antichrist:

"And out of one of them came forth a little horn, which waxed exceeding great, toward the south, and toward the east, and toward the pleasant land" (Dan. 8:9).

Without a doubt, Gabriel taught that the Antichrist (as seen in the little horn) would come out of one of those Greek generals. Here, for the first time, Daniel learned from where the Antichrist would come. However, there were several generals, four of whom ended up with their own kingdoms. Since Cassander and Lysimachus eventually lost their kingdoms through wars, our attention should be focused on Ptolemy and Seleucus. Will the Antichrist come out of Egyptian royalty or Syrian royalty? Actually, both men were from Greek descent.

Both Ptolemy and Seleucus adorned the trapping of a Macedonian monarch. They wore headbands similar to Alexander's, making them symbols of royalty and each calling himself "king." When visitors would come, they postured themselves in a "haughty" manner, while the guests were expected to gesture submission and respect.

Both men claimed descent from Greek gods. Ptolemy said that he was the progeny of Heracles and Dionysus, while Seleucus claimed lineage back to Apollo, son of Zeus. Where they actually came from is not clear. But John speaks of Apollo in Revelation 9:11 and 17:11. Apollo is shown as the destroyer who calls forth a plague of demonic locusts in Rev. 9; and as *"the beast that was, and is not ... the eighth ... and goeth into perdition"* (απωλειαν - i.e., Apollo) in Rev. 17. There are two other places in the New Testament where the Greek term for Apollo was used: in John 17:12, Jesus used the term *"son of perdition"* as a reference to Judas Iscariot; and in II Thessalonians 2:3, Paul referred to the Antichrist as the *"son of perdition."* In each case, the Greek term απωλειασ (Apollo) was used for the English *"perdition."* Therefore, it seems credible that Seleucus would be a good candidate for producing the future Antichrist.

In John's account, Apollyon possessed the key to a trans-dimensional gateway, bringing a horde of demonic locusts to plague the Earth for five months. In similar terms, Daniel discussed the little horn:

"And it waxed great, even to the host of heaven; and it cast down some of the host and of the stars to the ground, and stamped upon them" (Dan. 8:10).

This is a rather strange statement. The human race has never seen a battle between angels and demons before. It is a subject most theologians would rather not discuss, but Gabriel laid it out before Daniel in a way that cannot be denied. The Antichrist will descend from a family tree that has its roots in the seed of the serpent! In other words, he may not be completely human. We know that before the great Flood, a group of *"sons of God"* ... whom early theologians agreed were fallen angels, consorted with human women; and God sent the Flood to destroy them all. However, Genesis 6:4 tells us that some fallen angels returned after the Flood. Somewhere back in antiquity, the seed of the serpent made its way into another family dynasty.

Could they be represented by the clay in chapter two? Is that why Daniel told Nebuchadnezzar, *"they shall mingle with the seed of men"*? What would such a battle be like? Would there be casualties on both sides? If so, what kind of casualties could there be among immortals? Is Gabriel talking about the same battle that John saw between Michael and the dragon in the twelfth chapter of Revelation? Will angels and demons fight it out in our atmosphere — or, perhaps, in the inky blackness of space above our atmosphere? Will the stars that fall be natural or supernatural? This unusual description continues:

"Yea, he magnified himself even to the prince of the host, and by him the daily sacrifice was taken away, and the place of his sanctuary was cast down.

"And an host was given him against the daily sacrifice by reason of transgression, and it cast down the truth to the ground; and it practised, and prospered" (Dan. 8:11,12).

This is a reference to the abomination of desolation, here called *"transgression."* Bear in mind, the Holy Land became desolate during the Babylonian captivity in order to allow the land to enjoy its Sabbaths. Afterward, however, the Jews still did not repent, giving the Lord little choice but to continue the desolation of the land until the last days. Moses made it plain that if the people did not repent after the first exile, God would create another exile, and this time, He would multiply the desolation of the land seven times more:

"And if ye will not yet for all this hearken unto me, then I will punish you seven times more for your sins" (Lev. 26:18).

The final act of desolation will be on the Temple Mount. The Antichrist will take away the daily sacrifice and tear down the sanctuary. This should occur in the middle of the Tribulation Period. It seems as if the Antichrist will call upon demonic forces to help him stop the daily sacrifice. He will trample on the truth and allow the "transgression" to prosper. Gabriel explained:

"And in the latter time of their kingdom, when the transgressors are come to the full, a king of fierce countenance, and understanding dark sentences, shall stand up.

"And his power shall be mighty, but not by his own power: and he shall destroy wonderfully, and shall prosper, and practise, and shall destroy the mighty and the holy people.

"And through his policy also he shall cause craft to prosper in his hand; and he shall magnify himself in his heart, and by peace shall destroy many: he shall also stand up against the Prince of princes; but he shall be broken without hand" (Dan. 8:23-25).

These terms certainly fire the imagination! The descriptions seem somewhat cryptic, but enough can be gleaned for us to understand that the last half of the Tribulation will be horrendous! The *"latter time of their kingdom"* could refer to the last half of a seven-year Tribulation Period. By then, most of those who are going to believe the Gospel will believe. The rest of society will be generally wicked and unrepentant. The Antichrist will institute a system in which no one can participate in the economy unless there is a pledge of loyalty to the Antichrist. John called it the *"mark of the beast"* (Rev. 13:17).

Through his worldwide program, the Antichrist will set about to destroy *"the mighty and the holy people."* The *"mighty"* could refer to all nations who would try to stand in his way. The *"holy people"* are the Jews. Though the church will be translated before the Tribulation Period commences, millions of people, including Jews, will believe and be saved. They will become the target of the Antichrist.

Daniel learned that the Antichrist will talk of peace while destroying the Chosen People. Throughout the last half of the Tribulation, he will be slaughtering millions. Toward the end, he will foment the war of Armageddon for the purpose of genocide. He will try to rid the Earth of all Jews.

Some seven hundred years ago, a Jewish scholar, Rabbi Simeon (c. 1300), wrote that just after the turn of the seventh millennium, the sons of Ishmael would bring the whole world against Jerusalem:

"When the sixtieth year shall have passed over the threshold of the sixth millennium, the God of heaven will visit the daughter of Jacob with a preliminary remembrance. Another six and a half years will then elapse, and there will be a full remembrance of her.... Then all the nations shall combine together against the daughter of Jacob in order to drive her from the world. It is of that time that it is written: *'And it is a time of trouble unto Jacob, but out of it he shall be saved'* (Jer. 30:7). The children of Ishmael will ... rouse all the peoples of the world to come up to war against Jerusalem, as it is written: *'For I will gather all nations against Jerusalem to battle'* (Zech. 14:2)" (*Zohar*, vol 1, p. 370).

The 14th-century rabbi quotes enough Scripture to convince us that he definitely has Armageddon in mind. The rabbi continues: "God's glory will attach itself to the world ... cause souls to descend into the world and make them into new beings, so as to join the world into one" (Ibid).

Only the resurrection could be in mind, as Rabbi Simeon drew his commentary toward its conclusion. All of this is supposed to happen as the sixth millennium closes and the seventh millennium opens the great Sabbath, for which we all have been longing.

He writes: "Happy are those who will be left alive at the end of the sixth millennium to enter on the Sabbath, for that is the day set apart by the Holy One on which to effect the union of souls, and to cull new souls to join those that are still on earth. It is written: *'And it shall come to pass, that he that is left in Zion, and he that remains in Jerusalem, shall be called holy, even every one that is written into life in Jerusalem'* (Isaiah 4:3)" (Ibid).

How Long?

At this point in the vision, Daniel saw *"saints."* Two are on the banks of the river and another is on the river. Furthermore, the voice from between the banks of the river instructed Gabriel to explain the vision to Daniel. Their conversation is astounding:

"Then I heard one saint speaking, and another saint said unto that certain saint which spake, How long shall be the vision concerning the daily sacrifice, and the transgression of desolation, to give both the sanctuary and the host to be trodden under foot?

"And he said unto me, Unto two thousand and three hundred days; then shall the sanctuary be cleansed" (Dan 8:13,14).

One saint asked how long it would be from the abomination of desolation until the sanctuary could be cleansed. As we shall see, in chapter 12, Daniel had another similar situation. There, Daniel saw three men, one on each bank and another on the river. Note that the one on the river gave the answer. Practically the same question is asked, but the answer is different. In Daniel 8, the answer was, *"... two thousand and three hundred"* (Dan. 8:14). However, in Daniel 12, the answer was, *"... a thousand two hundred and ninety days. Blessed is he that waiteth and cometh to the thousand three hundred and five and thirty days"* (Dan. 12:11,12).

First, why was the question asked at all? I think the question was posed so that Daniel could include the answer in his book. That being the case, why was the answer 2,300, when the answer in chapter 12 was 1,290 and 1,335?

According to the Hebrew text, the number 2,300 is associated with two Hebrew words that should not have been translated *"days."* They are 2,300 ערב "evenings" and בקר "mornings." On the other hand, in Daniel 12:11,12, both the numbers 1,290 and 1,335 are associated with ימים the Hebrew word for "days." Therefore, we should translate this passage literally as 2,300 evenings and mornings.

Since this verse deals specifically with the "daily sacrifice," we should note that it was customary to offer a sacrifice at sunset, to mark the beginning of the next calendar day and at daybreak, to mark the beginning of the light for that day — a total of 1,150 days. In the marking of a calendar day, the night came first, followed by the day. This was a prophetic scenario that, in the process of human history, evil would be followed by good. The night of this old world would be turned into the day of resurrection and redemption.

As Gabriel concluded his interpretation, he mentioned the subject of the 2,300 evenings and mornings. He said:

"And the vision of the evening and the morning which was told is true: wherefore shut thou up the vision; for it shall be for many days.
"And I Daniel fainted, and was sick certain days; afterward I rose up, and did the king's business; and I was astonished at the vision, but none understood it." (Dan. 8:26,27).

Gabriel told Daniel that the Antichrist would commit the *"transgression of desolation"* — something so horrible against their beloved sacrifices that it would render the place desolate. Upon hearing about this terrible deed, Daniel fainted. For the next several days, Daniel was shaken to the point of illness. Remember, Daniel did not see this transgression take place in the vision. He only heard about it. But he was stunned by the news. It made him deathly ill. Later, in the next chapter, Gabriel coined the term, *"abomination."*

Antiochus IV Epiphanes

The rabbis of the first century believed that Daniel's despicable desolator was the king of Syria, Antiochus IV Epiphanes, who was from the lineage of Seleucus. He certainly seemed to fit the description. Louis Ginzberg, writing for *The Jewish Encyclopedia*, gives a brief history of Antiochus:

"Having thus made Jerusalem a Greek colony, the king's attention was next turned to the destruction of the national religion. A royal decree proclaimed the abolition of the Jewish mode of worship; Sabbaths and festivals were not to be observed … the sacred books were to be surrendered and the Jews were compelled to offer sacrifices to the idols that had been erected. The officers charged with carrying out these commands did so with great rigor; a veritable inquisition was established with monthly sessions for investigation. The possession of a sacred book or the performance of the rite of circumcision was punished with death. On Kislev (Nov.-Dec.) 25, 168 B.C., the *'abomination of desolation'* (Dan. xi. 31, xii. 11) was set up on the altar of burnt offering in the Temple, and the Jews were required to make obeisance to it. This was a statue to the Olympian Zeus. The rabbis think that the expression refers to the desecration of the Temple by the erection of a Zeus statue in its sacred precincts by Antiochus Epiphanes."

Antiochus IV Epiphanes set up a statue of Zeus (Jupiter) and sacrificed a sow on the altar of the Jerusalem Temple. Then he decreed that all Jews should offer pigs to his idol. No wonder Daniel was sick for a few days!

As we shall see, Antiochus offered only a prototype of the atrocity yet to be committed by the future Antichrist. Daniel is guiding us into a study on the bloodline of the Antichrist. He will be from the lineage of Antiochus, Seleucus, the Greeks, and possibly from the Spartans, who once called themselves Danaans.

There is a Jewish writing entitled, *Testaments of the Twelve Patriarchs*, purported to be the deathbed prophecies of all twelve sons of Jacob. In it, the dying Dan told his sons, "In the last days you will defect from the Lord ... I read in the Book of Enoch the Righteous that your prince is Satan ..." In the footnote of the *Old Testament Pseudepigrapha*, the editor, James Charlesworth, wrote: "No known Enochic text supports this, although Jewish and patristic speculation linked Dan and the Antichrist."

Is this why Dan is left out of the list of tribes in Revelation 7? Will Dan produce the Antichrist? I have a chapter on this subject in my book, *Guardians of the Grail*. Following circumstantial evidence, it is possible that Dan, whose symbol at first was a snake, will produce the Antichrist. More is given in chapter 2 of this book.

In Genesis 49, the dying Jacob gave prophecies concerning each son. When he came to Dan, Jacob attributed the symbol of the serpent to him, saying: *"Dan shall judge his people"* (Gen. 49:16). I am convinced that Daniel's book is a cryptic prophecy that will be opened and understood when the time is right. Who knows? Maybe even the name of this book — Daniel — holds a clue to the roots of the Antichrist!

The Mystery of the Seventy "Weeks"

During the Triumphal Entry, as Jesus started His descent from the Mount of Olives into the Kedron Valley, He wept over Jerusalem. Throngs of people stood along the road — a veritable sea of humanity was overflowing into the valley below, shouting and waving palm branches — yet, the Savior's heart was heavy. His disciples may have been delighted to see the crowd, but Jesus knew that it was not a throne that lay ahead, but a cross. Luke recorded His words:

"And when he was come near, he beheld the city, and wept over it,

"Saying, If thou hadst known, even thou, at least in this thy day, the things which belong unto thy peace! but now they are hid from thine eyes.

"For the days shall come upon thee, that thine enemies shall cast a trench about thee, and compass thee round, and keep thee in on every side,

"And shall lay thee even with the ground, and thy children within thee; and they shall not leave in thee one stone upon another; because thou knewest not the time of thy visitation" (Luke 19:41-44).

This lament alludes to something the archangel Gabriel

told Daniel, in this chapter. He said that after the seven weeks and the sixty-two weeks, the Messiah would be *"cut off"* and the *"… people of the prince that shall come, shall destroy the city and the sanctuary"* (Daniel 9:26). We know of no other Old Testament passage that could possibly have been on the Savior's mind that day. Furthermore, had their eyes not been blinded, Jewish scholars might have been able to calculate the *"time."* Jesus knew that, within a few days, He would be crucified. He knew that in A.D. 70, the Romans would destroy Herod's Temple along with the city of Jerusalem, thus fulfilling the prophecy.

Over the centuries, many attempts have been made to figure out the timing of Daniel's seventy weeks — and some calculations are quite remarkable. I suppose the study by Sir Robert Anderson is one of the most famous. He began with a royal Persian decree in 445 B.C.; calculated the number of days in 483 "biblical" years; converted them to solar years; and concluded with the day of the Savior's Triumphal Entry. However, there is something about these verses that he and most scholars have not considered. In this chapter, we shall attempt to put Gabriel's prophecy into perspective.

The First Year of Darius

The prophecy of the seventy weeks was given to Daniel within a year following Belshazzar's death. On that fateful night, Belshazzar bequeathed a political position to Daniel. Evidently, the conquering leaders of the Medes and Persians allowed him to retain a measure of that authority. It is possible that they were acquainted with stories of Daniel's wisdom and felt that he could be a valuable asset to their government. As this chapter opens, Darius had become king over a new Persian realm that encompassed the defeated empire of Babylon. Daniel was reading the scroll of Jeremiah:

"In the first year of Darius the son of Ahasuerus, of the seed of the Medes, which was made king over the realm of the Chaldeans;
"In the first year of his reign I Daniel understood by books

the number of the years, whereof the word of the LORD came to
Jeremiah the prophet, that he would accomplish seventy years in
the desolations of Jerusalem.
"And I set my face unto the Lord God, to seek by prayer and
supplications, with fasting, and sackcloth, and ashes" (Dan. 9:1-3).

Just how Daniel was able to obtain a copy of Jeremiah's writings is not known, but being a high-ranking government official, he probably sent a letter to the publisher of scrolls in Jerusalem requesting a copy. Not only was Daniel a prophet, but he also studied what other prophets had written.

Daniel, being of royal descent, probably read Jeremiah in order to learn details about the political history of his family and the Jewish kingdom in the years leading up to and during the Babylonian captivity. Daniel read about the things that occurred in the sacred city after his deportation. He might have been anxious to learn why Nebuchadnezzar had treated his family so harshly.

According to Babylonian accounts, during Nebuchadnezzar's seven-year insanity, his son, Evilmerodach, had befriended Israel's imprisoned king, Jeconiah. It is reported that Evilmerodach released Jeconiah and the blind Zedekiah from prison. It should be noted that Zedekiah mysteriously died that same day. We are not told whether he died of natural causes or was executed. But Jeconiah was allowed to live out his life comfortably in Babylon. Perhaps Daniel wanted to know what caused Jeconiah to be removed and why Zedekiah was installed in his place? If so, then he was probably saddened to read about Zedekiah's ill treatment of Jeremiah.

Whatever his reason for studying the scroll, we are told that he came across the passage where Jeremiah prophesied about the duration of the captivity being seventy years. Realizing that the seventieth year was fast approaching, Daniel put on sackcloth and ashes, a Jewish custom of mourning, and began to fast and pray.

Daniel's Prayer

"And I prayed unto the LORD my God, and made my confession, and said, O Lord, the great and dreadful God, keeping the covenant and mercy to them that love him, and to them that keep his commandments;

"We have sinned, and have committed iniquity, and have done wickedly, and have rebelled, even by departing from thy precepts and from thy judgments:

"Neither have we hearkened unto thy servants the prophets, which spake in thy name to our kings, our princes, and our fathers, and to all the people of the land" (Dan. 9:4-6).

Daniel reminded the Lord that He was a covenant-keeping God, and pleaded with Him to remember Jeremiah's prediction that the Jews could return after seventy years. Being from the royal family of Israel's kings, Daniel asked forgiveness on behalf of his family, who failed to require their subjects to keep the Mosaic Law regarding the Sabbatical Years; and for the way they had treated the prophets. Daniel realized that he would not have spent his life in a foreign land, had his family been men of integrity. I am sure that Daniel knew about King Manasseh, one of his previous relatives, desecrating the Temple and executing Isaiah. Overwhelmed with knowledge about the checkered history of his family and the desperation of the Jews in exile, Daniel prayed:

"O Lord, righteousness belongeth unto thee, but unto us confusion of faces, as at this day; to the men of Judah, and to the inhabitants of Jerusalem, and unto all Israel, that are near, and that are far off, through all the countries whither thou hast driven them, because of their trespass that they have trespassed against thee.

"O Lord, to us belongeth confusion of face, to our kings, to our princes, and to our fathers, because we have sinned against thee" (Dan. 9:7,8).

Daniel addressed the sins of his people, while realizing that his own royal family had failed to lead the nation in serving the Lord. It is the responsibility of kings to set the standard of conduct for their people. If the king does not lead in morality, honesty and integrity, the people will not aspire toward godly conduct. Realizing that God's righteous judgment had fallen upon his people, Daniel begged God for mercy:

"To the Lord our God belong mercies and forgivenesses, though we have rebelled against him;

"Neither have we obeyed the voice of the LORD our God, to walk in his laws, which he set before us by his servants the prophets.

"Yea, all Israel have transgressed thy law, even by departing, that they might not obey thy voice; therefore the curse is poured upon us, and the oath that is written in the law of Moses the servant of God, because we have sinned against him.

"And he hath confirmed his words, which he spake against us, and against our judges that judged us, by bringing upon us a great evil: for under the whole heaven hath not been done as hath been done upon Jerusalem" (Dan. 9:9-12).

Realizing the specific sin against the Law, Daniel admitted that his family and the wayward Jewish nation deserved their punishment. At the same time, however, suspending the sovereignty of the nation for seventy years was a punishment more severe than their forty years in the wilderness. There, all who were under twenty years of age when they left Egypt, were allowed to enter the Promised Land. Here, however, hardly anyone who remembered their homeland would survive to return. Seventy years was a lifetime for most. Daniel, himself, could not return. He was destined to live out the rest of his life in exile and die in Persia. Daniel reminded God that nothing so harsh had ever been done before. His prayer continued:

"As it is written in the law of Moses, all this evil is come upon us: yet made we not our prayer before the LORD our God, that we might turn from our iniquities, and understand thy truth.

"Therefore hath the LORD watched upon the evil, and brought it upon us: for the LORD our God is righteous in all his works which he doeth: for we obeyed not his voice" (Dan. 9:13,14).

Daniel did not blame God for the exile; he admitted that

the people could have repented and did not. None of his predecessors, or their subjects, had sought repentance. Daniel reminded God that He once delivered the nation from Egypt, and prayed that He would redeem them again:

"And now, O Lord our God, that hast brought thy people forth out of the land of Egypt with a mighty hand, and hast gotten thee renown, as at this day; we have sinned, we have done wickedly.

"O Lord, according to all thy righteousness, I beseech thee, let thine anger and thy fury be turned away from thy city Jerusalem, thy holy mountain: because for our sins, and for the iniquities of our fathers, Jerusalem and thy people are become a reproach to all that are about us.

"Now therefore, O our God, hear the prayer of thy servant, and his supplications, and cause thy face to shine upon thy sanctuary that is desolate, for the Lord's sake.

"O my God, incline thine ear, and hear; open thine eyes, and behold our desolations, and the city which is called by thy name: for we do not present our supplications before thee for our righteousnesses, but for thy great mercies.

"O Lord, hear; O Lord, forgive; O Lord, hearken and do; defer not, for thine own sake, O my God: for thy city and thy people are called by thy name" (Dan. 9:15-19).

Daniel begged God to turn His righteous anger away and have mercy upon Jerusalem and its people for His Holy name's sake. Perhaps thinking that his people could never expect God to love them as He once did, Daniel asked that God save the nation purely out of His own mercy and grace — for His *"own sake."*

Gabriel Responds to Daniel's Prayer

"And whiles I was speaking, and praying, and confessing my sin and the sin of my people Israel, and presenting my supplication before the LORD my God for the holy mountain of my God;

"Yea, whiles I was speaking in prayer, even the man Gabriel, whom I had seen in the vision at the beginning, being caused to fly swiftly, touched me about the time of the evening oblation.

"And he informed me, and talked with me, and said, O Daniel, I am now come forth to give thee skill and understanding" (Dan. 9:20-22).

Daniel had not closed his prayer. If Gabriel had not appeared, the prophet probably would have continued. On another occasion, Daniel prayed for twenty-one days. This prayer might have lasted that long, were it not for the archangel's appearance. Daniel recognized Gabriel as the same one who appeared to him some fifteen years earlier and told him about the ram and goat, and the little horn that would arise out of the Greeks. Now we find that Gabriel had returned to tell him more about this future Antichrist. More than that, however, the archangel told Daniel about the Jewish return to rebuild Jerusalem; about the Messiah and how He would be cut off; and about the Romans who would replace the Greeks. Furthermore, Gabriel referred to the Romans as *"the people of the prince that shall come"* (Dan. 9:26). Here is another clue to the genealogy of the Antichrist. Though he will ascend through Greek royalty (as we noted in chapter 8), he will also descend from the leaders of Rome! Gabriel explained:

> *"At the beginning of thy supplications the commandment came forth, and I am come to shew thee; for thou art greatly beloved: therefore understand the matter, and consider the vision.*
>
> *"Seventy weeks are determined upon thy people and upon thy holy city, to finish the transgression, and to make an end of sins, and to make reconciliation for iniquity, and to bring in everlasting righteousness, and to seal up the vision and prophecy, and to anoint the most Holy"* (Dan. 9:23,24).

God heard Daniel's prayer, and sent Gabriel to tell him about another extended period of time — this one would consist of three periods — 49 years followed by an interregnum period; 434 years followed by another interregnum of undisclosed length (at least two millennia); and 7 years of the final Tribulation Period. The English translation *"week"* should not be mistaken for a seven-day week. These seventy weeks are weeks of years. The Hebrew text refers to each *"week"* as a שבוע *shavuah*, a seven-year Sabbatical cycle. The term "interregnum" refers to a period of discontinuity in a government, organization, or social order.

Gabriel used the Leviticus (25-26) passage as a reference point. However, just as the original 490 years did not accrue consecutively, but rather accumulated over a period of 830 years, Daniel should expect these *"seventy weeks"* to stretch out over a longer period of time, as well. Gabriel divided these *"weeks"* into seven, sixty-two, and one; with gaps of unspecified years between the seventh and eighth *"weeks,"* and between the sixty-ninth and seventieth *"weeks."*

These *"weeks"* (Hebrew שבעים *shevuim*) were to be seven-year cycles, each beginning with year one and concluding with year seven as a Sabbatical Year — as was established in the Mosaic Law. In other words, the first year of the seventy could not begin in, say, the fourth or third or fifth year of a Jewish Sabbatical cycle, but in its first year. This is something that most scholars do not take into account when trying to calculate the time. Nor do they understand that there was a gap between the seventh and the eighth *"weeks."*

The ultimate goal of these Sabbatical cycles would be to complete the desolations of Jerusalem. Jeremiah had quoted the prophecy from Leviticus — that, if the people did not let the land rest every seventh year, God would drive them into exile. Only then could the land enjoy its Sabbaths. The land had been deprived of rest for seventy Sabbatical Years. That was the reason for the Babylonian captivity.

However, there was something about the Leviticus passage that Jeremiah did not address. God had promised: *"… if ye will not yet for all this hearken unto me, then I will punish you seven times more for your sins"* (Lev. 26:18). This was the reason for the seventy weeks in this chapter. Daniel was told that another exile would be coming; that it would begin when the Messiah was cut off; followed by the *"people of the prince"* destroying the city and the sanctuary. It will be concluded in the days of the *"prince that shall come"* — namely, the Antichrist.

There were six goals to be met during the course of the seventy weeks:

1. To finish the transgression — the violation of the Law of the Sabbatical Years.

2. To make an end of sins — to be accomplished by the sacrifice of God's Son for the sins of the world.

3. To make reconciliation for iniquity — God's plan to offer salvation by grace through faith.

4. To bring in everlasting righteousness — the future return of Christ to establish the Messianic kingdom.

5. To seal up the vision and prophecy — the final installment of the seventieth week.

6. To anoint the most Holy — the glorious appearing and official inauguration of the King of kings.

The First Seven Weeks

"Know therefore and understand, that from the going forth of the commandment to restore and to build Jerusalem unto the Messiah the Prince shall be seven weeks, ... the street shall be built again, and the wall, even in troublous times" (Dan. 9:25).

The *"commandment to restore and build Jerusalem"* has been dated to the decree of Artaxerxes in 445 B.C., as given in the opening chapter of Nehemiah. However, there was an earlier commandment — given only a year after Daniel received this vision. It was issued by King Cyrus in the late autumn of 537 B.C., within a few months following his ascension to the throne. King Darius only ruled one year (538-537 B.C.), then turned the throne over to his son-in-law, Cyrus, the Persian, as a dowry for marrying his daughter. This was the Cyrus of which Isaiah had prophesied:

"That saith of Cyrus, He is my shepherd, and shall perform all my pleasure: even saying to Jerusalem, Thou shalt be built; and to the temple, Thy foundation shall be laid" (Isa. 44:28).

"Thus saith the LORD to his anointed, to Cyrus, whose right hand I have holden, to subdue nations before him ..." (Isa. 45:1).

Isaiah wrote that Cyrus would say to Jerusalem, *"Thou shalt be built; and to the temple, Thy foundations shall be laid."* God called him *"my shepherd"* and *"his anointed."* Is it not obvious that this is the date God had in mind when Gabriel told Daniel about the *"commandment"* to restore and build Jerusalem?

Why should the Jews have to wait another 91 years (until 445 B.C.) for the *"commandment?"* The last verse of Daniel's opening chapter tells us that the prophet *"... continued even unto the first year of king Cyrus"* (Dan. 1:21). This was the year of the *"commandment."* It does not mean that Daniel died that year. Quite the contrary. It can only refer to the *"commandment"* that Cyrus delivered to Zerubbabel at the conclusion of the seventy-years exile.

A Jewish publication entitled, *The Jewish Time Line Encyclopedia: A Year-by-Year History from Creation to the Present*, by Mattis Kantor, said of Cyrus on page 69: "Cyrus became king and the power of the empire moved to Persia. Cyrus immediately encouraged the Jews of Babylon to return to the land of Israel and to rebuild the Temple. Over 40,000 people [49,697 to be exact] returned with Zerubbabel (who was of the royal family), including Joshua (the priest, a nephew of Ezra), Nehemiah, and Mordecai, but the majority remained behind."

In the spring of 536 B.C., Zerubbabel and Joshua led the initial return. In September, they rebuilt the altar in Jerusalem. Although the foundation stones of the second Temple were not yet laid, they began the daily sacrifice services on Rosh Hashanah (the new moon of September 24, 536 B.C.). More than a fourth of those who returned with Zerubbabel were from tribes other than Judah and Benjamin. Construction on the Temple began the following spring, in the month of Iyar (April/May 535 B.C.).

On September 14, 535 B.C., the people observed the beginning of a Sabbatical Year, which continued until October 2, 534 B.C., at which time the first year of Gabriel's first set of seven Sabbatical cycles commenced. We should note that the seventy weeks had to follow the Sabbatical cycles. Therefore, we should begin counting the first seven weeks (49 years) on October 2, 534 B.C., rather than in 536 B.C., the year of their initial return. In my opinion, Gabriel's first seven-week period ended with the death of King Ahasuerus, husband of Queen Esther, 49 years later — in the Sabbatical Year of 486/85 B.C.

When construction first began, the Samaritans volunteered to help, but were discouraged. After that, the Samaritans bribed certain courtiers of Cyrus and disrupted the Jews in their work of building the Temple. This was probably the reason why Daniel fasted for three weeks, as we shall see in chapter 10.

King Cyrus reigned for seven years, plus a month or so, and died in 529 B.C. His son, Artaxerxes (Cambyses), took the Medo/Persian throne in 529 B.C., and ruled for seven years. Bishop James Ussher tells us that in 522 B.C., the Samaritans wrote a letter asking Cambyses to "... forbid the further building of Jerusalem. They claimed it was a rebellious and wicked place which, if it were rebuilt would never pay tribute to the kings of Persia. Artaxerxes [Cambyses] sent a letter forbidding the rebuilding of Jerusalem until he should so order. The Samaritans, encouraged by this reply, came swiftly to Jerusalem and forced the Jews to stop building both the city and the Temple, although Cyrus had expressly ordered them to finish the Temple. They stopped all work until the second year of the reign of Darius [Ahasuerus]" (James Ussher, *TheAnnals of the World*, p. 124).

Cambyses, son of Cyrus, was mentally unstable. He married two of his sisters (one of whom was Atossa, also called Vashti); killed his brother; conquered Egypt; and then went stark raving mad. He came back to Persia and died of an accident (a self-inflicted wound with his sword while mounting his horse) in 522 B.C.

In 521 B.C., Darius (also called Artaxerxes the Great and Ahasuerus) began his reign. The next year (520 B.C.), Haggai and Zechariah challenged the people to finish rebuilding the Temple and its construction resumed. In 518 B.C., Ahasuerus banished Vashti (daughter of Cyrus and former wife of Cambyses). In 515 B.C., King Ahasuerus married Esther. In the spring of that same year, the new Jerusalem Temple was dedicated. In 510 B.C., Haman was hung on the gallows he had made for Mordecai. In 485 B.C., Ahasuerus died, having reigned for 36 years. We are not told what happened to Esther upon the death of Ahasuerus, but Vashti's son, Xerxes, may not have appreciated the woman who took his mother's place. However, if she had not been well treated, someone would have surely recorded it.

Xerxes, son of Ahasuerus and Vashti, ascended the Persian throne in 485 B.C., and was the richest monarch of his generation. We are told that he launched a battle against Greece with 1,700,000 soldiers, 80,000 horses, plus camels, and chariots. The Greeks never forgot this Persian intrusion. It took them 150 years to prepare for vengeance and, eventually, Alexander, son of Phillip of Macedon, would take up the challenge to crush the Persian monarchy. In my opinion, the first seven *"weeks"* of Gabriel's prophecy ended in 485 B.C., with the death of King Ahasuerus, husband of the famed Queen Esther. An ominous cloud of suspense may have swept over the Jewish community. Their future may have seemed in peril. A period of *"troublous times"* (v. 25) descended upon Jerusalem.

The 77-Year Interim Period

I see a gap of 77 years between the seventh and eighth weeks. The counting of the sixty-two weeks was resumed in 408/07 B.C., the 21st Jubilee Year. During the time of this gap, in 464 B.C., Artaxerxes (son of Xerxes) ascended the Persian throne. He sent Ezra with furnishings for the Temple in 457 B.C., and, in 445 B.C., sent Nehemiah to rebuild the walls and gates. Nehemiah built the walls of the fortified city in 52 days, amidst threats of war. I believe these were the *"troublous times"* mentioned by Gabriel in Daniel 9:25.

Ezra

According to most scholars, in 457 B.C., Ezra, a priest and scribe (lawyer) skilled in the Mosaic Law, obtained permission from King Artaxerxes (464-425 B.C.) to take seven counselors and a contingent of Jews to resettle in Judah and establish a government based upon their religion. This grant once again allowed all the Jews to return.

On the first day of the first month, in 457 B.C., Ezra left Babylon with a large number of Jews. After a journey of four months, they arrived in Jerusalem on the first day of the fifth month. They rested for three days, then weighed the gold and silver brought from Persia and stored the treasure in the Temple, along with other furnishings.

When Ezra discovered that many of the men had intermarried with Gentile women in the area, he demanded that they "put away their heathen wives and the children whom they had fathered" (Ussher). Over the next three months, his edict was carried out.

Nehemiah

Though Ezra had instituted many reforms, he did not fortify Jerusalem. The wall was still broken down and the gates burned. The city was in such ruin, it was difficult for a horse to find footing in the streets. The news of this reached Nehemiah in December (445 B.C.), at Shushan (modern Susa), the winter quarters of the Persian king. He was grieved at the report and began to fast and pray that God would help him do something about it.

Three months later, around the first of Nisan (444 B.C.), he took his turn as cupbearer to the king. But his countenance caught the attention of King Artaxerxes and Queen Damaspia. Nehemiah told them of the news about Jerusalem, and was given permission and supplies to go and rebuild the walls.

In spite of opposition from two governors, Sanballat (the Horonite of Moab) and Tobiah (the Ammonite), Nehemiah managed to rebuild the walls in 52 days. The workers worked with a trowel in one hand and a sword in the other.

The wall was finished on the 25th day of the sixth month (*Elul*). A week later, on the Feast of Trumpets (*Tishri* 1), the Jews came to Jerusalem to hear Ezra read and expound upon the Mosaic Law. It was an emotional time for the Jews, and a time of great revival. For the next three weeks, the Jews kept the festivals of the High Holy Days. Nehemiah wrote:

"And they found written in the law which the LORD had commanded by Moses, that the children of Israel should dwell in booths in the feast of the seventh month:

"And that they should publish and proclaim in all their cities, and in Jerusalem, saying, Go forth unto the mount, and fetch olive branches, and pine branches, and myrtle branches, and palm branches, and branches of thick trees, to make booths, as it is written.

"So the people went forth, and brought them, and made themselves booths, every one upon the roof of his house, and in their courts, and in the courts of the house of God, and in the street of the water gate, and in the street of the gate of Ephraim.

"And all the congregation of them that were come again out of the captivity made booths, and sat under the booths: for since the days of Jeshua the son of Nun unto that day had not the children of Israel done so. And there was very great gladness.

"Also day by day, from the first day unto the last day, he read in the book of the law of God. And they kept the feast seven days; and on the eighth day was a solemn assembly, according unto the manner" (Neh. 8:14-18).

In my opinion, these *"troublous times,"* predicted by Gabriel, were not part of the seven weeks, nor of the sixty-two weeks that followed, but of the interim period between the two prophecies. Artaxerxes and his wife, Damaspia, both died on the same day in 425 B.C., leaving the throne to his son, Xerxes, who reigned for one year. When he was "roaring drunk" on a festival day, he was killed in his chamber while sleeping. His brother, Secundianus, born of Aloguna, a Babylonian woman, murdered him with the aid of a eunuch.

In 424 B.C., Secundianus (second son of Artaxerxes) took over the throne. His army hated him for killing his brother. He also plotted to kill Ochus, his other brother, but was killed instead. In 423 B.C., Ochus/Darius (third son of Artaxerxes) lured Secundianus to meet him under the guise of making a treaty. Instead, Ochus captured and executed him for the murder of Xerxes. Ochus took the name Darius and reigned for 19 years. He died in 404 B.C., leaving the throne to his son, Arsicas. He gave his other son, Cyrus, rulership over the seacoast provinces of Ionia and Lydia, across the Aegean Sea, east of Greece.

The Sixty-Two Weeks

Near the end of the reign of the Persian king Ochus (Darius), Judah observed the Sabbatical Year of 409/08 B.C. This was the seventy-seventh year after the death of Ahasuerus, husband of the beloved and revered Queen Esther. This Sabbatical Year was followed by Judah's twenty-first Jubilee Year in 408/07 B.C. I think Gabriel intended to resume the counting of the next sixty-two Sabbatical cycles with the onset of this Jubilee Year.

Bishop James Ussher wrote that the twenty-first Jubilee was the last one seen by the prophets of the Old Testament. The period of the prophets came to an end. Malachi, thought to be a contemporary of Nehemiah, was the last of the Old Testament prophets. The first-century historian Flavius Josephus wrote:

"From the death of Moses to Artaxerxes, king of Persia, who succeeded Xerxes, the prophets wrote thirteen books. From Artaxerxes to our time, all things indeed have been likewise committed to writing, but not held in the same esteem as the former, because the succession of the prophets one after another has been uncertain" (Josephus, *Against Apion*, bk. 1, pp. 8).

Following Malachi, there were no biblical books until Matthew. Basically, we have 400 years of silence, with only

Malachi's promise that Elijah would return to introduce the Messiah. We need 434 years — the number of years in sixty-two Sabbatical cycles. If Gabriel's sixty-two *"weeks"* began in the Jubilee Year of 408/07 B.C., which ushered in the "silent years," then sixty-two Sabbatical cycles would bring us directly to the Sabbatical Year of A.D. 26/27, and the emerging ministries of John the Baptist and Jesus Christ.

Sir Robert Anderson

It is unlikely that Sir Robert Anderson's dating, concluding with the Triumphal Entry, was correct. He didn't take into account the Sabbatical cycles — the *"weeks."* Anderson wrote:

"The Julian date of that 10th Nisan was Sunday the 6th April, A.D. 32. What then was the length of the period intervening between the issuing of the decree to rebuild Jerusalem and the public advent of 'Messiah the Prince,' — between the 14th March, 445 B.C., and the 6th April, A.D. 32? The interval contained exactly and to the very day 173,880 days, or seven times sixty-nine prophetic years of 360 days, the first sixty-nine weeks of Gabriel's prophecy" (*The Coming Prince*, 1895).

He tried to squeeze 483 years into 477 years. To do this, he converted the 173,880 days in 483 years (claiming they were 360 days each) into 477 solar years of 365.25 days each. Unfortunately, he failed to understand the Mosaic Law concerning Sabbatical Years. He overlooked the *"weeks."* The seventh year of the sixty-second *"week"* ended in the year our Lord was baptized, not when He made His Triumphal entry. Gabriel continued:

"And after threescore and two weeks shall Messiah be cut off, but not for himself: and the people of the prince that shall come shall destroy the city and the sanctuary; and the end thereof shall be with a flood, and unto the end of the war desolations are determined" (Dan. 9:26).

Note that Gabriel said, אהרי *ahrei*, "*after* ...*,*" meaning that the death of our Lord would occur some time after the conclusion of the sixty-second "*week.*" Furthermore, Gabriel included the destruction of Jerusalem in the same statement. Yet, we know that the Romans destroyed Jerusalem in August of A.D. 70, some forty years after the Savior's crucifixion and resurrection.

The prophecy that the Messiah would "*be cut off, but not for himself*" can only refer to the crucifixion. Jesus was not executed because He was guilty of some crime. All of the charges leveled against Him were bogus. Pilate, a cynical and hardened procurator, could see through that. Jesus died completely innocent. He died for the rest of us, not for Himself. Gabriel could not have been more clear, without tipping off the Sanhedrin Court. The crucifixion was divinely ordained and orchestrated in order to pay for the sins of the world. Jesus expressed it perfectly when He said, "*If thou hadst known, even thou, at least in this thy day, the things which belong unto thy peace! but now they are hid from thine eyes*" (Luke 19:42).

The Prince that Shall Come

Gabriel gave Daniel a very important clue as to the lineage or background of the Antichrist. He said that Jerusalem would be destroyed by "*the people of the prince that shall come*" (Dan. 9:26). Since we know that the Romans destroyed Jerusalem and Herod's Temple in A.D. 70, we may assume that the future Antichrist will be from one of the royal families of the ancient Roman Empire. That could be a reference to European royalty or, for that matter, anyone with family ties to the royal bloodline.

In Daniel 7, the little horn rises out of the fourth beast — the Roman Empire. In Daniel 8, the little horn rises out of the he-goat — the Greek Empire. In Daniel 9, Gabriel returned to the subject of the Roman Empire as the source of the "*prince that shall come.*" How can the future Antichrist be both Roman and Greek? In Daniel's following chapters, we shall discuss this subject further.

Gabriel did not end the prophecy there. The gap between the sixty-ninth and the seventieth weeks began with the appearance of the Messiah, but will conclude with three signs: a flood, desolations, and war (Dan. 9:26). The world is still awaiting these signs. We do not know how or when these events will occur, but we can be certain that they will happen around the onset of the seventieth week. We cannot be dogmatic about these events, but it seems that the seventieth week could begin in the aftermath of some great war. The next verse explains that the Roman Prince will *"confirm"* or strengthen a *"covenant with many."*

The Seventieth Week

"And he shall confirm the covenant with many for one week: and in the midst of the week he shall cause the sacrifice and the oblation to cease, and for the overspreading of abominations he shall make it desolate, even until the consummation, and that determined shall be poured upon the desolate" (Dan. 9:27).

Most scholars agree that this seventieth week is the notorious Tribulation Period. The Roman Prince will feign to be a peacemaker. He will launch an effort to restore peace — but where? Gabriel said the covenant would be with *"many."* However, I think the *"covenant"* that will be *"confirmed"* (possibly through military strength) and will specifically concern the city of Jerusalem and its territory — the Holy Land. Let us not forget that the prophecy of the seventy weeks is all about the desolations of Jerusalem. That is what Daniel was praying about. And that was the subject addressed by Gabriel in this prophecy.

The future Antichrist will confirm or strengthen an existing covenant, setting the time-frame for its full deployment at seven years. In order to fall within the framework of the seventieth week, it must begin in the first year of a Sabbatical cycle and conclude in a Sabbatical Year, seven years later.

If the Antichrist follows Solomon's solution, he might seek to "divide the baby," so to speak. It is possible that Jerusalem will remain a divided city, but this time, Israel will be allowed to erect a sanctuary on the Temple Mount. According to Ezekiel, a wall will be built to make a separation between the sanctuary and the *"profane place"* (Ezk. 42:20). In Revelation 11, John was told to measure the area of Jewish worship, but to leave the Gentile area alone.

It is possible that current negotiations over the destiny of Jerusalem will result in a divided city and a divided Temple Mount. Since the Moslems have already developed the southern half of the Temple Mount, with three mosques in the area, perhaps Israel could be given the northern half of the compound for the restoration of Temple liturgy. Some kind of Jewish presence has to be there, because Gabriel links the abomination of desolation to the Antichrist stopping *"the sacrifice."* This will occur in the middle of the Tribulation Period.

The Desolation

The term *"desolation,"* as used in *"abomination of desolation,"* is a direct reference to the Mosaic Law of the Sabbatical Years:

"And I will bring the land into desolation: and your enemies which dwell therein shall be astonished at it.

"And I will scatter you among the heathen, and will draw out a sword after you: and your land shall be desolate, and your cities waste.

"Then shall the land enjoy her sabbaths, as long as it lieth desolate, and ye be in your enemies' land; even then shall the land rest, and enjoy her sabbaths.

"As long as it lieth desolate it shall rest; because it did not rest in your sabbaths, when ye dwelt upon it" (Lev. 26:32-35).

The Antichrist will fulfill this prophecy of desolation when he commits the *"abomination of desolation."* Evidently, the Babylonian captivity did not end the *"desolations"* of the land. It has continued down through the centuries — until the return of the Jews in the last century. Yet, even though the land now has trees and crops, the Temple Mount remains desolate of a Jewish sanctuary. Why has Israel continued to suffer over the past two millennia? Wasn't their Babylonian captivity enough? Moses tells us:

"And if ye will not yet for all this hearken unto me, then I will punish you seven times more for your sins" (Lev. 26:18).

It seems that Gabriel was addressing this very subject when he spoke about a future *"seventy weeks."* Going one step further, God may have multiplied those 490 years by seven! If so, the prophecy could be a reference to 490 Sabbatical cycles, or 70 Jubilees — 3,430 years.

Counting from Joshua's first Sabbatical Year in 1431/30 B.C., there have been 490 Sabbatical cycles (3,430 years) — leading up to the signing of the Israeli/Palestinian Peace Accord on September 13, 1993. The Peace Accord was signed a few days before Israel's 490th Sabbatical Year in 1993/94, which was followed by what should have been their 70th Jubilee in 1994/95.

Did a Jewish messiah arrive on the scene that year? If so, where is he? In any case, he could not have been the right one. We are still waiting for Jesus to return. However, while Israel awaits their messiah, Gabriel foretold that the Antichrist will come first. Perhaps this *"prince"* will try to revive the failed Peace Accord, divide the city, establish a Palestinian State, and deploy a multinational military garrison to keep the peace.

The Mysterious ו Vav in Jacob's Name

In Leviticus 26:40-42, we are told about the final conclusion of the Jewish exile in the end of days:

"If they shall confess their iniquity …
*"Then will I remember my covenant with **Jacob** [יעקוב], and also my covenant with Isaac, and also my covenant with Abraham will I remember; and I will remember the land"* (Lev. 26:40,42).

This passage deals with Israel's return after the land has fulfilled its years of desolation; and history attests to the fact that the Promised Land was desolate for many centuries —

until the Jews returned. In the Hebrew text of Leviticus 26:42, "Jacob," which is normally spelled יעקב Yac-v, here is spelled יעקוב Yacov with an added ו vav (pronounced as an "o"). This is the only time in the five Mosaic books where Jacob is spelled with a ו vav. However, Jeremiah used this spelling four times, each of them referring to the days of the final Jewish return to their homeland. Commenting on this, some have suggested that the ו vav stands for the Messiah. The numerical value of the ו vav is six — and, say the rabbis, the ו vav stands for six thousand years. They expect the Messiah to arrive at the end of the sixth millennium. Today, we also await the Second Advent of the Messiah. The four Jeremiah passages are:

> "Thus saith the LORD; Behold, I will bring again the captivity of Jacob's [יעקוב] tents, and have mercy on his dwellingplaces; and the city shall be builded upon her own heap, and the palace shall remain after the manner thereof" (Jer. 30:18).

> "Thus saith the LORD; If my covenant be not with day and night, and if I have not appointed the ordinances of heaven and earth;

> "Then will I cast away the seed of Jacob [יעקוב], and David my servant, so that I will not take any of his seed to be rulers over the seed of Abraham, Isaac, and Jacob: for I will cause their captivity to return, and have mercy on them" (Jer. 33:25,26).

> "But fear not thou, O my servant Jacob, and be not dismayed, O Israel: for, behold, I will save thee from afar off, and thy seed from the land of their captivity; and Jacob [יעקוב] shall return, and be in rest and at ease, and none shall make him afraid" (Jer. 46:27).

> "The portion of Jacob [יעקוב] is not like them; for he is the former of all things: and Israel is the rod of his inheritance: the LORD of hosts is his name" (Jer. 51:19).

Why would Jacob be spelled in this particular way? Moses and Jeremiah did not misspell his name. Furthermore, this is not the bungled work of some scribe. It seems that God placed a cryptic message in these verses to help Israel understand the timing of its fulfillment. In each case, the context points to the revival of the nation in the latter days — when the Messiah (typified by the ו vav) will come to Jacob.

The Peace Accord of 1993 occurred during a year of worldwide flooding, making it look like a perfect time for Daniel's seventieth week to commence. Though the timing seemed perfect, the Tribulation Period did not occur. Daniel's seventieth week still awaits a future fulfillment. The Interim period between the sixty-ninth and seventieth weeks continues to roll on. Surely, it cannot last much longer. Today, negotiations continue over the disposition of Jerusalem. Once the deal is struck, we will have a clearer picture of where it all fits in the fulfillment of the seventy weeks.

For a layout of Daniel's Seventy Weeks, consult the chart on pages 290-296.

Daniel's Last Incredible Vision

"In the third year of Cyrus king of Persia a thing was revealed unto Daniel ..." (Dan. 10:1).

Daniel's final vision, recorded in chapters 10-12, occurred in the third year of the reign of Cyrus, king of Persia. This was two years after Cyrus sent Zerubbabel with 49,697 Israelites (Ezra 2:64,65) back to Jerusalem. We should also note that this vision occurred two years after the date given in Daniel 1:21, which says: *"And Daniel continued even unto the first year of king Cyrus."* One would think that this verse should have referred to the death of the prophet, but that is not the case. Daniel was still alive two years later.

The reason Daniel included the statement that he *"continued ... unto the first year of king Cyrus,"* is that the date refers to the conclusion of the seventy years of captivity and the Persian king's commandment to restore Jerusalem. It seems strange to me that most scholars want to place the date for the beginning of the seventy weeks with Artaxerxes in 445 B.C., instead of with the decree of Cyrus in 537/536 B.C.

If the decree that launched the prophecy of the seventy weeks is not the one in the first year of Cyrus, then why did Daniel open his first chapter (Dan. 1:1) with Nebuchadnezzar besieging Jerusalem in the third year of Jehoiakim, and conclude the chapter (Dan. 1:21) in the first year of Cyrus? To me, the answer is obvious. Those were the years of the captivity. The seventy years were up in the first year of Cyrus.

Our chapter opens two years later (535/34 B.C.) — the Sabbatical Year prior to the onset of the seventy Sabbatical cycles given in chapter 9. Daniel was about 90; some say maybe as old as 93 years of age. As far as we know, Daniel was still active in government. He had been appointed as the chief of three rulers over the provinces of the Persian Empire, directly under the king.

I am confident that Daniel was a close adviser to Cyrus. However, a serious problem had developed. The Samaritans managed to bribe certain courtiers of the king and disrupt the Jews in their work of rebuilding the Temple. According to Flavius Josephus (Antiquities, IX, XIV, 3), the Samaritans were originally imported to Israel from Cuthah, a province in Persia. Naturally, these Persian settlers from Samaria had the ear of certain Persian politicians. Perhaps the mentally unbalanced Cambyses (prince and future king of the Persian Empire) was their proponent in this matter.

This chapter opens in the Jewish Passover season, a few months after the Samaritans had managed to halt construction on the Temple. According to Bishop James Ussher, this was the reason why Daniel had been fasting for three weeks.

The Revelation of a Heavenly Visitor

"In the third year of Cyrus king of Persia a thing was revealed unto Daniel, whose name was called Belteshazzar; and the thing was true, but the time appointed was long: and he understood the thing, and had understanding of the vision.

"In those days I Daniel was mourning three full weeks.

"I ate no pleasant bread, neither came flesh nor wine in my mouth, neither did I anoint myself at all, till three whole weeks were fulfilled.

"And in the four and twentieth day of the first month, as I was by the side of the great river, which is Hiddekel" (Dan. 10:1-4).

Daniel referred to this vision as a *"thing … revealed."* This term is used only three times in the book of Daniel. It was used twice in chapter two, when Daniel received details of Nebuchadnezzar's dream; and the third time is in the chapter before us. It is a term reminiscent of the Apostle John's last book, *The Revelation of Jesus Christ.* In John's opening chapter, we are told about a vision of the glorified Savior. And in this chapter, Daniel sees a remarkably similar scene. As we shall learn in the following verses, the heavenly visitor had a metallic appearance. The description is almost identical to John's view of Christ.

Daniel had fasted for three weeks, beginning on Nissan 3 and concluding on Nissan 24. Notice that Daniel did not partake in the observance of Passover that year. It was certainly a good time of the year to engage in a season of prayer; and Daniel probably did not intend to continue his fast for three full weeks. Perhaps he thought that God would send an answer much sooner. It had not taken that long before. Usually, God answered Daniel's prayers promptly.

I think there may have been a prophetic reason why it took 21 days for the answer to his prayer. Daniel explained that it was a vision whose appointed time *"was long"* (v.1). As we shall see, the vision points to Antiochus IV Epiphanes, the Syrian monarch who sacrificed a sow in the Temple courtyard. But then the vision moves us right into the latter days — to the future Antichrist — bypassing the gap between the sixty-ninth and seventieth weeks. The dispensation of Gentile Christianity is completely overlooked, unless these 21 days give us a clue to the timing of the gap. It is not an explicit teaching, nor can we find a reference to it anywhere else in the Bible. Daniel said that he *"understood the thing,"* but did not disclose any further information about those 21 days. However, Daniel used specific Hebrew terms to let us know that these three weeks were weeks of days, rather than weeks of years as in the previous chapter. The Hebrew text says, צנצשט שוהשיד שבעים ימים, meaning *"weeks of days"* (v. 2). It is possible, therefore, that those days represented centuries.

On the Banks of the Tigris River

On Nissan 24, Daniel took some friends down to the Tigris River for a season of prayer. Rabbinical sources, with no biblical proof, suggest that Daniel's companions were Haggai, Zechariah, and Malachi. Some rabbis see these three prophets as contemporary, though the Bible is silent on this subject. We see Haggai and Zechariah together in Ezra 5:1, but Malachi is nowhere mentioned. His name does not appear in Ezra, Nehemiah, or Esther. There is no proof that he was a contemporary with Haggai and Zechariah. Most theologians place his writing between 75 and 130 years later than the other two. It is possible that placing Malachi with Daniel was another step in a dishonest attempt to eliminate 243 years from the Jewish calendar.

Nevertheless, as we look in upon the scene, Daniel is not alone. Others were with him when the vision occurred. No one else saw the *"thing revealed,"* though they felt an earthquake and fled for safety:

"Then I lifted up mine eyes, and looked, and behold a certain man clothed in linen, whose loins were girded with fine gold of Uphaz:

"His body also was like the beryl, and his face as the appearance of lightning, and his eyes as lamps of fire, and his arms and his feet like in color to polished brass, and the voice of his words like the voice of a multitude.

"And I Daniel alone saw the vision: for the men that were with

me saw not the vision; but a great quaking fell upon them, so that they fled to hide themselves.

"Therefore I was left alone, and saw this great vision, and there remained no strength in me: for my comeliness was turned in me into corruption, and I retained no strength.

"Yet heard I the voice of his words: and when I heard the voice of his words, then was I in a deep sleep on my face, and my face toward the ground" (Dan. 10:5-9).

Daniel experienced some kind of trance-like state. He lifted up his eyes, but fell on his face before the apparition and was transfixed in a *"deep sleep"* (v. 9). Was this our Lord Jesus Christ that John saw in the first chapter of Revelation? Why not? The description is remarkably similar. John wrote:

"… the Son of man, clothed with a garment down to the foot, and girt about the paps with a golden girdle.

"His head and his hairs were white like wool, as white as snow; and his eyes were as a flame of fire;

"And his feet like unto fine brass, as if they burned in a furnace; and his voice as the sound of many waters" (Rev. 1:13-15).

Both looked like a man; both wore a white garment; both had a golden girdle; both had flesh that gave the appearance of brass; both had eyes like fire; both had a voice that sounded like *"a multitude"* or *"many waters"*; and both John and Daniel fell at his feet as if they were dead! The description is so similar, we should consider the possibility that Daniel saw the same Jesus that John saw. The question is, *"How'd He do that?"* The answer can only be that Jesus could have traveled back in time to visit Daniel. This was no pre-incarnate Christ. He had the same features as the one who took John on a journey to see events that would occur some two thousand years into the future. In like manner, Daniel also received a *"great vision"* (v. 8) about this same future.

As we shall see in the following verses, Daniel was petrified. Daniel was physically drained by the very sight of the heavenly visitor. However, something happened to Daniel that would be typical of what the Savior might do. This heavenly visitor touched the prophet and imparted physical strength. Suddenly, a great calm came over Daniel, allowing him the ability to converse with this spectacular being.

"And, behold, an hand touched me, which set me upon my knees and upon the palms of my hands.

"And he said unto me, O Daniel, a man greatly beloved, understand the words that I speak unto thee, and stand upright: for unto thee am I now sent. And when he had spoken this word unto me, I stood trembling" (Dan. 10:10,11).

Ten verses are taken up with Daniel's description on how he felt in the presence of this shining friend. By the way, similar experiences were described by Isaiah (6:5) and Ezekiel (1:28). It must be awesome to see such a marvelous view! No wonder Moses was told that no man could see God and live!

"And when he had spoken such words unto me, I set my face toward the ground, and I became dumb.

"And, behold, one like the similitude of the sons of men touched my lips: then I opened my mouth, and spake, and said unto him that stood before me, O my lord, by the vision my sorrows are turned upon me, and I have retained no strength.

"For how can the servant of this my lord talk with this my lord? for as for me, straightway there remained no strength in me, neither is there breath left in me.

"Then there came again and touched me one like the appearance of a man, and he strengthened me,

"And said, O man greatly beloved, fear not: peace be unto thee, be strong, yea, be strong. And when he had spoken unto me, I was strengthened, and said, Let my lord speak; for thou hast strengthened me" (Daniel 10:15-19).

In order to be seen of men, God would usually create an apparition or vision. Moses was the only man who ever saw what God really looked like. Even then, God told him, *"Thou canst not see my face: for there shall no man see me, and live"* (Ex. 33:20). Moses was shown God's back — Jehovah's real backside!

However, Moses was so affected, he retained that divine radiation for the rest of his life. When he descended Mount Sinai, the people saw his face emanating a strange glow about it, and became afraid. At the age of 120, *"his eye was not dim, nor his natural force abated"* (Deut. 34:7). Moses had to be put to death by God, Himself. Otherwise, say the rabbis, Moses would still be alive today.

While in this trance-like state, Daniel was extremely weak. He could not speak until an attending angel touched him and imparted physical strength.

The Great Conflict with Persia

"Then said he unto me, Fear not, Daniel: for from the first day that thou didst set thine heart to understand, and to chasten thyself before thy God, thy words were heard, and I am come for thy words."

"But the prince of the kingdom of Persia withstood me one and twenty days: but, lo, Michael, one of the chief princes, came to help me; and I remained there with the kings of Persia.

"Now I am come to make thee understand what shall befall thy people in the latter days: for yet the vision is for many days" (Dan. 10:12-14).

The strange visitor told Daniel that his prayer was heard on the first day. It is tempting here to explore how our prayers are transmitted and received. We know that no radio signals or light beams are used. If our prayers had to travel at the speed of such things, our bones would become dust long before God (if He were on the back side of the galaxy) could receive them. Yet, our prayers are heard in heaven the very instant we think them. In fact, our thoughts are monitored. But, tempting as it might be to explore this phenomenon, this is not the time. We have a greater issue before us. How was the *"prince"* of Persia able to withstand this heavenly warrior to the point that He called in Michael to help?

This type of question might be placed in the same category with, "If God is God, why does He allow disaster, war, disease, etc.?" We can only say that God has a plan and is in control of the plan. However, God has chosen to endow man with the ability to exert "free will." As all-powerful as God is, He allows mankind a certain measure of freedom in both thought and action that few other creatures in the universe have — even to the extent of opposing Him.

Just who was this *"prince of Persia"* anyway? Was he a demon? Or a man? Was there a battle in the heavens, like the one against Satan in Revelation 12? Or was this a conflict between the will of God and the will of man? The general consensus is that the battle involved demonic forces. It is possible that many political regimes are guided by the dark side of spiritual beings. We cannot discount the possibility that Satan has many emissaries in high places around this world.

However, let's explore the Hebrew text and consider a possible alternative. First of all, the text refers to the *"prince"* as a שר רקיד, meaning "leader" or "ruler." This prince of Persia could have been Cambyses, son of Cyrus. Someone in the Persian government had halted the construction of the Jerusalem Temple. After all, this may have been the cause of Daniel's mourning. God may have the heart of a king in His hand, but even the king has a free will. Secondly, after calling in Michael, this heavenly warrior remained with the מלכי *melek*, translated "kings" of Persia. Thirdly, the Hebrew text tells of a דסגשע שנשדא תצבא גדול, meaning "great conflict" (v. 1). Therefore, rather than becoming involved with hand-to-hand combat, being *"withstood"* may have been more of a conflict of ideas. Someone had halted the commandment that allowed Zerubbabel to rebuild the Temple.

In the case of man's free will, God's powers of persuasion are not mandatory. However, if the Persian prince should persist in disobeying the will of God, then mortal consequences could be forthcoming. Perhaps for that reason, Michael the archangel, who was privy to God's heavenly strategy (v. 21), was called upon to help. On the other hand, in verse 13, the heavenly visitor said, *"I remained there with the kings of Persia."* Notice that more than one king is implied. In all, there were 13 kings of Persia before the Greeks overthrew the empire. And even though the term *"remained"* appears to be past tense, a futurist view is implied by the following verse, in which the *"prince of Grecia"* was predicted to come — and that occurred some 200 years later:

"Then said he, Knowest thou wherefore I come unto thee? and now will I return to fight with the prince of Persia: and when I am gone forth, lo, the prince of Grecia shall come.

"But I will shew thee that which is noted in the scripture of truth: and there is none that holdeth with me in these things, but Michael your prince" (Dan. 10:20,21).

By saying that, besides Himself, only Michael was privy to this heavenly strategy, the implication is persuasive that this heavenly visitor was none other than Jesus, Himself. Who else could have formulated this classified information? The answer is in verse 21: *"none!"* It is possible that He would not force the Persian prince to do what is right. However, if this heavenly visitor was Jesus Christ, who had traveled from the future, He would have known that someday (about two hundred years later), Alexander, the prince of Greece, would conquer the Persians. All would be fulfilled in accordance with the prophecies of the seventy weeks. As we shall see, certain details of those seventy weeks are given in Daniel's remaining chapters.

Daniel's Last
Incredible Vision
... continued

Daniel had a heavenly guide to explain each of his visions. In chapter 7, his guide was unnamed. In chapters 8 and 9, his guide was the archangel Gabriel. However, it appears that in chapters 10 through 12, Daniel had a visit from none other than the Son of God, Himself! Daniel does not ask His name, nor was it given. We are left to speculate as to the identity of this heavenly visitor. But, the description in John's New Testament book of Revelation leaves little doubt. Daniel's last heavenly guide was most likely our Lord and Savior, Jesus Christ.

Chapter 11 opens with the heavenly guide explaining that He stood to confirm and strengthen Darius in the same manner that He was currently watching over Cyrus. No one could have had a better guardian angel than Christ, Himself!

"Also I in the first year of Darius the Mede, even I, stood to confirm and to strengthen him.
"And now will I shew thee the truth. Behold, there shall stand up yet three kings in Persia; and the fourth shall be far richer than they all: and by his strength through his riches he shall stir up all

against the realm of Grecia.

"And a mighty king shall stand up, that shall rule with great dominion, and do according to his will.

"And when he shall stand up, his kingdom shall be broken, and shall be divided toward the four winds of heaven; and not to his posterity, nor according to his dominion which he ruled: for his kingdom shall be plucked up, even for others beside those" (Dan. 11:1-4).

Daniel's heavenly visitor said that He personally stood by Darius during the king's first year. Let us recall that during that year (ch. 6), Darius was tricked into signing a bad law that required Daniel to be subjected to a den of lions. Perhaps the Lord, Himself, shut the mouths of those lions! The Lord could certainly keep demons away; and He could close the mouths of the lions to keep Daniel alive; but we know from Scripture that God chooses not to control the free will of men. Though He stood by to strengthen Darius, He chose not to stop him from being duped by Daniel's enemies. Therefore, in the current conflict that lasted 21 days, He may have chosen not to force the *"prince of Persia"* into submission. To me, this is a reasonable explanation, since He and Michael could surely succeed at anything they wanted to do. If this was an actual battle in the skies over Persia between spiritual forces of good and evil, then this heavenly visitor appeared to be woefully inadequate for the task. How could this be anything other than a proverbial wrestling match with the free will of Cambyses, the Persian prince?

Also, as we have noted, Daniel's heavenly guide may have been visiting him from the future. He had known that Darius would regretfully have to sentence Daniel to spend a night among lions. Maybe He chose to travel back through time, calm the lions and save Daniel.

While we're on the subject of time travel, we should note that these verses reveal the future. The heavenly visitor did not need to orchestrate every detail of events in order to dictate the outcome of His prophecy. Coming from the future, he could have simply told Daniel what would happen, from the perspective of having watched those events unfold. But be certain of this, He was in control of the timing and the outcome.

It was also in the first year of Darius (perhaps after Daniel's encounter with the lions) that he received the vision of the seventy weeks. When the angel Gabriel appeared (Dan. 9:21), he told the prophet that a *"commandment"* (Dan. 9:23) had come to him just as Daniel began to pray. That commandment may have come from this chapter's heavenly visitor, Himself; since we are told that He was personally handling the guardianship of Darius that year.

Now for the *"Truth"*

"And now will I shew thee the truth" (v.2).

Here is a term commonly used by the Savior, Himself. Throughout the Gospels, we read that Jesus used this or a similar phrase. Often, the phrase is translated as *"verily, verily."* In John's Gospel, the Greek terms *"Amen, Amen"* may be translated as, *"I tell you the truth"* Therefore, it is not out of character for this heavenly visitor to say, *"And now will I shew thee the truth."*

The heavenly visitor told Daniel that after Cyrus, three significant kings would rule in Persia — one after the other. The other Persian monarchs that followed them are not considered in this particular prophecy. Cyrus was the first Persian monarch. The fourth king (third following Cyrus) would be very wealthy and famous. He would stir up all the realm of Greece. The four kings in this prophecy were:

1. Cyrus (536-529 B.C.)
2. Artaxerxes (Cambyses) (529-522 B.C.)
3. Darius (Ahasuerus who married Esther) (521-485 B.C.)
4. Xerxes (son of Vashti and the richest of all the Persian kings) (485-474 B.C.)

The heavenly visitor is not saying that there would only be four kings. He simply explained that Xerxes would *"stir up"* the Greeks. After his failed invasion of Greece, 150 more years would come to pass, while the Greeks prepared to retaliate. There would be nine other Persian kings after Xerxes, but they are unimportant at this point. The intent of the prophecy was to direct Daniel's attention to the fourth king, Xerxes.

The Succession of Kings

1. Cyrus reigned for seven years and a month or so. In the winter of 529 B.C., while leading his army north to a land that, today, is called Khazakhstan, Cyrus was killed in battle. His eldest son, Cambyses, ascended the Persian throne and took the name Artaxerxes.

2. Artaxerxes (Cambyses) ruled for seven years, was mentally unstable, married two of his sisters, killed his brother, conquered Egypt, and then went stark raving mad. It is said that he opened many of Egypt's tombs just to gaze upon the embalmed bodies of those who lay buried there. He came back to Persia and died of an accident with his sword in 522 B.C. It is said that while swinging up to mount his horse, his own sword accidentally pierced him. Maybe Michael allowed that to happen. After all, Cambyses may have been the *"prince of Persia"* that gave heaven so much trouble! That year seven Magi tried to take over the kingdom, but were overthrown by Darius in 521 B.C.

3. Darius (also called Artaxerxes the Great and Ahasuerus) began his reign in 521 B.C. That year, he sent spies to map the coast of Greece and planned the first invasion. In 520 B.C., Haggai urged the Jews to finish building the Temple. With encouragement from Zerubbabel and Joshua, the people rallied and earnestly began to rebuild the Temple. In 518 B.C., the Persian monarch divorced Vashti and married Esther.

In 515 B.C., Esther was crowned queen of the Persian Empire, and the Jerusalem Temple was finished and dedicated. In 510 B.C., Haman plotted to exterminate all Jews throughout the kingdom, but was, himself, hanged on the gallows built for Esther's uncle, Mordecai.

In 501 B.C., trouble between the Greeks and Persians erupted into a war. Ussher says, "This was the beginning of all the wars which occurred between the Greeks and the Persians and which ended in the ruin of the Persian Empire" (*Annals*, p. 130). In 485 B.C., Darius (Ahasuerus) declared that Xerxes, his son by Vashti, would become Persia's new king. Vashti was the daughter of Cyrus, the founder of the Empire. Darius then left to invade Greece, but he died later that year and the war was put on hold.

4. Xerxes ascended the Persian throne in 485 B.C. He was the richest of all Persian kings, just as the prophecy indicated. In 480 B.C., after five more years of military preparations, he moved westward with 1,700,000 soldiers, 80,000 horses, plus many camels and chariots. He had 1,200 war ships, hundreds of cargo ships (some with thirty oars and others with fifty oars) and other smaller vessels to carry horses, adding up to a total of 3,000 ships. As he marched into Greece, he conscripted more soldiers, so that he invaded Athens in 480 B.C., with more than 5 million men. The Greeks never forgot nor forgave this Persian intrusion.

Over the next 150 years, Greece laid out a military strategy that would eventually bring Alexander the Great on a conquest of revenge. Xerxes fulfilled the prophecy that the fourth king would stir up all against the realm of Greece (v.2).

History records a total of 13 kings ruling the Medo/Persian Empire over a period of 207 years, from the death of Belshazzar and the installment of Darius in 538 B.C., to Alexander's victory over Darius in 331 B.C. Perhaps because Daniel is not told about the other Persian monarchs, second-century Jewish scholars saw the opportunity to discard the histories of the other kings. In writing the *Seder Olam Rabbah*, the Persian Empire was reduced from thirteen kings to five kings, and from 207 years to only 53 years. This accounts for a significant 154 years missing from the Jewish calendar. The thirteen Medo/Persian kings were:

1. Darius the Mede (538-537 B.C.)
2. Cyrus the Persian (nephew and son-in-law of Darius) (537-529 B.C.)
3. Artaxerxes (Cambyses, son of Cyrus) (529-522 B.C.)
4. Darius (Ahasuerus - banished Vashti and married Esther) (521-485 B.C.)
5. Xerxes (son by Vashti) (485-465 B.C.)
6. Artaxerxes (son of Xerxes) (465-425 B.C.)
7. Xerxes (son of Artaxerxes) (425-424 B.C.)
8. Secundianus (second son of Artaxerxes) (424-423 B.C.)
9. Ochus (Darius, third son of Artaxerxes) (423-404 B.C.)
10. Arsicas (Artaxerxes, son of Ochus Darius) (404-361 B.C.)
11. Ochus (son of Arsicas Artaxerxes) (361-338 B.C.)
12. Arses (son of Ochus) (338-336 B.C.)
13. Darius (son of Arsames the brother of Arsicas Artaxerxes) (336-331 B.C.)

Alexander the Great

Daniel had been told about the Greek invasion in the vision of the ram and goat (ch.8). However, in this chapter, Daniel learned what would happen after Alexander's death — here referred to as the *"mighty king"* (v.3). Alexander's untimely demise was very important to the fulfillment of the prophecy, both in chapter 8, and in this chapter. These details about the Persians and Greeks are also important to the overall story in the rise of the future Antichrist. Therefore, Daniel is reminded again about Alexander's death and the division of his kingdom. In all, Alexander was to rule for 12 years and die in 323 B.C.

The Ptolemy and Seleucid Dynasties

From this point, the heavenly visitor focused upon the Ptolemy and Seleucid dynasties. The *"king of the south"* represented the various kings of the Ptolemy dynasty that ruled over Egypt and the *"king of the north"* referred to the kings of the Seleucid dynasty that ruled over Syria:

"And the king of the south shall be strong, and one of his princes; and he shall be strong above him, and have dominion; his dominion shall be a great dominion" (Dan.11:5).

The *"king of the south"* in this verse referred to Ptolemy, king of Egypt, who reigned 40 years. It was commonly reported that Ptolemy was the half-brother of Alexander, being the illegitimate son of Philip. Ptolemy's mother, Arsinoe, had been Philip's mistress, but was cast off when she became pregnant, after which, she married Lagus.

The *"prince"* in this verse was Seleucus, who escaped from a confrontation with Antigonus and fled to Egypt for help. Ptolemy's troops joined Seleucus, Casander and Lysimachus for a military expedition against Antigonus. In 312 B.C., Antigonus gave up on trying to conquer Babylon and Persia and moved his troops back to Phrygia. Seleucus was able to return to Babylon and restore his kingdom. He began to enlarge his empire ... until it extended from India to Syria. Thus, the Syrian kingdom became stronger than Egypt. In 301 B.C., their combined armies were able to defeat and kill Antigonus. In Jewish historical writings, the establishment of the reign of Seleucus in 312 B.C., became the ordinal year from which Jewish history was calculated. This remained their official calendar of reckoning until the Ottoman Empire conquered Jerusalem in A.D. 1517. At that time, Israel adopted the date reckoning set forth in the *Seder Olam Rabbah*. The modern Jewish calendar, with its 243 missing years, was adopted in 1517.

Archbishop James Ussher published *The Annals of the World* in 1658, from which much of the following information is taken: Ptolemy and Seleucus could not agree on how to divide the spoils of Antigonus's kingdom. This made them and their future generations mortal enemies, whose conflicts are prophesied in this chapter:

"And in the end of years they shall join themselves together; for the king's daughter of the south shall come to the king of the

north to make an agreement: but she shall not retain the power of the arm; neither shall he stand, nor his arm: but she shall be given up, and they that brought her, and he that begat her, and he that strengthened her in these times" (Dan. 11:6).

The *"end of years"* in this verse refers to the descendants of the original two kings. This verse was fulfilled in 261 B.C., by the marriage of Berenice, daughter of Ptolemy Philadelphus II to Antiochus Theos, third king of Syria (285-247 B.C.). Ptolemy II insisted that Antiochus divorce his wife, Laodice, and declare his two children by her as illegitimate. The Egyptian monarch had hopes of putting his grandson on the Syrian throne and unifying the two nations. However, Ptolemy II died the following year and Antiochus Theos brought Laodice back while proclaiming that Berenice was a mere concubine. The spurned, then returned Laodice did not forgive her husband. She poisoned Antiochus and murdered Berenice and her son — thus fulfilling the prophecy that Berenice would not *"retain the power of the arm"* (v.6).

"But out of a branch of her roots shall one stand up in his estate, which shall come with an army, and shall enter into the fortress of the king of the north, and shall deal against them, and shall prevail:

"And shall also carry captives into Egypt their gods, with their princes, and with their precious vessels of silver and of gold; and he shall continue more years than the king of the north.

"So the king of the south shall come into his kingdom, and shall return into his own land" (Dan. 11:7-9).

The term *"a branch of her roots"* refers to Berenice's brother, Ptolemy Euergetes, who learned of her murder and invaded Syria for revenge. He decimated the land, destroyed the temples and confiscated Syria's treasury. Jerome said that the booty included 40,000 talents of silver, 4,000 talents of gold, and 2,000 costly statues.

The feud continued for generations. Verses 10-19 give a prophetic overview of the wars between Syria and Egypt, fought on a neutral battleground, namely, in poor little Israel.

No wonder Daniel told the heavenly guide, *"O my lord, by the vision my sorrows are turned upon me, and I have retained no strength"* (Dan. 10:16). Ptolemy Euergetes conquered all of Syria — everything west of the Euphrates River. In 245 B.C., he was called back to Egypt because of a rebellion among his own people. These verses cover a century of wars, from the death of Antiochus Theos in 246 B.C., to the rise of Antiochus IV Epiphanes:

> *"But his sons shall be stirred up, and shall assemble a multitude of great forces: and one shall certainly come, and overflow, and pass through: then shall he return, and be stirred up, even to his fortress"* (Dan. 11:10).

In 244 B.C., Seleucus Callinicus attacked Ptolemy Euergetes and was driven back, fulfilling the *"one* [who] *shall certainly come...."* In 243 B.C., Seleucus Callinicus tried and failed to make a pact with his brother Antiochus Hierax. These sons of Antiochus Theos by Laodice could have joined together to exact revenge upon Egypt, but Ptolemy Euergetes was able to forge a ten-year truce with Seleucus Callinicus, thus avoiding a fight with them both.

In 227 B.C., Antiochus Hierax was in trouble and fled to Ptolemy Euergetes in Egypt, who threw him into prison. He escaped, but fell into the hands of some thieves, who killed him. In 226 B.C., Seleucus Callinicus, the older brother, fell off his horse, broke his neck and died. He left two sons. The eldest was Seleucus Ceraunus, a physically weak man who could not keep order in his army. In 223 B.C., he was poisoned. The younger son was named Antiochus, who was later surnamed "the Great." Antiochus was 14 years old, living in Babylon, when the Syrian army invited him to accept the kingdom. He reigned for 36 years.

Ptolemy Euergetes, king of Egypt, died in 221 B.C., at the hands of his own son, Ptolemy Philopator.

"And the king of the south shall be moved with choler, and shall come forth and fight with him, even with the king of the north: and he shall set forth a great multitude; but the multitude shall be given into his hand.

"And when he hath taken away the multitude, his heart shall be lifted up; and he shall cast down many ten thousands: but he shall not be strengthened by it"

"For the king of the north shall return, and shall set forth a multitude greater than the former, and shall certainly come after certain years with a great army and with much riches" (Dan. 11:11-13).

In 217 B.C., Ptolemy Philopator led his army north to Syria and fought Antiochus over Coelosyria. In that battle, Antiochus lost almost ten thousand foot soldiers and more than three hundred cavalry, while more than four thousand were taken prisoner. Three elephants were killed in the battle and two died later from their wounds. Ptolemy lost 1,500 foot soldiers and 700 cavalry. Sixteen of his elephants were killed and the rest were captured. The people of Ceolosyria welcomed Ptolemy and pledged their loyalty to him. As soon as Antiochus returned to Antioch, he sent envoys to Ptolemy and bargained for peace. Ptolemy accepted the offer, pledged a truce, and returned to Egypt victorious. His subjects, knowing his lifestyle, marveled at his success in the war against Antiochus.

"And in those times there shall many stand up against the king of the south: also the robbers of thy people shall exalt themselves to establish the vision; but they shall fall" (Dan. 11:14).

Ussher, reported that Ptolemy Philopater returned to Egypt and "resumed his old lifestyle ... and wallowed in all manner of gluttony. He vexed the Jews of Alexandria and tried to turn them away from worshipping God. He expelled them from offices of dignity and branded them on the face with the sign of an ivy leaf — the sign of Baccus" (*Annals*, p. 379). By these atrocities, he fulfilled the prophecy: *"... the robbers of thy people."*

Finally, he put the Jews in the hippodrome for execution. He instructed the master of his 500 elephants to feed the beasts with wine mixed with myrrh until they were completely mad. He planned to trample the Jews the next day. However, the king slept through the day and awoke to find that the spectators had all gone home. On the third day, he launched the drunken elephants. According to the report, two fierce-looking angels came down in the sight of the spectators and spooked the elephants. Instead of attacking the Jews, the animals turned around and trampled the soldiers behind them. There was one sober king after that! He released all the Jews, with his apology, in 216 B.C., just as the prophecy said: *"... they shall fall."*

The War of 198 B.C.

"So the king of the north shall come, and cast up a mount, and take the most fenced cities: and the arms of the south shall not withstand, neither his chosen people, neither shall there be any strength to withstand.

"But he that cometh against him shall do according to his own will, and none shall stand before him: and he shall stand in the glorious land, which by his hand shall be consumed" (Dan. 11:15,16).

The *"king of the north,"* in verse 15, was Antiochus the Great. In the summer of 198 B.C., Antiochus took in all the cities of Coelosyria, which Ptolemy had controlled. He recovered all the cities of Syria and extended his hand of friendship to Judah. The Jews (here referred to as *"chosen people"*) received his whole army, with his elephants, into their city, and supported and helped the Syrians in the siege of the citadel where the Egyptians had a garrison. Josephus confirmed this from a letter, which Antiochus had written to Ptolemy, the captain of the garrison. Jerusalem (here called *"glorious land"*) voluntarily submitted to Antiochus. The Syrian king also destroyed Gaza, which had withstood him.

"He shall also set his face to enter with the strength of his whole kingdom, and upright ones with him; thus shall he do: and he shall give him the daughter of women, corrupting her: but she shall not stand on his side, neither be for him.

> *"After this shall he turn his face unto the isles, and shall take many: but a prince for his own behalf shall cause the reproach offered by him to cease; without his own reproach he shall cause it to turn upon him.*
>
> *"Then he shall turn his face toward the fort of his own land: but he shall stumble and fall, and not be found"* (Dan. 11:17-19).

Over the next five years Antiochus the Great tried to expand his kingdom toward the west into Greece. He made a league with Hannibal (whom the Romans had exiled from Carthage) and plotted a war against Rome. While in the process of his exploits, he offered his daughters to certain kings in the area to ensure their loyalty. In 193 B.C., he gave his daughter, Cleopatra, (here referred to as the *"daughter of women"*) to marry the Egyptian king, Ptolemy Philometor. Her dowry included an equal share of all tribute paid by Coelosyria and Israel, which had earlier been taken from Egyptian control. He offered his daughter Antiochis in marriage to Ariarathes, king of Cappadocia. He sent his third daughter to Eumenes, the king of Pergamum, but Eumenes was wise to his war plans and declined the marriage offer. The *"isles"* in verse 18, referred to Greece, and the *"prince"* referred to Scipio Asiaticus, brother of Publius Scipio Africanus. By the leadership of these two men, the power of Rome was felt in the East for the first time. The Roman army, with its allies, defeated Antiochus in every conflict fought over the next four years.

Finally, in 189 B.C., Antiochus the Great sued for peace with Rome and had to pay a thousand talents a year for the next twelve years and surrender 20 royal hostages to secure payment, among them was his youngest son, Antiochus. In 187 B.C., after plundering the temple of Zeus at Elymais to pay the Roman tax, Antiochus the Great was killed. Some say that he and his entire army were slaughtered by the peasants of Elymais, while others say that he was killed in a drunken brawl by some of his drinking companions. Cleopatra's brother, Seleucus Philopator (oldest son of Antiochus the Great), ascended the Syrian throne and inherited his father's tremendous debt. Seleucus (father of Demetrius) was the "raiser of taxes" referred to in the next verse:

"Then shall stand up in his estate a raiser of taxes in the glory of the kingdom: but within few days he shall be destroyed, neither in anger, nor in battle" (Dan. 11:20).

Seleucus Philopator heard that a vast amount of treasure was stored in the Jerusalem Temple. In 176 B.C., Seleucus sent his treasurer, Heliodorus, to Jerusalem to confiscate the treasure, which turned out to be a modest deposited collection for widows and orphans and amounted to only 400 talents of silver and 200 talents of gold. Onias (the high priest) begged the Syrians not to take God's treasure, but Heliodorus would not listen to reason. The Jews began to lament over the profaning of their Temple when, suddenly, Heliodorus was struck down by an angel on that very spot. His servants carried him half-dead to his lodging. After he recovered, through the prayers of Onias, he returned to Seleucus and magnified the holiness of the Temple and the power of God that dwelt there. Shortly after that, Heliodorus desired to take over the Syrian kingdom and had Seleucus killed. Eumenes, king of Pergamum, and Attalus, his brother, had Heliodorus expelled for treachery.

During the twelve years of Syria's reparations, Rome had demanded royal hostages to be imprisoned for three years at a stretch. Antiochus IV Epiphanes (youngest son of Antiochus the Great) served a three-year term in Rome. Shortly before his death, King Seleucus had secured the release of his brother, Antiochus, by sending his own son, Demetrius, to serve a three-year term. Demetrius, then ten years old, should have been the rightful heir to the Syrian throne, but he was languishing in a Roman prison. Therefore, Eumenes and Attalus offered the throne to Antiochus IV, hoping to obligate him as their friend. Antiochus IV took the name Epiphanes, meaning "Illustrious," but Polybius, the Greek historian (ca. 203-120 B.C.), thought he should more correctly be called Epimanes, meaning "the madman," because of his wild behavior.

Antiochus IV Epiphanes

As we shall see in the following verses, our attention is now focused upon the youngest brother of the assassinated Seleucus Philopator. He is our prototype for the Antichrist — Antiochus IV Epiphanes — thought to be the *"vile person"* in verse 21. However, as we shall see, it seems that in these verses, Daniel's heavenly visitor alludes to the end of days and compares Antiochus IV Epiphanes to the future Antichrist. The phrases *"arms of a flood"* and *"also the prince of the covenant"* are clear references to Daniel 9:26,27, and can only refer to the future Antichrist.

"And in his estate shall stand up a vile person, to whom they shall not give the honour of the kingdom: but he shall come in peaceably, and obtain the kingdom by flatteries.

*"And with the **arms of a flood** shall they be overflown from before him, and shall be broken; yea, **also the prince of the covenant**.*

"And after the league made with him he shall work deceitfully: for he shall come up, and shall become strong with a small people.

"He shall enter peaceably even upon the fattest places of the province; and he shall do that which his fathers have not done, nor his fathers' fathers; he shall scatter among them the prey, and spoil, and riches: yea, and he shall forecast his devices against the strong holds, even for a time" (Dan. 11:21-24).

Beginning with verse 21, this chapter seems to enlarge upon the prophecies concerning Daniel's seventieth week. As we encounter each verse, we cannot be sure which part refers to Antiochus IV Epiphanes and which part refers to the Antichrist — except to say that the bloodline of the Antichrist will find its roots in this family. First-century rabbis were convinced that this Syrian madman was the character described in these verses; therefore, we shall explore various historical writings about Antiochus IV Epiphanes and compare his exploits with those of the future Antichrist.

Antiochus ascended the Syrian throne at Antioch, in 175 B.C., and ruled for just over 11 years. According to First Maccabees, his reign began in the 137th year of the Greek kingdom and ended in the 149th year. This Jewish reckoning counts the years from 312 B.C., and the adoption of the *Minyan Shtarot*, the Greek calendar that dates back to a promise made to Alexander the Great by Shimon Ha Tzaddik (Simon the Righteous) and the Jewish priesthood.

It is said that Antiochus behaved most unusually for a king. Often, he would put on common clothes, take one or two companions and wander about the city, drinking and talking with the common people. If he heard about a party, he would show up for the wine and music. At first, he was not recognized as king, but sometime later, obtained the title — as if *"by flatteries."*

Jerusalem was already under Syrian domination when Antiochus became king. Jason, son of Simon II, coveted the position of high priest held by his brother, Onias. He went to see Antiochus and promised him 360 talents of silver, provided he could be awarded the office of high priest. Antiochus readily agreed. Jason went back and removed his brother. Then Jason began to treat the Jews badly and removed their royal privileges. With this intrusion into Judaism, Antiochus began to despise the Jews.

In 173 B.C., Antiochus sent an envoy to Rome with glowing reports about the Syrian king's loyalty to the Empire. The Syrian envoy stood before the Roman Senate and brought a gift of golden vessels weighing some 500 pounds. The Senate and the people treated the Syrian "as a king and not as a hostage" (Ussher, *Annals*, p. 415).

That year Antiochus sent Apollonius, son of Menestheus, as an envoy to Egypt to attend the coronation of Philometor (son of Cleopatra, who was the sister of Antiochus IV Epiphanes). When Antiochus realized that he was not welcome, he fortified himself against Egypt. Antiochus brought his army to Joppa, and then went to Jerusalem, where he was welcomed by Jason and the priesthood. He entered the city by torchlight, accompanied by great shouting. Jason proved to be a rogue politician, one who did not have the best interest of the Jewish people in mind.

In 172 B.C., Menelaus, another son of Simon II and brother to Onias and Jason convinced Antiochus to give him the office of high priest. Having secured the government of Judah, Menelaus drove his brother Jason from Jerusalem. Jason escaped to live across the Jordan River in Ammon.

In 171 B.C., Ptolemy prepared to go to war with Antiochus over Coelosyria. When Antiochus heard of this, he sent an envoy to Rome, telling the Senate that he was being wrongly invaded, and that since Ptolemy was an ally of Rome, just as he was, allies should not be fighting with each other. When the war began, the envoys of both kings came to Rome to negotiate a peace accord. Bishop Ussher tells what happened next and suggested that these events fulfilled verse 23: *"And after the league made with him he shall work deceitfully: for he shall come up, and shall become strong with a small people"* (Dan. 11:23). Ussher writes: "Antiochus defeated Ptolemy's commanders between Pelusium and Mount Casius. He spared the king because of his youth and pretended to be his friend. He went up to Memphis and took over the kingdom, claiming that he would be careful about the affairs of the land. Therefore, with a small company of people, he subdued all of Egypt" (*Annals*, p. 419).

Egypt is the subject of the following verses, but we should observe that verse 27 says, *"for yet the end shall be at the time appointed."* This could be a reference to the future Tribulation Period and the time when Egypt will become uninhabitable for 40 years, as prophesied in Ezekiel 29:11. Many prophetic passages contain references to both near and far fulfillments. Perhaps this is the case with Egypt:

> *"And he shall stir up his power and his courage against the king of the south with a great army; and the king of the south shall be stirred up to battle with a very great and mighty army; but he shall not stand: for they shall forecast devices against him.*
> *"Yea, they that feed of the portion of his meat shall destroy him, and his army shall overflow: and many shall fall down slain.*
> *"And both these kings' hearts shall be to do mischief, and they*

*shall speak lies at one table; but it shall not prosper: for yet the end
shall be at the time appointed"* (Dan. 11:25-27).

In 170 B.C., Antiochus prepared his second expedition into
Egypt. It is written that for forty days strange visions were
seen at Jerusalem. There were apparitions of armed horsemen
and of foot soldiers in battle in the air, portending their future
problems (*Annals*, p. 420). Antiochus planned to add Egypt to
his own empire. He entered Egypt with a vast company, with
chariots, elephants, horsemen and a large navy. He waged
war against Ptolemy, who turned and fled away. He seized the
fortified cities in the land and took the spoils of Egypt.

About this time a rumor began to circulate that Antiochus
was dead. Jason saw this as an opportunity to invade Jerusalem
and regain his position as high priest. He came with a small army
of about a thousand men, attacked Jerusalem, and slaughtered
many of his own people. Yet, he was unable to take the city and
fled back to Ammon. All of the kings of the area denounced
him. He was proclaimed a public enemy and had to wander
from place to place. He was hated by all men because he had
transgressed their laws.

Antiochus heard that the rumor of his death had caused the
people of Jerusalem to rejoice. This angered him and he came
up against Jerusalem with a large army. Josephus wrote that
he took the city without a battle, but slaughtered thousands of
people, regardless of age. By the end of three days some 80,000
men were missing; 40,000 had been killed and the rest sold into
slavery. Antiochus seized holy vessels, took the golden altar,
lamp stand, table of showbread and even collected the gold
from everything that was covered. He stole all the silver and all
the hidden treasures that he found.

Diodorus stated: "Antiochus … entered the Holy of Holies.
There he found a marble statue of a man with a long beard,
holding a book in his hand and sitting on an ass. He thought him
to be Moses…. He sacrificed a large sow to the statue … poured

blood on the altar ... boiled the flesh of the sow and commanded that the holy books ... be marred and obliterated with the broth.... He compelled ... the Jews to eat swine's flesh."

Antiochus returned to Antioch with 1,800 talents from the Jewish Temple.

"Then shall he return into his land with great riches; and his heart shall be against the holy covenant; and he shall do exploits, and return to his own land.

"At the time appointed he shall return, and come toward the south; but it shall not be as the former, or as the latter.

"For the ships of Chittim shall come against him: therefore he shall be grieved, and return, and have indignation against the holy covenant: so shall he do; he shall even return, and have intelligence with them that forsake the holy covenant.

"And arms shall stand on his part, and they shall pollute the sanctuary of strength, and shall take away the daily sacrifice, and they shall place the abomination that maketh desolate.

"And such as do wickedly against the covenant shall he corrupt by flatteries: but the people that do know their God shall be strong, and do exploits.

"And they that understand among the people shall instruct many: yet they shall fall by the sword, and by flame, by captivity, and by spoil, many days.

"Now when they shall fall, they shall be holpen with a little help: but many shall cleave to them with flatteries.

"And some of them of understanding shall fall, to try them, and to purge, and to make them white, even to the time of the end: because it is yet for a time appointed" (Dan. 11:28-35).

The *"abomination that maketh desolate,"* mentioned in verse 31, is a prophecy yet to be fulfilled by the future Antichrist. However, we should note that Antiochus also committed such atrocities. In 168 B.C., Antiochus sent Apollonius, his overseer, with an army to extract more treasure from Israel. He was ordered to kill all the mature young men and sell the women and children. Apollonius arrived at Jerusalem without any sign of hostility. He waited until the Sabbath day and then killed all who came to worship at the Temple. He plundered the city, set it on fire, and pulled down the houses and walls. They carried away some 10,000 women and children and seized the cattle. Judas Maccabeus and nine others fled to the wilderness where they began to raise an army to fight the Syrians. Jerusalem remained desolate for over three years.

In 167 B.C., the Syrians set up an idol of Zeus in the Temple. They cut to pieces all of the scrolls of the Holy Scriptures and burned them. On the 25th day of Kislev, sacrifices were offered to Zeus on an altar built in the Temple courtyard. Antiochus forced the people to eat unclean meat and renounce Judaism, under threat of execution. Then, the Syrians came to the city of Modin where Mattathias and his sons lived. Mattathias was a priest of the first of the 24 orders of the priesthood. When confronted with the order to sacrifice a pig to Zeus, Mattathias revolted, killing Apelles, the king's commissioner, throwing down the altar, and calling upon the people to help him throw out the Syrians. Over the next three years, the Maccabees, as they were known, led the battle against the Syrian forces. Eventually, they assembled 6,000 men and liberated Jerusalem.

On the 25th of Kislev, the third anniversary of the erection of the statue of Zeus, they rededicated the Jewish Temple. It is said that they built a menorah (lampstand) out of lead, but found only one day's supply of sacred olive oil. Knowing that it would take eight days to make another batch, they, nevertheless, lit the lamps; and were amazed that the lamps burned for eight days on one day's supply of oil. Judas Maccabeus honored the miracle by establishing the festival of Hanukkah — the Feast of Dedication.

Antiochus heard about the defeat of his troops when he arrived at the city of Ecbatana, on the banks of a tributary to the Tigris River — at the same place where Daniel had received this very vision. He left there and headed for Babylon. Near the border of Persia, he received word that the statue of Zeus had been removed from the Jerusalem Temple. Antiochus was so angry he ordered his chariots to go at full speed — to hasten toward home. Antiochus bragged that as soon as he arrived at Jerusalem, he would make that city a common burial place for the Jews. Scarcely had these words left his mouth when the Syrian king was struck with an incurable disease in his bowels. In spite of the extreme pain, he commanded his driver to go faster. The chariot went out of control and Antiochus was thrown out. With his body bruised and his bones out of joint, he had to be carried on a horse litter. Worms bred so fast in his body, that whole streaks of flesh would drop away from him. His men couldn't stand the stench.

In the spring of 164 B.C., Antiochus IV Epiphanes gave up all hope of recovery. He called his friends to him and publicly acknowledged that all these miseries had happened to him because of the harm he had done to the Jews. Now, to his great grief, he had to die in a strange land. When he could no longer endure his own smell, he said, "It is appropriate to be subject to God and a man who is mortal should not proudly think of himself as if he were God." He promised God that if he could recover, he would become a Jew. He promised to go through the entire inhabited world and declare the power of God. But that spring, Antiochus died a miserable death in a strange land on a mountain near Babylon. In the last days of his life, he told those around him that he was going to die because "he had robbed the Temple at Jerusalem and sent forces to destroy the Jews without any cause" (*Annals*, pp. 434-444).

Bloodline of the Antichrist

Verses 28-35 also allude to the future Antichrist, especially the part about stopping the Temple sacrifice and committing the abomination of desolation. However, Antiochus IV Epiphanes also desecrated the Temple in the same manner. At this point, the verses seem to allude to both evil men. However, the following verses seem to be reserved for the future Antichrist:

"And the king shall do according to his will; and he shall exalt himself, and magnify himself above every god, and shall speak marvelous things against the God of gods, and shall prosper till the indignation be accomplished: for that that is determined shall be done.

"Neither shall he regard the God of his fathers, nor the desire of women, nor regard any god: for he shall magnify himself above all.

"But in his estate shall he honour the God of forces: and a god whom his fathers knew not shall he honour with gold, and silver, and with precious stones, and pleasant things.

"Thus shall he do in the most strong holds with a strange god, whom he shall acknowledge and increase with glory: and he shall cause them to rule over many, and shall divide the land for gain" (Dan. 11:36-39).

In Revelation 12, John tells us that the Antichrist will set up some kind of image on the Temple Mount that will be brought to life. Everyone in the world will be forced to pay homage to the beast by receiving a mark in their forehead or right hand — either a mark, or the name, or the number of the name — or else they cannot buy and sell. In II Thessalonians 2:4, the Apostle Paul tells us that the Antichrist will enter the sanctuary and proclaim himself to be god. Also, Jesus referred to the abomination of desolation in the Olivet discourse: *"When ye therefore shall see the abomination of desolation, spoken of by Daniel the prophet, stand in the holy place, (whoso readeth, let him understand:) Then let them which be in Judea flee into the mountains…"* (Matt. 24:15,16).

These are some of the New Testament passages that refer to the abomination of desolation first given in Daniel 9:27. At this point, we need to understand that this vision contains background information about the bloodline of the Antichrist.

The two millennia between Daniel's sixty-ninth and seventieth weeks (ch. 9) were not addressed, but it seems apparent that the Antichrist should come out of the Seleucid dynasty discussed in these verses.

In Daniel's seventh chapter, the *"little horn"* is seen emerging out of the Roman Empire. In chapter 8, the *"little horn"* rises out of the Greek Empire. In chapter 9, the *"prince"* comes out of the Roman Empire. And in chapters 10-12, the *"vile person"* once again emerges out of the Greek Empire. How can the Antichrist come out of both Greek and Roman royal dynasties?

The answer may be found in the history of the Spartans. Alexander the Great claimed to be a relative of Achilles, the Spartan hero of the Trojan War. Ptolemy was his half brother. The house of Ptolemy intermarried with the Seleucid dynasty. In other words, they all carried Spartan blood. The Trojans had defected from Sparta. Aeneas, a Trojan prince, fled the burning of Troy and went to Italy, where he became the progenitor of Romulus and Remus, the founders of Rome. It seems that the royal families of both Greece and Rome had roots in a common ancestry — the Spartans.

Bishop Ussher tells about the Romans coming to the site of ancient Troy during their war with Antiochus the Great (190 B.C.) and rejoicing with the people as if they were long-lost relatives:

"There was much joy and mutual congratulations between the men of Illium and the Romans. They recounted how Aeneas and his captains, who had set out from Troy to eventually found Rome, were their countrymen. The Romans were just as proud that they were descended from them. They were like parents and children who had been separated by a long absence and were now joyfully reunited" (*Annals*, p. 398).

Amazing! The Romans were descendants of the Trojans, who descended from the Danaans/Spartans.

Verse 37 says that the Antichrist will not regard *"the God of his fathers,"* thus leading many to believe that he will be from the lineage of Jacob. We cannot imagine the Antichrist being from the royal tribe of Judah, but we can understand how he might be from the tribe of Dan. The dying Jacob gathered his children around his deathbed and prophesied what would befall each of the tribes in the last days. Of Dan, he said:

"Dan shall judge his people... Dan shall be a serpent by the way, an adder in the path, that biteth the horse heels, so that his rider shall fall backward" (Gen. 49:16,17).

In the opening chapters of I Chronicles, all the tribes are listed, with the exception of Dan. The Chronicler begins with Adam and brings the histories of all the tribes up-to-date, except Dan. Throughout history, the rabbis have admitted that the tribe of Dan is the only truly lost tribe. An ancient Jewish writing entitled *"The Testaments of the Twelve Patriarchs"* still exists, in which each of the sons gives their deathbed prophecies. It is recorded that Dan told his sons, "Your prince is Satan." A footnote in *The Old Testament Pseudepigrapha*, by James Charlesworth of Duke University, states that the rabbis speculated that, because of the statement, Dan would produce the Antichrist.

How can this be? How can the Antichrist descend from the Greeks and Romans, and be from the tribe of Dan at the same time? In Homer's Illiad and Odyssey, the Spartans were called Danaans. It is said that a family of Danaans came by boat from Phoenicia, the area where the Danites once lived, and settled on the southern Greek islands. At first, they called themselves Danaans. However, over the years, they changed the name of their tribe to Lacedemonians, and then to Spartans. Josephus records a letter sent from the king of this tribe to the high priest in Jerusalem, claiming to be from the "stock of Abraham" (*Antiquities*, XII, IV, 10). This letter can also be found in the Apocryphal book of I Maccabees (12:20,21), which records Jerusalem's letter saying that the Lacedemonians were recognized as "brethren" (I Maccabees 12:11). This letter from the king of the Spartans came to Onias during the reign of Antiochus IV Epiphanes.

One of the Spartan chieftains, Dardanus, took his family north to the Black Sea, built the city of Troy and developed the

kingdom of the Trojans. The rivers that empty into the Black
Sea from the north are called the Danube, Dniester, Dnieper,
and Don. The waterway between the Aegean Sea and the Black
Sea was called the Dardanelle. All of these names allude to the
possibility that Danites settled in those areas. One of the Trojan
princes, Aeneas, escaped the destruction of Troy and went to
central Italy, where his progeny produced Romulus and Remus,
the founders of Rome.

When building the Tabernacle in the wilderness, Moses
chose Bezaleel of the tribe of Judah and Aholiab of the tribe of
Dan to do the design work. Judah's motif was a lion and Dan's
was a snake. However, the tribe did not like the idea of a snake on
their flag, so they changed their symbol to an eagle. According
to the letter from the king of the Spartans, the symbol of their
tribe was an eagle with a serpent in its claws. Since both tribes
shared the construction of the Jewish sanctuary, representing
good and evil, perhaps Dan will produce the Antichrist —
through Greek and Roman royal families.

The following verses seem to allude to the final war that
will bring down the Antichrist — Armageddon:

*"And at the time of the end shall the king of the south push
at him: and the king of the north shall come against him like a
whirlwind, with chariots, and with horsemen, and with many
ships; and he shall enter into the countries, and shall overflow and
pass over.*

*"He shall enter also into the glorious land, and many countries
shall be overthrown: but these shall escape out of his hand, even
Edom, and Moab, and the chief of the children of Ammon.*

*"He shall stretch forth his hand also upon the countries: and the
land of Egypt shall not escape.*

*"But he shall have power over the treasures of gold and of silver,
and over all the precious things of Egypt: and the Libyans and the
Ethiopians shall be at his steps.*

*"But tidings out of the east and out of the north shall trouble
him: therefore he shall go forth with great fury to destroy, and*

utterly to make away many.

"And he shall plant the tabernacles of his palace between the seas in the glorious holy mountain; yet he shall come to his end, and none shall help him" (Dan. 11:40-45).

The eleventh chapter closes with the Antichrist converting the Jewish Tabernacle into his own and attempting to rule over the world from the Temple Mount. Like all those others who have touched the apple of God's eye, his judgment will be swift and sure.

It seems that Daniel alluded to the Seleucid/Greek dynasty for the lineage of the Antichrist. Though no complete record has been found through which to trace the genealogy, there are bits of evidence that the Seleucid dynasty found its way into the Roman Senate. After Antiochus IV, there was V, VI, VII, VIII, IX, X, and XIII. In 69 B.C., Lucullus of Rome awarded Antiochus XIII the rule over Syria. In 63 B.C., Pompey came to Syria and declared that it would become a Roman province. Descendants of the Seleucids became prominent politicians in Rome. For example, Vitellius, a Seleucid, was a Roman senator. Following the death of Nero (A.D. 68), Vitellius spent a few months as emperor. He was one of four emperors that year, along with his friend, Otho. In fact, Vitellius was the man who campaigned for the young Nero before the Roman Senate to become the next Caesar, following the death of Claudius. Claudius was Nero's stepfather, having married Nero's mother. The identity of Nero's father is obscure. Perhaps it was Vitellius. Who can tell? Vitellius had something to gain by helping Nero become Caesar. However, history is silent on that subject.

Tacitus, a Roman historian, in his publication of *"The Histories,"* reported that during a certain battle, the family of Vitellius was spared. He wrote: "... this delay gave the Vitellians a chance to retreat to a vineyard where a complex network of trellised vines impeded movement. There was a small woods close by, too. From this they ventured to stage a counter-attack, and in so doing managed to kill the most eager of the praetorian troopers. Among the wounded was Prince Epiphanes, who was eagerly leading his men into battle on Otho's side."

Here, we learn that one member of the family of Senator Vitellius was a Prince Epiphanes — a hero in the battle of Cremona, in northern Italy. He was the son of Antiochus IV, king of Commagene, located on the Euphrates River. His official title was Antiochus Epiphanes, in honor of the man who set up a statue of Zeus in the courtyard of the Jerusalem Temple, over a century before. For a time, Epiphanes had been engaged to marry Drusilla, the younger daughter of Herod Agrippa I. However, he would not embrace Judaism and Herod would not consent to the marriage.

Tacitus also tells us about the emperor that followed Vitellius. It was none other than Vespasian, the father of Titus: "By 15 July [A.D. 69] the whole of Syria had taken the oath of allegiance to Vespasian. He had also gained the adhesion of Sohaemus and his kingdom, whose resources were not to be despised, and that of Antiochus, who had great inherited wealth and was the richest client-king of all. Then Agrippa [Herod Agrippa II] arrived after a fast voyage from Rome, where secret emissaries from his people had brought him news, which recalled him home while Vitellius was still in the dark. Equal enthusiasm marked the support given to the cause by Queen Berenice. She was in her best years and at the height of her beauty, while even the elderly Vespasian appreciated her generosity."

Clearly, Vitellius, though little known among the famous, was emperor of the Roman Empire for a while. In an article entitled, *"Bloodline of the Antichrist,"* that appeared in our *Prophecy in the News* magazine, November 1994, Gary Stearman wrote: "In this historical moment, Vespasian, Herod Agrippa II, Berenice [his sister and consort, mentioned in Acts 25:13] and Antiochus IV, King of Commagene, are seen conspiring together as close confidants. It is a historical fact that the sons and daughters of the Seleucids merged into the royal families of

Rome, as did the Herodians."

Josephus mentions a letter from the Roman senate, which reads in part, "As to ourselves, although we have had many wars that have compassed us around, by reason of the covetousness of our neighbors, yet did not we determine to be troublesome either to you or to others that were related to us; but since we have now overcome our enemies, and have occasion to send Numenius, the son of Antiochus, and Antipater, the son of Jason, who are both honorable men belonging to our senate, to the Romans, we gave them this epistle to you also, that they might renew that friendship which is between us" (*Antiquities*, XIII, V, 8).

Numenius was from the Seleucid dynasty that preceded Antiochus IV, king of Commagene. He was also a member of the Roman senate.

In our book, *Guardians of the Grail,* I noted that Merovee, father of European royalty, claimed to be a descendant of the Trojans. Who knows? Perhaps that royal Spartan bloodline descended to the royal houses of Europe. Their progeny has also spread to other countries, including presidents of the United States. Therefore, it is not necessary that the Antichrist should come out of Assyria or any other country from ancient history. Perhaps the lost tribe of Dan has been busy populating many of the thrones of this world. So, where will the Antichrist come from? And who will he be?

Daniel's Last Incredible Vision
... continued

Daniel's fourth vision, which began in chapter ten, continues through this final chapter. It is Daniel's longest vision and one of the most comprehensive studies on the roots of the Antichrist in the Bible. It is also appropriate that God should introduce this study shortly after Judah's seventy-year exile. Nebuchadnezzar's invasion launched a protracted period of Gentile domination over Jerusalem, known as *"the times of the Gentiles,"* that will eventually be concluded with the coming of Israel's long-awaited Messiah to end the reign of the Antichrist.

It seems that Daniel's guide for this vision was the Messiah, Himself. Why should this guide be the Messiah? Because, the vision is about His enemy, the *"seed of the serpent."* It is only fitting that Christ should be the one to give us the details of the Antichrist — the imposter who will seek to imitate Him and bring the world down to Armageddon.

At Calvary, the serpent bruised the Messiah's *"heel,"* but here, we are taught about the conclusion of the story, when the Messiah will bruise the serpent's *"head!"* (Gen 3:15).

At this point, Daniel's vision is just about over. Only a few pertinent details need to be addressed, which we shall consider in this chapter.

The previous chapter explained Persia's fall to the Greeks and laid the groundwork for the emergence of the Antichrist. Antiochus IV Epiphanes became the prototype for the future Antichrist, but somewhere around verse 22, the scene shifts into the far future ... to the days of the seventieth *"week"* (Dan. 9:27).

As we concluded the eleventh chapter, the Antichrist had committed the abomination of desolation and planted his palace on the Temple Mount — *"But tidings out of the east and out of the north shall trouble him"* (Dan. 11:44). His kingdom will be short-lived. As we open chapter twelve, we are in the middle of the seventieth week. Michael is about to throw the great red dragon out of heaven.

Michael Stands Up

"And at that time shall Michael stand up, the great prince which standeth for the children of thy people: and there shall be a time of trouble, such as never was since there was a nation even to that same time: and at that time thy people shall be delivered, every one that shall be found written in the book.

"And many of them that sleep in the dust of the earth shall awake, some to everlasting life, and some to shame and everlasting contempt.

"And they that be wise shall shine as the brightness of the firmament; and they that turn many to righteousness as the stars for ever and ever" (Dan. 12:1-3).

Michael is the archangel in charge of Israel. He was the one consulted at the onset of this vision (Dan. 10:13). In Daniel 10:21, Daniel was told that Michael is *"your prince,"* meaning the prince of the Jewish nation. Were it not for him, the Chosen People would never have survived so many persecutions over the centuries. Michael was there to protect and care for them. In fact, Michael may be in charge of all the guardian angels assigned to saints. He is the leader of the heavenly troops that fight against Satan in Revelation 12:

"And there was war in heaven: Michael and his angels fought against the dragon; and the dragon fought and his angels,

"And prevailed not; neither was their place found any more in heaven.

"And the great dragon was cast out, that old serpent, called the Devil, and Satan, which deceiveth the whole world: he was cast out into the earth, and his angels were cast out with him" (Rev. 12:7-9).

When this *"time of trouble"* arrives, the Antichrist will commit the abomination of desolation and many Jews will flee into the wilderness. Michael will *"stand up"* (or make a stand) to press the battle against the evil forces of the dragon. We are told in the first verse that Michael will be called into action for the very reason that the time of trouble has arrived, the likes of which have never been seen before.

Daniel was assured that *"thy people,"* meaning the Jewish nation, will be *"delivered."* This must have been a great comfort to the old prophet. He had seen enough sorrow throughout his lifetime. In spite of the fact that Daniel had been a trusted adviser to several kings, he was still a captive, taken from his homeland and separated from his family and friends. Furthermore, Daniel never got to go home. He had to stay in Persia until he died.

Why did Daniel have to stay in captivity while others returned? Because God had said to King Hezekiah:

"Behold the days come, that all that is in thine house, and that which thy fathers have laid up in store until this day, shall be carried to Babylon: nothing shall be left, saith the LORD.

"And of thy sons that shall issue from thee, which thou shalt beget, shalll they take away, and they shall be eunuchs in the palace of the king of Babylon" (Isa. 39:6,7).

Daniel was from the royal lineage of Hezekiah. Therefore, he could not go home. The great hope for Daniel, in this chapter, was that he could look forward to the resurrection. At the end of days, the saints will be resurrected. This blessed hope was given in the opening of this chapter and repeated at the close of it. Daniel was promised that he would be among the saints on resurrection day.

Verse 2 may allude to all of the resurrections without being specific. But it does not teach a general resurrection as some believe. The New Testament reveals that Christians will be resurrected before the seventieth week commences; and yet, there is no specific reference to this in Daniel, because the gap between the sixty-ninth week and the seventieth week was sealed. The rapture of the church may not be specifically addressed here, but we will be among those who will *"shine as the stars,"* because Christianity is all about soulwinning. In this verse, we see two main groups — the saints who will be resurrected before the kingdom reign; and the ungodly who will be resurrected a thousand years later. The thousand-years gap between the two resurrections is not given to Daniel. Perhaps he does not need to see that now. He only needs to know that a glorious resurrection awaits his people; and that a resurrection of *"shame and everlasting contempt"* awaits those whose names are not written in the book.

Written in the Book

According to Jewish teaching, God has foretold a period of Tribulation as seen through the rituals of the Days of Awe (*Tishri* 1-10), beginning with *Rosh Hashanah* (the Feast of Trumpets), and ending with *Yom Kippur* (the Day of Atonement). It is said that when the time comes for the commencement of Daniel's seventieth week, God will sit down upon His throne of Judgment (on some future *Rosh Hashanah*) with three books — the "Book of Life," the "Book of Death" and the "Book for those who are neither totally virtuous nor totally evil."

Those written in the "Book of Death" will be punished and those whose names appear in the third book will be given seven years to repent. But, where will we be during this time? Will the church have to face the Days of Awe — the Tribulation Period — along with Israel? Must we, who have received eternal life by grace and grace alone, have to endure the punishment of these days? Must we, who have already repented and received the Holy Spirit as the *"earnest of our inheritance,"* still have to add something to our repentance during those future "days of repentance?"

Take heart. Rabbi Yosef Stern, author of a book entitled *Days of Awe*, has a word for us: "As it is well known, the righteous are written in the Book of Life on *Rosh Hashanah*. These worthy individuals can be vindicated on the basis of their own merit, they do not need to be saved. It is the intermediate category, the individuals who are neither totally virtuous nor totally evil, who are saved on *Yom Kippur*" (Yosef Stern, *Days of Awe*, p. 270).

These "worthy individuals" do not need to suffer during the "days of awe." We need no further repentance! This Jewish concept allows for a Pretribulation Rapture. We, whose names are written in the Lamb's Book of Life, do not need to wait until *Yom Kippur* to be saved!

According to rabbinical teachings, the wicked have been entered into the "Book of Death." At the onset of the Tribulation Period, their fate will be sealed. There is no hope for them during Daniel's seventieth week, as typified by the Jewish observance of the Days of Awe. For them, these days are days of affliction.

Yosef Stern also mentioned a third book in God's hand that holds the names of "those who are neither totally virtuous nor totally evil." They are given ten days to repent. And who are they? Rabbi Stern writes: "Whereas *Rosh Hashanah* is a day of judgment for all mankind, *Yom Kippur's* atonement is reserved for the Jewish people" (*Days of Awe*, p. 272). Yes, the rabbi writes that *Rosh Hashanah* is reserved for Gentiles. This Jewish concept makes room for righteous Gentiles! *Rosh Hashanah* is not primarily a "Jewish" day. *Yom Kippur* is exclusively a "Jewish" day. I am delighted to tell you that Gentile Christianity (the bride of Christ) will be taken on or before the onset of Daniel's seventieth week. According to Rabbi Stern's reasoning we will be raptured before the seven-year Tribulation Period, because our names are written in the "Lamb's Book of Life"!

The Jewish nation, having rejected Christ, will be left behind to endure the "days of repentance." They will be tempted by Satan's last chance to turn them away from God. They, who built the golden calf, will face another siege from the great tempter. He will desecrate the sacred sanctuary and commit the *abomination of desolation.* He will demand a *"mark"* in the right hand or forehead. He will claim to be Israel's messiah and try to force himself upon the Chosen People. But this time, it will not work. They will reject the pretender and bring his wrath upon them.

The story of the resurrection would not be complete if verse 3 was not there. When the resurrection comes, it will include all who have heard and responded to the Gospel. Every person included in the resurrection will have come in contact with a *"wise"* soul winner. Furthermore, soul winning is the most rewarding endeavor in this life. Solomon once said, *"The fruit of the righteous is a tree of life; and he that winneth souls is wise"* (Prov. 11:30). Daniel is told:

"And they that be wise shall shine as the brightness of the firmament; and they that turn many to righteousness as the stars for ever and ever" (Dan. 12:3).

This verse alludes to the teaching that there will be a Judgment Seat where rewards will be handed out for soulwinning. The one who saves a soul from hell will shine on that wonderful day!

The Sealed Book

"But thou, O Daniel, shut up the words, and seal the book, even to the time of the end: many shall run to and fro, and knowledge shall be increased" (Dan. 12:4).

Daniel has been one of the most mysterious books in the Bible.

For centuries, its prophetic message was clouded. However, since the Reformation, some theologians have recognized the need to return to a literal interpretation of Scripture. With the invention of the printing press, the Bible, once chained to pulpits, became available for the poorest families in society. In the past two centuries, the Bible has been translated into almost every language on the Earth.

It is true that scientific knowledge is expanding on an unprecedented scale. Until the twentieth century, there were no automobiles, no jet airplanes, no radios, no televisions, and certainly no computers. There have been more inventions in the past century than in all the previous centuries combined. Today, worldwide transportation has advanced beyond the wildest dreams of our forefathers. We can drive an automobile from the frozen tundra in Alaska to the southern tip of South America. We can board an airplane and be anywhere we want to go in the world in a matter of hours. Rockets propel men around the globe in less than 90 minutes.

Though these advancements are certainly included in this prophecy, I believe the primary purpose of this verse is to seal certain prophetic aspects of the book, and then to break those seals and open the book at the time of the end. Running *"to and fro"* means that men will be scanning the entire Bible from one end to the other, looking for answers to the mysteries of Scripture. The knowledge that will be increased at the time of the end is primarily a reference to the fulfillments of prophecy and our understanding of them.

A Final Word

Daniel's heavenly guide had to leave. He had other business to attend to among the kings of Persia. I am convinced that Christ was the man *"clothed in linen,"* which was upon the waters of the river. The reference to the *"linen"* (Dan. 10:5) is a clue to His identity. He was Daniel's guide for this final vision. We do not know what kind of craft He boarded, but assume that it was a boat of some kind. As He stepped into the boat and pushed away from shore, Daniel noticed two other people nearby:

"Then I Daniel looked, and, behold, there stood other two, the one on this side of the bank of the river, and the other on that side of the bank of the river.

"And one said to the man clothed in linen, which was upon the waters of the river, How long shall it be to the end of these wonders?

"And I heard the man clothed in linen, which was upon the waters of the river, when he held up his right hand and his left hand unto heaven, and sware by him that liveth for ever that it shall be for a time, times, and an half; and when he shall have accomplished to scatter the power of the holy people, all these things shall be finished.

"And I heard, but I understood not: then said I, O my Lord, what shall be the end of these things?" (Dan. 12:5-8).

We are not given the identities of the other two men in this vision, but there is a common thread running throughout prophetic Scriptures that implies that they were the two witnesses seen in Revelation 11. They may have been angels, but not necessarily. They could have been Israel's two most premier prophets of the Old Testament. They could have been the prophets that Malachi wrote about in his final chapter. They could have been the two who met with Jesus on the Mount of Transfiguration. They could have been the two men in white apparel in the first chapter of the book of Acts. If they were Moses and Elijah, it would certainly have been appropriate to the question they asked on Daniel's behalf. However, if Daniel recognized them, he didn't say.

They stood on either side of the river. Their question concerned the timing of events surrounding the abomination of desolation. *"How long shall it be to the end of these wonders?"* His question was not about the length of time between the onset and conclusion of Daniel's seventy weeks. That would have been nice to know, but those years are shrouded in mystery. Daniel was not told about the two millennia extending between the sixty-ninth and the seventieth weeks. The question, *"How long?"* (v. 6) concerned only three and a half years, beginning with the abomination of desolation.

The Lord held up His hands — not just His right hand, but both of them — and declared that the time will consist of three and a half years, the same *"time and times and the dividing of time"* mentioned in Daniel 7:25. During this time (the last half of the seventieth week) the Antichrist will remove the Jews from the Temple Mount and launch a campaign against those who refuse to worship him. Daniel must have been confused to hear about Michael standing up for his people, then hearing that their power will be scattered. Is that the end of it? Will the story end with the annihilation of the Jews? No wonder Daniel said, *"I understood not!"* Daniel spoke up and asked one last question: *"What shall be the end of these things?"* Please, finish the story! Don't leave me hanging!

"And he said, Go thy way, Daniel: for the words are closed up and sealed till the time of the end" (Dan. 12:9).

I can imagine Daniel saying, "Don't seal the words yet! Tell me more!" But the Savior replies, "Sorry, the rest is sealed. Well, maybe … one thing more …"

"Many shall be purified, and made white, and tried; but the wicked shall do wickedly: and none of the wicked shall understand; but the wise shall understand.

"And from the time that the daily sacrifice shall be taken away, and the abomination that maketh desolate set up, there shall be a thousand two hundred and ninety days.

"Blessed is he that waiteth, and cometh to the thousand three hundred and five and thirty days.

"But go thou thy way till the end be: for thou shalt rest, and stand in thy lot at the end of the days" (Dan. 12:10-13).

The purpose of it all is that *"many shall be purified, and made white, and tried."* This is no trivial statement. This reveals the whole divine plan for the human race from the beginning of Creation. The reason Daniel's guide (Jesus) created this world in the first place, is so that mankind would be put on this Earth and given a series of trials. The purpose was that we might be purified. The term *"made white"* is a metaphor for being purified. Beyond that, however, all men will be *"tried."* Ah-hah! Now we know! When asking the age-old question, "Why does God allow disaster, war, hunger, disease, etc.?" Here is the answer — that we might be *"tried."*

Oh yes, something else, Daniel — only the *"wise"* will understand why mankind is *"tried."* The wicked will not understand. They will just keep on asking, "Why?"

OK. That's not really the answer to Daniel's particular question. Daniel wanted to know: *"What shall be the end of these things?"* He was not referring to God's overall plan, but to the scattering of the saints. So the Savior explained, as he rowed out of sight:

From the day that the daily sacrifices are stopped and the *"abomination"* is set up, there will be "the days of the 1,290" — 30 days past the three and one half years (1,260 days). What will happen during those 30 days is not revealed. But, Daniel understands that it will come to pass.

After that will be "the days of the 1,335." Please notice the way these days are stated. They are not 1,290 days, or 1,335 days, but "in the days of the 1,290," and "in the days of the 1,335." In the Hebrew text, the term ימים *yomim* (days) is given before the numbers. This means that something from heaven will be happening every day of the extra 30 days — and something from heaven will be happening every day of the next 45 days. And, Daniel, you will be happy during those extra 45 days! Jesus also told Daniel that he would *"rest."* In other words, Daniel's time of testing would be over when he dies. His body would be laid to rest in a tomb until resurrection day. On that glorious day, Daniel will stand on holy ground. He will get to go back to live in Jerusalem!

The Extra Days

One can only speculate about these times. They appear to be seventy-five days past the 1,260 days. Exactly what will happen is not clear. However, we should note that they are divided into 30 days, then another 45 days. Beyond that, we should go back to another river and another question, as seen in Daniel 8:12-14. Daniel was in Shushan, (modern Susa) located on the banks of the Ulai River. The two saints addressed the same question to an unseen third man (guess who!), and the answer given was 2,300 evenings and mornings until the sanctuary is cleansed — for a total of 1,150 days. All of these days have the same starting point — the abomination of desolation. The question in chapter 8 was:

"How long shall be the vision concerning the daily sacrifice, and the transgression of desolation, to give both the sanctuary and the host to be trodden under foot?" (Dan. 8:13).

In both places, the same subject is addressed. But in chapter 8, Daniel is told that the sanctuary will be cleansed after 2,300 evenings and mornings. The Hebrew term for days is not used. According to the Hebrew text, the number 2,300 is associated with two Hebrew words that should not have been translated *"days."* They are 2,300 הקרק ערב (evenings) and רקלמנ בקר (mornings). On the other hand, in Daniel 12:11,12, both the numbers 1,290 and 1,335 are associated with ימים *yomim*, the Hebrew word for *"days."* Therefore, we should translate this term literally as 2,300 evenings and mornings. Since this passage deals specifically with the *"daily sacrifice,"* we should note that it was customary to offer a sacrifice at sunset, to mark the beginning of the next calendar day, and again at daybreak, to mark the beginning of the light for that day. In the marking of a calendar day, the night came first, followed by the day. This was a prophecy that, in the process of human history, evil (as depicted by night) would be followed by good (as depicted by day). The night of this old world would be turned into the day of resurrection and redemption. Many hymns refer to the day that follows night:

Some Golden Daybreak; I'll Meet You in the Morning; etc.

Basically, Daniel is told about a Great Tribulation that begins with the abomination of desolation. After 1,150 days, wherein Jerusalem will be *"trodden under foot,"* it is possible that the nations will have fielded their armies for the final battle — Armageddon. After another 110 days (accounting for the 1,260 days), Christ will appear. Over the next 30 days (accounting for the 1,290 days), birds will eat the flesh of the slain on the battlefields and Satan will be bound. During the next 45 days (accounting for a total of 1,335 days), the saints will be resurrected and Christ will establish heaven's kingdom. What particular event happens on which particular day is not revealed. We only know that during that last 45 days, Daniel will be rejoicing.

Conclusion

The book of Daniel is one of the most important prophetic books in the Bible. John's Apocalypse is based upon Daniel's prophecies. They compliment each other and aid in the understanding of both works. The general outline of the human dilemma is revealed in the four great Gentile world powers that would dominate Jerusalem — from the days of Nebuchadnezzar's Babylon, through the reigns of Medo/Persia, Greece and Rome — until the establishment of the Messianic Kingdom. The suffering of the Jewish people can be seen throughout this extended period of time — being revived *"after two days ... in the third"* (Hosea 6:2) millennial day. The times of their suffering are remarkably similar to the suffering of Christ who died and was resurrected on the third day. Though these mysteries are hidden in the sealed book and locked away from human understanding, we expect to be told all about it someday. The wars between the king of the north and the king of the south — fighting each other in the intermediate territory that lay between them (namely Israel) — offer a clue to the larger battles between heaven and hell. Their battles are being fought in this earthly realm. This third planet from the sun has become the designated battlefield for the two warring groups. An understanding of this gives meaning and purpose to all of human history — and God's greater plan of the ages.

In the following chapter, I have researched the history of the Jewish calendar and found where the Jews eliminated 243 years for the purpose of making Daniel's seventy weeks point to Bar Kokhbah as the messiah, rather than Jesus.

Be sure to study the chart of world history, from Creation to the year 2240. Many historical events are included on the time line. It will help you to date important events over the past 6,000 years. You can find the Sabbatical cycles, beginning with Joshua and continuing until this present day. You can see the Jubilees at the top of each column and understand where it all fits in with this generation. I have included the conjunction of Jupiter and Saturn over the past 6,000 years. It will also help you to understand the cosmologies of ancient cultures and why the rabbis believed that a triple conjunction between Jupiter and Saturn in the constellation Pisces would presage the birth of the Messiah. Finally, this chart will help you to understand the book of Daniel within the context of world history.

The Jewish Calendar's Missing Years

The book of Daniel can best be understood if one first obtains a working knowledge of human history over the past six-thousand years. In this study, we shall explore the past six millennia and attempt to reconcile the discrepancy of 243 years missing in the Jewish calendar.

Western civilization uses a calendar that dates from the birth of Christ. The term "A.D." is an acronym for *Anno Domini*, Latin for, "in the year of our Lord." All dates before the birth of Christ are marked as "B.C." (meaning Before Christ). The Jewish use of "B.C.E." refers to Before the Common Era, and "C.E." meaning after the Common Era, thus refusing to recognize the Christianized version of dating.

Though our Roman calendar dates from the First Advent of Christ, the Jewish calendar claims to date history from Creation, using the acronym "A.M." or *Anno Mundi*, Latin for "from the creation of the world" — and claiming that Adam was created 243 years later than our calendar suggests. The Jewish date for Creation is written as 1 *Anno Mundi*. Here is our first problem with the Jewish calendar. The year, 1 A.M., may have been the first year of Adam, but he was not one year old until twelve months later, in 2 A.M. Year 1 A.M. should not have been established until Adam was 1 year old. Therefore, the Jewish calendar added an extra year — a year that was actually not there.

Proof: the Jewish date for the death of Adam is 930 A.M. If that calendar date is correct, then Adam should have been only 929 years old when he died. Since the Bible tells us that Adam was 930 years old, the Jewish calendar added a year at its very beginning.

Furthermore, in the Julian calendar, December 31, 1 B.C. skips to January 1, A.D. 1, with the single tick of a clock. What happened to the twelve months from 1 B.C., to zero, and another twelve months from zero to A.D. 1? Combining these problems, we have no accounting for 36 months — 12 months during Adam's first year, and 24 months between 1 B.C., and A.D. 1. According to *The Jewish Time Line Encyclopedia* by Mattis Kantor, the Jewish year 3760 A.M. corresponds to our calendar year 1 B.C. In other words, we hold to 4003 years and 3 months, while the Jewish calendar records only 3760 years, a difference of 243 years. However, when our calendar turned to A.D. 1, the Jewish calendar was calculated to be 3761. From that point forward, the Jewish calendar has only 240 years missing.

Which calendar is closest to being right? Certainly not the Jewish calendar. Here's why. According to Jewish commentaries, their messiah was long ago predicted to come at the close of 6,000 years to establish their long-awaited "messianic kingdom," which should last throughout the "great Sabbath" — or seventh millennium. If we hold to the Jewish calendar, then the messiah cannot come until about A.D. 2240. This cannot be accurate. Long before then, life on this planet will be in great danger from the overwhelming volume of human population growth. In October 2000, the human population reached six billion, up from three billion in 1960.

The population doubled in only forty years. The previous doubling took 80 years; and before that, it took 200 years for the world's population to double. In other words, population growth has reached the proverbial "exponential curve." However, if the United Nations is successful in slowing population growth and keeping it stable at a forty-year doubling rate, then we are still facing a disaster of catastrophic proportions.

It is estimated that by 2240, there could be over 400 billion people on this planet! Obviously, that cannot be allowed to happen. There would not be enough air to breathe, not enough water to drink, and not enough food to eat to keep people alive. The human race cannot possibly continue to proliferate unabated. All efforts to avoid the catastrophe of population growth have thus far failed. God has to intervene. The Messiah has to come long before that happens. In light of these facts, the Jewish calendar could not possibly be accurate.

In the 1990s, billboards went up all over Israel, declaring that the messiah is coming. In January 1994, the Lubavitcher sect of Judaism declared that their aging leader, Menachem Schneerson, was the messiah. Unfortunately, he died that summer. In the spring of 2005, Rabbi Yitzchak Kaduri, a leading mystic in Israel, stated that the messiah should arrive, no later than September 13, 2007. If the Jewish calendar is correct, why are the Jews looking for their messiah at this time? Some 700 years ago, Jewish mystics wrote that the messiah would come shortly after the turn of the millennium. Rabbi Simeon ben Yohai wrote:

"When the sixtieth year crosses the threshold of the sixth millennium, the God of heaven will visit the daughter of Jacob with a preliminary remembrance.... In the year sixty-six, the messiah will appear in the land of Galilee" (*Zohar*, vol. 1, p. 370). Obviously, the "sixtieth year" was 5760, and the "threshold of the sixth millennium" was our year 2000. The prediction for the messiah appearing in the "year sixty-six" [5766 or 2006] may have provided the basis for Rabbi Kaduri's prediction. In the autumn of 2005, he received a visitor at his home in northern Galillee. When the man received a rabbinical blessing and left, Rabbi Kaduri turned to his aid and said, "I have just seen the messiah!" He wrote the man's name in a cryptic note and sealed it in an envelope, requesting that it be opened one year after his death. Kaduri died in late January 2006 and one year later, the envelope was opened, revealing the name of the expected messiah as *Yehoshua*! Yes, his messiah was named Jesus, but he was not the same Jesus we worship. Kaduri said that he would become more and more popular until he is asked to run for political office, at which time, he will win. It is obvious that the leading rabbis are not waiting until 2240 for their messiah to arrive. They believe He will soon establish the messianic kingdom.

The Jews have always known that their calendar was flawed. Though the rabbis will argue for the authenticity of their calendar, based upon the *Seder Olam Rabbah*, they know that their dates are wrong. Furthermore, some of them know the reason why.

What Happened to the Missing Years?

The Jews have not always used their current calendar. In fact, their system of "dating from Creation" did not become popular until 1517. Until then, it was common to date Jewish history from 312 B.C., the time of the establishment of the Seleucid dynasty — a system of dating that the Jews called *Minyan Shtarot*.

Alexander the Great died in the spring of 323 B.C., and his empire was divided among his generals. Seleucus claimed rulership over Babylon and Syria. However, in 315 B.C., Seleucus learned that Antigonus was planning to conquer the factions and reunite the Empire under his own leadership. Seleucus fled to Egypt and convinced Ptolemy to make a league with him in order to rid them both of their enemy. Seleucus and Ptolemy merged their armies with those of Cassander and Lysimachus and launched a campaign against Antigonus.

In 312 B.C., Antigonus gave up on Babylon and returned his troops to Phrygia. That year, Seleucus recovered his empire. Concerning 312 B.C., Bishop James Ussher (died 1656) wrote: "Seleucus had acquired this powerful army ... and easily subdued the provinces of Media, Susa and the other bordering countries.... **The story of the Maccabees' account of the Greek reign also began here** [emphasis mine]. Without a doubt this is from the autumn (September or October) of the year 312 B.C. The writer of the book[s] of Maccabees calculated his Greek years by starting at that time..." (*The Annals of the World*, first published in 1658, p. 329).

To confirm that, I read the book of First Maccabees (1:10) and noticed that it dates the events of 175 B.C., as being "137 years from the beginning of the kingdom of the Greeks" (312 B.C.). The Maccabean chronicle says that it was the year Antiochus returned from Rome where he had been held hostage. His brother Seleucus (not the original Seleucus) had been murdered through the treachery of Heliodorus. But Eumenes and Attalus expelled Heliodorus and gave Antiochus the kingdom.

Actually, the kingdom of Syria should have rightly belonged to Demetrius, the ten-year-old son of Seleucus, who was being held hostage at Rome, but Antiochus was not interested in installing the rightful king. He wanted to be king. In 175 B.C., Antiochus IV Epiphanes made a league with certain corrupt politicians in Jerusalem. This would soon lead to the desecration of the Temple in 168 B.C., and the Maccabean revolt that followed.

Jewish sources claim that their system of dating from 312 B.C., refers to a promise made to Alexander the Great. According to Josephus, Alexander requested that his statue be placed in the Temple at Jerusalem. Simon, the high priest, explained how unsettling this could be to Jewish religious law and suggested that the Jews could bestow an even greater honor on him by naming all the male babies born to the priesthood that year "Alexander." They also promised to accept the year (of his conquest of the empire) as the first year of counting in all legal documents. They called it the *Minyan Shtarot*. That system of dating was used by Jewish communities until as late as A.D. 1517.

A few Jewish communities had been using *Anno Mundi* as early as the ninth or tenth centuries, but in the sixteenth century, that form of dating became the officially accepted system. According to *The Jewish Time Line Encyclopedia*: "When the Turks conquered Egypt, in A.D. 1517, and the system of Jewish communal structure changed, Rabbi David ibn Zimra, became the leader of the Egyptian Jews and formally ended the *Minyan Shtarot*" (p. 185).

The *Seder Olam Rabbah*

The basis for the Jewish calendar lies in the *Seder Olam Rabbah* (The Book of the Order of the World), which was compiled in the mid-second century, by Yose ben Halafta (died A.D. 160). Halafta was a student of the famed Rabbi Akiva ben Joseph (the father of the *Mishnah*). During the Bar Kokhbah revolt against the Romans (A.D. 132-135), the 90-year-old Akiva gave his blessing to the revolution by proclaiming that Bar Kokhbah was the *"Star out of Jacob"* (Num. 24:17) — Israel's long awaited messiah!

Bar Kokhbah was killed in A.D. 135 and the Jewish revolt was crushed. The Roman general, Hadrian, plowed the city of Jerusalem and sowed salt in its furrows. He erected a statue to Zeus (Jupiter) on the Temple Mount and changed the name of Jerusalem to Aelia Capitolina, so that the name of Jerusalem would be lost to history. For spite, he changed the name of Israel to Palestine, after Israel's ancient enemies, the Philistines. He rounded up most of the Jewish population and sold them on the slave markets of the world. Over the next twenty years, Yose ben Halafta and his colleagues compiled the *Seder Olam Rabbah* for one primary purpose — to make Daniel's seventy weeks point to Bar Kokhbah as the Jewish Messiah.

Now for Details ... Beginning with Abraham

Some of the calculations in the *Seder Olam* may have been simple mistakes. For example, the *Seder Olam* claims that Terah fathered Abram at the age of 70. Genesis 11:26 says, *"Terah lived seventy years, and begat Abram, Nahor, and Haran."* What the Jewish scholars did not take into account is that three sons are named. Though Abram was named first, he was not necessarily the firstborn. Nor were all three children born the same year. For the date of the birth of Abram, we should consult the following verses: *"And the days of Terah were two hundred and five years: and Terah died in Haran"* (Gen. 11:32). Upon Terah's death, a 75-year-old Abram left Haran: *"So Abram departed, as the LORD had spoken unto him ... and Abram was seventy and five years old when he departed out of Haran"* (Gen 12:4). Abram was 75 years old when his father died at the age of 205. This would make Terah 130 years old when Abram was born — not 70. The *Seder Olam* simply overlooked those extra 60 years. Instead of Abram being born 1,948 years after the creation of Adam, he was actually born 2,008 years after Adam's creation.

Dating the Abrahamic Covenant

Secondly, the *Seder Olam* dates the Abrahamic Covenant in Abram's seventieth year. However, the Scripture states that Abram was seventy-five years old (Gen. 12:4). Here is another five-year mistake. To account for this, the *Seder Olam* has Moses being born five years earlier than he was. According to Mattis Kantor, author of *The Jewish Timeline Encyclopedia* (pg. 25), Moses was born on *Adar* 7, 1393 B.C. In our calendar, that would have been on February 18, 1576 B.C. However, according to most accepted calculations, the Exodus occurred on Passover (*Nissan* 14), April 12, 1491 B.C., when Moses was 80 years old. That would place Moses' birth in 1571 B.C., not 1576 B.C. There was a conjunction of Jupiter and Saturn on January 27, 1575, — too late to herald Moses' birth, had it occurred on February 18, 1576. Yet, Jewish scholar Abarbanel (A.D. 1437-1508) and others laid great stress on the importance of the conjunctions of Jupiter and Saturn. A conjunction of these two planets occurred about four years before Moses' birth, and was the reason Pharaoh ordered all newborn Hebrew males to be thrown into the Nile River. The conjunction caused Egyptian astrologers to think that a great redeemer was going to be born to the Jews — as Josephus puts it, "who ... would raise the Israelites ... excel all men in virtue, and obtain a glory that would be remembered through all ages" (Josephus, *Antiquities*, Book II, Chapter 9, Paragraph 2). This could not have happened in 1576 B.C., a year before the planetary conjunction of 1575, but could account for these events had they occurred after that. That would place Moses' birth in 1571 B.C.

The Reign of Amaziah

Thirdly, Yose ben Halafta removed 14 years from the reign of Amaziah (826-812 B.C.). King Amaziah reigned for 29 years, but the *Seder Olam* has him fleeing Jerusalem in his 15th year, leaving the throne to Azariah (also called Uzziah). Uzziah reigned 52 years (812-760 B.C.), but the *Seder Olam* has him reigning for the last 14 years of Amaziah's life and, therefore, Uzziah should have died in 773 B.C., rather than in 760 B.C. (see *"A Chart of Six Millennia"*). We know that the *Seder Olam* is wrong because II Kings 15:23 tells us *"In the fiftieth year of Azariah king of Judah Pekahiah the son of Menahem began to reign over Israel in Samaria, and reigned two years."* Pekahiah's reign only fits the calendar at 762-60 B.C., not 14 years earlier.

So far, we can assume that the dating differences in the *Seder Olam* were simple mistakes. However, from this point, we must agree that Yose ben Halafta and his colleagues deliberately cut 164 years out of the period of the Medo/Persian Empire.

The Cover-Up

The *Seder Olam* gives a chronology for its 53-year depiction of Persian history, thus eliminating 164 years from their calendar. The following is blatantly inaccurate:

1. **Darius** the Mede reigned 1 year – 3389-3390 A.M. (374-373 B.C.)
   - Babylon was conquered (the *Seder Olam* dates it at 374 B.C., rather than the accepted date of 538 B.C.)
   - Daniel was cast into the lion's den.
2. **Cyrus** reigned 3 years – 3390-3392 A.M. (373-371 B.C.)
   - The Jews returned to Jerusalem.
   - The second Temple construction began.
3. **Artaxerxes** (Cambyses) reigned 1/2 year – 3393 A.M. (370 B.C.)
   - Temple construction was halted.
4. **Ahasuerus** reigned 14 years – 3393-3407 A.M. (370-356 B.C.)
   - Esther was chosen queen
   - Esther bore Darius the Persian
5. **Darius** the Persian reigned 35 years – 3407-3442 A.M. (356-321 B.C.)
   - Temple construction was resumed – 3408 A.M. (355 B.C.)
   - Second Temple was dedicated – 3412 A.M. (351 B.C.)
   - Ezra came to Jerusalem – 3413 A.M. (350 B.C.)
   - Nehemiah came to Jerusalem – 3426 A.M. (337 B.C.)
   - Darius was defeated by Alexander – 3442 A.M. (321 B.C.)

Instead of 13 Medo/Persian kings over a period of 207 years, the *Seder Olam* lists only five kings over a period of 53 years. There are several historical writings on this point to prove that the *Seder Olam* is wrong.

The True Account

There were actually 13 Medo/Persian monarchs who reigned over a period of 207 years. I shall be as brief as possible, but, for a full reading, consult Bishop James Ussher's, *The Annals of the World*, pages 117-234:

1. Darius the Mede reigned one year (538-537 B.C.), then gave the throne to his son-in-law, Cyrus. He did not die that year, as the *Seder Olam* suggested, but retired instead.

2. Cyrus ascended the Medo/Persian throne in 537 B.C., as a dowry for marrying Darius's daughter. In the first year of his reign, Cyrus sent Zerubbabal to Jerusalem with 49,697 people to rebuild the kingdom and the Temple. Cyrus reigned for seven years (not three years as given in the *Seder Olam*) and died in 529 B.C., leaving the throne to his son, Cambyses.

3. Artaxerxes (Cambyses), son of Cyrus, ascended the Medo/Persian throne in 529 B.C. He was mentally unstable, married two of his sisters, killed his brother, conquered Egypt, and then went stark raving mad. He came back to Persia and died of an accident with his sword in 522 B.C. He reigned seven years, not a half-year as suggested in the *Seder Olam*.

4. Darius (also called **Artaxerxes the Great** and **Ahasuerus**) began his reign in 521 B.C. That year, he sent spies to map the coast of Greece and planned the first Persian invasion. In 518 B.C., he divorced Vashti and married Esther. In 485 B.C., he declared that his son, Xerxes, would be the next king, and left to invade Greece. But he died later that year, having reigned for a full 36 years (not 14 years as listed in the *Seder Olam*). His death stopped the *"Seventy Weeks"* prophetic clock after Gabriel's first seven weeks (49 years). Esther was no longer queen. Israel no longer had an advocate on the Persian throne. What followed was a period that Gabriel described as *"troublous times."* The gap between the seventh and eighth weeks lasted 77 years. Gabriel started the *"seventy weeks"* clock again in 408 B.C., and stopped it again 434 years later, in A.D. 27. That was the Sabbatical Year that Jesus began His ministry. The gap between the sixty-ninth week and the seventieth week continues until this present generation. The world awaits the beginning of the seventieth week — the Tribulation Period.

5. Xerxes ascended the Persian throne in 485 B.C. He was not Darius, son of Esther, as given in the *Seder Olam*. He was the son of Vashti. King Xerxes launched a battle against Greece with 1,700,000 soldiers; 80,000 horses, plus camels, and chariots. The Greeks never forgot this Persian intrusion. It took them about 150 years to prepare for vengeance, and Alexander the Great carried it out.

6. Artaxerxes (son of Xerxes) was made viceroy with his father in 474 B.C. Nine years later (465 B.C.), upon the death of Xerxes, Artaxerxes ascended the Persian throne. In his 20th year

(445 B.C.), he sent Nehemiah to rebuild Jerusalem. Artaxerxes and his wife, Damaspia, both died on the same day in 425 B.C., leaving the throne to his son, Xerxes.

7. Xerxes (son of Artaxerxes) reigned one year (425 B.C.). When he was "roaring drunk" on a festival day, he was killed in his chamber while sleeping. His brother, Secundianus, born of Aloguna, a Babylonian woman, murdered him with the aid of his eunuch.

8. Secundianus (second son of Artaxerxes) took over the throne in 424 B.C. His army hated him for killing his own brother. He also plotted to kill Ochus, his other brother, but was killed instead.

9. Ochus/Darius (third son of Artaxerxes) lured Secundianus to meet him and make a treaty. In 423 B.C., Ochus captured and executed Secundianus for the murder of Xerxes. Ochus took the name **Darius** and reigned for 19 years. He died in 404 B.C., leaving the throne to his son, Arsicas. He gave his other son, Cyrus, rulership over the Agean seacoast provinces of Ionia and Lydia, east of Greece.

10. Arsicas/Artaxerxes (son of Ochus/Darius) ascended the Persian throne in 404 B.C., and reigned for 43 years. He captured and chained his brother, Cyrus, with a "gold" chain, out of respect for his royalty, and thought about executing him, but their mother persuaded him to release Cyrus and let him return to his kingdom. Arsicas/Artaxerxes had two sons: Ochus, who was legitimate; and Arsames, by a concubine, whom he dearly loved. In 361 B.C., Ochus had Arsames murdered, and when Artaxerxes heard about it, he died of grief. Ochus concealed his father's death for ten months, while he sent letters into all the provinces with his father's name and seal, telling them to accept Ochus as their king. After everyone acknowledged him as their king, he announced his father's death and commanded a public mourning to be made for him.

11. Ochus assumed the name of his father, **Artaxerxes** in 361 B.C., and immediately had all of his relatives killed to eliminate any competition for the throne. After he reigned 23 years, he was poisoned by Bagoas, his chief eunuch. Bagoas, being an Egyptian, killed him as revenge for killing Egypt's bull god, Apis. Bagoas cut the king's body into pieces and fed it to cats. As the most powerful man in the kingdom, Bagoas made Arses, the king's youngest son, king of Persia, then executed all of his brothers.

12. Arses was given the throne in 338 B.C., but the young king had no one left to help him and, therefore, had to rely on Bagoas to rule the kingdom. However, he secretly planned to have his revenge against Bagoas. In 336 B.C. (the third year of his reign), Bagoas found out that Arses was plotting revenge against him. He had the king and all his children killed. Then Bagoas set up Darius, the son of Arsames, the brother of Artaxerxes, as the new Persian king.

13. Darius claimed the crown as next of kin in 336 B.C. This was the Persian monarch who was defeated by Alexander in 331 B.C. He was not a son of Esther as recorded in the *Seder Olam*. In fact, none of Esther's children (if she ever had any), became Persian kings. Xerxes, who ascended the throne in 485 B.C., was the son of Vashti, not Esther. For a complete overview of the Persian kings, see *"A Chart of Six Millennia."*

In all, 13 Medo/Persian monarchs reigned over a period of 207 years. Why did Yose ben Halafta exclude 164 years from the Persian monarchy? Rabbi Simon Schwab admitted the problem on page 188 of his book, *Comparative Jewish Chronology*:

"It should have been possible that our Sages — for some unknown reason — had covered up a certain historic period and purposely eliminated and suppressed all records and other material pertaining thereto. If so, what might have been their compelling reason for so unusual a procedure? Nothing short of a Divine command could have prompted ... those saintly 'men of truth' to leave out completely from our annals

a period of 165 years [actually 164 years] and to correct all data and historic tables in such a fashion that the subsequent chronological gap could escape being noticed by countless generations, known to a few initiates only who were duty-bound to keep the secret to themselves."

Schwab and others went on to suggest that they might have falsified the dates in order to confuse anyone who might try to use the prophecies of Daniel to predict the time of the Messiah's coming. The truth is, sometime between A.D. 135-160, Yose ben Halafta, student of Rabbi Akiva and admirer of Bar Kokhbah, changed the dating so that Daniel's seventy weeks would point to Bar Kokhbah as their predicted Messiah, rather than Jesus. He deliberately pointed generations of Jews away from Jesus, the true Messiah!

How could Halafta get away with this? The answer may lie in Daniel 11:1-4. The prophet is told that the fourth Persian king would wage war on Greece. Daniel's heavenly visitor said:

"Also I in the first year of Darius the Mede, even I, stood to confirm and to strengthen him.

"And now will I shew thee the truth. Behold, there shall stand up yet **three kings** *[after Cyrus] in Persia; and the* **fourth** *shall be far richer than they all: and by his strength through his riches he shall stir up all against the realm of Grecia.*

"And a mighty king **[Alexander the Great]** *shall stand up, that shall rule with great dominion, and do according to his will.*

"And when he shall stand up, his kingdom shall be broken, and shall be divided toward the four winds of heaven ..." (Dan. 11:1-4).

Because no other kings are mentioned in this passage, Halafta took the opportunity to suggest that there were only five Persian monarchs — the four in the prophecy, plus the one who would be defeated. However, Persian and Greek historians list eight more — a total of 13 Medo/Persian kings reigning over a period of 207 years. Why were they left out of Daniel's vision in chapter 11? It is because of a timed prophecy in Daniel's ninth chapter. Remember the first seven weeks in the prophecy of the seventy weeks? God scheduled a gap between the seventh and eighth Sabbatical cycles, which Christian theologians seem to have overlooked. Beginning with the death of Ahasuerus in the Sabbatical Year of 485 B.C., the counting of *"weeks"* stopped for the next 77 years of *"troublous times"* (Dan. 9:25), and commenced again in 408 B.C. This is the reason only four Persian kings are mentioned in Daniel's last vision in chapter 11.

Others have also written that the prophets ended with Malachi, marking an historical turn in Israel's history. Ussher wrote: "They were no longer to expect a continual succession of prophets, as before. Therefore, Malachi, in the last words of his prophecy, exhorted them to hold fast to the law of Moses until Christ, that great prophet of the church, should appear with his forerunner, John the Baptist" (*Annals*, p. 160). Malachi concluded his book with a prophecy of the return of Elijah to introduce the Messiah. Therefore, the counting down to the Messiah began again, after 77 years of *"troublous times."*

The Julian Calendar

Various historical accounts of changes in the Roman calendar also make calculations somewhat difficult. With the founding of the city of Rome (753 B.C.), their royal calendar contained only ten months of 304 days per year. Each Roman New Year began in March. That is why the Latin term for September refers to "seven" — seven months from March. October means "eight"; November stands for "nine"; and December contains a Latin root for "ten." Early Church tradition puts the year of Jesus' birth in 753 A.U.C. (a Latin abbreviation for an expression that meant "years from the founding of the city of Rome"). The Roman year 753 A.U.C., was later changed to 1 B.C.

In 707 A.U.C. (46 B.C.), the Greek astronomer, Sosigenes, conferred with Julius Caesar to reform the Roman calendar into a more manageable dating system. At that time, Julius also moved the beginning of the year from March to January 1. He changed the number of days in the months to achieve a 365-day year. In order to "catch up" with the seasons, Julius Caesar interposed 23 intercalary days to February (a previously common practice every other year), and two months (of 67 days) between November and December, expressly for that one year. (*Vardi*, 1991, p. 238). This gave the year 46 B.C., an odd number of 445 days, and was called "the last year of confusion." I wish it were so!

In the distribution of these extra days through several months, Julius Caesar adopted a simple arrangement. He ordered that the first, third, fifth, seventh, ninth, and eleventh months (that is January, March, May, July, September and November), should each have 31 days, and the other months, 30 — except for February, which in common years should have only 29days, but every fourth year, 30 days.

This order was interrupted in 8 B.C., to gratify the vanity of Augustus Caesar, by giving the month bearing his name (August) as many days as July (which had been re-named after Julius Caesar in 44 B.C.). A day was taken from February and given to August; and in order that three months of 31 days might not come together, September and November were reduced to 30 days, and 31 given to October and December.

The additional day, which occurred every fourth year, was given to February (being the shortest month) and was inserted in the calendar between the 24th and 25th day. In our modern calendar, the intercalary leap-day is still added to February, but only as the 29th day.

The Julian calendar consisted of a cycle of three 365-day years, followed by a 366-day leap year. In 8 B.C., it was found that the priests in charge of computing the calendar had been adding leap years every three years instead of four, as decreed by Julius Caesar (*Vardi* 1991, p. 239), resulting in 12 leap years instead of eight. There were four too many. As a result of this error, no more leap years were added until A.D. 8. From the onset of the Julian calendar, the leap years were: 42 B.C., 39 B.C., 36 B.C., 33 B.C., 30 B.C., 27 B.C., 24 B.C., 21 B.C., 18 B.C., 15 B.C., 12 B.C., 9 B.C., A.D.

8, A.D. 12, — and every fourth year, thereafter.

In A.D. 525 (1278 A.U.C.), Dionysius Exiguus proposed the system of *Anno Domini*, which—after it was adopted by Venerable Bede (672-735), the father of English history — gradually spread through the Western Christian world. Years were numbered from the supposed date of the incarnation or "annunciation" of Jesus on March 25, although this soon changed to Christmas, then back to Annunciation Day (March 25) in Britain.

Dionysius Exiguus, also known as "Dennis the Little" (470-540), was a 6th-century Dacian monk born in Scythia Minor, in what is now Dobruja, Romania. He is the man credited with our modern dating system, using "A.D.," instead of the Roman "A.U.C."

The Gregorian Calendar

The Gregorian calendar, adopted on October 4, 1582, is now used universally for civil purposes. The Julian calendar was its predecessor in the Western world. The two calendars have identical month names and number of days in each month, differing only in the rule for leap years. The Julian calendar had a leap year every fourth year, while the Gregorian calendar has a leap year every fourth year, except century-years not exactly divisible by 400. The changeover from the Julian calendar to the Gregorian calendar occurred in October 1582, instituted by Pope Gregory XIII. Specifically, for dates on or before October 4, 1582, the Julian calendar is used; for dates on or after October 15, 1582, the Gregorian calendar is used. Thus, there is a ten-day gap in calendar dates: October 4, 1582 (Julian) was on Thursday, and October 15, 1582 (Gregorian) was on Friday, the next day. The omission of ten days of calendar dates was necessitated by the astronomical error built up by the Julian calendar over its many centuries of use, due to its too-frequent leap years. The Julian calendar introduced an error of one day every 128 years. So every 128 years the tropical year shifted one day backwards with respect to the calendar. Furthermore, the method for

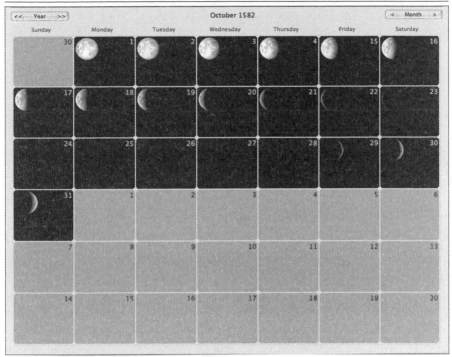

The Julian calendar is used for all dates prior to Thursday, October 4, 1582. Pope Gregory changed the next day, Friday, to October 15, the date for the beginning of the Gregorian calendar. *(Starry Night Pro)*

calculating the dates for Easter was inaccurate and needed to be refined. In order to remedy this, two steps were necessary: First, the Julian calendar had to be replaced by something more accurate; and secondly, the extra ten days that the Julian calendar had inserted had to be dropped.

The solution to the first problem was the Gregorian calendar. The solution to the second problem depended on the fact that it was felt that March 21 was the proper day for Vernal Equinox (because March 21 was the date for Vernal Equinox during the Council of Nicaea in A.D. 325). Therefore, the Gregorian calendar was calibrated to make March 21 the Vernal Equinox. At first, the changeover to the Gregorian calendar system occurred only in Roman Catholic countries. However, adoption of the Gregorian calendar in the rest of the world slowly progressed. For example, for England and its colonies, the change did not occur until September 1752.

I have prepared *A Chart of Six Millennia with Sabbatical Years and Jubilees*. It gives an overview of the centuries, and is arranged in columns of 49 years, so that the Sabbatical Years and Jubilees can be easily determined. Also, I have included the titles of the seven dispensations, many historical events, and the various eras of Church history as depicted in the letters to the seven churches. I have listed the kings of Israel and Judah, along with the Persian monarchs. I have changed the years that are missing in the Jewish calendar from black to gray, in order to show where they fit historically. Finally, I show the years of Daniel's *"seventy weeks"* as they fit in the calendar.

Conclusion

The authors of the second-century *Seder Olam* may have begun their chronology with good intentions, but their work became a dishonest cover-up of Daniel's seventy weeks — sixty-nine of which would lead up to Jesus as the Messiah, provided we recognize the 77-year gap between the seventh and eighth weeks. For Yose ben Halafta to shorten the period of the Persian monarchy from 207 years to only 53 years, goes beyond simple ignorance. He and his colleagues were determined that Jesus Christ would not be seriously considered as their Messiah. However, I think that someday soon, the Jews will be begging Jesus to come back. And when they do, He will!

The Legendary Saga of Jupiter and Saturn

The ancient Greeks had a legend about Jupiter and Saturn fighting over who would rule heaven and Earth. As the story goes, Saturn was king during Earth's "Golden Age." But he was evil, eating his own children to keep them from challenging his throne. However, when Jupiter was born, his mother hid him among friends, who nurtured him to manhood.

Saturn was head of the Titans, but Jupiter organized the Olympians and defeated his father. After making him release the children he had swallowed, Jupiter locked the Titans in Tartarus. The battle between these two immortals was seen in the night sky over the centuries. Their conjunctions, especially their triple conjunctions, became legendary. Saturn became the grim reaper, with a sickle in his hand, and Jupiter became a messiah figure.

The Greeks called Jupiter by his Greek name, Zeus, while Saturn was known as Cronus. In the letter to Pergamos (Revelation 2:13), Zeus/Jupiter is referred to as "Satan." Originally, however, it seems that the story was typical of the battle between Christ and Satan. With the development of idolatry during the days of the Tower of Babel, the story developed into the twisted legends of Babylonian, Egyptian, Greek and Roman mythologies.

The conjunctions of Jupiter and Saturn were known to every early civilization. Star gazers watched as Jupiter chased Saturn across the sky from constellation to constellation, and sometimes went round and round with him, in what was perceived as a continuing battle.

When Jupiter catches up with and crosses Saturn (something that happens about every 20 years), it is called a "conjunction." In Bible days, when a rare triple conjunction occurred, it was thought to be Jupiter's attempt to conquer Saturn and claim his throne. Intrigued with these conjunctions, I consulted my computer's astronomy program, locking on to Jupiter and watching the chase in a simulated night sky. Over a period of 6,000 years, from 3998 B.C., to A.D. 2001, I counted 303 conjunctions of Jupiter and Saturn.

Jupiter and Saturn in Creation Week

During Creation week, September 25-31, 4004 B.C., Jupiter was in Pisces. The newly created Adam could look up that first evening (sunset was on Friday, September 29, at 7:14 P.M.) and see Jupiter in the constellation Pisces rising above the eastern horizon. I can imagine that God might have said something like, "See that bright planet rising in the East. That is Jupiter in the constellation Pisces. Understand that it is a sign of the coming of My Son from among the people to whom Pisces will be assigned." As we now know, Pisces would be assigned to the house of Israel. In my thinking, God used the stars as signs (Gen. 1:14) — as the first Bible, so to speak, to explain various aspects of the human drama to Adam.

Precisely at midnight, Saturn arose above the eastern horizon. Adam could see the planet between the feet of Leo —

in the first of a triple conjunction with Regulus. I can imagine God saying, "Saturn is typical of Satan, an evil usurper, who will take the sceptre (the sickle in Leo's head) and rule over mankind. But Jupiter (My Son) will conquer him and save the world." This is essentially what Jacob said on his deathbed to his royal son, Judah:

"Judah is a lion's whelp: from the prey, my son, thou art gone up: he stooped down, he couched as a lion, and as an old lion; who shall rouse him up?

"The sceptre shall not depart from Judah, nor a lawgiver from between his feet, until Shiloh come; and unto him shall the gathering of the people be.

"Binding his foal unto the vine, and his ass's colt unto the choice vine; he washed his garments in wine, and his clothes in the blood of grapes" (Genesis 49:9-11).

Adam could see Jupiter rising in Pisces at sunset and watch as it traveled upward in the night sky. Then, at midnight, he could see Saturn rise in Leo, having Leo's sickle in his grasp. It could have been a fascinating lesson he learned that first night! For the next six years, Adam could watch as Jupiter pursued Saturn, getting closer and closer, until the royal planet caught up with the usurper in Virgo!

The First Conjunction

The very first conjunction of these two planets occurred on September 26, 3998 B.C., in the seventh year after Adam was created. I was somewhat surprised to see the two planets cross paths in the very first constellation — Virgo! To me, it is only fitting that these two should show up in the constellation that prophesies the coming of God's promised messiah as the "Seed" of the woman. Virgo represents the house of Israel and, more specifically, Mary of the tribe of Judah (daughter of the lion) — God's virgin bride, who was destined to give birth to the Messiah.

Furthermore, this first conjunction of Jupiter and Saturn

following Creation is in, not in the fifth, seventh or eleventh conjunctions, etc., but in Virgo — the very first one, thus telling us where to begin to read the story in this most ancient of scrolls — the night sky! This was God's first Bible — divinely inspired — 2,500 years before Moses wrote Genesis.

The First Triple Conjunction

Jupiter and Saturn's first triple conjunction occurred when Adam was 105 years old. It was on March 7, August 4, and September 2, 3899 BC, in Aquarius. The constellation of the water bearer is fitting, because it seems to foretell a time when God would pour out water upon the Earth in the form of a great Flood. Josephus tells us that Seth and his sons "were the inventors of that peculiar sort of wisdom which is concerned with the heavenly bodies, and their order. And that their inventions might not be lost before they were sufficiently known, upon Adam's prediction that the world was to be destroyed at one time by the force of fire, and at another time by the violence and quantity of water, they made two pillars; the one of brick, the other of stone; they inscribed their discoveries on them both, that in case the pillar or brick should be destroyed by the flood, the pillar of stone might remain, and exhibit those discoveries to mankind" (Antiquities of the Jews, bk. 1, ch. 2).

So, when Adam was 105 years old, he looked up at the night sky and observed Jupiter going back and forth over Saturn in the constellation of the Water Bearer pouring out his water. Maybe that is when he received a revelation that the world would someday be destroyed by a Flood.

The Birth of Enoch

Enoch was born in 3382 B.C., the year of the 32nd Jupiter/Saturn conjunction (August 5, 3382 B.C.) — this time in Virgo. Among these 32 conjunctions, only two were triple conjunctions, and both of them occurred in Aquarius, the water-bearer, foretelling the destructive power of a coming Flood. In the year of Enoch's birth, Jupiter and Saturn were fighting it out again — in the constellation Virgo. It is fitting that Virgo should be the constellation, since it depicts the birth of a messiah figure. This time, it was the birth of Enoch — a man who would walk with God for 365 years, then be raptured alive into heaven.

When Enoch was 19 years old, he saw a triple conjunction of these two warring planets in the constellation Aries. Jupiter had pursued Saturn through Aquarius and Pisces — and caught up with him on July 7, 3363 B.C., in Aries. Jupiter passed Saturn, then turned around and came back for another pass on August 26, 3363 B.C.; then turned around and passed him again the third time on January 12, 3362 B.C. Why did it take place in Aries? Perhaps because Aries represented the Lamb of God who would become victorious over Satan. Through the death of the sacrificial Lamb, Christ would save the world.

The Fallen Angels

When Noah was 142 years old, there was a triple conjunction in Pisces (2807 B.C.), and another 40 years later, in Leo (2767/66 B.C.). These two triple conjunctions seem to tell the story of the First and Second Advents of the Messiah. The triple conjunction in Pisces predicted the birth of the Messiah in the house of Jacob, while Satan tried to destroy Him. The triple conjunction in Leo depicts the Second Coming of Christ. As the Lion of the tribe of Judah, He will conquer Satan and rule over the Earth as King of kings. In this last constellation, Leo pounces on Hydra, the many-headed serpent, while Crater pours out a bowl of wrath upon the serpent and Corvus (the bird) eats his flesh — all of which is depicted in the book of Revelation.

It is possible that fallen angels helped to pervert these ancient constellations into idolatry — the worship of Satan. But, the prophecy that emerged from this triple conjunction in Pisces was that this would be the sign of the birth of the Messiah.

The Days of Noah

When Noah was 480 years old, another incredible triple conjunction occurred. There were three conjunctions of Jupiter and Saturn — on October 24, 2469 B.C., March 8, 2468 B.C., and May 13, 2468 B.C., in Virgo. That was the year that Noah was warned of a coming Flood. Over the next 120 years he built the Ark.

When Noah was 599 years old, another triple conjunction occurred — on December 11, 2350 B.C., February 3, 2349 B.C., and June 28, 2349 B.C., — also in Virgo. A few months later, the Flood destroyed the world! How much more perfect can it get? Noah looked up and saw these two triple conjunctions — both in Virgo! God warned him about the coming "birth pangs" of a new world, using the virgin to demonstrate a watery and painful birth ahead. It was as if God was saying, "Hurry, Noah! The water is about to break!"

The Birth of Moses

The famous fifteenth-century rabbi, Abarbanel (c. 1480), and other Jewish writers noted that a planetary conjunction of Jupiter and Saturn seemed to the Egyptians as a prediction for the birth of a great Jewish leader — as Josephus puts it, "who … would raise the Israelites … excel all men in virtue, and obtain a glory that would be remembered through all ages" (Antiquities, bk. 2, ch. 9). For this reason, it is reported that Pharaoh ordered all newborn Jewish males to be thrown into the Nile River. The conjunction in question was a single conjunction that occurred on January 28, 1575 B.C., in Sagittarius, just four years before the birth of Moses on February 19 (Adar 7), 1571 B.C. Because of errors in early calculations, astronomers thought the planetary conjunction occurred in Pisces and that it was a triple conjunction. The ancient legend was universally believed that a triple conjunction in Pisces would precede the birth of mankind's long-awaited Messiah. Each generation was looking for a Messiah — a virgin-born Son of God. He would conquer Satan and rule over mankind as King of kings.

A Pattern Emerges

The German astronomer, Johannes Kepler (died 1630) suggested that a Jupiter/Saturn conjunction coincided with the approach of each climacteric in human affairs — the revelation to Adam, the birth of Enoch, Noah's Flood, the birth of Moses, the birth of Cyrus, the birth of Christ, the birth of Charlemagne, the birth of Martin Luther, etc. As you can see thus far, I began to notice a pattern emerging from these conjunctions. Out of 303 conjunctions of Jupiter and Saturn, over the span of 6,000 years, only 36 encounters were triple conjunctions. Five of these were triple conjunctions in Pisces.

The Christmas Star

According to Joseph A. Seiss (1823-1904), in his book, *The Gospel in the Stars*, a specific triple conjunction would herald the Messiah. Jupiter and Saturn would meet each other in Pisces, the constellation assigned to Jacob, father of the Twelve Tribes. Seiss wrote, "Three things here come out with great clearness ... which deserve to be particularly noted: first, that the star-reading of a conjunction between Jupiter and Saturn betokened the birth of a great, virtuous, princely, and glorious operator among men, and the beginning or starting of a new order of things; second, that the sign in which the conjunction occurred indicated the people among whom the child was to be born; and third, that the children of Israel were already at that early period associated with the sign of Pisces."

Thus far, we have both Jewish rabbis and Egyptian astrologers concurring in the interpretation of the conjunctions of Jupiter and Saturn. Seiss continued, "Abarbanel, in his Commentary on Daniel, affirms it as a settled thing that the conjunction of Jupiter and Saturn always betokens some great event or beginning in human affairs, and because such a conjunction occurred in his day (Nov. 18, 1484 in Libra), he expected the speedy birth of the Messiah, as still expected by the Jews" (Seiss, p. 163).

Just prior to the birth of Christ, a triple conjunction of Jupiter and Saturn occurred in Pisces, on June 3, September 22, and December 13, 7 B.C. Please understand, out of 36 triple conjunctions, over a period of 6,000 years, only five triple conjunctions occurred in Pisces. The first triple conjunction happened in 2807 B.C., as we have previously noted. The second triple conjunction happened in 980 B.C., four years before Solomon died. The third triple conjunction happened in 861 B.C. The fourth one, in 7 B.C., is the special one before us, whom some have dubbed "the Christmas Star." The fifth triple conjunction of Jupiter and Saturn in Pisces happened in A.D. 967/68, which may have led to the organization of the European Knights, the quest for the Holy Grail and the Crusades to liberate the Holy Land.

During the Middle Ages, several orders of knighthood were founded by various monarchs across Europe. Some of these orders have persisted into the 20th century. Perhaps the best-known is the Order of the Garter, established by Edward III of England about 1348. In France, the Order of the Golden Fleece was founded in 1430. In Jerusalem, in A.D. 1118, a special religious order was established — the Poor Knights of Christ and of the Temple of Solomon, also known as the Knights Templar.

Out of five triple conjunctions in Pisces, only one fulfilled the ancient prophecy — the one in 7 B.C. Many speculations have been made about the Christmas Star, but the legend of a triple conjunction in Pisces seems to be the one that permeated the mythologies of every ancient civilization since the Flood.

The Births of Jacob and Esau

Jacob and Esau were twins, born in 1836 B.C., to Isaac and Rebekah. When they were two years old, a remarkable and historic triple conjunction occurred in Pisces. Remember, it was believed that a Pisces conjunction would herald the birth of the Messiah. Jupiter chased Saturn into Pisces and passed him on May 29, 1834 B.C. A few months later, on August 7, he came back for a second pass. Jupiter returned from retrograde motion for a third pass on December 6, 1834 B.C. The fact that this battle between the planets occurred in Pisces, signalled that Pisces was awarded to Jacob as his constellation. Furthermore, Jacob and Esau were twins. Is it not remarkable that Pisces represents two fish with their tails tied together!? Wow! Twin fish for twin boys — both tied together with umbilical cords in their mother's womb! Furthermore, Rebekah complained that they fought each other — even before birth! Again, this triple constellation points to the First Advent of Christ, who would come out of Jacob.

Jacob was 43 years old when he saw Jupiter chase Saturn into Leo for another 3-round fight. Jupiter's first conjunction happened on October 8, 1794 B.C., moved forward for a couple of months, then turned around and passed Saturn again on January 19, 1793. Moving in retrograde for another couple of months, Jupiter moved forward again for a third conjunction on May 1, 1793. This triple conjunction in Leo seems to be another prophecy of the Second Advent of Christ.

The Days of Moses

When Moses was 35 years old, he observed a triple conjunction of Jupiter and Saturn in Taurus, the bull. Taurus represents Christ as the coming Judge. Moses first noticed it on June 28, 1536 B.C., then again on October 30, and two months later, on January 9, 1535 B.C. Perhaps this battle between Jupiter and Saturn had an effect on him. He became restless in his role as the military general of the Egyptian forces. Five years later, he would slay an Egyptian caught persecuting the Israelites and bury him in the sand. The next day, while trying to settle an argument between two Hebrews, they turned upon him and asked, *"Who made you a judge over us?"* (Ex. 2:14). Fearing that his secret slaying would get back to Pharaoh, he fled to the wilderness of Midian.

The Exodus

Four years before the Exodus, Moses observed another battle between Jupiter and Saturn — this time, in the constellation Virgo. It seems that God was about to tell Moses to go back to Egypt, confront Pharaoh, and bring His virgin bride back to Mount Sinai for a divine wedding. On the night of November 21, 1496 B.C., Moses saw Jupiter pass Saturn in Virgo. A few months later, on March 8, 1495 B.C., Jupiter turned around and came back for another pass by Saturn. He continued to regress, turn and pass Saturn a third time on June 15, 1495 B.C. Shortly thereafter, Moses met God in the burning bush, went back to Egypt and, on Nissan 15, 1491 (Passover), brought the virgin bride back to Mount Sinai.

Nine Conjunctions in Virgo

Out of 36 triple conjunctions in 6,000 years, nine of them were in Virgo. They point to Israel, the virgin bride. We have already discussed the two prior to Noah's Flood and the one connected with the Exodus. Now let us look at the virgin bride in the days of the Judges. It was 1376 B.C., and Israel was under the oppression of the Moabites. Soon Ehud will liberate the Chosen People from Moab's oppression. The first conjunction occurred on January 9; the second on February 3, and the third on July 20, 1376 B.C. As with all Virgo triple conjunctions, it also pointed to another bride — Ruth. In 1323 B.C., Naomi and family moved to Moab and took Ruth, a beautiful virgin bride, into their family. She remained loyal to Naomi through trying circumstances and helped her regain her lost inheritance. Ruth married Boaz, her kinsman redeemer and member of the royal tribe of Judah. She would produce the lineage of the house of David and, eventually, the Messiah!

The next occurrence of a triple conjunction in Virgo happened in 523 B.C., the year before Ahaseurus became the king of Persia. Soon, he would seek out Esther, the virgin bride of Israel, and marry her. How fitting that the triple conjunction should be in Virgo! The first encounter between Jupiter and Saturn happened on December 16, 523 B.C.; the second on March 14, 522 B.C.; and the third on July 10, 522 B.C. The overriding prophecy points to Israel as the wife of Jehovah, but it is incredible that it should occur in the year before the new Persian king would begin his rule, and find himself in need of a queen.

The next triple conjunction in Virgo occurred in A.D. 1007, with Israel, the virgin bride, in exile. Europe was steeped in the Dark Ages; Bibles were chained to pulpits; European Christians were kept ignorant on theology and dependant on the Roman Church. The Bride of Christ was in a sorry state, though they thought that God had forsaken His Israelite bride for a Gentile bride. In 1007, with riots across France, many Jews were killed and many were forced to convert to Christianity. Most of these converts returned to Judaism a few years later, after the riots had ceased. In 1012, when a priest converted to Judaism in Mainz, Germany, the Jews were forced to convert or leave. However, the expulsion order was withdrawn within the year. Many Jews were killed when the Berbers conquered Cordova and divided Spain into provinces. Soon, the Crusaders would launch a war in the Holy Land and set up a Crusader kingdom.

The latest triple conjunction in Virgo happened in 1980/81, 33 years after the birth of the state of Israel. The first conjunction occurred on December 31, 1981; the second on March 3, 1981; and the third on July 23, 1981. At the age of 33, the virgin bride awaits her Messiah. In 1981, a nuclear reactor near Baghdad was destroyed by Israeli planes. Iraq, which had always sent troops into the wars against Israel, was threatening to gain a nuclear arms capacity. Soon, all of the prophecies depicted by these triple conjunctions will be fulfilled. Christ will defeat Satan and chain him in Tartarus — the bottomless pit! We await the establishment of the kingdom of heaven on Earth.

A Chart of Six Millennia

Major Historical Events,
Daniel's 70 Weeks,
Sabbatical Years and Jubilees,
Jupiter/Saturn Conjunctions,
243 Missing Years in the Jewish
Calendar, and more . . .

QUESTIONABLE DATES AND NAMES IN RED
The following names and dates, shown in red, are from the *Book of Jubilees*, containing some errors in dating, but are included in this chart to show an early Jewish dating scheme using Sabbatical cycles (called "weeks") and 49-year Jubilee cycles. The book claims that it was dictated by an angel and penned by Moses during his stay atop Mount Sinai. It is a bogus, yet clever attempt to cover human history from Creation to the Exodus. It is important to note that the weeks and Jubilees in this book do not correspond to the Sabbatical Years and Jubilees from Joshua to the present.

S=Sabbatical Year. J=Jubilee.

4004/03 BC (J1) **Adam was created** on the 6th day. This is
4003/02   marked on the Jewish calendar as 1AM. (Anno
4002/01   Mundi, Latin for "from Creation").
4001/00   On the sixth day of the second week, God brought
4000/99   the animals for Adam to name. This lasted for five
3999/98   days. On the 13th day, God made Eve.
3998/97 S   Jupiter and Saturn's first conjunction after Creation
3997/96   was on Sept. 26, 3998 BC, in Virgo. They will have a
3996/95   conjunction about every 20 years, but a triple con-
3995/94   junction is rare.
3994/93
3993/92

The First Dispensation
of Innocence
ended in the Fall of Adam

3991/90 S
3990/89   Adam entered the Garden 40 days after his recov-
3989/88   ery from surgery. Eve entered Eden 80 days after
3988/87   she was made from Adam's rib. After exactly 7
3987/86   years, on the 17th day of the 2nd month, the ser-
3986/85   pent beguiled Eve (3997 BC).

3985/84
3984/83 S
3983/82
3982/81
3981/80
3980/79
3979/**78**   Jupiter/Saturn conj. - May 5, 3978 in Gemini
3978/77
3977/76 S
3976/75
3975/74   Adam's name means "red," as in the ground from
3974/73   which he was made. The names of the first 10 gen-
3973/72   erations have meanings that represent a prophetic
3972/71   scenario of 7 millennia. Adam represents the first
3971/70   thousand years. The shame of his guilt is alluded
3970/69 S   to in the meaning of his name. He lived 930 years of
3969/68   the first millennium.
3968/67   **Genesis 5:**
3967/66   *1. This is the book of the generations of Adam. In*
3966/65   *the day that God created man, in the likeness of*
3965/64   *God made he him;*
3964/63   *2. Male and female created he them; and blessed*
3963/62 S   *them, and called their name Adam, in the day when*
3962/61   *they were created.*
3961/60
3960/59
3959/58   Jupiter/Saturn conj. - Dec. 8, 3959 in Capricorn
3958/57
3957/56
3956/55 S   The 49th year concludes the first Jubilee period.
3955/54 J2   The 50th year celebrates the first Jubilee and com-
3954/53   mences the 2nd Jubilee period. They appear in this
3953/52   chart as "red numbers" because they are not to be
3952/51   trusted.
3951/50
3950/49
3949/48 S
3948/47
3947/46
3946/45
3945/44
3944/43
3943/42
3942/41 S
3941/40   In the 3rd week of the 2nd Jubilee, Eve gave birth
3940/39   to Cain.
3939/**38**   Jupiter/Saturn conj. - July 26, 3938 in Virgo
3938/37
3937/36

The Second Dispensation
of Conscience
ended with the Flood of Noah

Saturday Evening/Sunday, September 24/25, 4004 B.C. is a choice date for the first day of Creation. Three months later, on January 1, the year 4003 BC began. Therefore, 4004 BC was not a full year. In this chart 315 Jupiter/Saturn conjunctions (J/S) are listed, including 37 triple conjunctions, along with the constellation in which each conjunction occurred. Possibly as many as seven of these triple conjunctions occurred in Pisces. The dates are: 2807 BC, 1834 BC, 981 BC, 862 BC, 7 BC, AD 967 and AD 1821.

3936/35		
3935/34	S	
3934/33		In the 4th week of the 2nd Jubilee, Eve gave birth
3933/32		to Abel.
3932/31		
3931/30		
3930/29		
3929/28		
3928/27	S	
3927/26		In the 5th week of the 2nd Jubilee, Eve gave birth
3926/25		to a daughter, Awan.
3925/24		
3924/23		
3923/22		
3922/21		
3921/20	S	
3920/19		
3919/**18**		Jupiter/Saturn conj. - Mar. 13, 3918 in Gemini
3918/17		
3917/16		
3916/15		
3915/14		
3914/13	S	
3913/12		
3912/11		
3911/10		
3910/09		
3909/08		
3908/07		
3907/06	S	
3906/05	J3	In the 1st year of the 3rd Jubilee Cain killed Abel.
3905/04		Adam and Eve grieved for 4 weeks (28 years).
3904/03		
3903/02		
3902/01		
3901/00		
3900/**99**	S	Jupiter and Saturn's first triple conjunction was on
3899/98		Mar. 7, Aug. 4, & Sept. 2, 3899 BC, in Aquarius
3898/97		
3897/96		
3896/95		
3895/94		
3894/93		
3893/92	S	
3892/91		
3891/90		
3890/89		
3889/88		
3888/87		

3887/86		
3886/85	S	
3885/84		
3884/83		
3883/82		
3882/81		
3881/80		
3880/79		
3879/**78**	S	Jupiter/Saturn conj. - Oct. 18, 3879 in Libra
3878/77		
3877/76		
3876/75		
3875/**74**		**Adam begat Seth** (4th year of the 5th week)
3874/73		**Genesis 5:**
3873/72		*3. And Adam lived an hundred and thirty years, and*
3872/71	S	*begat a son in his own likeness, and after his image;*
3871/70		*and called his name Seth:*
3870/69		*4. And the days of Adam after he had begotten Seth*
3869/68		*were eight hundred years: and he begat sons and*
3868/67		*daughters:*
3867/66		*5. And all the days that Adam lived were nine hun-*
3866/65		*dred and thirty years: and he died.*
3865/64	S	
3864/63		In the 6th week of the 3rd Jubilee, Eve gave birth to
3863/62		a daughter, Azura.
3862/61		
3861/60		
3860/**59**		Jupiter/Saturn conj. - June 17, 3859 in Gemini
3859/58		
3858/57	S	Seth's name means "substitute." He seems to
3857/56	J4	represent the 2nd millennium, in which the Flood
3856/55		washed away the wicked and started again with a
3855/54		substitute human race.
3854/53		
3853/52		
3852/51		
3851/50	S	
3850/49		
3849/48		
3848/47		
3847/46		
3846/45		
3845/44		
3844/43	S	
3843/42		
3842/41		
3841/40		
3840/39		Jupiter/Saturn conj. - Dec. 29, 3840 in Aquarius
3839/38		

The Jewish calendar claims to date its years from the creation of Adam in what became known as the 7th month (*Sept* is Latin for "seven"). The *Seder Olam Rabbah* has Adam being created in 1 AM (*Anno Mundi*) without allowing for the first 12 months of his life. This accounts for the first of 243 years missing from the Jewish calendar.

According to the *Book of Jubilees*, Cain was born around 3941 (in the 3rd week of the 2nd Jubilee); Abel was born around 3934 (in the 4th week of the 2nd Jubilee); and a daughter, Awan, was born around 3927 (in

3838/37		3789/88	
3837/36 s		3788/87 s	
3836/35		3787/86	
3835/34		3786/85	
3834/33		3785/84	
3833/32		3784/83	
3832/31		3783/82	
3831/30		3782/81	
3830/29 s		3781/**80** s	Jupiter/Saturn - second triple conjunction on Apr. 7,
3829/28		**3780**/79	July 18, & Oct. 18, 3780 in Aquarius
3828/27		3779/78	In the 5th week of the 5th Jubilee Seth took his sis-
3827/26		3778/77	ter, Azura, to be his wife.
3826/25		3777/76	
3825/24		3776/75	
3824/23		3775/74	
3823/22 s		3774/73 s	
3822/21		3773/72	
3821/20		3772/71	
3820/**19**	Jupiter/Saturn conj. - Aug. 12, 3819 in Libra	3771/70	
3819/18		**3770/69**	**Seth begat Enos** (4th year of the 6th week)
3818/17		3769/68	**Genesis 5:**
3817/16		3768/67	*6. And Seth lived an hundred and five years, and*
3816/15 s		3767/66 s	*begat Enos:*
3815/14		3766/65	*7. And Seth lived after he begat Enos eight hundred*
3814/13		3765/64	*and seven years, and begat sons and daughters:*
3813/12		3764/63	*8. And all the days of Seth were nine hundred and*
3812/11		3763/62	*twelve years: and he died.*
3811/10		3762/61	
3810/09	Cain took his sister, Awan, to be his wife and she	3761/60	
3809/08 s	gave birth to Enoch at the close of the 4th Jubilee.	**3760**/59 s	Jupiter/Saturn conj. - Oct. 30, 3760 in Libra
3808/07 J5	At the beginning of the 5th Jubilee, Cain built hous-	3759/58 J6	
3807/06	es and a city named after his son, Enoch.	3758/57	Enos means "another," also "mortal." He seems to
3806/05		3757/56	represent the 3rd millennium, at the beginning of
3805/04		3756/55	which God chose a special lineage (Abraham) for
3804/03		3755/54	producing the promised Messiah.
3803/02		3754/53	
3802/01 s		3753/52 s	
3801/00		3752/51	
3800/**99**	Jupiter/Saturn conj. - May 2, 3799 in Cancer	3751/50	
3799/98		3750/49	
3798/97		3749/48	
3797/96		3748/47	
3796/95		3747/46	
3795/94 s		3746/45 s	
3794/93		3745/44	
3793/92		3744/43	
3792/91		3743/42	
3791/90		3742/41	
3790/89		3741/**40**	Jupiter/Saturn conj. - Aug. 8, 3740 in Cancer

the 5th week of the 2nd Jubilee). She became Cain's wife. After Cain killed Abel, he left the area and began to produce children. After the birth of Seth (another male heir), Adam and Eve produced sons and daughters (Gen. 5:4). The *Book of Jubilees* suggests only 9 sons. How much of the *Book of Jubilees* is bogus information cannot be determined, but the dates in the book are obviously in error. The names of the women may also be concocted, but we include them here as possibly emerging from some ancient Jewish source.

3740/39	
3739/38 s	
3738/37	
3737/36	
3736/35	
3735/34	
3734/33	
3733/32	
3732/31 s	
3731/30	
3730/29	
3729/28	
3728/27	
3727/26	
3726/25	
3725/24 s	
3724/23	
3723/22	
3722/21	
3721/20	Jupiter/Saturn conj. - Jan. 30, 3720 BC in Pisces
3720/19	
3719/18	
3718/17 s	
3717/16	
3716/15	
3715/14	
3714/13	
3713/12	
3712/11	
3711/10 s	
3710/09 J7	
3709/08	
3708/07	
3707/06	
3706/05	
3705/04	
3704/03 s	
3703/02	
3702/01	
3701/00	
3700/99	Jupiter/Saturn conj. - Sep. 3, 3700 BC in Scorpio
3699/98	
3698/97	
3697/96 s	
3696/95	In the 3rd week of the 7th Jubilee Enos took his
3695/94	sister, Noam, to be his wife.
3694/93	
3693/92	
3692/91	

3691/90	
3690/89 s	
3689/88	
3688/87	
3687/86	
3686/85	
3685/84	
3684/83	
3683/82 s	
3682/81	
3681/80	Jupiter/Saturn conj. - Jun. 22, 3680 BC in Leo
3680/79	**Enos begat Cainan** (3rd year of the 5th week)
3679/78	**Genesis 5:**
3678/77	9. And Enos lived ninety years, and begat Cainan:
3677/76	10. And Enos lived after he begat Cainan eight hundred
3676/75 s	and fifteen years, and begat sons and daughters:
3675/74	11. And all the days of Enos were nine hundred and
3674/73	five years: and he died.
3673/72	
3672/71	
3671/70	Cainan means "a fixed nest." His name seems to
3670/69	represent a prophetic view of the Promised Land,
3669/68 s	which the Chosen People settled in the mid-3rd
3668/67	millennium and established the Davidic kingdom
3667/66	at the beginning of the 4th millennium.
3666/65	
3665/64	
3664/63	
3663/62	
3662/61 s	
3661/60 J8	Jupiter/Saturn conj. - Dec. 7, 3661 BC in Pisces
3660/59	
3659/58	A legend was told that Saturn ate his children, but
3658/57	Jupiter was hidden by his mother until he came of
3657/56	age and defeated his father. In Greek culture Saturn
3656/55	was head of the Titans. He ruled the earth during its
3655/54 s	golden era. Jupiter was head of the Olympians. It is
3654/53	said that he conquered the Titans and locked them
3653/52	in Tartarus. The conjunctions of Jupiter and Saturn
3652/51	appeared as "wars" in heaven. This may have been
3651/50	why Egyptian astrologers believed that these two
3650/49	planets foretold the rise of the Jewish Messiah,
3649/48	and told Pharaoh to kill the newborn male Jews.
3648/47 s	
3647/46	
3646/45	
3645/44	
3644/43	
3643/42	

Adam means "red." Seth means "substitute." Enos means "mortal." Cainan means "nest." Mahalaleel means "Praise of God." Jared means "descent." Enoch means "initiated." Methuselah means "man of the dart or javelin" (perhaps referring to the coming Tribulation). Lamech has no known meaning. Noah means "rest." Each name seems to refer to the prophetic events of human history, from the first millennium to the messianic era. In the first millennium, Adam sinned. His name "red" denotes a blushing face — ashamed of his sin. In the second

3642/41	3593/92
3641/40 S Jupiter/Saturn conj. - Nov. 24, 3641 BC in Scorpio	3592/91 S
3640/39	3591/90
3639/38	3590/89
3638/37	3589/88
3637/36	3588/87
3636/35	3587/86
3635/34	3586/85
3634/33 S	3585/84 S
3633/32	3584/83
3632/31	3583/82
3631/30	3582/81
3630/29	3581/80 Jupiter/Saturn conj. - Sept. 27, 3581 BC in Scorpio
3629/28	3580/79
3628/27	3579/78
3627/26 S	3578/77 S
3626/25	3577/76
3625/24	3576/75
3624/23	3575/74
3623/22	3574/73
3622/21	3573/72
3621/20 Jupiter/Saturn conj. - May 7, 3620 BC in Leo	3572/71
3620/19 S	3571/70 S
3619/18	3570/69
3618/17	3569/68
3617/16	3568/67
3616/15	3567/66
3615/14	3566/65
3614/13	3565/64
3613/12 S In the close of the 8th Jubilee Cainan took his sis-	3564/63 S
3612/11 J9 ter, Mualeleth, to be his wife.	3563/62 J10
3611/10	3562/61 Jupiter/Saturn conj. - Aug. 12, 3561 BC in Leo
3610/09 Cainan begat Mahalaleel (3rd year of the 1st	3561/60
3609/08 week of the 9th Jubilee)	3560/59
3608/07 **Genesis 5:**	3559/58
3607/06 *12. And Cainan lived seventy years and begat Mahalaleel:*	3558/57
3606/05 S *13. And Cainan lived after he begat Mahalaleel eight hun-*	3557/56 S
3605/04 *dred and forty years, and begat sons and daughters:*	3556/55 In the 2nd week of the 10th Jubilee Mahalaleel took
3604/03 *14. And all the days of Cainan were nine hundred*	3555/54 to wife Dinah, daughter of Barakiel, his father's
3603/02 *and ten years: and he died.*	3554/53 brother.
3602/01 Jupiter/Saturn conj. - Mar. 14, 3601 BC in Pisces	3553/52
3601/00	3552/51
3600/99	3551/50
3599/98 S Mahalaleel means "praise of God." His name	3550/49 S
3598/97 seems to represent a prophetic view of the 4th	3549/48
3597/96 millennium, in which Solomon built the Temple for	3548/47
3596/95 worship and praise.	3547/46
3595/94	3546/45
3594/93	**3545/44**

millennium the Flood destroyed the human race and left a substitute in Noah's family. In the third millennium the Jews occupied the land of Cainan. In the fourth millennium Solomon built the Temple for praise and worship. In the fifth millennium Jesus came. He died and rose again for our salvation. In the sixth millennium, Christians awaited the Tribulation Period. Methuselah also means "when he is gone, it will come," denoting God's patience. In the seventh millennium, Christ will establish His kingdom — the great Sabbath Rest.

3544/43   **Mahalaleel begat Jared** (6th year of 3rd week)

3543/42 s

3542/41   Jupiter/Saturn conj. - Jan 24, 3541 BC in Pisces

3541/40   **Genesis 5:**

3540/39   *15. And Mahalaleel lived sixty and five years, and*

3539/38   *begat Jared:*

3538/37   *16. And Mahalaleel lived after he begat Jared eight*

3537/36   *hundred and thirty years, and begat sons and*

3536/35 s   *daughters:*

3535/34   *17. And all the days of Mahalaleel were eight hun-*

3534/33   *dred ninety and five years: and he died.*

3533/32

3532/31   Jared was born when Adam was 460 years old. His

3531/30   name means "Descent," because of the descent

3530/29   of the fallen angels in his days. He also seems to

3529/28 s   represent a prophecy of the descent of Christ at

3528/27   the beginning of the fifth millennium. The following

3527/26   names of Enoch, Methuselah, Lamech and Noah

3526/25   also seem to represent prophecies — the events

3525/24   that will attend the return of Christ.

3524/23

3523/22

3522/21 s   Jupiter/Saturn conj. - Dec. 18, 3522 BC in Sagit-

3521/20   When Adam was approaching his 500th year, fallen

3520/19   angels descended to Mount Hermon and began to

3519/18   corrupt the human race, inserting the "seed" of the

3518/17   serpent into the human genome, producing giants.

3517/16   These fallen angels were the gods of Greek mythol-

3516/15   ogy known as "Titans." Their offspring, the "Neph-

3515/14 s   ilim" were known in Greece as "Olympians."

3514/13 J11

3513/12   Flavius Josephus (c. A.D. 90) wrote: "Many angels

3512/11   of God accompanied with women, and begat sons

3511/10   that proved unjust, and despisers of all that was

3510/09   good, on account of the confidence they had in their

3509/08   own strength; for the tradition is, that these men did

3508/07 s   what resembled the acts of those whom the Gre-

3507/06   cians call giants. But Noah was very uneasy at what

3506/05   they did." (*Antiquities of the Jews*, bk 1, ch 3)

3505/04

3504/03

3503/02

3502/01   Jupiter/Saturn conj. - Jun. 27, 3501 BC in Leo

3501/00 s

3500/99

3499/98

3498/97

3497/96

3496/95

3495/94

3494/93 s

3493/92   In the 4th week of the 11th Jubilee Jared took to

3492/91   wife Baraka, daughter of Rasujal, his father's

3491/90   brother.

3490/89

3489/88

3488/87

3487/86 s

3486/85

3485/84

3484/83

3483/82   Jupiter/Saturn conj. - May 4, 3482 BC in Aries

3482/81   According to the Book of Jubilees, in the 4th year

3481/80   of the 5th week of the 11th Jubilee Jared and Ba-

3480/79 s   raka gave birth to Enoch. Here is a 100-year error

3479/78   in the *Book of Jubilees*. The Bible has Enoch being

3478/77   born in 3383 BC (622 AM), not 3483 BC (522 AM) as

3477/76   given in the *Book of Jubilees*.

3476/75

3475/74

3474/73

3473/72 s

3472/71

3471/70

3470/69

3469/68

3468/67

3467/66

3466/65 s

3465/64 J12

3464/63

3463/62

3462/61   Jupiter/Saturn conj. - Oct. 19, 3462 BC in Sagittarius

3461/60

3460/59

3459/58 s

3458/57

3457/56

3456/55

3455/54

3454/53

3453/52

3452/51 s

3451/50

3450/49

3449/48

3448/47

3447/46

Until Jared, the dates in the *Book of Jubilees* corresponded with the Bible. But the *Book of Jubilees* says that Jared was 62 years old when Enoch was born. The Bible says that Jared was 162 years old. This fundamental error gets worse from here, showing that this is not just a translator's mistake. There is an error of 122 years in the birth of Methuselah and another error of 133 years in the birth of Lamech. Furthermore, *Jubilees* has Lamech only 49 years old, instead of 182 years, when Noah was born. The *Book of Jubilees* has Noah born around 701 to 707

3446/45		3397/96	
3445/44 s		3396/95 s	
3444/43		3395/94	
3443/42		3394/93	
3442/41	Jupiter/Saturn conj. - Sept. 27, 3442 BC in Virgo	3393/92	
3441/40		3392/91	
3440/39		3391/90	**Genesis 5:**
3439/38		3390/89	*18. And Jared lived an hundred sixty and two years,*
3438/37 s		3389/88 s	*and he begat Enoch:*
3437/36		3388/87	*19. And Jared lived after he begat Enoch eight hun-*
3436/35		3387/86	*dred years, and begat sons and daughters:*
3435/34		3386/85	*20. And all the days of Jared were nine hundred*
3434/33		3385/84	*sixty and two years: and he died.*
3433/32		3384/83	
3432/31		**3383/82**	**Jared begat Enoch.**
3431/30 s		3382/81 s	Enoch's name means "dedicated one." He was
3430/29		3381/80	born in the year of a Jupiter/Saturn conjunction,
3429/28		3380/79	which occurred on Aug. 5, 3382 BC, in Virgo. The
3428/27		3379/78	German astronomer, Johannes Kepler (d.1630)
3427/26		3378/77	suggested that a Jupiter/Saturn conjunction co-
3426/25		3377/76	incided with the approach of each climacteric in
3425/24		3376/75	human affairs - the revelation to Adam, the birth of
3424/23 s		3375/74 s	Enoch, Noah's Flood, the birth of Moses, the birth
3423/22	Jupiter/Saturn conj. - Mar. 10, 3422 BC in Aries	3374/73	of Cyrus, the birth of Christ, the birth of Charle-
3422/21	The Book of Jubilees says that Enoch took a wife,	3373/72	magne, the birth of Luther, etc.
3421/20	Edna, in the 7th week of the 12th Jubilee.	3372/71	Enoch was taken alive into heaven, and seems
3420/19		3371/70	to represent a prophecy — the future Rapture of
3419/18		3370/69	believers. Christ will descend from heaven with a
3418/17	Edna gave birth to Methuselah in 3418/17 BC, in the	3369/68	shout. The dead will be raised and we who are alive
3417/16 s	6th year of this week. But the Bible has Methuselah	3368/67 s	will be translated - taken alive into heaven.
3416/15 J13	being born a hundred years later, in 3318/17 BC.	3367/66 J14	
3415/14	This is a 122-year error.	3366/65	
3414/13		3365/64	
3413/12		3364/63	Jupiter/Saturn triple conjunction - July 7, Aug. 26,
3412/11		3363/62	3363 BC, and Jan. 12, 3362 in Aries
3411/10		3362/61	According to the Book of Jubilees, in the 14th Ju-
3410/09 s		3361/60 s	bilee Methuselah took a wife, also named Edna,
3409/08		3360/59	the daughter of Azrial, the daughter of his father's
3408/07		3359/58	brother.
3407/06		3358/57	
3406/05		3357/56	
3405/04		3356/55	
3404/03		3355/54	
3403/02 s	Jupiter/Saturn conj. - Jan. 10, 3402 BC in Sagittarius	3354/53 s	
3402/01		3353/52	In 3353/52 BC, the 1st year of the 3rd week of the
3401/00		3352/51	14th Jubilee Methuselah and Edna gave birth to
3400/99		3351/50	Lamech. But the Bible has Lamech born in 3131/30
3399/98		3350/49	BC. Here, Methuselah is 65, but the Bible says he
3398/97		3349/48	was 187 years old when Lamech was born.

AM (3303 - 3297 BC), instead of the biblical 1056 AM (2949/48 BC). This puts the *Book of Jubilees* in as much as 355 years at variance with the dates of the Bible.

w/ Sabbatical Years & Jubilees

Year		Note	Year		Note
3348/47			3299/98		Methuselah means "man of the dart, spear or jav-
3347/46	S		3298/97	S	elin." His name seems to represent a prophecy —
3346/45			3297/96		the Tribulation Period that will follow the rapture.
3345/44			3296/95		His name alludes to an instrument of war.
3344/43		Jupiter/Saturn conj.-Nov. 6, 3343 BC in Sagittarius	3295/94		
3343/42			3294/93		
3342/41			3293/92		
3341/40			3292/91		
3340/39	S		3291/90	S	
3339/38			3290/89		
3338/37			3289/88		
3337/36			3288/87		
3336/35			3287/86		
3335/34			3286/85		
3334/33			3285/84		
3333/32	S		3284/83	S	Jupiter/Saturn conj. - Jan. 29, 3283 BC in Sagittarius
3332/31			3283/82		
3331/30			3282/81		
3330/29			3281/80		
3329/28			3280/79		
3328/27			3279/78		
3327/26			3278/77		
3326/25	S		3277/76	S	
3325/24			3276/75		
3324/23			3275/74		
3323/22		Jupiter/Saturn triple conjunction - Nov. 12, 3323 BC,	3274/73		
3322/21		Feb 1, 3322 and Jun 3, 3322 in Virgo	3273/72		
3321/20			3272/71		
3320/19			3271/70		
3319/18	S		3270/69	S	
3318/17	J15	**Enoch begat Methuselah.**	3269/68	J16	
3317/16		**Genesis 5:**	3268/67		
3316/15		*21. And Enoch lived sixty and five years, and begat*	3267/66		
3315/14		*Methuselah:*	3266/65		
3314/13		*22. And Enoch walked with God after he begat Me-*	3265/64		
3313/12		*thuselah three hundred years, and begat sons and*	3264/63		Jupiter/Saturn conj. - Aug. 29, 3263 BC in Virgo
3312/11	S	*daughters:*	3263/62	S	
3311/10		*23. And all the days of Enoch were three hundred*	3262/61		
3310/09		*sixty and five years:*	3261/60		
3309/08		*24. And Enoch walked with God: and he was not;*	3260/59		
3308/07		*for God took him.*	3259/58		
3307/06			3258/57		
3306/05			3257/56		
3305/04	S		3256/55	S	
3304/03		Jupiter/Saturn conj. - Apr. 23, 3303 BC in Taurus	3255/54		
3303/02		In the 3rd week of the 15th Jubilee Methuselah and	3254/53		
3302/01		Edna gave birth to Noah (3304/03 BC). But the Bible	3253/52		
3301/00		has him born in 2949/48 BC.	3252/51		
3300/99			3251/50		

3250/49	3201/00
3249/48 s	3200/99 s
3248/47	3199/98
3247/46	3198/97
3246/45	3197/96
3245/44	3196/95
3244/43 Jupiter/Saturn conj. - Mar. 3, 3243 BC in Taurus	3195/94
3243/42	3194/93
3242/41 s	3193/92 s
3241/40	3192/91
3240/39	3191/90
3239/38	3190/89
3238/37	3189/88
3237/36	3188/87
3236/35	3187/86
3235/34 s	3186/85 s
3234/33	3185/84 Jupiter/Saturn conj. - June 7, 3184 BC in Taurus
3233/32	3184/83
3232/31	3183/82
3231/30	3182/81
3230/29	3181/80
3229/28	3180/79
3228/27 s	3179/78 s
3227/26	3178/77
3226/25	3177/76
3225/24	3176/75
3224/23 Jupiter/Saturn conj. - Nov. 22, 3224 BC in Capricorn	3175/74
3223/22	3174/73
3222/21	3173/72
3221/20 s	3172/71 s
3220/19 J17	3171/70 J18
3219/18	3170/69
3218/17	3169/68
3217/16	3168/67
3216/15	3167/66
3215/14	3166/65
3214/13 s	3165/64 s Jupiter/Saturn conj. - Feb. 13, 3164 BC in Capricorn
3213/12	3164/63
3212/11	3163/62
3211/10	3162/61
3210/09	3161/60
3209/08	3160/59
3208/07	3159/58
3207/06 s	3158/57 s
3206/05	3157/56
3205/04	3156/55
3204/03 Jupiter/Saturn conj. - July 3, 3203 BC in Virgo	3155/54
3203/02	3154/53
3202/01	3153/52

3152/51		3103/02		
3151/50 s		3102/01 s		
3150/49		3101/00		
3149/48		3100/99		
3148/47		3099/98		
3147/46		3098/97		
3146/45		3097/96		
3145/44		3096/95		
3144/43 s	Jupiter/Saturn conj. - Sept. 23, 3144 BC in Virgo	3095/94 s		
3143/42		3094/93		
3142/41		3093/92		
3141/40		3092/91		
3140/39		3091/90		
3139/38	**Genesis 5:**	3090/89		
3138/37	25. And Methuselah lived an hundred eighty and	3089/88		
3137/36 s	seven years, and begat Lamech.	3088/87 s		
3136/35	26. And Methuselah lived after he begat Lamech	3087/86		
3135/34	seven hundred eighty and two years, and begat	3086/85		
3134/33	sons and daughters:	3085/84	Jupiter/Saturn conj. - July 21, 3084 BC in Virgo
3133/32	27. And all the days of Methuselah were nine hun-	3084/83		
3132/31	dred sixty and nine years: and he died.	3083/82		
3131/30	**Methuselah begat Lamech.**	3082/81		
3130/29 s	Lamech's name has no known meaning, but he	3081/80 s		
3129/28	lived 777 years. It seems that his name represents	3080/79		
3128/27	a prophecy — the glorious appearing of Christ at	3079/78		
3127/26	the battle of Armageddon.	3078/77		
3126/25		3077/76		
3125/24	Jupiter/Saturn conj. - Apr. 15, 3124 BC in Taurus	3076/75		
3124/23		**3075/74**	Adam died when he was 930 years old.
3123/22 s		3074/73 s	In the Book of Jubilees Cain died after Adam in the
3122/21 J19		3073/72 J20	same year. His house fell on him. He was killed by
3121/20		3072/71	stones falling on him.
3120/19		3071/70		
3119/18		3070/69		
3118/17		3069/68		
3117/16		3068/67		
3116/15 s		3067/66 s		
3115/14		3066/65	Jupiter/Saturn triple conjunction - July 20, 3065,
3114/13		3065/64	Dec. 6, 3065 and Feb. 1, 3064 BC in Gemini
3113/12		3064/63		
3112/11		3063/62		
3111/10		3062/61		
3110/09		3061/60		
3109/08 s		3060/59 s		
3108/07		3059/58		
3107/06		3058/57		
3106/05		3057/56		
3105/04	Jupiter/Saturn conj. - Dec. 6, 3105 BC in Capricorn	3056/55		
3104/03		3055/54		

Adam died at 930 years old. Jewish sages say that God showed him all of human history, and that when Adam saw that David would die at birth, he offered to give the last 70 years of his life to David — the reason given for Adam living only 930 years. They say that David was born on Pentecost and died on his 70th birthday.

3054/53	3005/04
3053/52 S	3004/03 S Its been a thousand years since Adam's creation.
3052/51	3003/02
3051/50	3002/01
3050/49	3001/00
3049/48	3000/99
3048/47	2999/98
3047/46	2998/97
3046/45 S Jupiter/Saturn conj. - Feb. 29, 3045 BC in Capricorn	2997/96 S
3045/44	2996/95
3044/43	2995/94
3043/42	2994/93
3042/41	2993/92
3041/40	2992/91
3040/39	2991/90
3039/38 S	2990/89 S
3038/37	2989/88
3037/36	2988/87
3036/35	2987/86
3035/34	2986/85 Jupiter/Saturn conj. - Dec. 23, 2986 BC in Aquarius
3034/33	2985/84
3033/32	2984/83
3032/31 S	2983/82 S
3031/30	2982/81
3030/29	2981/80
3029/28	2980/79
3028/27	2979/78
3027/26	2978/77
3026/25	2977/76
3025/24 S Jupiter/Saturn conj. - Oct. 8, 3025 BC in Libra	2976/75 S
3024/23 J21	2975/74 J22
3023/22	2974/73
3022/21	2973/72
3021/20	2972/71
3020/19	2971/70
3019/18	2970/69
3018/17 S Enoch was translated.	2969/68 S
3017/16	2968/67
3016/15	2967/66
3015/14	2966/65 Jupiter/Saturn conj. - Aug. 8, 2965 BC in Libra
3014/13	2965/64
3013/12	2964/63
3012/11	**2963/62** Seth died.
3011/10 S	2962/61 S
3010/09	2961/60
3009/08	2960/59
3008/07	2959/58
3007/06	2958/57
3006/05 Jupiter/Saturn conj. - May 27, 3005 BC in Gemini	2957/56

2956/55	Noah means "rest." He seems to represent the 7th
2955/54 S	millennium, in which Christ will establish the king-
2954/53	dom rest - the great Sabbath. These first 10 men
2953/52	depict major events over the course of 7,000 years,
2952/51	thus completing God's plan of the ages.
2951/50	
2950/49	
2949/48	**Lamech begat Noah.**
2948/47 S	
2947/46	
2946/45	Jupiter/Saturn conj. - Apr. 5, 2945 BC in Gemini
2945/44	**Genesis 5:**
2944/43	28. And Lamech lived an hundred eighty and two
2943/42	years, and begat a son:
2942/41	29. And he called his name Noah, saying, This same
2941/40 S	shall comfort us concerning our work and toil of
2940/39	our hands, because of the ground which the LORD
2939/38	hath cursed.
2938/37	30. And Lamech lived after he begat Noah five
2937/36	hundred ninety and five years, and begat sons and
2936/35	daughters:
2935/34	31. And all the days of Lamech were seven hundred
2934/33 S	seventy and seven years: and he died.
2933/32	
2932/31	
2931/30	
2930/29	
2929/28	
2928/27	
2927/26 S	Jupiter/Saturn conj. - Mar. 23, 2926 BC in Aquarius
2926/25 J23	
2925/24	
2924/23	
2923/22	
2922/21	
2921/20	
2920/19 S	
2919/18	
2918/17	
2917/16	
2916/15	
2915/14	
2914/13	
2913/12 S	
2912/11	
2911/10	
2910/09	
2909/08	
2908/07	

2907/06	
2906/05 S	Jupiter/Saturn conj. - Oct. 28, 2906 BC in Libra
2905/04	
2904/03	
2903/02	
2902/01	
2901/00	
2900/99	
2899/98 S	
2898/97	
2897/96	
2896/95	
2895/94	
2894/93	
2893/92	
2892/91 S	
2891/90	
2890/89	
2889/88	
2888/87	
2887/86	Jupiter/Saturn conj. - July 11, 2886 BC in Cancer
2886/85	
2885/84 S	
2884/83	
2883/82	
2882/81	
2881/80	
2880/79	
2879/78	
2878/77 S	
2877/76 J24	
2876/75	
2875/74	
2874/73	
2873/72	
2872/71	
2871/70 S	
2870/69	
2869/68	
2868/67	
2867/66	Jupiter/Saturn conj. - Jan. 17, 2866 BC in Aquarius
2866/65	
2865/64	Enos died.
2864/63 S	
2863/62	
2862/61	
2861/60	
2860/59	
2859/58	

Noah was born 127 years after Adam's death, 69 years after the translation of Enoch, and 14 years after the death of Seth. However, Enos (3rd generation); Cainan (4th); Mahalaleel (5th); Jared (6th); Methusaleh (8th); and Lamech (9th) were all still alive and could tell Noah about Adam and Eve and the generations up until his time. Noah was the tenth generation from Adam. These patriarchs all died before the flood. It is said that Methu-

2858/57	
2857/56 S	
2856/55	
2855/54	
2854/53	
2853/52	
2852/51	
2851/50	
2850/49 S	
2849/48	
2848/47	
2847/46	Jupiter/Saturn conj. - Aug. 30, 2846 BC in Scorpio
2846/45	
2845/44	
2844/43	
2843/42 S	
2842/41	
2841/40	
2840/39	
2839/38	
2838/37	
2837/36	
2836/35 S	
2835/34	
2834/33	
2833/32	
2832/31	
2831/30	
2830/29	
2829/28 S	
2828/27 J25	
2827/26	Jupiter/Saturn conj. - May 27, 2826 BC in Cancer
2826/25	
2825/24	
2824/23	
2823/22	
2822/21 S	
2821/20	
2820/19	
2819/18	
2818/17	
2817/16	
2816/15	
2815/14 S	
2814/13	
2813/12	
2812/11	
2811/10	
2810/09	

2809/08	
2808/07 S	Jupiter/Saturn triple conjunction - May 2, 2807 BC
2807/06	in Pisces, July 30 on the border and Nov 11, 2807
2806/05	in Aquarius
2805/04	
2804/03	
2803/02	
2802/01	
2801/00 S	
2800/99	In the 1st year of the 5th week of the 25th Jubilee
2799/98	Noah took a wife, Emzara, the daughter of Rake'el,
2798/97	the daughter of his father's brother. In the 3rd year
2797/96	of it, she gave birth to Shem. In the 5th year of it
2796/95	she gave birth to Ham, and . . .
2795/94	
2794/93 S	
2793/92	. . . in the first year in the 6th week she gave birth to
2792/91	Japheth. This is a 349-year error. According to the
2791/90	Bible, Shem was born around 2449-2446 BC.
2790/89	
2789/88	
2788/87	
2787/86 S	Jupiter/Saturn conj. - Nov. 18, 2787 BC in Scorpio
2786/85	
2785/84	
2784/83	
2783/82	
2782.81	
2781/80	
2780/79 S	
2779/78 J26	
2778/77	
2777/76	
2776/75	
2775/74	
2774/73	
2773/72 S	
2772/71	
2771/70	
2770/69	Cainan died.
2769/68	
2768/67	
2767/66	Jupiter/Saturn triple conjunction - Sept. 5, 2767 BC,
2766/65 S	Jan. 26, 2766 and Mar. 22, 2766 in Leo
2765/64	
2764/63	
2763/62	
2762/61	
2761/60	

saleh died one week before the Flood. Josephus wrote that Lamech "appointed Noah, his son, to be ruler of the people. Noah was born to Lamech when he was one hundred and eighty-two years old." (*Ant.* bk 1, ch 3)

2760/59		2711/10	
2759/58 S		2710/09 S	
2758/57		2709/08	
2757/56		2708/07	Jupiter/Saturn conj. - July 22, 2707 BC in Leo
2756/55		2707/06	
2755/54		2706/05	
2754/53		2705/04	
2753/52		2704/03	According to the *Book of Jubilees*, Noah's Flood
2752/51 S		2703/02 S	happened in 2704/03 BC.
2751/50		2702/01	Arphaxad was born 2 years after the Flood. At this
2750/49		2701/00	point *Jubilees* has an error of 355 years in dating.
2749/48		2700/99	If the Flood occurred in 2704/03 BC, then Jared, La-
2748/47	Jupiter/Saturn conj. - Feb. 22, 2747 BC in Pisces	2699/98	mech and Methuselah could not have lived out their
2747/46		2698/97	years on Earth as given in the Bible. They would
2746/45		2697/96	have perished in the Flood. The *Book of Jubilees*
2745/44 S		2696/95 S	does not date their deaths, but says that Jared was
2744/43		2695/94	62 (not 162) when Enoch was born; that Methuselah
2743/42		2694/93	was 65 (not 187) when Lamech was born; and that
2742/41		2693/92	Lamech was 49 (not 182) when Noah was born. At
2741/40		2692/91	the time of this Flood Jared would be 840 years old
2740/39		2691/90	(not 962); Lamech was 649 years old (not 777); and
2739/38		2690/89	Methuselah was 714 years old (not 969).
2738/37 S		2689/88 S	
2737/36		2688/87	Jupiter/Saturn conj. - Dec. 31, 2688 BC in Pisces
2736/35		2687/86	
2735/34		2686/85	
2734/33		2685/84	
2733/32		2684/83	
2732/31		2683/82	
2731/30 S		2682/81 S	
2730/29 J27		2681/80 J28	
2729/28		2680/79	
2728/27	Jupiter/Saturn conj. - Sept. 23, 2727 BC in Scorpio	2679/78	
2727/26		2678/77	
2726/25		2677/76	
2725/24		2676/75	
2724/23 S		2675/74 S	
2723/22		2674/73	
2722/21		2673/72	
2721/20		2672/71	
2720/19		2671/70	
2719/18		2670/69	
2718/17		2669/68	
2717/16 S		2668/67 S	Jupiter/Saturn conj. - Dec. 15, 2668 BC in Pisces
2716/15		2667/66	
2715/14	Mahalaleel died.	2666/65	
2714/13		2665/64	
2713/12		2664/63	
2712/11		2663/62	

2662/61	
2661/60 S	
2660/59	
2659/58	
2658/57	
2657/56	
2656/55	
2655/54	
2654/53 S	
2653/52	
2652/51	
2651/50	
2650/49	
2649/48	
2648/47	Jupiter/Saturn conj. - June 5, 2647 BC in Leo
2647/46 S	
2646/45	
2645/44	
2644/43	
2643/42	
2642/41	
2641/40	
2640/39 S	
2639/38	
2638/37	
2637/36	
2636/35	
2635/34	
2634/33	
2633/32 S	
2632/31 J29	In the beginning of the 1st week of the 29th Jubilee
2631/30	Arphaxad took a wife, Rasu'eja, daughter of Elam.
2630/29	In the 3rd year, they had a son, Kainam, . . .
2629/28	Jupiter/Saturn conj. - Apr. 7, 2728 BC in Pisces
2628/27	. . . 74 years after the Flood. According to the Book
2627/26	of Jubilees, Kainam's son was Salah (born in the
2626/25 S	4th year of the 2nd week of the 30th Jubilee). But
2625/24	Genesis 11:12 says that Arphaxad's son was Salah.
2624/23	There is no mention of Kainam in Genesis, but
2623/22	Luke 3:36 does include "Cainan" in the list:
2622/21	"...Sala, which was the son of Cainan, which was
2621/20	the son of Arphaxad ..." (Luke 3:35,36).
2620/19	This is strange. Could Luke have been quoting the
2619/18 S	Book of Jubilees? Why did Moses leave him out of
2618/17	the family tree? I checked a premier Jewish com-
2617/16	mentary on Genesis, Flavius Josephus, and the
2616/15	Zohar, but none mention Cainan. Thus far, Luke is
2615/14	the only other source with Jubilees that mentions
2614/13	Cainan being the son of Arphaxad.

2613/12	
2612/11 S	
2611/10	
2610/09	
2609/08	
2608/07	Jupiter/Saturn conj. - Oct. 16, 2608 BC in Sagit-
2607/06	
2606/05	
2605/04 S	
2604/03	
2603/02	
2602/01	
2601/00	
2600/99	
2599/98	
2598/97 S	
2597/96	
2596/95	
2595/94	
2594/93	
2593/92	
2592/91	
2591/90 S	
2590/89	
2589/88	Jupiter/Saturn conj. - Sept. 7, 2588 BC in Leo
2588/87	
2587/86	
2586/85	
2585/84	
2584/83 S	
2583/82 J30	Jared died.
2582/81	
2581/80	
2580/79	
2579/78	
2578/77	
2577/76 S	
2576/75	In the 1st year of the 2nd week of the 30th Jubilee
2575/74	Kainam took a wife, Melka, daughter of Madai, who
2574/73	was the son of Japheth,
2573/72	Melka gave birth to Salah in the 4th year. At this
2572/71	point Jubilees has an error of 261 years in dating.
2571/70	
2570/69 S	
2569/68	Jupiter/Saturn conj. - Feb. 17, 2568 BC in Aries
2568/67	
2567/66	
2566/65	
2565/64	

2564/63		2515/14	
2563/62 S		2514/13 S	
2562/61		2513/12	
2561/60		2512/11	
2560/59		2511/10	
2559/58		2510/09	Jupiter/Saturn triple conjunction - May 29, 2509,
2558/57		2509/08	Nov 7, and Nov 16, 2509 BC in Aries
2557/56		2508/07	
2556/55 S		2507/06 S	
2555/54		2506/05	In the 1st year of the 5th week of the 31st Jubilee
2554/53		2505/04	Salah took a wife, Mu'ak, daughter of Kesed, his
2553/52		2504/03	father's brother.
2552/51		2503/02	
2551/50		2502/01	Mu'ak gave birth to Eber in the 5th year. At this
2550/49		2501/00	point, *Jubilees* has an error of 220 years in dating.
2549/48 S	Jupiter/Saturn conj. - Jan. 8, 2548 BC in Sagittarius	2500/99 S	
2548/47		2499/98	
2547/46		2498/97	
2546/45		2497/96	
2545/44		2496/95	
2544/43		2495/94	
2543/42		2494/93	
2542/41 S		2493/92 S	
2541/40		2492/91	
2540/39		2491/90	
2539/38		2490/89	
2538/37		2489/88	Jupiter/Saturn conj. - Nov. 6, 2489 BC in Sagittarius
2537/36		2488/87	
2536/35		2487/86	
2535/34 S		2486/85 S	
2534/33 J31		2485/84 J32	
2533/32		2484/83	
2532/31		2483/82	
2531/30		2482/81	
2530/29		2481/80	
2529/28	Jupiter/Saturn conj. - July 22, 2528 BC in Virgo	2480/79	
2528/27 S		2479/78 S	
2527/26		2478/77	
2526/25		2477/76	
2525/24		2476/75	
2524/23		2475/74	
2523/22		2474/73	
2522/21		2473/72	
2521/20 S		2472/71 S	
2520/19		2471/70	
2519/18		2470/69	
2518/17		**2469/68**	Jupiter/Saturn triple conj. - Oct. 24, 2469 BC, Mar. 8, 2468
2517/16		2468/67	BC and May 13, 2468 BC in Virgo. This year, Noah was
2516/15		2467/66	warned of a coming flood and began to build the Ark.

2466/65	
2465/64 S	
2464/63	
2463/62	
2462/61	
2461/60	
2460/59	
2459/58	
2458/57 S	
2457/56	
2456/55	
2455/54	In *Jubilees*, Noah died, being 950 yrs old.
2454/53	
2453/52	
2452/51	
2451/50 S	
2450/49	Jupiter/Saturn conj. - Apr. 4, 2449 BC in Taurus
2449/48	Noah begat Japheth first,
2448/47	then Ham,
2447/46	then Shem.
2446/45	**Genesis 5:**
2445/44	*32. And Noah was five hundred years old: and Noah*
2444/43 S	*begat Shem, Ham, and Japheth.*
2443/42	
2442/41	
2441/40	In the 3rd year of the 7th week of the 32nd Jubilee
2440/39	Eber took a wife, Azurad, daughter of Nebrod.
2439/38	
2438/37	Azurad gave birth to Peleg in the 6th year. At this
2437/36 S	point, we have an error of 190 years in dating.
2436/35 J33	In the beginning of the 33rd Jubilee, the children
2435/34	of Noah divided the earth into 3 parts, for Shem,
2434/33	Ham and Japheth.
2433/32	
2432/31	
2431/30	
2430/29 S	Jupiter/Saturn conj. - Jan. 31, 2647 BC in Sagittarius
2429/28	In the 1st year of the 2nd week of the 33rd Jubilee
2428/27	Peleg took a wife, Lomna, daughter of Sina'ar.
2427/26	
2426/25	Lomna gave birth to Reu in the 4th year, for she
2425/24	said, "Look the children of men are planing to build
2424/23	a city and a tower in the land of Shinar for an evil
2423/22 S	purpose."
2422/21	
2421/20	At this point *Jubilees* has an error of 208 years in
2420/19	dating. Jubilees has Peleg only 9 years old when he
2419/18	married, and only 12 when his son, Rue, was born,
2418/17	instead of the biblical 30 years old at his son's birth.

2417/16	
2416/15 S	
2415/14	They started building in the 4th week and spent 43
2414/13	years building the tower of Babel.
2413/12	
2412/11	
2411/10	
2410/09	Jupiter/Saturn conj. - Aug. 27, 2409 BC in Virgo
2409/08 S	
2408/07	
2407/06	
2406/05	
2405/04	
2404/03	
2403/02	
2402/01 S	
2401/00	
2400/99	
2399/98	
2398/97	
2397/96	
2396/95	
2395/94 S	
2394/93	
2393/92	
2392/91	
2391/90	
2390/89	Jupiter/Saturn conj. - Feb. 12, 2389 BC in Taurus
2389/88	
2388/87 S	
2387/86 J34	
2386/85	
2385/84	
2384/83	
2383/82	
2382/81	
2381/80 S	
2380/79	
2379/78	
2378/77	
2377/76	
2376/75	
2375/74	
2374/73 S	
2373/72	
2372/71	
2371/70	
2370/69	Jupiter/Saturn conj. - Nov. 25, 2370 BC in Capricorn
2369/68	

2368/67	
2367/66 S	
2366/65	In the 1st year of the 4th week of the 34th Jubilee
2365/64	they were dispersed from the land of Shinar. The
2364/63	whole land of Shinar is called Babel, because the
2363/62	Lord confounded their language.
2362/61	
2361/60	
2360/59 S	
2359/58	
2358/57	
2357/56	
2356/55	
2355/54	
2354/53	Lamech died.
2353/52 S	
2352/51	
2351/50	Jupiter/Saturn triple conjunction - Dec. 11, 2350 BC,
2350/49	Feb. 3, 2349 BC and June 28, 2349 BC in Virgo
2349/48	**FLOOD** - Methuselah died 1 week
2348/47	before the flood.
2347/46	**Shem begat Arphaxad** 2 years after the Flood.
2346/45 S	
2345/44	

The Third Dispensation of Human Government
ended with the Tower of Babel

2344/43	
2343/42	
2342/41	
2341/40	
2340/39	**Genesis 11:**
2339/38 S	10. These are the generations of Shem: Shem was
2338/37 J35	an hundred years old, and begat Arphaxad two
2337/36	years after the flood:
2336/35	11. And Shem lived after he begat Arphaxad five
2335/34	hundred years, and begat sons and daughters.
2334/33	
2333/32	
2332/31 S	
2331/30	Jupiter/Saturn conj. - May 19, 2330 BC in Taurus
2330/29	
2329/28	
2328/27	
2327/26	
2326/25	
2325/24 S	
2324/23	In the 1st year of the 3rd week of the 35th Jubi-
2323/22	lee Reu took a wife, Ora, daughter of Ur, the son
2322/21	of Kesed.
2321/20	
2320/19	

2319/18	Ora gave birth to Serug in the 7th year. At this
2318/17 S	point, *Jubilees* has an error of 132 years
2317/16	**Genesis 11:**
2316/15	12. And Arphaxad lived five and thirty years, and be-
2315/14	gat Salah:
2314/13	13. And Arphaxad lived after he begat Salah four hun-
2313/12	dred and three years, and begat sons and daughters.
2312/11	**Arphaxad begat Salah.**
2311/10 S	Jupiter/Saturn conj. - Feb. 16, 2310 BC in Capricorn
2310/09	"Unto Shem also, the father of all the children of
2309/08	Eber, the brother of Japheth the elder, even to him
2308/07	were children born. The children of Shem; Elam,
2307/06	and Asshur, and Arphaxad, and Lud, and Aram.
2306/05	And the children of Aram; Uz, and Hul, and Gether,
2305/04	and Mash. And Arphaxad begat Salah; and Salah
2304/03 S	begat Eber. And unto Eber were born two sons:
2303/02	the name of one was Peleg; for in his days was
2302/01	the earth divided; and his brother's name was Jok-
2301/00	tan. and Joktan begat Almodad, and Sheleph, and
2300/99	Hazarmaveth, and Jerah, And Hadoram, and Uzal,
2299/98	and Diklah, and Obal, and Abimael, and Sheba, and
2298/97	Ophir, and Havilah, and Jobab: all these were the
2297/96 S	sons of Joktan. And their dwelling was from Me-
2296/95	sha, as thou goest unto Sephar a mount of the east.
2295/94	These are the sons of Shem, after their families, af-
2294/93	ter their tongues, in their lands, after their nations."
2293/92	(Gen. 10:22-31).
2292/91	
2291/90	Jupiter/Saturn conj. - Sept. 23, 2290 BC in Virgo
2290/89 S	At some point after the Flood, other fallen angels
2289/88 J36	descended to Mount Hermon and once again be-
2288/87	gan to breed giants - the Anakim, Emim, Zamzum-
2287/86	mim, etc. The Hebrew suffix "im" means the term
2286/85	is plural. Og of Bashan was a giant who ruled from
2285/84	Mount Hermon. Goliath was also a Rapha (singular
2284/83	for Raphaim; i.e., giant).
2283/82 S	
2282/81	**Salah begat Eber.**
2281/80	**Genesis 11:**
2280/79	14. And Salah lived thirty years, and begat Eber:
2279/78	15. And Salah lived after he begat Eber four hundred
2278/77	and three years, and begat sons and daughters.
2277/76	
2276/75 S	
2275/74	
2274/73	
2273/72	
2272/71	
2271/70	Jupiter/Saturn conj. - Mar. 29, 2270 BC in Taurus

Luke 3:35,36 says, *"Salah, which was the son of Cainan, which was the son of Arphaxad ..."* Yet, Genesis 11 says *"Arphaxad begat Salah."* Where did Cainan come from? Dr. Floyd Nolan Jones (*The Chronology of the Old Testament*) suggests five possibilities, any of which could account for Luke's inclusion of Cainan without contradicting Scripture. Notice Luke did not say that Arphaxad begat Cainan, but that Cainan was the "son of" Arphaxad. This could have been a matter of adoption, family blessing or inheritance. Jones says, "Cainan was

2270/69		"The sons of Japheth; Gomer, and Magog, and
2269/68	S	Madai, and Javan, and Tubal, and Meshech, and
2268/67		Tiras. And the sons of Gomer; Ashkenaz, and
2267/66		Riphath, and Togarmah. And the sons of Javan; El-
2266/65		ishah, and Tarshish, Kittim, and Dodanim. By these
2265/64		were the isles of the Gentiles divided in their lands;
2264/63		every one after his tongue, after their families, in
2263/62		their nations." (Gen. 10:2-5).
2262/61	S	
2261/60		In the 1st year of the 5th week of the 36th Jubilee
2260/59		Serug took a wife, Melka, She gave birth to Nahor
2259/58		in the 1st year. At this point, *Jubilees* has an error
2258/57		of 105 years in dating.
2257/56		
2256/55		
2255/54	S	
2254/53		
2253/52		
2252/51		
2251/50		Jupiter/Saturn conj. - Dec. 9, 2251 BC in Leo
2250/49		
2249/48		
2248/47	S	**Eber begat Peleg.**
2247/46		**Genesis 11:**
2246/45		16. And Eber lived four and thirty years, and begat Peleg:
2245/44		17. And Eber lived after he begat Peleg four hundred
2244/43		and thirty years, and begat sons and daughters.
2243/42		# Nimrod's Tower of Babel
2242/41		Nimrod had been born to Cush, Ham's son.
2241/40	S	After God judged Nimrod's Babel, Japhath's tribe
2240/39	J37	migrated north into central Russia. One group
2239/38		moved westward into Europe, while another
2238/37		group moved eastward, across the Berring Strait
2237/36		and populated North, Central and South America.
2236/35		Ham's tribe moved westward to the territory
2235/34		around Mount Hermon. Some went further south
2234/33	S	into Egypt and Africa, and others migrated to the
2233/32		South Sea Islands and Australia.
2232/31		
2231/30		Jupiter/Saturn conj. - July 21, 2230 BC in Virgo
2230/29		
2229/28		
2228/27		
2227/26	S	
2226/25		
2225/24		
2224/23		
2223/22		
2222/21		

2221/20		
2220/19	S	
2219/18		
2218/17		**Peleg begat Reu.**
2217/16		**Genesis 11:**
2216/15		18. And Peleg lived thirty years, and begat Reu:
2215/14		19. And Peleg lived after he begat Reu two hundred
2214/13		and nine years, and begat sons and daughters.
2213/12	S	
2212/11		Jupiter/Saturn conj. - June 30, 2211 BC in Gemini
2211/10		
2210/09		
2209/08		
2208/07		
2207/06		
2206/05	S	
2205/04		In the 1st year of the 6th week of the 37th Jubilee
2204/03		Nahor took a wife, Ijaska, daughter of Nestag of the
2203/02		Chaldees.
2202/01		
2201/00		
2200/99		
2199/98	S	Ijaska gave birth to Terah in the 7th year. At this
2198/97		point, Jubilees has an error of 72 years in dating.
2197/96		
2196/95		
2195/94		
2194/93		
2193/92		
2192/91	S	Jupiter/Saturn conj. - Feb. 28, 2191 BC in Leo
2191/90	J38	
2190/89		
2189/88		Egypt was founded by Mizraim, son of Ham.
2188/87		
2187/86		
2186/85		**Reu begat Serug.**
2185/84	S	**Genesis 11:**
2184/83		20. And Reu lived two and thirty years, and begat
2183/82		Serug:
2182/81		21. And Reu lived after he begat Serug two hundred
2181/80		and seven years, and begat sons and daughters.
2180/79		
2179/78		
2178/77	S	
2177/76		
2176/75		
2175/74		
2174/73		
2173/72		

probably either (a) a son by adoption and/or a son-in-law, not a direct son — hence he is not listed in Genesis 10:24 or (b) Cainan is not mentioned in Genesis as the blessing passed over him, going directly from Arphaxad to Salah who is almost certainly Cainan's younger brother."

2172/71	Jupiter/Saturn conj. - Oct 11, 2171 BC in Libra
2171/70 S	"And the sons of Ham; Cush, and Mizraim, and Phut,
2170/69	and Canaan. And the sons of Cush; Seba, and Havilah,
2169/68	and Sabtah, and Raamah, and Sabtechah: and the
2168/67	sons of Raamah; Sheba, and Dedan. And Cush begat
2167/66	Nimrod: he began to be a mighty one in the earth. He
2166/65	was a mighty hunter before the LORD: wherefore it
2165/64	is said, Even as Nimrod the mighty hunter before the
2164/63 S	LORD. And the beginning of his kingdom was Babel,
2163/62	and Erech, and Accad, and Calneh, in the land of Shi-
2162/61	nar. Out of that land went forth Asshur, and builded
2161/60	Nineveh, and the city Rehoboth, and Calah, and Resen
2160/59	between Nineveh and Calah: the same is a great city"
2159/58	(Gen. 10:6-12).
2158/57	
2157/56 S	**Genesis 11:**
2156/55	**Serug begat Nahor.**
2155/54	22. And Serug lived thirty years, and begat Nahor:
2154/53	23. And Serug lived after he begat Nahor two hun-
2153/52	dred years, and begat sons and daughters.
2152/51	Jupiter/Saturn conj. - May 8, 2151 BC in Gemini
2151/50	"And Mizraim begat Ludim, and Anamim, and Lehabim,
2150/49 S	and Naphtuhim, And Pathrusim, and Casluhim, (out of
2149/48	whom came Philistim,) and Caphtorim. And Canaan begat
2148/47	Sidon his first born, and Heth, and the Jebusite, and the
2147/46	Amorite, and the Girgasite, and the Hivite, and the Arkite,
2146/45	and the Sinite, and the Arvadite, and the Zemarite, and
2145/44	the Hamathite: and afterward were the families of the Ca-
2144/43	naanites spread abroad. And the border of the Canaanites
2143/42 S	was from Sidon, as thou comest to Gerar, unto Gaza; as
2142/41 J39	thou goest, unto Sodom, and Gomorrah, and Admah, and
2141/40	Zeboim, even unto Lasha" (Gen. 10:13-19).
2140/39	
2139/38	
2138/37	
2137/36	
2136/35 S	
2135/34	In the 1st year of the 2nd week of the 39th Jubilee
2134/33	Terah took a wife, Edna, daughter of Abram (not
2133/32	Abraham), the daughter of his father's sister.
2132/31	Jupiter/Saturn conj. - Dec. 22, 2132 BC in Aquarius
2131/30	
2130/29	
2129/28 S	Edna gave birth to Abram (Abraham) in the 7th
2128/27	year. *Jubilees* has an error of 132 years.
2127/26	**Nahor begat Terah.**
2126/25	
2125/24	
2124/23	

2123/22	**Genesis 11:**
2122/21 S	24. And Nahor lived nine and twenty years, and
2121/20	begat Terah:
2120/19	25. And Nahor lived after he begat Terah an hundred
2119/18	and nineteen years, and begat sons and daughters.
2118/17	
2117/16	
2116/15	
2115/14 S	
2114/13	
2113/12	
2112/11	Jupiter/Saturn conj. - Aug. 9, 2111 BC in Libra
2111/10	
2110/09	For the generations, from Shem to Abram, the Book
2109/08	of Jubilees does not match the biblical dating.
2108/07 S	Examples:
2107/06	Shem was B-100 (not J-96) at the birth of Arphaxad.
2106/05	Arphaxad was B-35 at the birth of Salah.
2105/04	Jubilees has Arphaxad J-72 at the birth of Cainan.
2104/03	Jubilees has Cainan J-57 at the birth of Salah.
2103/02	Salah was B-30 (not J-71) at the birth of Eber.
2102/01	Eber was B-34 (not J-64) at the birth of Peleg.
2101/00 S	Peleg was B-30 (not J-12) at the birth of Reu.
2100/99	Reu was B-32 (not J-118) at the birth of Serug.
2099/98	Serug was B-30 (not J-57) at the birth of Nahor.
2098/97	Nahor was B-29 (not J-62) at the birth of Terah.
2097/96	Terah was B-130 (not J- 70) at the birth of Abram.
2096/95	
2095/94	
2094/93 S	
2093/92 J40	Jupiter/Saturn triple conjunction - Aug. 13, 2092,
2092/91	Dec. 13, 2092 and Mar. 2, 2091 BC in Gemini
2091/90	
2090/89	
2089/88	
2088/87	
2087/86 S	
2086/85	
2085/84	
2084/83	
2083/82	
2082/81	
2081/80	
2080/79 S	In the 7th year of the 2nd week of the 40th Jubilee
2079/78	Abram took a wife, Sarai, his half sister - his fa-
2078/77	ther's daughter by another wife.
2077/76	In the 3rd year of the 3rd week, Haran, Abram's
2076/75	brother, took a wife, who bore a son in the 7th year
2075/74	and called his name Lot.

2074/73		
2073/72	S	Jupiter/Saturn conj. - Mar. 16, 2072 BC in Aquarius
2072/71		
2071/70		
2070/69		
2069/68		
2068/67		
2067/66		
2066/65	S	
2065/64		
2064/63		
2063/62		
2062/61		
2061/60		
2060/58		
2059/58	S	
2058/57		
2057/56		**Terah begat Haran.**
2056/55		**Genesis 11:**
2055/54		26. And Terah lived seventy years, and begat Abram,
2054/53		Nahor, and Haran.
2053/52		
2052/51	S	Jupiter/Saturn conj. - Oct. 28, 2052 BC in Libra
2051/50		
2050/49		**60 missing years in the**
2049/48		**Jewish calendar**
2048/47		These are grayed out because they were left
2047/46		out of the *Sedar Olam* - a second-century
2046/45		Jewish account of the history of the world.
2045/44	S	
2044/43	J41	
2043/42		
2042/41		In the 3rd year of the 1st week of the 41st Jubilee,
2041/40		Abram returned from living 7 years in Egypt. In
2040/39		the 4th year, Lot parted from him to live in Sodom.
2039/38	S	Also, on the new moon of the 3rd month, God made
2038/37	S	a covenant with Abram in the same way God made
2037/36		the covenant with Noah in this month — at Pente-
2036/35		cost — and Abram renewed the festival and laws of
2035/34		Pentecost for himself. And Sarah took Hagar, her
2034/33		maid, the Egyptian, and gave her to ...
2033/32		Jupiter/Saturn conj. - Jun. 18, 2032 BC in Cancer
2032/31		... Abram, her husband, to be his wife. In the 5th
2031/30	S	year of this week, Hagar gave birth to Ishmael; and
2030/29		this was the 86th year in the life of Abram.
2029/28		
2028/27		
2027/26		
2026/25		

2025/24		
2024/23	S	
2023/22		
2022/21		
2021/20		
2020/19		
2019/18		In the 5th year of the 4th week, in the middle of
2018/17		the 3rd month, Abram celebrated the feast of the
2017/16	S	first-fruits of the grain harvest (Pentecost). God
2016/15		changed Abram's name to Abraham and Sarai's
2015/14		name to Sarah. On the new moon of the 4th month,
2014/13		the LORD and two angels and promised ...
2013/12		Jupiter/Saturn conj. - Jan. 10, 2012 BC in Aquarius
2012/11		... Sarah a son the next year. In this month the Lord
2011/10		judged Sodom. In the seventh month Abraham cel-
2010/09	S	ebrated the Feast of Tabernacles. Isaac was ...
2009/08		Peleg died.
2008/07		... born on Pentecost the following year - 2017 BC.
2007/06		At this point, Jubilees has an error of 121 years in
2006/05		dating, because the biblical date of Isaac's birth is
2005/04		1896 BC.
2004/03		
2003/02	S	
2002/01		On the 12th day of the 1st month, in the 1st year of
2001/00		the 7th week of the 41st Jubilee God told Abraham
2000/99		to sacrifice Isaac, who was not yet 16 years old.
1999/98		They traveled to Mount Moriah, and on the 3rd day
1998/97		(Passover's date) a ram was substituted.
1997/96		**Terah begat Abram.**
1996/95	S	Abraham celebrated this day every year. Now we
1995/94	J42	have 3 festivals, Passover, Pentecost and Taber-
1994/93		nacles being observed by Abraham.
1993/92		Jupiter/Saturn conj. - Aug. 27, 1992 BC in Libra
1992/91		In the 1st year of the 1st week of the 42nd Jubi-
1991/90		lee, Abraham moved to Kirjath Arba, near Hebron
1990/89		where he lived for 14 years.
1989/88	S	
1988/87		
1987/86		**Terah begat Sarai of another wife.**
1986/85		
1985/84		
1984/83		
1983/82		
1982/81	S	
1981/80		In the 1st year of the third week, Sarah died and
1980/79		was buried at Hebron in the cave of Machpelah.
1979/78		Reu died.
1978/77		In the 4th year, Isaac was given Rebecca for his
1977/76		wife.

The Jewish calendar (*Seder Olam Rabbah*) records the birth of Abraham in 1948 *Anno Mundi*, when Terah was 70 years old, rather than 130, thus eliminating 60 years. These years (2056/55 B.C.-1997/96 B.C., shown above) are light gray, but given in this chart in order to correct the mistake in the Jewish calendar.

1976/75	**Genesis 11:**
1975/74 s	27. Now these are the generations of Terah: Terah be-
1974/73	gat Abram, Nahor, and Haran; and Haran begat Lot.
1973/72	Jupiter/Saturn conj.-May 1, 1972 BC in Cancer
1972/71	28. And Haran died before his father Terah in the
1971/70	land of his nativity, in Ur of the Chaldees.
1970/69	29. And Abram and Nahor took them wives: the
1969/68 s	name of Abram's wife was Sarai; and the name of
1968/67 s	Nahor's wife, Milcah, the daughter of Haran, the fa-
1967/66	ther of Milcah, and the father of Iscah.
1966/65	30. But Sarai was barren; she had no child.
1965/64	31. And Terah took Abram his son, and Lot the son of
1964/63	Haran his son's son, and Sarai his daughter in law,
1963/62	his son Abram's wife; and they went forth with them
1962/61	from Ur of the Chaldees, to go into the land of Ca-
1961/60 s	naan; and they came unto Haran, and dwelt there.
1960/59	
1959/58	In the 2nd year of the 6th week Rebecca had two
1958/57	sons — Jacob and Esau. At this point, the *Book of*
1957/56	*Jubilees* has an error of 122 years.
1956/55	Serug died.
1955/54	
1954/53 s	Jupiter/Saturn double conjunction - Apr. 11, 1953 BC
1953/52	and Sept 23, 1953 BC in Aquarius
1952/51	
1951/50	
1950/49	
1949/48	
1948/47	In the 6th year of the 7th week of the 42nd Jubilee,
1947/46 s	Abraham died at 175 years old — 1948/47 BC. But
1946/45 J43	if we follow the date of Abram's birth in the *Book of*
1945/44	*Jubilees* (7th year of the 2nd week of the 39th Ju-
1944/43	bilee — 2129/28 BC), then Abraham was 181 years
1943/42	old on this date. This marks a 6-year error in the
1942/41	*Book of Jubilees.*
1941/40	
1940/39 s	
1939/38	
1938/37	
1937/36	
1936/35	
1935/34	
1934/33	
1933/32 s	Jupiter/Saturn conj. - Nov. 16, 1933 BC in Scorpio
1932/31	
1931/30	
1930/29	
1929/28	
1928/27	
1927/26	5 missing years are grayed out because they were
1926/25 s	removed from the *Sedar Olam.*
1925/24	In 1925/24 BC, the 1st year of the 4th week of the
1924/23	43rd Jubilee, Jacob bought Esau's birthright.
1923/22	Abram's covenant. Terah died.
1922/21	**Genesis 11:**
1921/20	32. And the days of Terah were two hundred and five
1920/19	years: and Terah died in Haran.
1919/18 s	
1918/17	**The Fourth Dispensation of Promise** — ended with the Exodus
1917/16	
1916/15	
1915/14	
1914/13	Jupiter/Saturn conj. - Aug. 6, 1913 BC in Leo
1913/12	
1912/11 s	Chedorlaomer captured Sodom.
1911/10	
1910/09	**Ishmael was born.** Abram was 86 years old.
1909/08	Arphaxad died.
1908/07	
1907/06	
1906/05	
1905/04 s	
1904/03	In the 1st year of the 7th week, after 21 years in
1903/02	Gerar, Isaac moved away from the Philistines.
1902/01	
1901/00	
1900/99	In the 7th year (1897 BC), Jacob stole Esau's bless-
1899/98	ing and Isaac sent Jacob to Mesopotamia.
1898/97 S	**Isaac was born.** God added a ה *hay* to each
1897/96 J44	name. Thus, Abram became Abraham and Sarai
1896/95	became Sarah.
1895/94	
1894/93	Jupiter/Saturn conj. - Feb. 7, 1893 BC in Pisces
1893/92	
1892/91	In the 1st year of the 3rd week, Jacob was tricked
1891/90 s	and given Leah for his wife. Seven days later, he
1890/89	was given Rachel, but worked another 7 years.
1889/88	Reuben b. 1883 BC (14th day, 9th mo.)
1888/87	Simeon b. 1881 BC (21st day, 10th mo.)
1887/86	Levi b. 1877 BC (1st day, 1st mo.)
1886/85	Judah b. 1875 BC (15th day, 3rd mo.)
1885/84	Dan b. 1877 BC (9th day, 6th mo.)
1884/83 s	Naphthali b. 1875 BC (5th day, 7th mo.)
1883/82	Gad b. 1874 BC (12th day, 8th mo.)
1882/81	Asher b. 1871 BC (2nd day, 11th mo.)
1881/80	Issachar b. 1872 BC (4th day, 5th mo.)
1880/79	Zabulon and Dinah b. 1871 BC (7th day, 7th mo.)
1879/78	Joseph b. 1870 BC. (1st day, 4th mo.)

Also, 5 years (1927/26-1922/21) are light gray to show the second mistake in the Jewish calendar. The *Seder Olam* claims that Abraham received the Abrahamic covenant in his 70th year, instead of his 75th year. However, they show him moving to Canaan at the age of 75. To account for this, they removed five years from the calendar, thus allowing the Exodus to occur 430 years from the 70th year of Abraham, rather than the correct 75th year.

1878/77		1829/28		
1877/76 s		1828/27 s		
1876/75		1827/26		
1875/74		1826/25		
1874/73		1825/24		
1873/72	Jupiter/Saturn conj. - Sept. 17, 1873 BC in Scorpio	1824/23		
1872/71	Isaac was offered.	1823/22		
1871/70	Joseph was born in the 6th year of the 4th week.	**1822/21**	Abraham died.	
1870/69 s	In the 7th year of the 4th week, Jacob left Laban's	1821/20 s		
1869/68	ranch and headed home with his wives and chil-	1820/19		
1868/67	dren. Laban overtook him on the 13th day of the	1819/18		
1867/66	3rd month (time of Pentecost) in 1869 BC. On the	**1818/17**	Eber died.	
1866/65	15th day, they had a feast and made a covenant.	1817/16	Jacob died in 1817 BC, the 4th year of the 5th week of	
1865/64	Jacob passed over the Jabbok River on the 11th	1816/15	the 45th Jubilee at the age of 147 years. But this year,	
1864/63	day of the 9th month (1869 BC). On that day, Esau	1815/14	in *Jubilee* dating, Jacob was only 142 years old.	
1863/62 s	came to him. In 1869 BC, the 1st year of the 5th	1814/13 s	Jupiter/Saturn conj. - Dec. 10, 1814 BC in Ophiuchus	
1862/61	week, he crossed the Jordan River and pastured	1813/12		
1861/60	his sheep from Bethshan to Dothan.	1812/11		
1860/59	Sarah died. In 1860/59 BC, the 3rd year of the	1811/10		
1859/58	6th week of the 44th Jubilee Jacob moved into the	1810/09		
1858/57	house of Abraham to be near Isaac and Rebecca.	1809/08		
1857/56	Isaac married Rebekah.	1808/07		
1856/55 s	On the 11th day of the 8th month (1862 BC) Rachael	1807/06 s		
1855/54	gave birth to Benjamin and died.	1806/05		
1854/53	Jupiter/Saturn conj. - Jun. 24, 1853 BC in Leo	1805/04		
1853/52	In the 1st day of the 7th month (date of Rosh Hasha-	1804/03		
1852/51	nah 1852 BC) Jacob and family went to Bethel, built	1803/02		
1851/50	an altar and celebrated the Feast of Tabernacles.	1802/01		
1850/49	On the 22nd, God changed his name to Israel.	1801/00		
1849/48 s	In the 7th year (1849 BC) Joseph was sold. Jacob	1800/99 s		
1848/47 J45	was shown his bloody coat on Tishri 10.	1799/98 J46		
1847/46	Shem died.	1798/97		
1846/45	Both Bilhah and Dinah died within a month while	**1797/96**	Esau married 2 wives.	
1845/44	grieving over Joseph's supposed death — adding	1796/95		
1844/43	to Jacob's grief. Both were buried next to Rachel's	1795/94		
1843/42	tomb in Bethlehem.	1794/93	Jupiter/Saturn triple conjunction - Oct. 8, 1794 BC,	
1842/41 s	In the 1st year of the 1st week of the 45th Jubilee	1793/92 s	Jan. 19, 1793 BC and May 1, 1793 BC in **Leo**	
1841/40	(1848/47 BC), Rebecca said, "I shall die this year."	1792/91		
1840/39	Joseph stood before Pharoah (1840 BC).	1791/90		
1839/38	In 1838 BC, the 4th year of the 2nd week of the 45th	1790/89		
1838/37	Jubilee, Leah died.	1789/88		
1837/36	**Isaac begat Jacob and Esau** in 1836 BC.	1788/87		
1836/35		1787/86		
1835/34 s	Jupiter/Saturn triple conjunction - May 29, Aug 7	1786/85 s		
1834/33	and Dec 6, 1834 BC in **Pisces**	1785/84		
1833/32	The Great 7-year famine began in the 1st year of	1784/83		
1832/31	the 3rd week of the 45th Jubilee (1834/33 BC). His	1783/82		
1831/30	brothers came into Egypt to buy grain. Jacob ar-	1782/81		
1830/29	rived in Egypt Tammuz 1, 1832 BC.	1781/80		

The triple conjunctions of Jupiter and Saturn in Pisces became the defining prediction for the birth of the Messiah. These conjunctions occurred when Jacob was two years old. Forty years later, there was a triple conjunction in Leo, probably the source of the prophecy used by Jacob on his deathbed in Genesis 49. He said that Judah would produce the Messiah, who would rule with the sceptre between the feet of Leo.

1780/79		
1779/78	S	
1778/77		
1777/76		
1776/75		
1775/74		Jupiter/Saturn conj. - Mar. 17, 1774 BC in Pisces
1774/73		Ishmael died.
1773/72		
1772/71	S	
1771/70		
1770/69		
1769/68		
1768/67		
1767/66		
1766/65		
1765/64	S	
1764/63		
1763/62		Joseph died in the 2nd year of the 6th week of the
1762/61		46th Jubilee at the age of 110 years.
1761/60		Jacob stole Isaac's blessing, went to Laban and
1760/59		married Leah & Rachel that year — before he
1759/58		worked 14 years to pay Laban, otherwise, Jacob's
1758/57	S	children would be too young when Jacob returned
1757/56		home after 20 years. **Leah gave birth to Reuben**
1756/55		**(1758 BC), Simeon, Levi, Judah (1755 BC), Is-**
1755/54		**sachar and . . .**
1754/53		Jupiter/Saturn conj. - Oct. 12, 1754 BC in Sagittarius
1753/52		**Bilhah gave birth to Dan and Naphtali.**
1752/51		
1751/50	S	**Zilpah gave birth to Gad and Asher.**
1750/49	J47	
1749/48		**Leah bore Zebulun and, afterward, Dinah.**
1748/46		
1747/44		
1746/45		**Rachel gave birth to Joseph** in 1745 BC.
1745/44		
1744/43	S	
1743/42		
1742/41		
1741/40		Jacob returned to Canaan.
1740/39		**Rachel died giving birth to Benjamin** in 1739
1739/38		BC. He had to be born this early, otherwise, he
1738/37		would have been too young to have 10 sons when
1737/36	S	Jacob moved to Egypt in 1706 BC.
1736/35		
1735/34		Jupiter/Saturn conj. - Aug. 16, 1734 BC in Leo
1734/33		
1733/32		
1732/31		

1731/30		
1730/29	S	Jacob moved to Shalem. Dinah (18 yrs old) raped.
1729/28		Joseph (17 yrs old) was sold into slavery.
1728/27		
1727/26		
1726/25		
1725/24		
1724/23		
1723/22	S	
1722/21		
1721/20		
1720/19		
1719/18		
1718/17		
1717/16		Isaac died.
1716/15	S	Joseph became 2nd to the Pharaoh.
1715/14		Jupiter/Saturn conj. - Jan. 25, 1714 BC in Pisces
1714/13		
1713/12		
1712/11		
1711/10		
1710/09		
1709/08	S	The seven-year famine began.
1708/07		The brothers went to Egypt.
1707/06		Jacob moved to Egypt in 1706 BC.
1706/05		
1705/04		Though their birth dates are not certain, Issachar
1704/03		begat Tola, Phuvah, **Job** and Shimron. It is likely
1703/02		that Job is the character in the book that bears his
1702/01	S	name. It seems the book was written about his life
1701/00	J48	to encourage the slaves in Egypt. It's message is
1700/99		that God will restore them after their trial is over.
1699/98		
1698/97		
1697/96		
1696/95		
1695/94	S	Jupiter/Saturn conj. - Jan. 5, 1694 BC in Sagittarius
1694/93		
1693/92		
1692/91		
1691/90		
1690/89		Jacob died.
1689/88		As he lay dying, Jacob called his sons around his
1688/87	S	bed and gave prophecies about the future of each
1687/86		tribe. The two most important were about Judah,
1686/85		the lion, from whom the Messiah would come, and
1685/84		Dan, the snake, from whom the Antichrist would
1684/83		rise (see Genesis 49).
1683/82		

On the first day of Creation, Saturn was in its first of three conjunctions with Regulus, thus obtaining the ruling sceptre. At the same time, Jupiter was in Pisces. Thus began a long series of Jupiter/Saturn conjunctions that portrayed a war in the heavens between the two planets. This battle was known in all early civilizations, particularly in Greek mythology, which says that Saturn ruled the earth during its golden years, but that Jupiter conquered Saturn and became the king of the gods. This corresponds to the prophecy of the battle between the

1682/81		
1681/80 S		
1680/79		
1679/78		
1678/77		
1677/76		
1676/75		
1675/74	Jupiter/Saturn conj. - July 3, 1674 BC in Leo	
1674/73 S	Moses was born in the 6th year of the 4th week of	
1673/72	the 48th Jubilee (1674 BC). At this point *Jubilees*	
1672/71	has a dating error of 103 years.	
1671/70		
1670/69		
1669/68		
1668/67		
1667/66 S		
1666/65		
1665/64		
1664/63		
1663/62		
1662/61		
1661/60		
1660/59 S		
1659/58		
1658/57		
1657/56		
1656/55		
1655/54	Jupiter/Saturn conj. - May 4, 1655 BC in Aries	
1654/53		
1653/52 S		
1652/51 J49		
1651/50		
1650/49		
1649/48		
1648/47		
1647/46		
1646/45 S		
1645/44		
1644/43		
1643/42	Joseph died.	
1642/41		
1641/40		
1640/39		
1639/38 S		
1638/37		
1637/36		
1636/35		
1635/34	Jupiter/Saturn conj. - Nov. 4, 1635 BC in Sagittarius	
1634/33		

1633/32	Moses fled to Midian in the 6th year of the 3rd week
1632/31 S	of the 49th Jubilee and lived there 40 years.
1631/30	
1630/29	
1629/28	
1628/27	
1627/26	
1626/25	
1625/24 S	
1624/23	
1623/22	
1622/21	
1621/20	
1620/19	Levi died and the enslavement began.
1619/18	
1618/17 S	
1617/16	
1616/15	
1615/14	Jupiter/Saturn conj. - Oct. 4, 1615 BC in Virgo
1614/13	
1613/12	
1612/11	
1611/10 S	
1610/09	
1609/08	
1608/07	
1607/06	
1606/05	
1605/04	
1604/03 S	
1603/02 J50	
1602/01	
1601/00	
1600/99	
1599/98	
1598/97	
1597/96 S	
1596/95	Jupiter/Saturn conj. - Mar. 15, 1595 BC in Aries
1595/94	**EXODUS** - In the *Book of Jubilees*. It ends
1594/93	with a dating error of 103 years. We are not at liberty
1593/92	to try to reconcile the dating errors between the Bi-
1592/91	ble and the *Book of Jubilees*. We only report them. If
1591/90	there is any value to this ancient Jewish book, it lies
1590/89	in the names of the wives not listed in the Bible, and
1589/88	in the general concept of a Jewish dating method
1588/87	for Sabbatical cycles and Jubilees. Namely, that the
1587/86	Jubilee year is also the first year of the next Sabbati-
1586/85	cal cycle. This is a dating scheme used in the Jew-
1585/84	ish calendar from Bible days to the present.

seed of the woman and the seed of the serpent. In the commentaries of Abarbanel (A.D. 1437-1508) great stress was laid on the conjunctions of the planets Jupiter and Saturn. It was believed that a triple conjunction of the two planets in the constellation Pisces would presage the birth of the Messiah. One of five such triple conjunctions (possibly seven) in Pisces occurred in 7 B.C., and could have been the "star in the East" seen by the Magi.

1584/83	Levi begat Kohath and Kohath begat Amram (I	1535/34	
1583/82	Chron. 6:1,18), but their dates and ages are not	**1534/33**	Joshua was born.
1582/81	given.	1533/32	
1581/80		**1532/31**	Moses fled to Midian.
1580/79		**1531/30**	Caleb was born.
1579/78	**Amram begat Miriam.**	1530/29	
1578/77		1529/28	
1577/76		1528/27	
1576/75	Jupiter/Saturn conj. - Jan. 28, 1575 BC in Sagittarius	1527/26	
1575/74	Amram begat Aaron.	1526/25	
1574/73		1525/24	
1573/72		1524/23	
1572/71	**Amram begat Moses** (b. Adar 7, 1571 BC)	1523/22	
1571/70	To account for 5 years missing between Abraham's	1522/21	
1570/69	70th and 75th year, the *Seder Olam* listed Moses'	1521/20	
1569/68	birth five years earlier, in what would be 1576 in	1520/19	
1568/67	stead of 1571 BC, but the conjunction of Jupiter/	1519/18	
1567/66	Saturn on Jan. 27, 1575 BC, shows that Moses could	1518/17	
1566/65	not have been born that early. Abarbanel (c. 1480)	1517/16	
1565/64	and other Jewish writers noted that a planetary con-	1516/15	Jupiter/Saturn conj. - Nov. 25, 1516 BC in Sagittarius
1564/63	junction of Jupiter and Saturn seemed to the Egyp-	1515/14	
1563/62	tians as a prediction of the birth of a great Jewish	1514/13	
1562/61	leader — as Josephus puts it, "who ... would raise	1513/12	
1561/60	the Israelites ... excel all men in virtue, and obtain a	1512/11	
1560/59	glory that would be remembered through all ages."	1511/10	
1559/58	A triple conjunction of Jupiter and Saturn occurred	1510/09	
1558/57	again just before the birth of Christ — May 29, Oct.	1509/08	
1557/56	1 and Dec. 5, in 7 BC in Pisces.	1508/07	
1556/55	Jupiter/Saturn conj. - Aug. 16, 1555 BC in Virgo	1507/06	
1555/54		1506/05	
1554/53		1505/04	
1553/52		1504/03	
1552/51		1503/02	
1551/50		1502/01	
1550/49		1501/00	
1549/48		1500/99	
1548/47		1499/98	
1547/46		1498/97	
1546/45		1497/96	
1545/44		1496/95	Jupiter/Saturn triple conjunction - Nov. 21, 1496 BC,
1544/43		1495/94	Mar. 8, 1495 BC and Jun. 15, 1495 BC in Virgo
1543/42		1494/93	
1542/41		1493/92	
1541/40		**1492/91**	**The Exodus** - Nisan 15
1540/39		1491/90	
1539/38		1490/89	**5th Dispensation of Law**
1538/37		1489/88	ended with the crucifixion of Christ
1537/36	Jupiter/Saturn triple conjunction - Jun. 28, 1536 BC,	1488/87	
1536/35	Oct. 30, 1536 BC and Jan. 9, 1535 BC in Taurus	1487/86	

According to Jewish sources, Moses was born on Adar 7, and died on that same date, on his 120th birthday. Abarbanel suggested that the conjunction of Jupiter and Saturn 4 years before Moses' birth, caused the Egyptian astrologers to tell Pharaoh that a deliverer would be born to the Jews, causing the deaths of the male infants. The triple conjunction of Jupiter and Saturn in Virgo, three years before the Exodus, occurred in Virgo. It seemed that God was telling Moses to go to Egypt and bring his bride out to Mount Sinai for a spiritual historic marriage.

1486/85		1437/36	**Israel planted their first crop.**	
1485/84		1436/35	Jupiter/Saturn conj. - Sept. 18, 1436 BC in Virgo	
1484/83		1435/34		
1483/82		1434/33		
1482/81		1433/32		
1481/80		1432/31		
1480/79		**1431/30S**	**1st Sabbatical Year**	
1479/78		1430/29		
1478/77		1429/28		
1477/76	Jupiter/Saturn conj. - Apr. 30, 1476 BC in Taurus	1428/27		
1476/75		1427/26		
1475/74		**1426/25**	Dan was driven from the valley to live in the	
1474/73		1425/24	mountains.	
1473/72		**1424/23S**	Joshua died-Nisan 26. The Elders ruled 17 years,	
1472/71		1423/22	until the first judge.	
1471/70		1422/21	The Dannites, having been driven out of their	
1470/69		1421/20	land in 1425 BC (Joshua 1:34), eventually	
1469/68		1420/19	moved to Laish (Judges 18). It is possible that	
1468/67		1419/18	the Danites later migrated to the Greek islands	
1467/66		1418/17	and became known as Danaans or Spartans.	
1466/65		**1417/16S**	Jupiter/Saturn conj. - Mar. 8, 1416 BC in Taurus	
1465/64		1416/15		
1464/63		1415/14		
1463/62		1414/13		
1462/61		1413/12		
1461/60		1412/11		
1460/59		1411/10		
1459/58		**1410/09S**		
1458/57		1409/08		
1457/56	Jupiter/Saturn conj. - Feb. 17, 1456 BC in Capricorn	1408/07		
1456/55		**1407/06**	**Othniel** - 1st judge	
1455/54		1406/05	Judges ruled Israel until Saul became king.	
1454/53		1405/04	They were the *Shoftim* meaning "judges."	
1453/**52**	Aaron ascended Mt. Hor, at the age of 123 years, on	1404/03		
1452/51	Av 1, *"the 1st day of the 5th month"* (Num. 33:38),	**1403/02S**		
1451/50	1452 BC. and died there. Moses conquered Hesh-	1402/01		
1450/49	bon and the area of Gilead from the Arnon River to	1401/00		
1449/48	the Jabbok River. Moses died about 7 months after	1400/99		
1448/47	Aaron on Adar 7. Joshua crossed over Jordan on	1399/98		
1447/46	Nisan 10, 1451 BC. They fought for seven years to	1398/97		
1446/45	gain control of the country. Joshua began to divide	1397/96	Jupiter/Saturn conj. - Dec. 11, 1397 BC in Capricorn	
1445/44	the territory among the tribes, but the logistics of	**1396/95S**		
1444/43	dividing the land must have taken another seven	1395/94		
1443/42	years. This would have cause the first Sabbatical	1394/93		
1442/41	Year to be observed in 1431 BC rather than 1438 BC.	1393/91		
1441/40	Using the Bar Kochba letters, found in a cave near	1392/91		
1440/39	the Dead Sea in 1960, we counted back from AD	1391/90		
1439/38	132/33, the last recorded Jubilee, in order to deter-	1390/89		
1438/37	mine when the first Sabbatical cycle began.	**1389/88S**		

The first Sabbatical Year, **1431/30S**, began with the new moon of September in 1431 B.C., and ended in September 1430 B.C. The "S" designates a Sabbatical Year. This chart conforms with modern Jewish obser- vances of Sabbatical cycles. The last record of a Jubilee was at the beginning of the Bar Kochba revolt in A.D. 132/33. That indicates when the first Jubilee cycle ended in **1388/87 B.C.** This first Jubilee followed the seventh Sabbatical cycle. It was the fiftieth year and first year of the next seven-year cycle. For convenience, the Jubilee

1388/87 J	End of 1st Jubilee	**1339/98 J**	End of 2nd Jubilee
1387/86		1338/37	Jupiter/Saturn conj. - Mar. 3, 1337 BC in Capricorn
1386/85		1337/36	
1385/84	King Eglon of Moab opressed Israel 18 yrs.	1336/35	
1384/83		1335/34	
1383/82		1334/33	
1382/81S		**1333/32S**	
1381/80		1332/31	
1380/79		1331/30	
1379/78		1330/29	
1378/77		1329/28	
1377/76	Jupiter/Saturn triple conjunction - Jan. 9, 1376 BC,	1328/27	
1376/75	Feb. 3, 1376 BC and July 20, 1376 BC in Virgo	1327/26	
1375/74S		**1326/25S**	
1374/73		1325/24	The tribe of Benjamin was almost wiped out.
1373/72		1324/23	
1372.71		1323/22	Naomi and family went to Moab. During their ten-
1371/70		**1322/21**	year stay, her husband and two sons died. Naomi
1370/69		1321/20	was left with two daughters-in-law, Orpah and Ruth.
1369/68		1320/19	Orpah stayed in Moab, but Ruth accompanied Nao-
1368/67S		**1319/18S**	mi back to Bethlehem in 1312 BC.
1367/66	**Ehud** - 2nd judge. He killed King Eglon and defeated	1318/17	Jupiter/Saturn conj. - Oct. 10, 1317 BC in Libra
1366/65	Moab. The land had rest for 80 yrs. We don't know	1317/16	Naomi had lost her land as well as her family. Boaz,
1365/64	how long Ehud lived, but are told that **Shamgar** fol-	1316/15	her kinsman could redeem the land, so Naomi sent
1364/63	lowed him and defeated the Philistines.	1315/14	Ruth into his fields. On Pentecost night, Ruth ap-
1363/62		1314/13	proached the kinsman redeemer, asking him to
1362/61		1313/**12**	help Naomi regain her inheritance. Boaz redeemed
1361/60S		**1312/11S**	Naomi's land and married Ruth in 1312 BC. Their
1360/59		1311/10	son was Obed, who was the father of Jesse and
1359/58		1310/09	grandfather of King David.
1358/57	Jupiter/Saturn conj. - June 11, 1357 BC in Taurus	1309/08	
1357/56		1308/07	
1356/55		1307/06	
1355/54		**1306/05**	King Jaban oppressed Israel 20 years.
1354/53S		**1305/04S**	
1353/52		1304/03	
1352/51		1303/02	
1351/50		1302/01	
1350/49		1301/00	
1349/48		1300/99	
1348/47		1299/98	
1347/46S		**1298/97S**	Jupiter/Saturn conj. - Apr. 20, 1297 BC in Gemini
1346/45		1297/96	
1345/44		1296/95	
1344/43		1295/94	
1343/42		1294/93	
1342/41		1293/92	
1341/40		1292/91	
1340/39S		**1291/90S**	

is placed at the top of each column containing 49 years. If the *Book of Jubilees*, which claims to show Sabbatical cycles and Jubilees from Creation, had actually been dictated by an angel and penned by Moses on top of Mount Sinai, then Joshua would have followed that dating system. However, there seems to be no correlation between the two systems. Fragments of *Jubilees*, also called *"Little Genesis"* and *"The Apocalypse of Moses,"* were found among the Dead Sea Scrolls, but Its origin is unknown.

1290/89 J	End of 3rd Jubilee
1289/88	
1288/87	
1287/86	
1286/85	Shamgar died and **Deborah** became the 4th judge.
1285/84	She and Barak defeated King Jabin.
1284/83S	
1283/82	
1282/81	
1281/80	
1280/79	
1279/78	
1278/77	Jupiter/Saturn conj. - Dec. 25, 1278 BC in Taurus
1277/76S	
1276/75	
1275/74	
1274/73	
1273/72	
1272/71	
1271/70	
1270/69S	
1269/68	
1268/67	
1267/66	
1266/65	
1265/64	
1264/63	
1263/62S	
1262/61	
1261/60	
1260/59	
1259/58	
1258/57	Jupiter/Saturn conj. - Aug. 10, 1257 BC in Libra
1257/56	
1256/55S	
1255/54	
1254/53	
1253/52	
1252/51	
1251/50	
1250/49	
1249/48S	
1248/47	
1247/46	
1246/45	**Gideon** - 5th judge
1245/44	
1244/43	
1243/42	
1242/41S	

1241/40 J	End of 4th Jubilee
1240/39	
1239/38	Jupiter/Saturn conj. - July 24, 1238 BC in Gemini
1238/37	
1237/36	Gideon died.
1236/35	**Abimelech** - 6th judge and short-lived king (Judges 9)
1235/34S	
1234/33	
1233/32	**Tola** - 7th judge
1232/31	
1231/30	
1230/29	
1229/28	
1228/27S	
1227/26	
1226/25	
1225/24	Merneptah, son of Rameses II (1224-1214 BC) con-
1224/23	quered Canaan in the spring of his 5th year (1219
1223/22	BC). A black granite Stele at the Cairo Museum
1222/21	says, "Plundered is Canaan with every evil. Carried
1221/20S	off is Askelon; siezed upon is Gezer; Yanoam is
1220/**19**	made as that which does not exist . . .
1219/18	Jupiter/Saturn conj. - Mar. 17, 1218 BC in Aquarius
1218/17	. . . **Israel is laid waste**, his seed is not; Hurru
1217/16	(Palestine) has become a widow for Egypt! All lands
1216/15	together, they are pacified ... by King Merneptah."
1215/14	Semiramis rebuilt the city of Babylon
1214/13S	Eli was born
1213/12	
1212/11	
1211/10	
1210/09	Jair - 8th judge
1209/08	
1208/07	
1207/06S	
1206/05	
1205/04	
1204/03	
1203/02	
1202/01	
1201/00	
1200/99S	
1199/98	Jupiter/Saturn conj. - Oct. 30, 1198 BC in Libra
1198/97	
1197/96	
1196/95	
1195/94	
1194/93	
1193/92S	

The *Book of Jubilees* starts out with a 100-year error at the birth of Enoch, worsens to a 349-year error at the birth of Noah, a 355-year error at the birth of Arphaxad and ends with eliminating only 103 years at the time of the Exodus. Therefore, the Book of Jubilees could not have been dictated by an angel atop Mt. Sinai. It is the flawed work of a Jew, probably in the second century BC. Only the Bible offers perfectly accurate information and the best framework for a study of the first 4,000 years from Adam to Christ.

1192/91 J	End of 5th Jubilee
1191/90	
1190/89	
1189/88	
1188/87	**Jephath** - 9th judge (see note at 1152 BC)
1187/86	
1186/85S	
1185/84	
1184/83	Troy was destroyed by the Spartans (i.e., Danaans).
1183/82	
1182/81	**Ibzan** - 10th judge
1181/80	
1180/79	
1179/78S	Jupiter/Saturn conj. - June 2, 1178 BC in Gemini
1178/77	
1177/76	
1176/75	
1175/74	**Elon** - 11th judge
1174/73	
1173/72	
1172/71S	
1171/70	
1170/69	
1169/68	
1168/67	
1167/66	
1166/65	
1165/64S	**Abdon** - 12th judge
1164/63	
1163/62	
1162/61	
1161/60	
1160/59	
1159/58	Jupiter/Saturn conj. - Jan. 9, 1158 BC in Aquarius
1158/57S	
1157/56	**Eli** was High Priest at the Tabernacle in Shiloh
1156/55	Samson was born.
1155/54	
1154/53	
1153/52	
1152/51	NOTE: In Judges 11:25,26, Jephath said, "Did he
1151/50S	[Moab] ever strive against Israel ... while Israel dwelt
1150/49	in Heshbon ... three hundred years?" It is likely that
1149/48	this was an approximate figure. Had it been literally
1148/47	300 years since the Israelites took their land from
1147/46	the Amorites, then Jephath would have become
1146/45	judge in 1152 BC, rather than 1188 BC., and there
1145/44	would not be enough years for the remaining judges
1144/43S	leading up to King Saul.

1143/42 J	End of 6th Jubilee
1142/41	
1141/40	
1140/39	
1139/38	Jupiter/Saturn conj. - Aug. 28, 1138 BC in Libra
1138/37	**Samson** - 13th judge
1137/36S	The Danite tribe had moved north to the foothills of
1136/35	Mount Hermon around 1425 BC. Some 300 years lat-
1135/34	er, Samson, a Danite whose family still lived near the
1134/33	Gaza strip (the land allotted to the Danites, but oc-
1133/32	cupied by the Philistines), took up the fight against
1132/31	their old enemy. The Philistines were "sea people"
1131/30	who had come from Kittim, thought to be Greece.
1130/29S	Now, it seems that the Danites had migrated from
1129/28	Northern Israel to Greece, the very place where the
1128/27	Philistines came from, and settled in Sparta. Hom-
1127/26	er's *Illiad* called the Spartans "Danaans." During the
1126/25	40 years that the Philistines dominated Israel, Sam-
1125/24	son fought their common enemy. His war with the
1124/23	Philistines covered a period of 20 years.
1123/22S	**Samuel** was born.
1122/21	
1121/20	
1120/19	Jupiter/Saturn triple conjunction - Sept. 11, 1119 BC,
1119/18	Dec. 14, 1119 BC, and Apr. 3, 1118 BC in Cancer
1118/17	Samson died.
1117/16	Eli died. The Philistines kept the Ark for seven
1116/15S	months, then sent it back with gifts. It was placed
1115/14	in the home of Aminadab until David fetched it 70
1114/13	years later.
1113/12	
1112/11	
1111/10	
1110/09	
1109/08S	
1108/07	
1107/06	
1106/05	
1105/04	
1104/03	Barzillai was born. He was 80 yrs old when Absa-
1103/02	lom died.
1102/01S	
1101/00	
1100/99	Jupiter/Saturn conj. - Apr. 4, 1099 BC in Aquarius
1099/98	
1098/97	
1097/96	Samuel was told to choose a king for Israel.
1096/95	**Saul** - the 1st king ruled 40 years.
1095/94S	

Boaz had married Ruth in his later years. Exactly when is not certain, but their son, Obed, was the father of Jesse, who begat David. Ussher says that Saul became king in 1095/94 B.C., and ruled for 40 years. If so, then Saul, David and Solomon ruled for 40 years each.

1094/93 J	End of 7th Jubilee
1093/92	
1092/91	
1091/90	
1090/89	
1089/88	
1088/87S	
1087/86	
1086/85	**David was born.**
1085/84	
1084/83	
1083/82	
1082/81	
1081/80S	
1080/79	
1079/78	Jupiter/Saturn conj. - Nov. 16, 1079 BC in Scorpio
1078/77	
1077/76	
1076/75	
1075/74	
1074/73S	
1073/72	
1072/71	
1071/70	
1070/69	
1069/68	
1068/67	
1067/66S	
1066/65	
1065/64	
1064/63	
1063/62	David (23 years old) was anointed by Samuel
1062/61	
1061/60	
1060/59S	Jupiter/Saturn conj. - July 15, 1059 BC in Cancer
1059/58	
1058/57	
1057/56	
1056/55	Saul died and **David** became the 1st king in the
1055/54	lineage of Jesus (Matthew 1:6). David ruled Judah
1054/53	from Hebron for seven years, then all Israel for the
1053/52S	next 33 years — a total of 40 years.
1052/51	
1051/50	
1050/49	
1049/48	David became king of all Israel.
1048/47	Jerusalem became the new capital of Israel.
1047/45	
1046/45S	David retrieved the Ark.

1045/44 J	End of 8th Jubilee
1044/43	
1043/42	
1042/41	
1041/40	
1040/39	Jupiter/Saturn conj. - Jan. 29, 1039 BC in Pisces
1039/38S	
1038/37	
1037/36	
1036/**35**	David's sin with Bathsheba
1035/**34**	Their first baby died.
1034/33	Solomon was born of Bathsheba.
1033/32	
1032/31S	Tamar was raped by Amnon.
1031/30	
1030/29	Absalom killed Amnon for raping his sister.
1029/28	
1028/27	
1027/26	
1026/25	
1025/24S	
1024/23	
1023/22	Absalom died.
1022/21	
1021/20	
1020/19	Jupiter/Saturn conj. - Sept. 16, 1019 BC in Ophiuchus
1019/18	
1018/17S	David bought Ornan's threshingfloor.
1017/16	
1016/15	**Solomon** - 3rd king - was 18 years old.
1015/14	(2nd in Matthew's royal lineage).
1014/13	
1013/12	**I Kings 6:**
1012/11	**Temple begun in 480th year after the Exodus.**
1011/10S	1. And it came to pass in the four hundred and
1010/09	eightieth year after the children of Israel were come
1009/08	out of the land of Egypt, in the fourth year of Solo-
1008/07	mon's reign over Israel, in the month Zif, which is
1007/06	the second month, that he began to build the house
1006/05	of the LORD.
1005/04	Temple was dedicated.
1004/03S	
1003/02	
1002/01	
1001/00	
1000/99	Jupiter/Saturn conj. - May 30, 999 BC in Leo
999/98	
998/97	
997/96S	

David became king of Judea in 1056/55 B.C., and king of all tribes in 1049/48 B.C. There were 23 Judean kings, beginning with Saul of the tribe of Benjamin, replaced by David of the tribe of Judah. Also, there were 20 northern kings, making a total of 43 kings.

996/95 J	End of 9th Jubilee
995/94	
994/93	
993/92	
992/91	
991/90	
990/89S	
989/88	
988/87	
987/86	
986/85	
985/84	
984/83	
983/82S	
982/81	
981/80	Jupiter/Saturn triple conjunction - May 4, 980 BC,
980/79	Sept. 28, 980 BC and Nov. 3, 980 BC in Pisces
979/78	
978/77	
977/76	
976/75S	Solomon died. **Rehoboam** - 4th S. king
975/74	**Jeroboam** split the kingdom - Israel's 1st N. king
974/73	
973/72	
972/71	
971/70	
970/69	
969/68S	
968/67	
967/66	
966/65	
965/64	
964/63	
963/62	
962/61S	
961/60	
960/59	Jupiter/Saturn conj. - Dec. 5, 960 BC in Ophiuchus
959/58	
958/57	**Abijah** - 5th S. king
957/56	
956/55	**Asa** - 6th S. king (spring)
955/54S	**Nadab** - 2nd N. king
954/53	**Baasha** - 3th N. king
953/52	
952/51	
951/50	
950/49	
949/48	
948/47S	

947/46 J	End of 10th Jubilee
946/45	
945/44	
944/43	
943/42	
942/41	
941/40S	Jupiter/Saturn conj. - Sept. 3, 940 BC in Leo
940/39	
939/38	
938/37	
937/36	
936/35	
935/34	
934/33S	
933/32	
932/31	
931/30	**Elah** - 4th N. king (summer)
930/29	**Zimri, Tibna, Omri** N. kings
929/28	
928/27	
927/26S	
926/25	**Omri** (only) - 7th N. king
925/24	
924/23	
923/22	
922/21	
921/20	Jupiter/Saturn conj. - Mar. 1, 920 BC in Pisces
920/19S	
919/18	**Ahab** - 8th N. king
918/17	
917/16	
916/15	
915/14	**Jehoshaphat** - 7th S. king
914/13	
913/12S	
912/11	
911/10	
910/09	
909/08	
908/07	
907/06	
906/05S	
905/04	
904/03	
903/02	
902/01	
901/00	Jupiter/Saturn conj. - Oct. 8, 900 BC in Ophiuchus
900/99	
899/98S	

In the 35th year of Solomon's reign there was a triple conjunction of Jupiter and Saturn in Pisces — something believed to presage the birth of the Messiah. Solomon was a prototype and progenitor of the Messiah. A previous triple conjunction had occurred in 1834 BC, when Jacob was 2 years old. It seems that God was confirming the lineage of the Savior. A triple conjunction of Jupiter and Saturn in the constellation Pisces has occurred throughout history about a thousand years apart.

898/97 J	End of 11th Jubilee **Ahaziah** - 9th N. king
897/96	**Joram** - 10th N. king
896/95	
895/94	
894/93	
893/92	**Jehoram** - 8th S. king
892/91S	
891/90	
890/89	
889/88	
888/87	
887/86	**Ahaziah** - 9th S. king (skipped by Matthew)
886/85	**Athaliah** - 10th S. queen & **Jehu** - 11th N. king
885/84S	
884/83	
883/82	
882/81	
881/80	Jupiter/Saturn conj. - July 22, 880 BC in Leo
880/79	**Joash** - 11th S. king (skipped by Matthew)
879/78	Matthew's genealogy skipped 3 southern kings
878/77S	— Ahaziah, Joash and Amaziah. Matthew said
877/76	that Jehoram begat Uzziah (Matt. 1:8), his great-
876/75	great-grandson. II Chron. 21 tells us that Jehoram
875/74	married Ahab's daughter, Athaliah, contaminating
874/73	David's bloodline. He was so wicked, he murdered
873/72	his brothers. The Ten Commandments decree that
872/71	the iniquities of the father will be visited upon the
871/70S	children until the third and fourth generations. Aha-
870/69	ziah was killed by Jehu while visiting relatives in
869/68	Samaria. Joash killed the son of the high priest, and
868/67	was assassinated in a palace coup. Amaziah was
867/66	also assassinated. Uzziah was struck with leprosy
866/65	in the Temple. None of these kings, Jehoram, Aha-
865/64	ziah, Joash, Amaziah or Uzziah, were allowed to be
864/63S	buried among the kings of Judah. But it seems that
863/62	David's lineage could have been purged of Ahab's
862/61	DNA by the time of the fourth generation. That is my
861/60	suggestion as to why 3 kings were skipped.
860/59	Jupiter/Saturn triple conjunction - July 1, 861 BC,
859/58	Aug. 8, 861 BC, Jan. 1, 860 BC in Pisces
858/57	
857/56S	**Jehoahaz** - 12th N. king
856/55	
855/54	
854/53	
853/52	
852/51	
851/50	
850/49S	

849/48 J	End of 12th Jubilee
848/47	
847/46	
846/45	
845/44	
844/43	
843/42S	
842/41	
841/40	**Amaziah** - 12 S. king (skipped by Matthew)
840/39	Jupiter/Saturn conj. - Dec. 29, 841 BC in Sagittarius
839/38	He reigned for 29 years, but the *Seder Olam* said he
838/37	fled in his 15th year.
837/36	**Jehoash** - 13th N. king
836/35S	
835/34	
834/33	
833/32	
832/31	
831/30	
830/29	
829/28S	
828/27	
827/26	
826/25	**Jeroboam** - 14th N. king. Did Amaziah flee?
825/24	
824/23	
823/22	
822/21S	
821/20	Jupiter/Saturn triple conjunction - Nov. 16, 821 BC,
820/19	Jan. 7, 820 BC, June 4, 820 BC in Leo
819/18	
818/17	
817/16	
816/15	
815/14S	
814/13	
813/12	
812/11	**Uzziah** - 13th S. king reigned 52 years. However, the
811/10	*Seder Olam* has him reigning for the last 15 years of
810/09	Amaziah's life, and dying in 773/72 BC, rather than
809/08	in 760/59 BC, leaving 14 missing years.
808/07S	
807/06	
806/05	
805/04	
804/03	
803/02	
802/01	Jupiter/Saturn conj. - Apr. 11, 801 BC in Pisces
801/00S	

14 missing years

800/799 J	End of 13th Jubilee		**751/50 J**	End of 14th Jubilee
799/98			750/49	
798/97			749/48	8th Greek Olympiad - **Rome founded by Romulus**
797/96			**748/47**	**on Apr. 10, 748BC.**
796/95			747/46	
795/94			746/45	
794/93S			**745/44S**	9th Greek Olympiad
793/92			**744/43**	**Ahaz** - 15th S. king
792/91			743/42	
791/90			**742/41**	Jupiter/Saturn conj. - Feb. 22, 741 BC in Aries
790/89			741/40	10th Greek Olympiad
789/88			**740/39**	Pekah died and an interregnum followed
788/87			739/38	with no N. king for 9 years.
787/86S			**738/37S**	
786/85			737/36	11th Greek Olympiad
785/84	Jeroboam died, and an Interregnum followed		736/35	
784/83	with no N. king for 12 years.		735/34	
783/82			734/33	
782/81	Jupiter/Saturn conj. - Oct. 31, 781 BC in Sagittarius		733/32	12th Greek Olympiad
781/80			732/31	
780/79S			**731/30S**	**Hoshea** - 20th N. king
779/78			730/29	
778/77			729/28	13th Greek Olympiad
777/**776**	1st Greek Olympiad (July 776BC) (Greek Games)		**728/27**	**Hezekiah** - 16th S. king
776/75	Greek mythology ends and true Greek history		727/26	
775/74	begins.		726/25	
774/73	**Zachariah** (6mo) 15th N. king		725/24	14th Greek Olympiad
773/72S	**Shallum** (1mo), **Menachem** became 17th N. king.		**724/23S**	
772/71			723/22	
771/70			**722/21**	**Assyrian captivity**
770/69			721/20	Jupiter/Saturn conj. - Jan. 24, 721 BC in Sagittarius
769/68	3rd Greek Olympiad		720/19	(The northern tribes had a total of 20 kings.)
768/67			719/18	
767/66			718/17	
766/65S			**717/16S**	16th Greek Olympiad
765/64	4th Greek Olympiad		716/15	
764/63			715/14	
763/62			714/13	
762/61	**Pekahiah** - 18th N. king		**713/12**	Hezekiah's illness -God healed and gave him
761/60	Jupiter/Saturn conj. - Sept. 12, 761 BC in Virgo		712/11	another 15 years to live.
760/59	**Jotham** - 14th S. king & **Pekah** - 19th N. king		711/10	
759/58S			**710/09S**	
758/57			709/08	18th Greek Olympiad
757/56	6th Greek Olympiad		708/07	
756/55			707/06	
755/54			706/05	**Sennacherib** ascended the Assyrian throne.
754/53			705/04	19th Greek Olympiad
753/52	7th Greek Olympiad - Carthage built		704/03	
752/51S			**703/02S**	Sennacherib surrounds Jerusalem.

Scholars differ on the date of Sennacherib's invasion. But in telling King Hezekiah that Sennacherib would not succeed in conquering Judah, Isaiah referred to the 49th and fiftieth years of the Jubilee cycle: *"Ye shall eat this year such as groweth of itself; and the second year that which springeth of the same: and in the third year sow ye, and reap, and plant vineyards, and eat the fruit thereof"* (Isa. 37:30). This year had to be 703/02 B.C.,

702/01 J	End of 15th Jubilee
701/00	Jupiter/Saturn conj. - July 30, 701 BC in Virgo
700/99	
699/98	
698/97	**Manesseh** - 17th S. king
697/96	He put idols in Temple, the Ark was removed, and
696/95S	Isaiah was killed.
695/94	
694/93	
693/92	22nd Greek Olympiad
692/91	
691/90	
690/89	
689/88S	23rd Greek Olympiad
688/87	
687/86	
686/85	
685/84	24th Greek Olympiad
684/83	
683/82	Jupiter/Saturn conj. - May 31, 682 BC in Aries
682/81S	
681/80	25th Greek Olympiad
680/79	
679/78	
678/77	
677/76	26th Greek Olympiad
676/75	
675/74S	
674/73	
673/72	27th Greek Olympiad
672/71	
671/70	
670/69	
669/68	28th Greek Olympiad
668/67S	
667/66	
666/65	
665/64	29th Greek Olympiad
664/63	
663/62	Jupiter/Saturn conj. - Nov. 24, 662 BC in Sagittarius
662/61	Ashurbanipal was joined by Jewish mercenaries on
661/60S	his way to conquer Egypt. Afterward, the Jews set-
660/59	tled on Elephantine Island and built a large temple.
659/58	It is possible that they had the Ark.
658/57	
657/56	
656/55	
655/54	
654/53S	

653/52 J	End of 16th Jubilee - 32nd Greek Olympiad
652/51	
651/50	
650/49	
649/48	33rd Greek Olympiad
648/47	
647/46S	
646/45	
645/44	34th Greek Olympiad
644/43	**Amon** - 18th S. king
643/42	**Josiah** - 19th S. king
642/41	Jupiter/Saturn conj. - Nov. 1, 642 BC in Virgo
641/40	35th Greek Olympiad
640/39S	
639/38	
638/37	
637/36	36th Greek Olympiad
636/35	
635/34	
634/33	
633/32S	37th Greek Olympiad
632/31	
631/30	
630/29	Temple cleansed
629/28	38th Greek Olympiad
628/27	
627/26	
626/25S	
625/24	39th Greek Olympiad
624/23	Josiah kept Passover. The Ark was missing.
623/22	Jupiter/Saturn conj. - Apr. 11, 622 BC in Taurus
622/21	
621/20	40th Greek Olympiad
620/19	
619/18S	
618/17	
617/16	41st Greek Olympiad
616/15	
615/14	
614/13	
613/12	42nd Greek Olympiad
612/11S	
611/10	**Jehoahaz** - 20th S. king (3mo)
610/09	**& Jehoiakim** - 21th S. king
609/08	43rd Greek Olympiad
608/07	
607/06	**1st Babylonian Exile**
606/05	(Daniel among deportees)
605/04S	44th Greek Olympiad

rather than 710/09 B.C., as Ussher suggested. According to Dr. Floyd Nolen Jones, Sennacherib didn't ascend the Assyrian throne until 705 B.C.

604/03 J	End of 17th Jubilee Daniel reveals King		**555/54 J**	End of 18th Jubilee
603/02	Nebuchadnezzar's dream in his second year.		**554/53**	He was succeeded by **Nabonidus**, grandson of
602/01	Jupiter/Saturn conj. - Feb. 16, 602 BC in Capricorn		553/52	Nebuchadnezzar by Evilmerodach. Nabonidus
601/00	45th Greek Olympiad		552/51	was also known as **Belshazzar** (r.555-538 BC).
600/99	**2nd Exile**		551/50	(555 BC) Daniel's vision of four beasts.
599/98	**Coniah** - 22nd S. king (3mo)		550/49	(553 BC) Daniel's vision of the ram and goat.
598/97S	**Zedekiah** - 23nd S. king		**549/48S**	58th Greek Olympiad
597/96	(Ezekiel was among the deportees)		548/47	
596/95			547/46	
595/94			546/45	
594/93			545/44	59th Greek Olympiad
593/92	47th Greek Olympiad		544/43	
592/91			543/42	Jupiter/Saturn conj. - Dec. 13, 543 BC in Capricorn
591/90S			542/41S	
590/89			541/40	60th Greek Olympiad
589/88	**3rd Exile**		540/39	
588/87	(Solomon's Temple was burned Av 9, 588 BC)		**539/38**	Belshazzar died.
587/86			538/37	1. **Darius** ruled 1 yr. Daniel's vision of 70 weeks.
586/85	The S. kingdom ended after 390 years and 23 kings,		537/36	2. **Cyrus** - Decree - Zerubbabal returned to Judea.
585/84	for a total of 43 kings in the N. & S. kingdoms.		536/35	
584/83S			**535/34S**	Daniel's last vision (ch. 10-12)
583/82	Jupiter/Saturn conj. - Sept. 10, 582 BC in Virgo		**534/33**	**Seventy weeks began**
582/81			**533/32**	62nd Greek Olympiad
581/80	50th Greek Olympiad		**532/31**	
580/79	Nebuchadnezzar's image of gold		**531/30**	
579/78			**530/29**	Cyrus died. 3. **Cambyses** became king of Persia.
578/77			**529/28**	63rd Greek Olympiad
577/76S	51st Greek Olympiad		**528/27S**	1st week ended
576/75			**527/26**	
575/74			**526/25**	
574/73			**525/24**	64th Greek Olympiad
573/72	52nd Greek Olympiad		**524/23**	Jupiter/Saturn triple conjunction - Dec. 16, 523 BC,
572/71			**523/22**	Mar. 14, 522 BC, and July 10, 522 BC in Virgo
571/70			**522/21**	4. **Ahasuerus** became the king of Persia.
570/69S	The dream of a tree ... Neb. was insane 7 years.		**521/20S**	65th Greek Olympiad - (Daniel's 2nd week ended)
569/68			**520/19**	
568/67			**519/18**	
567/66			**518/17**	**Esther became the queen of Persia.**
566/65			**517/16**	66th Greek Olympiad
565/64	Jupiter/Saturn triple conjunction - July 26, 563 BC,		**516/15**	
564/63	Nov. 2, 563 BC and Feb. 9, 562 BC in Taurus		**515/14**	The Jerusalem Temple was dedicated.
563/62S	Nebuchadnezzar was restored, ruled 1 year and died.		**514/13S**	3rd week ended
562/61	His son, **Evilmerodach**, ruled 2 yrs and was		**513/12**	67th Greek Olympiad
561/60	murdered by Neriglissar, his sister's husband.		**512/11**	
560/59	**Neriglisssar** became king and ruled 4 yrs, then		**511/10**	
559/58	was succeded by his son Laborosoarchodus.		**510/09**	Haman's Edict
558/57			**509/08**	Haman was hung.
557/56	56th Greek Olympiad		**508/07**	
556/55S	**Laborosoarchodus** ruled 9 months.		**507/06S**	Daniel's 4th week ended

Sixty-nine of Daniel's *"seventy weeks"* are listed in enlarged type, with the first seven weeks (49 years) beginning in 534 B.C. (the first year of a seven-year cycle) and concluding with the seventh Sabbatical Year in 486/85 B.C., at which time Ahasuerus died and Esther was no longer the Jewish queen of Persia. I suggest a gap of 11 weeks (*shavuim* of 77 years) (485-409 B.C.) as a period of *"troublous times"* (Dan. 9:25), and a return to the counting of the 62 weeks from the 21st Jubilee in 408/07 B.C., with Malachi, to AD 26/27, the beginning of Jesus' ministry.

506/05 J	End of 19th Jubilee
505/04	69th Greek Olympiad
504/03	
503/02	Jupiter/Saturn conj. - May 25, 503 BC in Taurus
502/01	
501/00	70th Greek Olympiad
500/99S	Daniel's 5th week ended
499/98	
498/97	
497/96	71st Greek Olympiad
496/95	
495/94	
494/93	
493/92S	72nd Olympiad - Daniel's 6th week ended
492/91	
491/90	
490/89	
489/88	73rd Greek Olympiad
488/87	
487/86	
486/85S	Daniel's 7th week ended - Ahasuerus died. Esther
485/84	disappeared. Gabriel's 70-weeks counting stopped.
484/83	Jupiter/Saturn conj. - Mar. 5, 483 BC in Capricorn
483/82	
482/81	
481/80	5. **Xerxes** (485 BC)-These were "troublous times."
480/79	The *Seder Olam* skipped the next 164 years and
479/78S	claims that Alexander defeated Persia in 321 BC.
478/77	
477/76	
476/75	
475/74	
474/73	Artaxerxes was made viceroy with his father.
473/72	
472/71S	
471/70	
470/69	
469/68	78th Greek Olympiad
468/67	
467/66	Ezra returned to Judea.
466/65	
465/64S	6. **Artaxerxes** was made king of Persia
464/63	Jupiter/Saturn conj. - Oct. 9, 463 BC in Libra
463/62	
462/61	
461/60	80th Greek Olympiad
460/59	
459/58	
458/57S	

457/56 J	End of 20th Jubilee - 81st Greek Olympiad
456/55	
455/54	
454/53	
453/52	82nd Greek Olympiad
452/51	
451/50S	
450/49	
449/48	83rd Greek Olympiad
448/47	
447/46	
446/45	Artaxerxes sent Nehemiah to Judea.
445/44	
444/43S	Jupiter/Saturn conj. - Apr. 3, 443 BC in Taurus
443/42	
442/41	
441/40	85th Greek Olympiad
440/39	
439/38	
438/37	
437/36S	86th Greek Olympiad
436/35	
435/34	**164 years missing**
434/33	**in the *Seder Olam***
433/32	**(gray numbers)**
432/31	
431/30	
430/29S	88th Greek Olympiad
429/28	
428/27	
427/26	
426/25	
425/24	7. **Xerxes** became the king of Persia.
424/23	8. **Secundianus** became the king of Persia.
423/22S	9. **Ochus** became the king of Persia.
422/21	Jupiter/Saturn conj. - Dec. 28, 424 BC in Capricorn
421/20	90th Greek Olympiad
420/19	
419/18	
418/17	
417/16	91st Greek Olympiad
416/15S	
415/14	
414/13	
413/12	92nd Greek Olympiad
412/11	
411/10	
410/09	
409/08S	93rd Greek Olympiad

The *Seder Olam Rabbah* removed 65 years from Abraham's lifetime (2056 to 1996 B.C., and 1927 to 1922 B.C); truncated 14 years from the reign of Amaziah (826 to 812 B.C.); and 164 years from the Persian Empire (485 to 321 B.C.), moving Alexander's conquest of Persia from 331 B.C. to 321 B.C. — a total of 243 years missing in the Jewish calendar. The 164 years (above) are a light gray color to signify that they were left out of the Jewish calendar.

408/07 **J**	End of 21st Jubilee - Malachi was the last	
407/06	prophet of the Old Testament period. The counting	
406/05	of the 70 weeks resumed after a 77-year gap.	
405/04		
404/03	10. **Arsicas** became the king of Persia.	
403/02	Jupiter/Saturn conj. - Aug. 9, 403 BC in Libra	
402/01**S**	Daniel's 8th week ended	
401/00	95th Greek Olympiad	
400/99		
399/98		
398/97		
397/96	96th Greek Olympiad	
396/95		
395/94**S**	Daniel's 9th week ended	
394/93		
393/92	97th Greek Olympiad	
392/91		
391/90		
390/89		
389/88	98th Greek Olympiad	
388/87**S**	Daniel's 10th week ended	
387/86		
386/85		
385/84	Jupiter/Saturn conj. - July 5, 384 BC in Gemini	
384/83		
383/82		
382/81		
381/80**S**	100th Olympiad - Daniel's 11th week ended	
380/79		
379/78		
378/77		
377/76	101st Greek Olympiad	
376/75		
375/74		
374/73**S**	Daniel's 12th week ended	
373/72	102nd Greek Olympiad	
372/71		
371/70		
370/69		
369/68	103rd Greek Olympiad	
368/67		
367/66**S**	Daniel's 13th week ended	
366/65		
365/64	Jupiter/Saturn conj. - Mar. 19, 364 BC in Aquarius	
364/63		
363/62		
362/61		
361/60	11.**Ochus** - 105th Greek Olympiad	
360/59**S**	Daniel's 14th week ended	

359/58 **J**	End of 22nd Jubilee
358/57	
357/56	106th Greek Olympiad
356/55	
355/54	
354/53	
353/52**S**	107th Olympiad - Daniel's 15th week ended
352/51	
351/50	
350/49	
349/48	108th Greek Olympiad
348/47	
347/46	
346/45**S**	Daniel's 16th week ended
345/44	109th Greek Olympiad
344/43	Jupiter/Saturn conj. - Oct. 30, 344 BC in Libra
343/42	
342/41	
341/40	110th Greek Olympiad
340/39	
339/38**S**	Daniel's 17th week ended
338/37	12. **Arses** became the king of Persia.
337/36	111th Greek Olympiad
336/35	13. **Darius** became the king of Persia.
335/34	**Alexander** made king of Greece (336 BC)
334/33	
333/32	112th Greek Olympiad
332/31**S**	Daniel's 18th week
331/30	**Alexander** won and the Persian King Darius died.
330/29	
329/28	
328/27	
327/26	
326/25	
325/24**S**	114th Greek Olympiad - Daniel's 19th week ended
324/23	Jupiter/Saturn conj. - May 16, 324 BC in Gemini
323/22	Alexander died in Babylon at the age of 33 years..
322/21	Ptolemy took his body to Egypt for burial.
321/20	115th Greek Olympiad
320/19	
319/18	
318/17**S**	Daniel's 20th week ended
317/16	116th Greek Olympiad
316/15	
315/14	
314/13	
313/12	117th Greek Olympiad
312/11	Seleucus's kingdom. Jews adopt Greek calendar.
311/10**S**	Daniel's 21st week ended

Malachi was the last Old Testament prophet. But, he left a promise that Elijah would come to announce the Messiah. This seems to designate this period of sixty-two weeks — Malachi would start the counting and John the Baptist (a fulfillment of the promised Elijah) would appear at the end of it. We now await the final future return of Elijah as promised by Jesus (Matt. 17:11). He will appear in the 70th week.

310/09 J	End of 23rd Jubilee	
309/08	118th Greek Olympiad	
308/07		
307/06		
306/05		
305/04	Jupiter/Saturn conj. - Jan. 10, 304 BC in Aquarius	
304/03 S	Daniel's 22nd week	
303/02		
302/01		
301/00	120th Greek Olympiad	
300/99		
299/98		
298/97		
297/96 S	Daniel's 23rd week ended - 121st Olympiad	
296/95		
295/94		
294/93		
293/92	122nd Greek Olympiad	
292/91		
291/90		
290/89 S	Daniel's 24th week ended	
289/88	123rd Greek Olympiad	
288/87		
287/86		
286/85		
285/84	Jupiter/Saturn conj. - Aug. 29, 284 BC in Libra	
284/83		
283/82 S	Daniel's 25th week ended	
282/81		
281/80	125th Greek Olympiad	
280/79		
279/78		
278/77		
277/76	126th Greek Olympiad	
276/75 S	Daniel's 26th week ended	
275/74		
274/73		
273/72	127th Greek Olympiad	
272/71		
271/70		
270/69		
269/68 S	Daniel's 27th week ended - 128th Greek Olympiad	
268/67		
267/66		
266/65	Jupiter/Saturn conj. - Aug. 17, 265 BC in Cancer	
265/64	129th Greek Olympiad	
264/63		
263/62		
262/61 S	Daniel's 28th week ended	

261/60 J	End of 24th Jubilee - 130th Greek Olympiad	
260/59		
259/58		
258/57		
257/56	131st Greek Olympiad	
256/55		
255/54 S	Daniel's 29th week ended	
254/53		
253/52	132nd Greek Olympiad	
252/51		
251/50		
250/49		
249/48	133rd Greek Olympiad	
248/47 S	Daniel's 30th week ended	
247/46		
246/45	Jupiter/Saturn conj. - Apr. 2, 245 BC in Aquarius	
245/44	134th Greek Olympiad	
244/43		
243/42		
242/41		
241/40 S	Daniel's 31st week ended - 135th Greek Olympiad	
240/39		
239/38		
238/37		
237/36	136th Greek Olympiad	
236/35		
235/34		
234/33 S	Daniel's 32nd week ended	
233/32	137th Greek Olympiad	
232/31		
231/30		
230/29		
229/28	138th Greek Olympiad	
228/27		
227/26 S	Daniel's 33rd week ended	
226/25		
225/24	Jupiter/Saturn conj. - Nov. 17, 225 BC in Scorpio	
224/23		
223/22		
222/21		
221/20	140th Greek Olympiad	
220/19 S	Daniel's 34th week ended	
219/18		
218/17		
217/16	141st Greek Olympiad	
216/15		
215/14		
214/13		
213/12 S	Daniel's 35th week ended - 142nd Olympiad	

Between Malachi and Matthew, there were about 400 silent years when no prophet arose until John. The Persian Empire fell in 330 BC, and the Greek/Syrian (Seleucus) established his kingdom in 312 BC. At that time, Judea adopted the Greek calendar (Minyan Shterot) as they had promised to Alexander. Jews used the Greek calendar's dating system until AD 1517, when they adopted their modern calendar with its 243 missing years.

212/11 J	End of 25th Jubilee		163/62 J	End of 26th Jubilee
211/10			162/61	
210/09			161/60	155th Olympiad
209/08	143rd Olympiad		160/59	
208/07			159/58	
207/06			158/57	
206/05S	Daniel's 36th week		157/56S	Daniel's 43rd week ended - 156th Olympiad
205/04	Jupiter/Saturn conj. - June 26, 205 BC in Cancer		156/55	
204/03			155/54	
203/02			154/53	
202/01			153/52	157th Olympiad
201/00	145th Olympiad		152/51	
200/99			151/50	
199/98S	Daniel's 37th week ended		150/49S	Daniel's 44th week ended
198/97			149/48	158th Olympiad
197/96	146th Olympiad		148/47	
196/95			147/46	
195/94			146/45	Jupiter/Saturn triple conjunction - Oct. 17, 146 BC,
194/93			145/44	Dec. 11, 146 BC, and May 4, 145 BC in Cancer
193/92	147th Olympiad		144/43	
192/91S	Daniel's 38th week ended		143/42S	Daniel's 45th week
191/90			142/41	
190/89			141/40	160th Olympiad
189/88	148th Olympiad		140/39	
188/87			139/38	
187/86			138/37	
186/85	Jupiter/Saturn conj. - Jan. 27, 185 BC in Aquarius		137/36	161st Olympiad
185/84S	Daniel's 39th week ended - 149th Olympiad		136/35S	Daniel's 46th week ended
184/83			135/34	
183/82			134/33	
182/81			133/32	162nd Olympiad
181/80	150th Olympiad		132/31	
180/79			131/30	
179/78			130/29	
178/77S	Daniel's 40th week ended		129/28S	Daniel's 47th week ended - 163rd Olympiad
177/76	151st Olympiad		128/27	
176/75			127/26	Jupiter/Saturn conj. - Apr. 24, 126 BC in Pisces
175/74	Antiochus IV Epiphanes - king		126/25	
174/73			125/24	164th Olympiad
173/72	152nd Olympiad		124/23	
172/71			123/22	
171/70S	Daniel's 41st week ended		122/21S	Daniel's 48th week ended
170/69			121/20	165th Olympiad
169/68	Antiochus besieged Jerusalem - 153rd Olympiad.		120/19	
168/67			119/18	
167/66	Kislev 25 - A sow was sacrificed and a statue of		118/17	
166/65	Zeus was erected.		117/16	166th Olympiad
165/64	Jupiter/Saturn conj. - Sept. 15, 165 BC in Ophiuchus		116/15	
164/63S	Daniel's 42nd week ended		115/14S	Daniel's 49th week ended

In 1856, Benedict Zuckermann published a table of Sabbatical Years in ancient times. His table is considered by scholars to be the standard position. However, in 1973, Rabbi Ben Zion Wacholder, published a table of Sabbatical Years as being one year later, suggesting that John the Baptist began baptizing at Passover A.D. 28. The modern Jewish calendar agrees with Zuckermann's table. This chart follows Zuckermann's table.

114/13 J	End of 27th Jubilee		**65/64 J**	End of 28th Jubilee - 179th Greek Olympiad
113/12	167th Greek Olympiad		**64/63**	Pompey conquered Jeruusalem Dec. 28, 64 BC.
112/11			**63/62**	
111/10			**62/61**	
110/09			**61/60**	180th Greek Olympiad (July 60BC)
109/08	168th Greek Olympiad		**60/59**	
108/07S	Daniel's 50th week ended		**59/58S**	Daniel's 57th week ended
107/06			**58/57**	
106/05	Jupiter/Saturn conj. - Dec. 5, 106 BC in Ophiuchus		**57/56**	181st Greek Olympiad (July 56BC)
105/04	169th Greek Olympiad		**56/55**	
104/03			**55/54**	
103/02			**54/53**	
102/01			**53/52**	182nd Greek Olympiad (July 52BC)
101/00S	Daniel's 51st week ended - 170th Greek Olympiad		**52/51S**	Daniel's 58th week ended
100/99			**51/50**	
99/98			**50/49**	
98/97			**49/48**	183rd Greek Olympiad (July 48BC)
97/96	171st Greek Olympiad		**48/47**	
96/95			**47/46**	Jupiter/Saturn conj. - Oct. 6, 46 BC in Ophiuchus
95/94			**46/45**	Julius Ceasar's calendar
94/93S	Daniel's 52nd week ended		**45/44S**	Daniel's 59th week ended - 184th Greek Olympiad
93/92	172nd Greek Olympiad		**44/43**	
92/91			**43/42**	
91/90			**42/41**	
90/89			**41/40**	185th Greek Olympiad (July 40BC)
89/88	173rd Greek Olympiad		**40/39**	Herod received royal title.
88/87			**39/38**	
87/86S	Daniel's 53rd week ended		**38/37S**	Daniel's 60th week - Herod took Jerusalem
86/85	Jupiter/Saturn conjunction - Aug. 11, 86 BC in Leo.		**37/36**	on Jan. 1, 37BC.
85/84	Both Jupiter and Saturn had triple conjunctions with		**36/35**	
84/83	Regulus between the feet of Leo ... Jupiter: Sept. 9,		**35/34**	
83/82	86 BC, Feb. 28, 85 BC, & Apr. 28, 85 BC. Saturn; Oct.		**34/33**	
82/81	9, 86 BC, Dec. 23, 86 BC, & Jun. 24, 85 BC.		**33/32**	187th Greek Olympiad (July 32 BC)
81/80	175th Greek Olympiad		**32/31**	Caesar fights Anthony in the battle at Actium.
80/79S	Daniel's 54th week		**31/30S**	Daniel's 61st week ended
79/78			**30/29**	
78/77			**29/28**	188th Greek Olympiad (July 28BC)
77/76	176th Greek Olympiad		**28/27**	
76/75			**27/26**	Jupiter/Saturn conjunction - June 29, 26 BC in Leo.
75/74			**26/25**	(Saturn/Regulus June 16 & Jupiter/Regulus June 22,
74/73			**25/24**	just before their conjunction - each a week apart.)
73/72S	Daniel's 55th week ended - 177th Greek Olympiad		**24/23S**	Daniel's 62nd week
72/71			**23/22**	
71/70			**22/21**	
70/69	Hyrcanus became high priest.		**21/20**	Herod starts the Temple construction (18th year)
69/68	178th Greek Olympiad		**20/19**	
68/67			**19/18**	
67/66	Jupiter/Saturn conj. - Feb. 20, 66 BC in Pisces		**18/17**	
66/65S	Daniel's 56th week		**17/16S**	Daniel's 63rd week ended - 191st Greek Olympiad

The birth of Christ must precede the death of Herod. Flavius Josephus leaves no doubt that Herod died in 4 B.C., following the lunar eclipse of March 13, 4 B.C. We see no way around the many Roman references of Herod's rise to power (39-37 BC), his construction of the temple (19 BC), and the Greek Olympiads. These point to the likelihood of Christ's birth in 5 BC.

16/15 J	End of 29th Jubilee	
15/14 S	These bogus Sabbatical Years (red) correspond	
14/13	with the dating scheme in the *Book of Jubilees*.	
13/12	192nd Olympiad	
12/11		
11/10		
10/09S	Daniel's 64th week ended	
09/08	193rd Olympiad	
08/07 S	Jupiter/Saturn triple conjunction - May 29, 7 BC,	
07/06	Oct. 1, 7 BC, and Dec. 5, 7 BC in **Pisces**	
06/05		
05/04	***Jesus born Oct 3, 5 BC?**	
04/03	Herod died on Kislev 7, which was Nov 25, 4 BC?	
03/02S	Daniel's 65th week ended	
02/01		
01BC/AD01	S 195th Greek Olympiad	
01/02		
02/03		
03/04		
04/05		
05/06S	Daniel's 66th week ended	
06/07		
07/08 S		
08/09		
09/10		
10/11		
11/12		
12/13S	Daniel's 67th week ended	
13/14		
14/15 S	Jupiter/Saturn conj. - Dec. 26, 14 AD in Sagittarius	
15/16 J		
16/17		
17/18		
18/19		
19/20S	Daniel's 68th week ended	
20/21		
21/22 S		
22/23		
23/24		
24/25		
25/26		
26/27S	Daniel's 69th week concluded. Jesus was baptized.	
27/28		
28/29 S	Passover: Wed/Thu Apr 16/17, AD 29	
29/30	*Passover: Thursday/Friday Apr 6/7, AD 30	
30/31	Passover: Mon/Tue Mar 26/27, AD 31	
31/32	Passover: Sun/Mon Apr 13/14, AD 32	
32/33	Passover: Thu/Fri Apr 2/3, AD 33	
33/34S	(210th Sabbatical Year)	

34/35 J	End of 30th Jubilee
35/36	Jupiter/Saturn conjunction - Oct. 5, 34 AD in Leo -
36/37	almost another on Apr. 9, 35 AD
37/38	**The Age of**
38/39	
39/40	**Ephesus**
40/41S	
41/42	
42/43	**6th Dispensation of Grace**
43/44	will end with the Rapture
44/45	
45/46	
46/47	
47/48S	
48/49	
49/50	
50/51	
51/52	
52/53	
53/54	Jupiter/Saturn conj. - Mar. 25, 54 AD in Pisces
54/55S	Nero - emperor
55/56	
56/57	
57/58	
58/59	
59/60	
60/61	
61/62S	
62/63	
63/64	
64/65	
65/66	Apostle Paul beheaded
66/67	
67/68	Nero - suicide June 9. Vespasian became emperor
68/69S	
69/70	Temple burned Av 9. Titus took 100,000 captives.
70/71	
71/72	
72/73	
73/74	Masada fell.
74/75	Jupiter/Saturn conj. - Oct. 74, 74 AD in Sagittarius
75/76S	**The Age of**
76/77	
77/78	**Smyrna**
78/79	
79/80	Titus - emperor
80/81	
81/82	Domitian - emperor
82/83S	

Daniel's 69th week ended with the Sabbatical Year of A.D. 26/27; with the crucifixion during the Sabbatical cycle that followed. The **210th Sabbatical Year** was in A.D. 33/34, and the **30th Jubilee** in A.D. 34/35. Neither the birth nor crucifixion of Jesus can be definitely fixed.

*Our best guess places His birth in 5 B.C., His baptism (October 10, A.D. 26) shortly after His 30th birthday (Sept. 30, A.D. 26), and with His crucifixion on Friday, April 7, A.D. 30.

83/84 J	End of 31st Jubilee	**132/33 J**	End of 32nd — Last Jubilee recorded
84/85		133/34	Jupiter/Saturn conj. - Jan. 20, 134 AD in Sagittarius
85/86		134/35	Bar Kokhbah killed.
86/87		**135/36**	**Israel's Final Exile**
87/88		136/37	Hadrian changed name of Jerusalem to Alia
88/89		137/38	Capitolina, and Israel to Palestine.
89/90S		**138/39S**	
90/91		139/40	
91/92		140/41	
92/93		141/42	
93/94	Jupiter/Saturn conj. - Aug. 20, 94 AD in Leo	142/43	
94/95		143/44	
95/96	**John writes the Apocalypse**	144/45	
96/97S	Domitian killed A.D. 96.	**145/46S**	
97/98		146/47	
98/99		147/48	
99/100		148/49	
100/01		**149/50**	In this year, Yose ben Halafta was arrested. He was
101/02		150/51	the author of the *Seder Olam.*
102/03		151/52	
103/04S		**152/53S**	
104/05		153/54	Jupiter/Saturn conj. - July 7, 154 AD in Virgo
105/06		154/55	Papias martyred (70-155)
106/07	Ignatius fed to wild beasts in Rome (30-107)	155/56	Polycarp burned at the stake (69-155)
107/08		156/57	
108/09		157/58	
109/10		158/59	
110/11S		**159/60S**	
111/12		160/61	
112/13		161/62	
113/14	Jupiter/Saturn conj. - Jan. 29, 114 AD in Aries	162/63	
114/15		163/64	
115/16		164/65	Justin Martyr executed (110-165)
116/17		165/66	
117/18S		**166/67S**	
118/19		167/68	
119/20		168/69	
120/21		169/70	
121/22		170/71	
122/23		171/72	
123/24		172/73	Jupiter/Saturn conj. - May 8, 1173 AD in Aries
124/25S		**173/74S**	
125/26		174/75	
126/27		175/76	
127/28		176/77	
128/29		177/78	
129/30		178/79	
130/31		179/80	
131/32S		**180/81S**	

The last Jubilee recorded in history was A.D. 132/33. The evidence for this Jubilee was found in some rental receipts belonging to Simon Bar Kochbah, discovered in a cave near the Dead Sea and reported in 1961. This was pointed out in an article entitled, *"Chronomessianism"* by Rabbi Ben Zion Wacholder, in the 1975 *Hebrew Union College Annual Handbook.* From this date (A.D. 132/33), one can calculate all previous Jubilees.

181/82 J		**230/31 J**	
182/83		231/32	
183/84		232/33	Jupiter/Saturn conj, - Mar. 20, 233 AD in Taurus
184/85		233/34	
185/86		234/35	
186/87		235/36	
187/88S		**236/37S**	
188/89		237/38	
189/90	Mishna was completed	238/39	
190/91		239/40	
191/92		240/41	
192/93		241/42	
193/94	Jupiter/Saturn conj. - Nov. 21, 193 AD in Sagittarius	242/43	
194/95S		**243/44S**	
195/96		244/45	
196/97		245/46	
197/98		246/47	
198/99		247/48	
199/200		248/49	
200/01		249/50	
201/02S	Irenaeus died (120-202)	**250/51S**	
202/03		251/52	
203/04		252/53	Jupiter/Saturn conj. - Feb. 13, 253 AD in Capricorn
204/05		253/54	Origen died (185-254)
205/06		254/55	
206/07		255/56	
207/08		256/57	
208/09S		**257/58S**	
209/10		258/59	
210/11		259/60	
211/12		260/61	
212/13		261/62	
213/14	Jupiter/Saturn conj. - Oct. 10, 213 AD in Virgo	262/63	
214/15		263/64	
215/16S		**264/65S**	Dionysius died (200-265)
216/17	Clement (153-217) of Alexandria died	265/66	
217/18		266/67	
218/19		267/68	
219/20	Writing the Talmud was begun	268/69	
220/21	Tertullian died (145-220)	269/70	
221/22		270/71	
222/23S		**271/72S**	Constantine was born.
223/24		272/73	Jupiter/Saturn conj. - Aug. 27, 273 AD in Virgo
224/25		273/74	
225/26		274/75	
226/27		275/76	
227/28		276/77	
228/29		277/78	
229/30S		**278/79S**	

279/80 J	
280/81	
281/82	
282/83	
283/84	
284/85	
285/86S	
286/87	
287/88	
288/89	
289/90	
290/91	
291/92	Jupiter/Saturn conj. - June 27, 292 AD in Taurus
292/93S	
293/94	
294/95	
295/96	
296/97	
297/98	
298/99	
299/300S	
300/01	
301/02	
302/03	
303/04	
304/05	
305/06	
306/07S	
307/07	
308/09	
309/10	
310/11	
311/12	Jupiter/Saturn conj. - Dec. 13, 312 AD in Capricorn
312/13	Constantine saw a cross in the sky and became a
313/14S	Christian.
314/15	
315/16	
316/17	**The Age of**
317/18	**Pergamos**
318/19	
319/20	
320/21S	
321/22	
322/23	
323/24	
324/25	
325/26	The Council of Nicaea
326/27	
327/28S	

328/29 J	
329/30	
330/31	
331/32	
332/33	Jupiter/Saturn triple conjunction - Nov. 27, 332 AD,
333/34	Apr. 23, 333 AD and June 14, 333 AD in Virgo
334/35S	
335/36	
336/37	Constantine died (272-337)
337/38	
338/39	
339/40	
340/41	Eusebius (260-341)
341/42S	
342/43	
343/44	
344/45	
345/46	
346/47	
347/48	
348/49S	
349/50	
350/51	
351/52	Jupiter/Saturn conj. - May 7, 352 AD in Taurus
352/53	
353/54	
354/55	
355/56S	
356/57	
357/58	
358/59	
359/60	
360/61	
361/62	
362/63S	
363/64	
364/65	
365/66	
366/67	
367/68	
368/69	
369/70S	
370/71	
371/72	Jupiter/Saturn conj. - Mar. 6, 372 AD in Capricorn
372/73	
373/74	
374/75	
375/76	
376/77S	

377/78 J	
378/79	
379/80	
380/81	
381/82	
382/83	
383/84S	
384/85	
385/86	
386/87	
387/88	
388/89	
389/90	
390/91S	
391/92	
392/93	Jupiter/Saturn conj. - Oct. 2, 392 AD in Virgo
393/94	
394/95	
395/96	
396/97	
397/98S	
398/99	
399/400	
400/01	
401/02	
402/03	
403/04	
404/05S	
405/06	
406/07	
407/08	
408/09	
409/10	
410/11	Jupiter/Saturn triple conjunction - Aug. 27, 411 (with
411/12S	the Moon), Nov. 2, 411, and Mar. 11, 412 AD in Taurus
412/13	
413/14	
414/15	
415/16	
416/17	
417/18	
418/19S	
419/20	
420/21	
421/22	
422/23	
423/24	
424/25	
425/26S	

426/27 J	
427/28	Gamara was compiled.
428/29	
429/30	
430/31	
431/32	Jupiter/Saturn conj. - Dec. 31, 431 AD in Capricorn
432/33S	
433/34	
434/35	
435/36	
436/37	
437/38	
438/39	
439/40S	
440/41	
441/42	
442/43	
443/44	
444/45	
445/46	
446/47S	
447/48	
448/49	
449/50	
450/51	
451/52	Jupiter/Saturn triple conjunction - Jan. 13, 452,
452/53	Mar. 18, 452 and Aug. 3, 452 AD in Libra
453/54S	
454/55	
455/56	
456/57	
457/58	
458/59	
459/60	
460/61S	
461/62	
462/63	
463/64	
464/65	
465/66	
466/67	
467/68S	
468/69	
469/70	
470/71	Jupiter/Saturn conj. - June 20, 471 AD in Gemini
471/72	
472/73	
473/74	
474/75S	

475/76 J	The Talmud was finished.		**524/25 J**	
476/77			525/26	
477/78			526/27	
478/79			527/28	
479/80			528/29	
480/81			529/30	
481/82S			**530/31S**	Jupiter/Saturn conj. - Apr. 29, 531 AD in Gemini
482/83			531/32	
483/84			532/33	
484/85			533/34	
485/86			534/35	
486/87			535/36	
487/88			536/37	
488/89S			**537/38S**	
489/90			538/39	
490/91	Jupiter/Saturn conj. - Mar. 23, 491 AD in Aquarius		539/40	
491/92			540/41	
492/93			541/42	
493/94			542/43	
494/95			543/44	
495/96S			**544/45S**	
496/97			545/46	
497/98			546/47	
498/99			547/48	
499/500			548/49	
500/01			549/50	
501/02	**The Age of**		550/51	Jupiter/Saturn conj. - Jan. 14, 551 AD in Aquarius
502/03S	**Thyatira**		**551/52S**	
503/04			552/53	
504/05			553/54	
505/06			554/55	
506/07			555/56	
507/08			556/57	
508/09			557/58	
509/10S			**558/59S**	
510/11			559/60	
511/12	Jupiter/Saturn conj. - Oct. 30, 511 AD in Libra		560/61	
512/13			561/62	
513/14			562/63	
514/15			563/64	
515/16			564/65	
516/17S			**565/66S**	
517/18			566/67	
518/19			567/68	
519/20			568/69	
520/21			569/70	
521/22			570/71	Jupiter/Saturn conj. - Aug. 30, 571 AD in Libra
522/23			571/72	
523/24S			**572/73S**	

573/74 J		
574/75		
575/76		
576/77		
577/78		
578/79		
579/80S		
580/81		
581/82		
582/83		
583/84		
584/85		
585/86		
586/87S		
587/88		
588/89		
589/90	Jupiter/Saturn conj. - July 30, 590 AD in Gemini	
590/91		
591/92		
592/93		
593/94S		
594/95		
595/96		
596/97		
597/98		
598/99		
599/600		
600/01S		
601/02		
602/03		
603/04		
604/05		
605/06		
606/07		
607/08S		
608/09		
609/10	Jupiter/Saturn conj. - Apr. 14, 610 AD in Aquarius	
610/11		
611/12		
612/13		
613/14		
614/15S		
615/16		
616/17		
617/18		
618/19		
619/20		
620/21		
621/22S		

622/23 J	
623/24	
624/25	
625/26	
626/27	
627/28	
628/29S	
629/30	
630/31	Jupiter/Saturn conj. - Nov. 18, 630 AD in Scorpio
631/**32**	Mohammed died (570-632)
632/33	
633/34	
634/35	
635/36S	
636/37	
637/38	Islam conquered Israel.
638/39	
639/**40**	Alexandria Library burned in 640 by Calif Omar.
640/41	
641/42	
642/43S	
643/44	
644/45	
645/46	
646/47	
647/48	
648/49	
649/50S	Jupiter/Saturn conj. - Jun. 10, 650 AD in Cancer
650/51	
651/52	
652/53	
653/54	
654/55	
655/56	
656/57S	
657/58	
658/59	
659/60	
660/61	
661/62	The Mosque of Omar was built out of wood.
662/63	
663/64S	
664/65	
665/66	
666/67	
667/68	
668/69	
669/70	Jupiter/Saturn conj. - Jan. 27, 670 AD in Aquarius
670/71S	

671/72 J	
672/73	
673/74	
674/75	
675/76	
676/77	
677/78S	
678/79	
679/80	
680/81	
681/82	
682/83	
683/84	
684/85S	
685/86	
686/87	
687/88	
688/89	
689/90	Jupiter/Saturn conj. - Sept. 16, 690 AD in Scorpio
690/**91**	The Mosque of Omar was given a lead roof.
691/92S	
692/93	
693/94	
694/95	
695/96	
696/97	
697/98	
698/99S	
699/700	
700/01	
701/02	
702/03	
703/04	
704/05	
705/06S	
706/07	
707/08	
708/09	
709/10	Jupiter/Saturn triple conjunction - Sept. 14, 709,
710/11	Feb. 4, 710, and Mar. 30, 710 in Cancer
711/12	
712/13S	
713/14	
714/15	
715/16	
716/17	
717/18	
718/19	
719/20S	

720/21 J	
721/22	
722/23	
723/24	
724/25	
725/26	
726/27S	
727/28	
728/29	Jupiter/Saturn conj. - Apr. 20, 729 AD in Pisces
729/30	
730/31	
731/32	
732/33	
733/34S	
734/35	
735/36	
736/37	
737/38	
738/39	
739/40	
740/41S	
741/42	
742/43	
743/44	
744/45	
745/46	
746/47	
747/48S	
748/49	
749/50	Jupiter/Saturn conj. - Dec. 5, 749 AD in Ophiuchus
750/51	
751/52	
752/53	
753/54	
754/55S	
755/56	
756/57	
757/58	
758/59	
759/60	
760/61	
761/62S	
762/63	
763/64	
764/65	
765/66	
766/67	
767/68	
768/69S	Jupiter/Saturn conj. - July 22, 769 AD in Leo

769/70 J	**818/19 J**
770/71	819/20
771/72	820/21
772/73	821/22
773/74	822/23
774/75	823/24
775/76S	**824/25S**
776/77	825/26
777/78	826/27
778/79	827/28
779/80	828/29 Jupiter/Saturn conj. - June 4, 829 AD in Leo
780/81	829/30
781/82	830/31
782/83S	**831/32S**
783/84	832/33
784/85	833/34
785/86	834/35
786/87	835/36
787/88	836/37
788/89 Jupiter/Saturn conj. - Feb. 14, 789 AD in Pisces	837/38
789/90S	**838/39S**
790/91	839/40
791/92	840/41
792/93	841/42
793/94	842/43
794/95	843/44
795/96	844/45
796/97S	**845/46S**
797/98	846/47
798/99	847/48 Jupiter/Saturn conj. - May 14, 848 AD in Pisces
799/800	848/49
800/01	849/50
801/02	850/51
802/03	851/52
803/04S	**852/53S**
804/05	853/54
805/06	854/55
806/07	855/56
807/08	856/57
808/09	857/58
809/10 Jupiter/Saturn conj. - Oct. 5, 809 AD in Ophiuchus	858/59
810/11S	**859/60S**
811/12	860/61
812/13	861/62
813/14	862/63
814/15	863/64
815/16	864/65
816/17	865/66
817/18S	**866/67S**

867/68 J		**916/17 J**	
868/69	Jupiter/Saturn conj. - Dec. 24, 868 AD in Sagittarius	917/18	
869/70		918/19	
870/71		919/20	
871/72		920/21	
872/73		921/22	
873/74S		**922/23S**	
874/75		923/24	
875/76		924/25	
876/77		925/26	
877/78		926/27	
878/79		927/28	
879/80		928/29	Jupiter/Saturn conj. - Oct. 25, 928 AD in Sagittarius
880/81S		**929/30S**	
881/82		930/31	
882/83		931/32	
883/84		932/33	
884/85		933/34	
885/86		934/35	
886/87		935/36	
887/88S		**936/37S**	
888/89	Jupiter/Saturn conj. - Sept. 8, 888 AD in Leo	937/38	
889/90		938/39	
890/91		939/40	
891/92		940/41	
892/93		941/42	
893/94		942/43	
894/95S		**943/44S**	
895/96		944/45	
896/97		945/46	
897/98		946/47	
898/99		947/48	Jupiter/Saturn conj. - July 28, 948 AD in Leo
899/900		948/49	
900/01		949/50	
901/02S		**950/51S**	
902/03		951/52	
903/04		952/53	
904/05		953/54	
905/06		954/55	
906/07		955/56	
907/08	Jupiter/Saturn conj. - Mar. 13, 908 AD in Pisces	956/57	
908/09S		**957/58S**	
909/10		958/59	
910/11		959/60	
911/12		960/61	
912/13		961/62	
913/14		962/63	
914/15		963/64	
915/16S		**964/65S**	

965/66 J	
966/67	Jupiter/Saturn triple conjunction - June 25, 967,
967/68	Oct. 5, 967, and Jan. 4, 968 in Pisces
968/69	
969/70	
970/71	
971/72S	
972/73	
973/74	
974/75	
975/76	
976/77	
977/78	
978/79S	
979/80	
980/81	
981/82	
982/83	
983/84	
984/85	
985/86S	
986/87	
987/88	Jupiter/Saturn conj. - Jan. 16, 988 AD in Sagittarius
988/89	
989/90	
990/91	
991/92	
992/93S	
993/94	
994/95	
995/96	
996/97	
997/98	
998/99	
999/1000S	
1000/01	
1001/02	
1002/03	
1003/04	
1004/05	
1005/06	
1006/07S	
1007/08	Jupiter/Saturn triple conjunction - Nov. 7, 1007,
1008/09	May 7, 1008 and June 2, 1008 AD in Virgo
1009/10	
1010/11	
1011/12	
1012/13	
1013/14S	

1014/15 J	
1015/16	
1016/17	
1017/18	
1018/19	
1019/20	
1020/21S	
1021/22	
1022/23	
1023/24	
1024/25	
1025/26	
1026/27	Jupiter/Saturn conj. - Apr. 20, 1027 AD in Aries
1027/28S	
1028/29	
1029/30	
1030/31	
1031/32	
1032/33	
1033/34	
1034/35S	
1035/36	
1036/37	
1037/38	
1038/39	
1039/40	
1040/41	Rashi was born.
1041/42S	
1042/43	
1043/44	
1044/45	
1045/46	
1046/47	
1047/48	Jupiter/Saturn conj. - Nov. 18, 1047 AD in Sagittarius
1048/49S	
1049/50	
1050/51	
1051/52	
1052/53	
1053/54	
1054/55	
1055/56S	
1056/57	
1057/58	
1058/59	
1059/60	
1060/61	
1061/62	
1062/63S	

1063/64 J	
1064/65	
1065/66	
1066/67	Jupiter/Saturn conj. - Sept. 19, 1067 AD in Virgo
1067/68	
1068/69	
1069/70S	
1070/71	
1071/72	
1072/73	
1073/74	
1074/75	
1075/76	
1076/77S	
1077/78	
1078/79	
1079/80	
1080/81	
1081/82	
1082/83	
1083/84S	
1084/85	
1085/86	
1086/87	Jupiter/Saturn conj. - Feb. 26, 1087 AD in Aries
1087/88	
1088/89	
1089/90	
1090/91S	
1091/92	
1092/93	
1093/94	
1094/95	
1095/96	
1096/97	
1097/98S	
1098/99	
1099/1100	Crusaders captured Jerusalem.
1100/01	Godfrey de Bouillon, crusader leader died. His
1101/02	brother Baldwin became king of Jerusalem.
1102/03	
1103/04	
1104/05S	
1105/06	Rashi died.
1106/07	Jupiter/Saturn conj. - Feb. 9, 1107 AD in Sagittarius
1107/08	
1108/09	
1109/10	
1110/11	
1111/12S	

1112/13 J	
1113/14	
1114/15	
1115/16	
1116/17	
1117/18	
1118/19S	
1119/20	
1120/21	
1121/22	
1122/23	
1123/24	
1124/25	
1125/26S	
1126/27	Jupiter/Saturn conj. - Aug. 7, 1127 AD in Virgo
1127/28	Knights Templar return to Europe, wealthy beyond
1128/29	belief. They invent check-writing and establish in-
1129/30	ternational banking.
1130/31	
1131/32	
1132/33S	
1133/34	
1134/**35**	Maimonides was born on Mar 30, 1135.
1135/36	
1136/37	
1137/38	
1138/39	
1139/40S	
1140/41	
1141/42	
1142/43	
1143/44	
1144/45	
1145/46	Jupiter/Saturn conj. - June 4, 1146 AD in Taurus
1146/47S	
1147/48	
1148/49	
1149/50	
1150/51	
1151/52	
1152/53	
1153/54S	
1154/55	
1155/56	
1156/57	
1157/58	
1158/59	
1159/60	
1160/61S	

1161/62 J		**1210/11 J**	
1162/63		1211/12	
1163/64		1212/13	
1164/65		1213/14	
1165/66		1214/15	
1166/67	Jupiter/Saturn conj. - Dec. 11, 1166 AD in Capricorn	1215/16	
1167/68S		**1216/17S**	
1168/69		1217/18	
1169/70		1218/19	
1170/71		1219/20	
1171/72		1220/21	
1172/73		1221/22	
1173/74		1222/23	
1174/75S		**1223/24S**	
1175/76		1224/25	
1176/77		1225/26	Jupiter/Saturn conj. - Mar. 5, 1226 AD in Capricorn
1177/78		1226/27	
1178/79		1227/28	
1179/80		1228/29	
1180/81		1229/30	
1181/82S		**1230/31S**	
1182/83		1231/32	
1183/85		1232 /33	
1184/85		1233/34	
1185/86	Jupiter/Saturn conj. - Nov. 8, 1186 AD in Virgo	1234/35	
1186/**87**	Battle of Hattin - Saladin beat the Crusaders	1235/36	
1187/88	on July 4, 1187.	1236/37	
1188/89S		**1237/38S**	
1189/90		1238/39	
1190/91		1239/40	
1191/92	Radak wrote a commentary on the Torah.	1240/41	
1192/93		1241/42	
1193/94		1242/43	
1194/95		1243/44	
1195/96S		**1244/45S**	
1196/97		1245/46	
1197/98		1246/47	Jupiter/Saturn conj. - Sept. 21, 1246 AD in Virgo
1198/99		1247/48	
1199/1200		1248/49	
1200/01		1249/50	
1201/02		1250/51	
1202/03S		**1251/52S**	
1203/04		**1252/53**	The Inquisition used torture.
1204/05	Maimonides died (1135-1204)	1253/54	
1205/06	Jupiter/Saturn conj. - Apr. 16, 1206 AD in Taurus	1254/55	
1206/07		1255/56	
1207/08		1256/57	
1208/09		1257/58	
1209/10S		**1258/59S**	

1259/60 J	
1260/61	
1261/62	
1262/63	
1263/64	
1264/65	Jupiter/Saturn conj. - July 25, 1265 AD in Taurus
1265/66S	
1266/67	
1267/68	
1268/69	
1269/70	
1270/71	Moses deLeon found the *Zohar* in a cave in Israel.
1271/72	
1272/73S	
1273/74	
1274/75	
1275/76	
1276/77	
1277/78	
1278/79	
1279/80S	
1280/81	
1281/82	
1282/83	
1283/84	
1284/85	Jupiter/Saturn conj. - Dec. 31, 1285 AD in Capricorn
1285/86	
1286/87S	
1287/88	
1288/89	
1289/90	
1290/91	England expelled Jews.
1291/92	
1292/93	
1293/94S	
1294/95	
1295/96	
1296/97	
1297/98	
1298/99	
1299/1300	Ottoman Empire was established.
1300/01S	
1301/02	
1302/03	
1303/04	
1304/05	Jupiter/Saturn triple conjunction - Dec. 25, 1305,
1305/06	Apr. 20, 1306, and July 19, 1306 AD in Libra
1306/07	France expelled Jews.
1307/08S	

1308/09 J	
1309/10	
1310/11	
1311/12	
1312/13	
1313/14	
1314/15S	
1315/16	
1316/17	
1317/18	
1318/19	
1319/20	
1320/21	
1321/22S	
1322/23	
1323/24	
1324/25	Jupiter/Saturn conj. - June 1, 1325 AD in Taurus
1325/26	
1326/27	
1327/28	
1328/29S	
1329/30	
1330/31	
1331/32	
1332/33	
1333/34	
1334/35	
1335/36S	
1336/37	
1337/38	
1338/39	
1339/40	
1340/41	
1341/42	
1342/43S	
1343/44	
1344/45	Jupiter/Saturn conj. - Mar. 24, 1345 AD in Aquarius
1345/46	
1346/47	
1347/48	
1348/49	
1349/50S	Black death plagues Europe. Jews blamed.
1350/51	
1351/52	
1352/53	
1353/54	
1354/55	
1355/56	
1356/57S	

1357/58 J			**1406/07 J**	
1358/59			1407/08	
1359/60			1408/09	
1360/61			1409/10	
1361/62			1410/11	
1362/63			1411/12	
1363/64S			**1412/13S**	
1364/65			1413/14	
1365/66	Jupiter/Saturn conj. - Oct. 25, 1365 AD in Libra		1414/15	
1366/67			1415/16	
1367/68			1416/17	
1368/69			1417/18	
1369/70			1418/19	
1370/71S			**1419/20S**	
1371/72			1420/21	
1372/73			1421/22	
1373/74			1422/23	
1374/75			1423/24	
1375/76			1424/25	Jupiter/Saturn triple conjunction - Feb. 14, 1425,
1376/77			1425/26	Mar. 18, 1425, and Aug. 26, 1425 AD in Libra
1377/78S			**1426/27S**	
1378/79			1427/28	
1379/80			1428/29	
1380/81			1429/30	
1381/82			1430/31	
1382/83			1431/32	
1383/84			1432/33	
1384/85S	Jupiter/Saturn triple conjunction - Oct. 9, 1384,		**1433/34S**	
1385/86	Oct. 25, 1384, and Apr. 8, 1385 AD in Gemini		1434/35	
1386/87			1435/36	
1387/88			1436/37	
1388/89			**1437/38**	Abarbanel was born.
1389/90			1438/39	
1390/91			1439/40	
1391/92S			**1440/41S**	
1392/93			1441/42	
1393/94			1442/43	
1394/95			1443/44	Jupiter/Saturn conj. - July 14, 1444 AD in Gemini
1395/96			1444/45	
1396/97			1445/46	
1397/98			1446/47	
1398/99S			**1447/48S**	
1399/1400			1448/49	
1400/01			1449/50	
1401/02			**1450/51**	Gutenburg invented the printing press.
1402/03			1451/52	
1403/04			1452/53	
1404/05	Jupiter/Saturn conj. - Jan. 16, 1405 AD in Aquarius		1453/54	
1405/06S			**1454/55S**	

1455/56 J	
1456/57	
1457/58	
1458/59	
1459/60	
1460/61	
1461/62S	
1462/63	
1463/64	Jupiter/Saturn conj. - Apr. 8, 1464 AD in Aquarius
1464/65	
1465/66	
1466/67	
1467/68	
1468/69S	
1469/70	
1470/71	
1471/72	
1472/73	
1473/74	
1474/75	
1475/76S	
1476/77	
1477/78	
1478/79	
1479/80	
1480/81	
1481/82	Spanish inquisition
1482/83S	
1483/84	
1484/85	Jupiter/Saturn conj. - Nov. 18, 1484 AD in Libra
1485/86	
1486/87	
1487/88	
1488/89	
1489/90S	
1490/91	
1491/**92**	Christopher Columbus discovered America.
1492/93	Spain expelled the Jews.
1493/94	
1494/95	
1495/96	
1496/97S	
1497/98	
1498/99	
1499/1500	
1500/01	
1501/02	
1502/03	
1503/04S	Jupiter/Saturn conj. - May 25, 1504 AD in Gemini

1504/05 J	
1505/06	
1506/07	
1507/08	
1508/09	Abarbanel died.
1509/10	
1510/11S	
1511/12	

The Age of Sardis

1512/13	
1513/14	
1514/15	
1515/16	
1516/17	Ottoman Turks conquer Israel. Jews declare end of
1517/18S	*Minyan Shtarot* (dating from 312 BC).
1518/19	*Also, on Oct 31, 1517, Martin Luther nailed 95
1519/20	Thesis to the door of the Wittenburg Church.
1520/21	
1521/22	
1522/23	
1523/24	Jupiter/Saturn conj. - Jan. 31, 1524 AD in Aquarius
1524/25S	
1525/26	
1526/27	Hungary expelled Jews.
1527/28	
1528/29	
1529/30	
1530/31	
1531/32S	
1532/33	
1533/34	
1534/35	
1535/36	
1536/37	
1537/38	
1538/39S	
1539/40	
1540/41	
1541/42	
1542/43	
1543/44	
1544/45	Jupiter/Saturn conj. - Sept. 18, 1544 AD in Scorpio
1545/46S	
1546/47	
1547/48	
1548/49	
1549/50	
1550/51	
1551/52	
1552/53S	

1553/54 J		**1602/03 J**	
1554/55		1603/04	Jupiter/Saturn conj. - Dec. 18, 1603 AD in Ophi-
1555/56		1604/05	
1556/57		1605/06	
1557/58		1606/07	
1558/59		1607/08	
1559/60S		**1608/09S**	
1560/61		1609/10	
1561/62		1610/11	
1562/63	Jupiter/Saturn conj. - Aug. 25, 1563 AD in Cancer	1611/12	
1563/64		1612/13	
1564/65		1613/14	
1565/66		1614/15	
1566/67S		**1615/16S**	
1567/68		1616/17	
1568/69		1617/18	
1569/70		1618/19	
1570/71		1619/20	
1571/72		1620/21	
1572/73		1621/22	
1573/74S		**1622/23S**	Jupiter/Saturn conj. - July 16, 1623 AD in Cancer
1574/75		1623/24	
1575/76		1624/25	
1576/77		1625/26	
1577/78		1626/27	
1578/79		1627/28	
1579/80		1628/29	
1580/81S		**1629/30S**	
1581/82		1630/31	
1582/83	Jupiter/Saturn conj. - May 2, 1583 AD in Pisces	1631/32	
1583/84		1632/33	
1584/85		1633/34	
1585/86		1634/35	
1586/87		1635/36	
1587/88S		**1636/37S**	
1588/89		1637/38	
1589/90		1638/39	
1590/91		1639/40	
1591/92		1640/41	
1592/93		1641/42	
1593/94		1642/43	Jupiter/Saturn conj. - Feb. 24, 1643 AD in Pisces
1594/95S		**1643/44S**	
1595/96		1644/45	
1596/97		1645/46	
1597/98		1646/47	
1598/99		1647/48	
1599/1600		1648/49	
1600/01		1649/50	
1601/02S		**1650/51S**	

1651/52 J	
1652/53	
1653/54	
1654/55	Jews settle in New York.
1655/56	
1656/57	Jews allowed to live in England again.
1657/58S	
1658/59	
1659/60	
1660/61	
1661/62	
1662/63	
1663/64	Jupiter/Saturn conj. - Oct. 16, 1663 AD in Ophiuchus
1664/65S	
1665/66	
1666/67	
1667/68	
1668/69	
1669/70	
1670/71	
1671/72S	
1672/73	
1673/74	
1674/75	
1675/76	
1676/77	Shabbetai Tzvi died. He claimed to be the Messiah,
1677/78	but was forced to convert to Islam or be killed.
1678/79S	
1679/80	
1680/81	
1681/82	
1682/83	Jupiter/Saturn triple conjunction - Oct. 23, 1682,
1683/84	Feb. 9, 1683, and May 18, 1683 in Leo
1684/85	
1685/86S	
1686/87	
1687/88	
1688/89	
1689/90	
1690/91	
1691/92	
1692/93S	
1693/94	
1694/95	
1695/96	
1696/97	
1697/98	
1698/99	Baal Shem Tov was born.
1699/1700S	

1700/01 J	
1701/02	Jupiter/Saturn conj. - May 21, 1702 AD in Pisces
1702/03	
1703/04	
1704/05	
1705/06	
1706/07S	
1707/08	
1708/09	
1709/10	
1710/11	
1711/12	
1712/13	
1713/14S	
1714/15	
1715/16	
1716/17	
1717/18	
1718/19	
1719/20	
1720/21S	Vilna Gaon was born.
1721/22	
1722/23	Jupiter/Saturn conj. - Jan. 5, 1723 AD in Capricorn
1723/24	
1724/25	
1725/26	
1726/27	
1727/28S	The Moravian Church in Saxony began around-
1728/29	the-clock prayer meetings that lasted a hundred
1729/30	years. By 1791 thy had sent 300 missionaries
1730/31	around the world.
1731/32	
1732/33	
1733/34	John Kay's Fly Shuttle sparked the Industrial
1734/35S	Revolution.
1735/36	
1736/37	
1737/38	
1738/39	
1739/40	
1740/41	
1741/42S	Jupiter/Saturn conj. - Aug. 30, 1742 AD in Leo
1742/43	
1743/44	
1744/45	
1745/46	
1746/47	
1747/48	
1748/49S	

The Ages of Philadelphia and Laodicea

The letters to the seven churches in Revelation seem to give a prophetic overview of the Church age. Ephesus depicted the Apostolic era of the 1st century; Smyrna, the persecutions of the 2nd and 3rd centuries; Pergamos, the church under Imperial favor (A.D.316+); Thyatira, A.D. 500-1500; Sardis, the Reformation; Philadelphia, the age of missions; and Laodicea, the period of liberal theology.

1749/50 J	
1750/51	
1751/52	
1752/53	
1753/54	
1754/55	
1755/56S	
1756/57	
1757/58	
1758/59	
1759/60	
1760/61	Baal Shem Tov died.
1761/62	Jupiter/Saturn conj. - Mar. 18, 1762 AD in Pisces
1762/63S	
1763/64	
1764/65	
1765/66	
1766/67	
1767/68	
1768/69	
1769/70S	Napoleon was born.
1770/71	
1771/72	
1772/73	
1773/74	
1774/75	
1775/76	
1776/77S	American Revolution
1777/78	
1778/79	
1779/80	
1780/81	
1781/82	
1782/83	Jupiter/Saturn conj. - Nov. 5, 1782 AD in Sagittarius
1783/84S	
1784/85	
1785/86	
1786/87	
1787/88	
1788/89	
1789/90	French Revolution
1790/91S	
1791/92	
1792/**93**	William Carey sailed for India in April. He was
1793/94	the "Father of Modern Missions.
1794/95	
1795/96	
1796/97	
1797/98S	Vilna Gaon died.

1798/99 J	
1799/1800	
1800/01	
1801/02	Jupiter/Saturn conj. - July 17, 1802 AD in Leo
1802/03	
1803/04	Napoleon (1769-1821) emperor - May 18, 1804
1804/05S	
1805/06	
1806/07	
1807/08	
1808/09	
1809/10	
1810/11	
1811/12S	
1812/13	
1813/14	
1814/15	
1815/16	Napoleon was defeated at Waterloo
1816/17	
1817/18	
1818/19S	
1819/20	
1820/21	Jupiter/Saturn conjunction - July 19, 1821 AD in Pi-
1821/22	sces The two planets returned for what was almost
1822/23	another conjunction on December 1-3, 1821. Some
1823/24	might classify it as a triple conjunction.
1824/25	
1825/26S	
1826/**27**	John Nelson Darby (1800-1882) organized the
1827/28	Plymouth Brethren in 1827.
1828/29	
1829/30	
1830/31	
1831/32	
1832/33S	
1833/34	
1834/35	
1835/36	
1836/37	
1837/38	
1838/39	
1839/40S	
1840/41	
1841/42	Jupiter/Saturn conj. - Jan. 26, 1842 AD in Sagittarius
1842/43	
1843/44	
1844/45	
1845/46	
1846/47S	

1847/48 J	
1848/49	
1849/50	
1850/51	
1851/52	
1852/53	
1853/54S	Charles Hadden Spurgeon (1834-1892) became
1854/55	pastor of New Park Street Chappel (later named
1855/56	Metropolitan Baptist Tabernacle).
1856/57	
1857/58	
1858/59	
1859/60	
1860/61S	Theodor Herzl born
1861/62	Jupiter/Saturn conj. - Oct 21, 1861 AD in Leo
1862/63	
1863/64	
1864/65	
1865/66	
1866/67	
1867/68S	
1868/69	
1869/70	
1870/71	
1871/72	
1872/73	
1873/74	
1874/75S	
1875/76	
1876/77	
1877/78	
1878/79	Petah Tikvah was built as Israel's 1st kibbutz.
1879/80	
1880/81	Jupiter/Saturn conj. - Apr. 18, 1881 AD in Aries
1881/82S	Russian pograms against Jews
1882/83	
1883/84	
1884/85	
1885/86	
1886/87	
1887/88	
1888/89S	
1889/90	
1890/91	
1891/92	
1892/93	
1893/94	
1894/95	
1895/96S	

1896/97J	World Zionist Congress held in Basel Switzerland
1897/98	
1898/99	
1899/1900	
1900/01	
1901/02	Jupiter/Saturn conj. - Nov. 29, 1901 AD in Sagittarius
1902/03S	
1903/04	
1904/05	Theodor Herzl died.
1905/06	Another Russian pogram against the Jews
1906/07	
1907/08	
1908/09	
1909/10S	
1910/11	
1911/12	
1912/13	
1913/14	
1914/15	**World War I** (1914-18)
1915/16	
1916/17S	
1917/18	Jerusalem was liberated Dec. 9, 1917.
1918/19	The Russian Revolution overthrew the Czar.
1919/20	
1920/21	Jupiter/Saturn conj. - Sept. 10, 1921 AD in Virgo
1921/22	
1922/23	
1923/24S	
1924/25	
1925/26	
1926/27	
1927/28	
1928/29	
1929/30	
1930/31S	
1931/32	
1932/33	
1933/34	
1934/35	
1935/36	
1936/37	
1937/38S	
1938/39	
1939/40	**World War II** Jewish Holocaust (1939-45)
1940/41	Jupiter/Saturn triple conjunction - Aug. 8, 1940,
1941/42	Oct. 20, 1940, and Feb. 15, 1941, in Aries
1942/43	
1943/44	Six million Jews died at the hands of the Nazis.
1944/45S	Hitler committed suicide on April 30, 1945.

1897 (68th Jubilee Year) - Theodor Herzl hosted the first World Zionist Congress, held in Basel, Switzerland, in August 1897.

1917 (Following a Sabbatical Year, shortly after the beginning of the 1st year of a new Sabbatical cycle) - The Brittish Army, under the command of General Edmund Allenby, liberated Jerusalem.

1945/46 J	
1946/47	
1947/**48**	**Birth of Israel**
1948/49	1st Arab War
1949/50	
1950/51	
1951/52S	
1952/53	
1953/54	
1954/55	
1955/56	
1956/57	Israel's war with Egypt
1957/58	
1958/59S	
1959/60	Three billion population counted on Earth.
1960/61	Jupiter/Saturn conj. - Feb. 18, 1961 in Sagittarius.
1961/62	Within Six weeks, the Encke Comet circled the event
1962/63	as the sun covered Jupiter on Jan. 5, and Saturn on
1963/64	Jan. 11, 1961. The comet disappeared on Feb. 3, 1961.
1964/65	
1965/66S	
1966/**67**	The Six-Day War
1967/68	Jerusalem was united.
1968/69	
1969/70	
1970/71	
1971/72	
1972/73S	
1973/74	The Yom Kippur War
1974/75	
1975/76	
1976/77	
1977/78	
1978/79	
1979/80S	
1980/81	Jupiter/Saturn triple conjunction - Dec. 31, 1980,
1981/82	Mar. 3, 1981 and July 23, 1981 AD in Virgo
1982/83	The Lebanon War
1983/84	
1984/85	
1985/86	
1986/87S	
1987/88	1st Intafada in Israel
1988/89	
1989/90	
1990/91	
1991/92	
1992/93	The Peace Accord between Rabin and Arafat
1993/94S	490th Sabbatical Year

1994/95 J	- This could have marked the 70th Jubilee.
1995/96 s	These bogus Sabbatical Years (red) correspond
1996/97	with the dating scheme in the *Book of Jubilees*.
1997/98	
1998/99	
1999/2000	Six billion population counted on Earth.
2000/01S	2nd Intafada in Israel.
2001/02	On Sept. 11, Islamic Terrorists struck New York City.
2002/03	Jupiter/Saturn conj. - May 28, 2001 AD in Aries
2003/04	
2004/05	Jewish settlements were dismantled in an effort to
2005/06	please the Moslems.
2006/07	
2007/08S	The *Zohar* suggests that the time of Jacob's trouble
2008/09	will commence in the 73rd year (5773 or 2012/13),
2009/10 s	They say that the kings of Earth will gather in Rome
2010/11	and be killed by meteoric stones from the sky. Some
2011/12	kings, who have not yet arrived, will survive, and
2012/13	that the sons of Ishmael will bring the whole world
2013/14	against Jerusalem to drive the Jews from the Earth.
2014/15S	Two solar eclipses and four lunar eclipses will occur
2015/16	in 2014/2015: Lunar-Passover 4/15/2014; Lunar-Suk-
2016/17 s	kot 10/8/2014; Solar (total) Adar 29/Nisan 1-3/20/2015;
2017/18	Lunar-Passover 4/4/2015; Solar (partial) Rosh Ha-
2018/19	shanah 9/13/15; and Lunar-Sukkot 9/28/2015.
2019/20	
2020/21	Jupiter/Saturn conj. - Dec. 21, 2020 AD in Capricorn
2021/22S	
2022/23	
2023/24 s	
2024/25 J	
2025/26	
2026/27	
2027/28	
2028/29S	
2029/30	
2030/31	
2031/32	
2032/33	
2033/34	
2034/35	
2035/36S	
2036/37	
2037/38	
2038/39	
2039/40	Projected 12 billion population
2040/41	Jupiter/Saturn conj. - Oct. 31, 2040 AD in Virgo
2041/42	
2042/43S	

We await the future ...
7th Dispensation of the
Messianic Kingdom
It will end at the Final Judgment

Notice that the Sabbatical Years in the *Book of Jubilees* occur two years after the Sabbatical Years in the modern Jewish calendar, and that the Jubilees are twenty years earlier than the accepted dates for the years of Jubilee. If we followed the Book of Jubilees, the next Jubilee would be 2024/25.

The 20th century witnessed the revival of Israel, wars on a global scale, widespread famines, earthquakes and diseases unlike any previous century. In 1945, the United Nations was formed for the purpose of establishing a world government with a goal of controling population growth, economic development, food distribution, transportation and communications. The ancient prophecies are being fulfilled.

2043/44 J		**2092/93 J**	
2044/45		2093/94	
2045/46		2094/95	
2046/47		2095/96	
2047/48		2096/97	
2048/49		2097/98	
2049/50S		**2098/99S**	
2050/51		2099/2100	Jupiter/Saturn conj. - Sept. 18, 2100 AD in Virgo
2051/52		2100/01	
2052/53		2101/02	
2053/54		2102/03	
2054/55		2103/04	
2055/56		2104/05	
2056/57S		**2105/06S**	
2057/58		2106/07	
2058/59		2107/08	
2059/60	Jupiter/Saturn conj. - Apr. 7, 2060 AD in Taurus	2108/09	
2060/61		2109/10	
2061/62		2110/11	
2062/63		2111/12	
2063/64S		**2112/13S**	
2064/65		2113/14	
2065/66		2114/15	
2066/67		2115/16	
2067/68		2116/17	
2068/69		2117/18	
2069/70		2118/19	Jupiter/Saturn conj. - July 15, 2119 AD in Taurus
2070/71S		**2119/20S**	
2071/72		**2120/21**	Projected 48 billion population
2072/73		2121/22	
2073/74		2122/23	
2074/75		2123/24	
2075/76		2124/25	
2076/77		2125/26	
2077/78S		**2126/27S**	
2078/79		2127/28	
2079/80	Jupiter/Saturn conj. - Mar. 14, 2080 AD in Capricorn	2128/29	
2080/81	Projected 24 billion population	2129/30	
2081/82		2130/31	
2082/83		2131/32	
2083/84		2132/33	
2084/85S		**2133/34S**	
2085/86		2134/35	
2086/87		2135/36	
2087/88		2136/37	
2088/89		2137/38	
2089/90		2138/39	
2090/91		2139/40	Jupiter/Saturn conj. - Jan. 14, 2140 AD in Capricorn
2091/92S		**2140/41S**	

Someday, the Antichrist will rise and bring all these prophetic developments together. Then Daniel's prophecies will be complete. According to Daniel, this *"vile person"* (Daniel 11:21) will come out of Greek and Roman royalty, the descendent of a royal family with roots in both ancient kingdoms. Though Daniel does not specifically treat the subject, his name implies that the Antichrist will come from Dan.

2143/44 J	
2144/45	
2145/46	
2146/47	
2147/48	
2148/49	
2149/50S	
2150/51	
2151/52	
2152/53	
2153/54	
2154/55	
2155/56	
2156/57	
2157/58	
2158/59	
2159/60	Jupiter/Saturn conj. - Dec. 20, 2159 AD in Virgo
2160/61	Projected 96 billion population
2161/62	
2162/63	
2163/64S	
2164/65	
2165/66	
2166/67	
2167/68	
2168/69	
2169/70	
2170/71S	
2171/72	
2172/73	
2173/74	
2174/75	
2175/76	
2176/77	
2177/78S	
2178/79	Jupiter/Saturn conj. - May 28, 2179 AD in Taurus
2179/80	
2180/81	
2181/82	
2182/83	
2183/84	
2184/85S	
2185/86	
2186/87	
2187/88	
2188/89	
2189/90	
2190/91	
2191/92S	

2192/93 J	
2193/94	
2194/95	
2195/96	
2196/97	
2197/98	
2198/99S	Jupiter/Saturn conj. - Apr. 7, 2199 AD in Capricorn
2199/2100	
2200/01	Projected 192 billion population
2201/02	
2202/03	
2203/04	
2204/05	
2205/06S	
2206/07	
2207/08	
2208/09	
2209/10	
2210/11	
2211/12	
2212/13S	
2213/14	
2214/15	
2215/16	
2216/17	
2217/18	
2218/19	
2219/20S	Jupiter/Saturn conj. - Oct .31, 2219 AD in Libra
2220/21	
2221/22	
2222/23	
2223/24	
2224/25	
2225/26	
2226/27S	
2227/28	
2228/29	
2229/30	
2230/31	
2231/32	
2232/33	
2233/34S	
2234/35	
2235/36	
2236/37	
2237/38	Jupiter/Saturn triple conjunction - Sept. 7, 2238,
2238/39	Jan. 13, 2239, and Mar. 23, 2239 in Taurus
2239/40	
2240/41S	Projected 384 billion population

The Talmud teaches that their Messiah will come at the close of 6,000 years, to establish a Messianic kingdom and reign for 1,000 years. If their calendar is correct, then by their date of 6000 A.M. (A.D. 2240), there should be almost 400 billion people on this planet — provided the population continues to double every 40 years as it did from 1960 to 2000. Obviously, the Jewish calendar is wrong. We must be much closer to the end times and the return of Jesus Christ.